THE ONCE UPON
A TIME WORLD

THE
ONCE UPON
A TIME WORLD

THE DARK AND SPARKLING STORY
OF THE FRENCH RIVIERA

Jonathan Miles

PEGASUS BOOKS
NEW YORK LONDON

THE ONCE UPON A TIME WORLD

Pegasus Books, Ltd.
148 West 37th Street, 13th Floor
New York, NY 10018

First Pegasus Books cloth edition September 2023

ISBN: 978-1-63936-495-4

10 9 8 7 6 5 4 3 2 1

Printed in the United States of America
Distributed by Simon & Schuster
www.pegasusbooks.com

For Katiu

Following *St Petersburg: Three Centuries of Murderous Desire*,
I offer the second volume of an informal trilogy dedicated to
phenomenal places created by strangers.

Contents

The Voices of Paradise

A secret for centuries, the south-eastern coast of France became the Riviera. It brazenly created and recreated itself in the image of successive visitors attracted by its sun, sea and fragrant air. To become so famous, so desired, and yet prove incapable of satisfying everybody's dreams, is a tough destiny. Paradise was threatened – but there was much passion, wit, intrigue and splendour along the way. This strip of land hosted cultural phenomena well in excess of its tiny size. A mere handful of towns and villages transformed by foreigners enticed the talented, rich and famous – as well as those who wanted to be. For two centuries of opulence, scandal, war and corruption, the Riviera was a temptation.

Nineteenth-century visitors came south to keep themselves alive or to die on a temperate coast that one Belle Époque writer called 'an outdoor hospital'. These winter residents were often overbearing. Foreigners with spending power, they imposed their will and their languages. There was palpable xenophobia on all fronts. The English mocked their hosts, while the French were amused by English self-importance, German pedanticism and Russian bombast. By 1870, Nice – a medium-sized town of 50,000 plus – hosted consulates and therefore visitors from countries as widespread as Turkey, Chile, Mexico and Uruguay. The list grew.[1] The early quest for self-preservation was succeeded by a drive for dangerous living that reverberated through the first decades of the twentieth century. High-octane, the Riviera was spurred by hedonism and cultural frenzy as the English and American impact on the region made waves across the world.

The territory had been frequently contested. The French and Italians had been bickering over the frontier for centuries. When Antonio de Beatis visited in 1517, he recorded the prevailing wisdom that Nice, being on the border, was so-called because it was 'neither here nor there' – '*ni ici, ni là*'. The claim has been questioned, but it is significant that, at the beginning of the sixteenth century, the Nice coat of arms displayed an eagle whose raised claws seemed undecided about what to clutch.[2]

The area's motley and squabble-ridden past is echoed by its medley of voices. Before the French Revolution, the astronomer Jérôme Lalande observed Nice's linguistic indecision. Polite society spoke French, the laws were in Italian, and the ordinary people spoke a verbal salmagundi. The larger Provençal dialect has been described as 'French rubbed with garlic',[3] whereas the local lingo – Nissart – derives from almost any language but French. If 'laundry' is *lessive* in French, in Nissart it is *bugada* – as it is in Catalan. The Niçois use *cabossa* for 'head' – close to the Spanish *cabeza*. Spanish *agua* for 'water' is corrupted into *daigua*, and so it goes on.[4] The philosopher and art critic John Ruskin, visiting briefly in 1845, heard the Greek *ara* for 'now' and *Aspai ma picciota?* – 'Where are you going, my little girl?'– in which he considered *aspai* to be a corruption of *apercevoir*, and *picciota* from the Italian *picciola*.[5] There were also borrowings from Arabic, the Provençal *langue d'oc* and a slow corruption of Latin.[6] As foreigners came south, the babble of sounds became even more diverse. Travelling to Genoa in 1878, the French writer Laurent Germain's train stopped in Nice to pick up gamblers bound for Monte Carlo. His compartment was invaded by a gaggle of aristocratic gentlemen who rattled away in English, German, Russian, Spanish – even French. No matter which language they used, their discourse was predictable. 'Did you win yesterday?' 'No, I lost a lot of money.'[7]

In autumn 1922, James Joyce – about to have leeches applied to drain the pressure of his glaucoma – took a room at Nice's Hôtel Suisse and began to assemble ideas for what became his huge and forbidding multilingual pun, *Finnegans Wake*. He took inspiration from a polyglot city which, throughout its chequered history, hosted languages that came and went according to political circumstance. Russian diminished after the 1917 Revolution only to reappear on restaurant menus in the 1990s. German vanished after the Second World War and came back in the early 1970s, as hordes of West Germans came south to grill themselves lobster orange.

Earlier ages largely ignored the potential of the southern French coast. It took the British desire for a sympathetic climate for bronchitis and the Romantic attraction to untamed nature to make the Riviera a destination. The British saw paradise in a wilderness and created a pleasure ground. Over the decades, other nations followed and turned this thin strip of Shangri-La – snow-capped mountains towering on one side, the azure Mediterranean on the other – into a singular treasure. The Aga Khan spoke of meeting members of the aristocracy and plutocracy 'over and over again' in London, Rome, Berlin, Monte Carlo, Cannes and Nice[8] – three capitals widely separated and three resorts only miles apart.

There was an Anglo-Saxon land grab aided and abetted by the Russians, Germans, Belgians, Americans and a scatter of Scandinavians. The Parisian French also colonized the coast – seeking either commercial opportunity or enjoyment in resorts that boasted a wonderful winter climate and an international reputation. They found no indigenous high-cultural tradition – just a convivial lifestyle and a landscape in which to create a modern paradise; one full of temptations in which those who fell were rarely doomed to expulsion. As entrepreneurs recognized the commercial scope of the Riviera, they built restaurants and hotels in the grand French style while cunningly making strategic concessions to foreign tastes. Later, American improvisations on the themes of Gallic style and bohemianism modified the character of the coast. Later still, all levels of the French population grew to love and hate the Côte d'Azur.

As the 'outdoor hospital' became a pleasure ground, it grew famous for its frivolity. The Riviera was a world of indolent aristocracy and Noël Coward's poor little rich girls. It was also an attractive destination, where important decisions could be taken

by powerful people relaxing at a remove and out of context –
Winston Churchill was addicted. The Riviera provided a haven
where the Duke and Duchess of Windsor went to escape reality.
The landscape and the influx of international visitors made for a
potent cultural cocktail that worked its magic on the likes of Hector
Berlioz, Friedrich Nietzsche, Pablo Picasso, Coco Chanel, F. Scott
Fitzgerald, James Baldwin, Katherine Mansfield, Jean-Paul Sartre,
Igor Stravinsky and the Rolling Stones – to name but a few. Colours
and forms cut by the strong Mediterranean light were inspirational
to modern painters. The Riviera hosted the exceptional. 'Out of
time's monotone', recorded the American writer Allen Tate in a poem
honouring a picnic at which 16 adults – in an act of intoxicated
inversion – downed 61 bottles of wine.[9] Tate and friends put into a
small cove full of 'amethyst fishes and octopuses darting, like closed
parasols'. Over a driftwood fire, they started to cook a bouillabaisse
– its ingredients lately caught. Lurching down the craggy goat track
of the red cliff came an eighty-two-year-old peasant on a horse
carrying all those bottles.[10]

Drink has always been a feature of this festive enclave. Celebrated
lush F. Scott Fitzgerald arrived hours late for a dinner with the
writer Michael Arlen. The delay had been caused by Fitzgerald's
inability to pull himself away from a bottle. He sat down and
declared, 'This is how I want to live… This is how I want to live,'
laid his head on the table and fell asleep.[11]

This wayward coast – once a temptation for pirates and brigands –
has attracted profiteers, corrupt politicians and the mafia – Italian
and Russian. David Dodge's book *To Catch a Thief*, which inspired
Alfred Hitchcock's film of the same name, demonstrated that
wealth lavishly displayed provided great opportunities for crime.
The coast, wrote Dodge elsewhere, was 'lousy with situations and
characters'.[12] Among these were notable crooks, from the man who
broke the bank at Monte Carlo to the famously corrupt mayor
of Nice, Jacques Médecin, and the underworld that sustained
him. Somerset Maugham's celebrated quip 'a sunny place for
shady people', believed to have targeted Monte Carlo but perhaps

provoked by the unsavoury quarters of wartime Marseille – or by his disreputable lover Gerald Haxton – has become the motto for a dark yet sparkling coast.

The locals were swept up into the international scene that engulfed them. The 1960s *École de Nice* was a group of artists inhabiting the worlds of Pop Art and Conceptualism. In one of Nice's most surprising hotels, some rooms are decorated by local artists. I remember standing in the foyer, listening to an American guest despair about the room she had been given. In true Pop style, the walls were covered with American license plates. 'That's what I came away to escape,' the guest groaned. 'Perhaps the Louis XIV room would suit Madame better?' Indeed. I also overheard a couple of travelling companions suggest that having the bathroom facilities creatively exposed in the middle of their room was a teensy bit too 'modern'.

This sunny coast lifts the spirit. Picasso found that Antibes and Golfe-Juan rekindled his delight in the joyous visual pun which had lain largely dormant during the years of the Second World War. Marc Chagall let his antic spirit loose in the installations he made for the Musée National Message Biblique. Yves Klein of the *École de Nice* signed the air above the Mediterranean, calling it a work of art.

Verbal wit has also embellished most aspects of life on the Côte d'Azur. Charlotte Dempster, who lived near Cannes in the second half of the nineteenth century, mocked the energetic attempts of Protestants to establish their own churches: 'At Nice and Monte Carlo I dare say there are not many persons as devout as the Praying Mantis'.[13] Even when they were ill, visitors could be witty. The ailing author of *Treasure Island*, Robert Louis Stevenson, wrote to an old friend from Hyères in March 1884: 'Dover sounds somewhat shiveringly in my ears. You should see the weather *I* have – cloudless, clear as crystal... aromatic air, all pine and gum tree. You would be ashamed of Dover; you would scruple to refer, sir, to a spot so paltry... pray, how do you warm yourself?'[14] Comparisons of southern sun and northern chilliness are legion. Vita Sackville-West suggested that 'her lover, Violet Trefusis, was the Mediterranean while her husband, Harold Nicolson, was Kent'. Ford Madox Ford thought the south of France was Eden whereas the north meant Brussels sprouts.[15]

Social observation was spiked. The French writer and archaeologist Prosper Mérimée spoke of the arrival in Nice of a certain Madame de Vogüé, 'who left her husband somewhere en route but who has replaced him with impressive specimens from here or there'.[16] Etiquette often gave rise to risible situations. A shabbily dressed, socially diffident and absent-minded Englishman attempted to enter the Casino in Monte Carlo. He was asked for his passport. 'A passport? I'm sorry but I haven't got one.' 'No passport! Then you cannot enter.' 'You see, I am the man who issues them.' 'You! That's a good one.' The Englishman left. When it was discovered that the thwarted visitor was Lord Salisbury, thrice prime minister and – at the time of the incident – Secretary of State for Foreign Affairs, the fear of bad publicity sent a frock-coated, top-hatted deputation from the Casino administration to Salisbury's villa in nearby Beaulieu to apologize.[17] The Foreign Secretary had merely been amused by the rebuff.

As performers began to adorn the coast in the 1920s and '30s, the homosexual contingent – often fleeing from the stringent laws that pertained in England – prompted the actress Maxine Elliott to refer to the coast as an 'Adamless Eden'. She sometimes found it refreshing to invite heterosexuals like Douglas Fairbanks Sr or Johnny 'Tarzan' Weissmuller. True to character, Tarzan dived from her top terrace, over the dining patio, into her huge pool.

A legend about the lemon-scented border town of Menton claimed that its citrus trees were a gift from Eve. Expelled from paradise for eating the forbidden apple, the mother of us all grabbed a lemon and – wandering over the earth – threw it down in the countryside near Menton, where it created a new Eden.[18] Unlike Eve, many later visitors arrived not with lemons, but with oodles of their own forbidden fruit.

I

Jagged, Tormented and Tiny

In 1902, a French writer suggested that it was 'cruel to use barbaric scientific terms' to describe the dazzling landscape of the Côte d'Azur.[1] Yet such description helps to explain how a shy strip of coast, inaccessible for millennia, possesses qualities to attract both the ailing and the pleasure-seeking. This difficult terrain was made alluring by the way philosophers, artists and writers helped people to look at landscapes differently. It was chosen for its life-giving properties by doctors seeking a cure for consumption, their efforts aided by improvements in transport. For the first rich visitors, the very seclusion of the Riviera made it a privileged 'space apart' – a place where people could recover their health or misbehave. Once a wilderness, this coast became a place where people could go wild.

This secluded paradise was created just over five million years ago – at the outset of the Pliocene epoch – when the flooding of the Mediterranean started. Our ancestors had already begun to separate from the chimpanzee, and modern mammals and bird families had developed into species recognizable today. The creation and mutation of the Alps had been ongoing for hundreds of millions of years. In the western part of that range, towering above the coast from Nice to Menton, there was tremendous volcanic activity. This created a geological mash-up, a crush of different rocks, resulting in a region of powerful beauty. Folds and faults made for a jagged, tormented and tiny coastal shelf, the drama of which is diminished to the east beyond the Italian frontier, and hardly exists to the west, beyond Cannes. It is a hectic stretch of coastline, an exciting space for hedonistic, frenzied eruptions.

The physique of modern Europe became recognizable in the Pliocene, during which Alpine regions became glaciated and formed an imposing frontier between the creatures and vegetation of the north and the south. In the twentieth century, holiday-makers who visited the Riviera would delight in this climatic confrontation, which permitted skiing on the slopes of the Alps and water-skiing on the adjacent Mediterranean. Orogeny sculpted paradise – it was only left for man to discover, enjoy, exploit and ruin.

One of the earliest indications of human habitation in Europe was found in a small cave at Roquebrune-Cap-Martin, towards the eastern end of the Riviera. Dating from about one million years ago, when the level of the Mediterranean was a hundred metres higher than it is today, the cave contained – along with the rudimentary tools of scavenging humans – remains of panthers, sabre-toothed tigers and jaguars.

Another ancient site is now buried beneath a 1960s apartment block in central Nice. Terra Amata – hastily excavated so as not to delay the construction of the modern building – dates from about 400,000 years ago. By then, hunters had established homes and summer camps. Round cabins were assembled with branches dragged onto the shore – only thirty metres higher than today's pebble beach. The denizens hunted rhinoceros, deer and elephants.

In the hills at Tourrettes-sur-Loup, there are remains dating from the end of the Neolithic period – about 3000 BC. These include evidence of burials, suggesting ceremony. Other Bronze and then Iron Age sites reveal the beginnings of a tribal society – the Ligurians, who were land-dwellers. They stretched along the coast from south-eastern Gaul to south-western Italy. Among their tribes, occupying what is now the Riviera, were the Oxybii and Deciates to the west of Nice and the Vediantii east of the Var, a river which would act, for many centuries, as the natural barrier between Italy and France.[2] The Ligurians left clear signs of 'Man the Maker'. They were the first artists to work on the Côte d'Azur, carving horned animals, geometrical figures and rare human forms on rocks. When Picasso sketched his head of a faun in Antibes in the aftermath of the Second World War, he was the heir to Prehistoric stylization, but his subject matter drew on the mythology of the region's invaders from the eastern Mediterranean.

After founding Carthage in 814 BC, the Phoenicians – who generally hugged the North African coast to trade with Iberia – appear to have settled in several well-chosen havens along the Riviera. At Monaco and Villefranche they built temples to Melkarth, protector of the universe, god of the underworld and lord of their richest city-state, Tyre. At Antibes, where much pottery originating in the eastern Mediterranean has been found, Astarte – the Phoenician goddess of fertility, sexuality and war – guarded the port.[3] Most significantly, the discovery in Marseille of coins and medals from Tyre and Carthage, along with an acropolis and stone shrines in a pre-Greek style, confirm a Phoenician presence predating the Greek founding of Massalia – the ancient name for Marseille – around 600 BC.[4] The Phocaeans – Ionian Greeks from Asia Minor – created a settlement in Massalia and smaller ports at Nice and Antibes, planting olive trees and vines along the coast.[5] They called their settlement at Nice *niki*, which means 'victory'. It proved an ironic choice for a city that stood close to a shifting frontier and was frequently invaded or crushed.

As a busy trading port, Massalia absorbed foreign pleasures and vices. It fell into a moral decadence witnessed by the Romans called upon to help the Greeks after Antibes and Nice were harassed by the Oxybii and Deciates in 144 BC. When the Ligurians threatened Massalia itself nineteen years later, Rome provided further assistance and established a greater presence. Although subsequently robbed of its political role, the old Phocaean city remained a thriving port, and its school of philosophy and rhetoric tutored young Romans from patrician families.[6] The hectic pace of life and racy morality persisted down through the ages. In 1786, the English botanist James Edward Smith noted that nothing struck a visitor to the city as much as the omnipresence of business – 'In this respect, Marseilles resembles Amsterdam'.[7] Sounding a rare note of approval for the city, an American businessman, visiting in 1869, wrote that the 'women are handsomer, houses taller, streets wider and people look more like New-Yorkers than I have seen elsewhere'.[8] Its port and frenetic commercial activity ensured that Marseille would remain beyond the bounds of the serene appeal of the Riviera. However, given its importance in opening up the south coast to foreigners – and given the proximity of Bandol, Sanary and Hyères – it is reasonable to claim Marseille as the original gateway to what we call the Riviera. In 1938, the Compagnie des Chemins de fer de Paris à Lyon et à la Méditerranée, the railway company that did so much to make the region accessible, defined the Riviera as extending from Marseille to the Italian border.[9]

The Romans consolidated their presence along the south coast in order to improve communications between their capital and the recently conquered Iberian Peninsula. The first Roman province in Gaul was created in an area blessed by a coast where they were happy to build villas and could enjoy a climate that was milder than Rome's in the winter and less harsh in the summer. They drove two important roads across the province to complement time-honoured transport by boat. The Via Aurelia ran through Menton, La Turbie and Cimiez to Antibes and Fréjus. It then struck out across country to Aix and Arles. Their second major road, the Via Julia Augusta, started at La Turbie and ran through Vence, reconnecting with the Via Aurelia at Fréjus or Forum Julii – an impressive port established by Julius Caesar. The splendour of Roman times was a far cry from the ruined state in which eighteenth- and nineteenth-century visitors found the town. Aubin-Louis Millin, the French antiquary and naturalist, described its best inn as 'disgusting', serving 'putrid water from badly rinsed flasks'. Millin had a miserable stay and – with the silting of the River Argens – found a sandy plain instead of a port. As for the ruins – they looked ruined.[10]

Two decades before the birth of Christ, the emperor Augustus had imposed Roman authority on the peoples of the western Alps from the Mediterranean to Lake Geneva. That considerable achievement on difficult terrain was commemorated at La Turbie with a huge monument commissioned by the Roman Senate. Originally fifty metres high, it was capped by a statue of the warring emperor who had brought peace to the Roman world. Over the centuries, this monument was plundered by Vandals and Visigoths, and then desecrated by a group opposed to any kind of tribute to pagan gods – the monks from the Île Saint-Honorat, off Cannes. The ruins – fortified by locals in the late Middle Ages – were then shelled by Louis XIV's troops when war broke out between France and Savoy in 1705. Partially restored by an American financier in the 1920s, the stunted monument is upstaged by the spectacular coastline beyond.

While this 'Trophy of the Alps' was being constructed, the Romans created the military province of Alpes Maritimae and made its capital at Cemenelum – later Cimiez, above Nice. There, during the first century AD, they built a modest amphitheatre, and in the third century, public baths. It was at that time that the obscure and gory origins of Christianity took root in the region. St Bassus is believed by some to be the first Bishop of Nice. More likely, he was Bishop of Cimiez, as Nice was not, at that time, a *civitas*. Martyred in 253, Bassus was burned with red-hot blades and transpierced from head to foot by large shipbuilding nails. These atrocities were followed, only four years later, by the torture of St Pontius, who proved difficult to kill. He was placed on a rack and the rack broke. Next, he was thrown to the lions, but they licked and caressed his feet. Bound on a funeral pyre, the flames danced safely around him in a circle. This was too much for his oppressors, so they chopped off his head, which was swept down Nice's River Paillon and out to sea – where it drifted, for some reason best known to legend, to Marseille. Such an awful fuss and fate when, only fifty-six years later, in 313, the emperor Constantine declared toleration and freedom for Christians.[11]

In the centuries following the decline and fall of the Roman Empire, the south was assailed by Visigoths, Ostrogoths and Lombards, who pillaged and destroyed. Nothing remains along the southern coast to compare with the magnificent Roman structures at Arles, Nîmes, or elsewhere in the former empire. The region remained a wilderness for many centuries. Attacked, sacked and traversed by armies, it never established a grand centre of culture.

The marauders from the north were followed by the Moors from Spain, who harassed the southern French coastline, wasting the small fishing village of Cannes and murdering – in around 732 – the abbot and 500 monks in the monastery on Île Saint-Honorat.[12] Inspired by Egyptian monasticism, the monks there had followed a solitary style of obedience and prayer. Among them a most important scholar, who had been born in Britain, had studied on the continent and who – after purging the Île Saint-Honorat of snakes – would go on to found the Celtic Church in Ireland and become St Patrick. The Moors established their stronghold at the fort of La Garde-Freinet above the Gulf of Saint-Tropez in the Maures – hills most probably named to mark their occupation or deriving from the Provençal *mauro* – the dark trunks of pine trees.[13] Few records survive this period, suggesting that, as the invaders sallied forth to plunder, the destruction throughout the region was wanton.

If those years are obscure, the succeeding centuries are a tangle of largely local conflicts contributing to the development of mongrel customs. In 973, Guillaume the Liberator rid the area of its Arab invaders. In recompense, he was made Comte de Provence, a position thereafter occupied – as a result of royal marriages – by Catalans and distant Angevins. Along the Riviera, these rulers of Provence exercised little influence on the persistent local struggles between the Republic of Genoa and the Duchy of Savoy.

Blessed with a magnificent port, the Genoese were a seafaring people who occupied trading posts westward along the coast as far as Nice, while Savoy grew from its humble origins south of Lake Geneva during the early years of the thirteenth century. Genoa and Savoy – and the later Kingdom of Sardinia – were shapeshifting states whose fortunes ebbed and flowed in response to territorial ambition, conflict, or betrayal. By 1562, Turin had become the capital of a much-enlarged Duchy of Savoy that included the Aosta Valley, the strategic Mont-Cenis pass over the Alps, Piedmont and the Comté de Nice. Its frontier with Provence – absorbed into France in 1481 – was established on the River Var.

The Habsburg Charles V – son of Philip the Handsome and Joanna the Mad of Spain – inherited great swathes of Europe and territories in the Americas. It is hardly surprising that he was a Holy Roman Emperor obsessed by the concept of universal monarchy. Conflict between Charles and François I brought Habsburg armies

Barbarossa's Ottoman fleet help the French besiege Savoyard Nice in August 1543.

into France and took French troops into Italy – the route passing through Nice. In 1524, the treacherous Constable de Bourbon led 25,000 Habsburg soldiers into Provence, pillaging as he went. When he failed to capture Marseille, the French hounded his retreat and cut off his supplies. Twelve years later, the Habsburgs again attempted to invade France via its Mediterranean coast, marching through a countryside which they found to be a 'vast solitude'. As before, their army was beaten at Marseille and suffered another slow and painful retreat, losing many men to ambushes in the Esterel, the range of hills between Fréjus and the Bay of Cannes.[14]

Ridding Nice of the Savoyards became strategically important for François I. In 1543, he organized a coordinated attack with a surprising ally. The Ottoman emperor Suleiman the Magnificent was no friend to the Habsburgs, and allowed his Grand Admiral, Barbarossa, to participate in the Siege of Nice. On 12 August, the French commenced their bombardment from cannon sited on the hill of Cimiez and amid the pines and olive trees on the heights of Mont Boron. Meanwhile, the Ottoman fleet fired from the sea and stormed the fort. The heaviest fighting was seen on the 15th, when the defenders – outnumbered – stood horrified as the invaders began to scale their walls. As a Turk surmounted the parapet to plant his standard, Catherine Ségurane entered the fray, armed with a washerwoman's wooden beater. Nicknamed Donna Maufacia – Nissart for a 'poorly made' or even 'deformed' woman[15] – Ségurane struck the head of the Ottoman standard-bearer, snatched his flag and screamed, 'Victory!' It was a legendary intervention. In its most fanciful telling, the laundress bared her backside to the enemy and scared them off. Ségurane's bravery inspired the defenders to fight on, until the army of the Duke of Savoy arrived to repel the French.[16]

After 1559, when the Treaty of Cateau-Cambrésis ended the French European wars and split the Habsburg Empire in two, the relative stability and prosperity of the Comté de Nice endured for nearly 150 years. Not that the region was totally free of panic and strife. In the year following the treaty, 500 pirates burned Roquebrune, in the hills north-east of Monaco. Algerian raiders frequently plundered coastal villages, carrying off inhabitants to be sold as slaves.[17]

After the House of Savoy entered into a coalition against Louis XIV in the War of the Grand Alliance, Louis later wreaked his revenge by sending troops to attack the fort at Nice. During the second and third week of December 1705, the bombardment by sixty cannon and twenty-four mortars was intense. In early January 1706, the commander defending Nice capitulated, and the citadel was – according to the wishes of Louis XIV – wiped from the face of the earth. No longer a fortified town, Nice slowly began to develop a new double identity: that of sanatorium and resort.[18]

Military insignificance, however, did not stop Victor Amadeus II of Savoy from retaking Nice. By the time of his death in 1732, Victor Amadeus had become ruler of the Kingdom of Piedmont-Sardinia and done much to embellish its capital at Turin and consolidate his presence in the western Alps. Both Genoa and Turin grew into administrative and cultural centres. There was no such splendid city along the Riviera. The impact of invading troops and marauders had textured the region, as Greeks, Romans, Moors, Italians, Spanish, French and Savoyards each left their footprint. Through it all, the locals got on with their lives as best they could, their roots reaching deep beneath the topsoil of political brinkmanship.

While the area had little to offer the cultured visitor, like all back of beyonds it was thick with folklore. In the first century, Torpes – a steward at Nero's palace in Pisa – refused to renounce his Christian beliefs. He was decapitated – the head tossed into the River Arno. The rest of the body was set to sea in a boat with a dog, a pig, a viper and a cock. It floated all the way to the little port to which the body in the boat gave its name – Saint-Tropez. Equally firm in her Christian convictions, Maxima, sister of Torpes, was also martyred. Her boat – either by amazing coincidence or sibling solidarity – was carried to what is now Sainte-Maxime, across the small gulf from where her brother's body blew ashore.

There were also legends of figures from the gospels who fetched up in the south of France. Mary and Martha, who welcomed Christ into their home, were said to have arrived on the shores near Marseille in 37 AD. Balthazar, after visiting the baby Jesus, left his two fellow Wise Men and kept following the star – which, curiously, took him all the way to Les Baux in Provence. Lazarus, raised from the dead, came west to 'present the truths of immortality' to the heathen of the southern littoral. When the Jews of Palestine became irked because a new religion was beginning to take hold, they rounded up Mary Magdalene and Joseph of Arimathea and set them adrift in the Mediterranean, until 'under divine protection' they landed in the south of France. Mary Magdalene came ashore close to where former convent girl Coco Chanel's villa La Pausa would be sited; the name commemorated the rest stop made by Mary.[19] Sailing from Marseille to Genoa in 1699, the English essayist Joseph Addison was shown the deserts made famous 'by the penance of Mary Magdalene, who… is said to have wept away the rest of her life among these solitary rocks and mountains'.[20]

In the mid-sixth century, a chained penitent and healer who lived on a diet of dry bread and dates inhabited an ancient, unused signal tower at Pointe Saint-Hospice on Cap Ferrat. When the Lombards invaded and one of the attackers prepared to decapitate the hermit, his arms became suddenly paralysed. Astonished, a number of the intruders became disciples of the man who had been miraculously saved.[21] Nice espoused the cult of the Umbrian St Rita. A contemporary of Jeanne d'Arc and patroness of lost causes – her own life had been miserable – she was praying in a church when one of the thorns of Christ's crown fell and pierced her forehead. The stench emanating from the wound led to her solitary confinement until, one day, the odour of roses filled the convent and Rita was discovered dead, her face restored to its former beauty.[22]

In the mid-eighteenth century, the Scottish writer Tobias Smollett remarked on the glut of superstition in Nice, which revealed 'the darkest shades of ignorance and prejudice'.[23] Well-funded establishments in and around the town – Smollett counted ten convents and three nunneries – were evidence of a superstitious peasantry who gave what they could ill afford for masses, processions and benedictions in desperate attempts to secure good harvests.[24] Peasants thought miracles highly probable. In Notre-Dame des Oiseaux at Hyères, Adolphe Smith found hundreds of 'abominably painted' images testifying to the miraculous powers of this church. There was a man 'whose gun burst while shooting wild ducks on Dec 2nd 1773', who 'owed his life solely to his devotion to the shrine'. A mason who fell through five storeys of a house – having first dropped the heavy cask that made the hole into which he tumbled – was saved. A man's arm, gnawed by 'an infuriated mule', was healed. A carriage full of people skidded off a bridge without fatality. There were a host of other road accidents and more exploding guns – all incidents in which, miraculously, no one was hurt.[25]

The traditional origin for the name of Nice's Baie des Anges was the legend of a peasant girl who was sculling on the water when a storm blew up and her boat was overturned. Angels appeared to waft her to dry land before disappearing into the clouds. The following day, she became a Christian.[26] A more plausible explanation is that the bay is named after the huge, repulsive and inedible angel shark – *lou pei-ange* in Nissart.[27] The walkway along the bay at Nice was called the *Camin dei Anges* by the locals. This mutated into the *Camin dei Anglès* – which, in French, became the *Promenade des Anglais*.

However, the legend that has most excited the imagination is the imprisonment of the 'man in the iron mask', who died in the fortress on the Île Sainte-Marguerite off Cannes in 1703. The mystery has inspired rumours, novels, silent films, colour films, a TV movie, three TV series, a Russian musical film and a song by Billy Bragg. Few elements of the story are certain, except that the 'iron mask' was made from black velvet.

Late in April 1687, the new governor of the fort and prison on Sainte-Marguerite arrived with a masked prisoner who had been moved from gaol to gaol while his rebellious instincts were tamed by torture. Upon arrival in his new dungeon – with walls three metres thick, one triple-barred opening, and an adjacent corridor where he could exercise unobserved – the prisoner fell sick and took to his bed. It was noted that he spoke French with a foreign accent, and sang. Beyond that, we encounter an increasingly elaborate tissue of theories – or, at least, we did until 2015, when documents previously thought to have been destroyed by the Paris Commune in 1871 surfaced in the Archives Nationales in Paris.

Left: Walls three metres thick, a triple-barred opening. *Right*: The elusive man 'in the iron mask'.

Voltaire was responsible for converting the black velvet covering to an iron mask, thereby pricking people's curiosity. He claimed the prisoner was the illegitimate half-brother of Louis XIV – the son of Anne of Austria and the Italian cardinal Mazarin. That would explain the foreign accent. Alexandre Dumas, in *The Man in the Iron Mask* – the third part of *The Vicomte of Bragelonne: Ten Years Later* – claimed the prisoner was none other than an identical twin of Louis XIV, fathered by Louis XIII and Anne of Austria: a wild idea that would spark the imagination of filmmakers. Yet another explanation was that the man in the iron mask was the issue of Anne of Austria after an illicit affair with the English ambassador, the Duke of Buckingham.

The mystery of the prisoner became mired in the shifting sands of fiction. Not only identified as the 'improbable' twin brother of Louis XIV, he was also held to be the son of the king. Some thought him 'the Duke of Monmouth, son of Charles II' – though Monmouth was hanged in 1685, when the man in the velvet mask was still alive. Another candidate was the Armenian patriarch Avédic, captured by the French and taken to Marseille, but he was seen alive and living in Turkey three years after the death of the elusive prisoner. Perhaps the fantasy that caps the lot is a rumour stating that the man in the iron mask was the father of a little boy whose mother, Julie de Bonpart, was the daughter of one of the officials in the fortress. Their child 'was sent over to Corsica... the only message transmitted to his new guardians was, "Il fanciullo vi viene da buona parte"' – 'This youngster is from a good family'. Thus the man in the iron mask – perhaps a member of the French royal family – would have originated the Napoleonic dynasty.[28]

There have been countless different identities assigned to the prisoner – some more credible than others. Suspicion fell on Ercole Antonio Mattioli, an agent of the Duke of Mantua. But this figure was well known across Europe, and there was no secrecy about his imprisonment and punishment. A more plausible candidate was Monsieur de Marchiel, an agent involved in a conspiracy to poison Louis XIV. Marchiel – a man with many aliases and identities – was captured at the end of March 1673 and taken to the Bastille. Yet his positive identification as the man in the iron mask remained impossible, because of the lack of documentation. Then, the papers rediscovered in 2015 disclosed that the gaoler, Saint-Mars – who guarded the prisoner in isolation for over thirty years – had siphoned off funds provided by the king, and allowed his captive to languish in a spartan if sizeable cell. The prisoner was named as Eustache Dauger. There are many variations including Daugier, Dogiers, d'Auger, d'Oger – making identification even more difficult. The Eustache Dauger incarcerated on Sainte-Marguerite was most probably a valet to someone in a high position – perhaps Cardinal Mazarin. As such, he would have known too many secrets, having witnessed debauchery, black masses and poisonings in court circles. Such knowledge combined with a proclivity for political muckraking would have taken him to gaol.

But the truth remains in the shadows. A story as slippery as Mary Magdalene's rest at La Pausa or Joseph of Arimathea's journey break on his way to Glastonbury, the man in the iron mask is certainly the most sensational yarn spun before this stunning coast buzzed with society gossip.

2

This 'Wild and Tremendous Region of the Globe'

I n late November 1517, Don Antonio de Beatis gave a
surprisingly modern response to the natural qualities of the
Riviera – observations heralding the manner in which it would
be appreciated by later travellers. Cannes, he wrote, 'offers
magnificent views... and is charming'. Antibes was 'pretty', and
Nice 'very beautiful and big' and 'full of pretty women whose
skirts reach only to their knees'.[1] More than a century later, the
first English visitors began to pass through the region, en route to
Italy. Among them was a young man escaping the rigours of the
English Civil War – the diarist John Evelyn. His first impressions
of the Mediterranean coast, recorded on 7 October 1644, were
of a countryside 'full of vineyards and olive-yards, orange trees,
myrtles, pomegranates, and the like sweet plantations'.[2]

At Marseille, Evelyn was struck by the crocodile skins hanging
in the chapel of Notre-Dame de la Garde, and noted that 'the
chief trade of the town' was 'in silks and drugs out of Africa, Syria
and Egypt'. Evelyn was astonished by the number of slaves in the
streets and by the 'jingling of their huge chains' as they dragged
enormous loads about the town. He was received by the captain
of a galley that was 'richly carved and gilded' and manned by 'so
many hundreds of miserably naked persons... doubly chained about
their middle and legs'.

With unchecked marauders preying on small craft, Evelyn
could not find a galley bound for Genoa, and his party was
obliged to continue on muleback as far as Fréjus and 'the small
port' of Cannes – where they found a boatman who was willing

to carry them on along the coast, past Antibes, Nice, Monaco and Menton.[3]

The appreciation of untouched nature that would engage the Romantic traveller was still over a century away, but contemplative visitors were starting to signal their attraction for a region through which they could access Italy without crossing the Alps. At the time, mountains were considered a treacherous barrier rather than a scenic beauty. Italy, with its classical culture, Renaissance treasures and new architectural wonders, was the destination of those on the 'Grand Tour'. From the early years of the eighteenth century, this coming-of-age journey for British gentlemen was undertaken not only for the chance to whore, but also to enrich the mind and improve judgement – neither of which could be done in the underdeveloped and war-torn region of southern France. To the Grand Tourist, such as the 'Person of Quality' who passed through the region in 1691, the mountains between Marseille and Toulon appeared 'dismal as well as barbarous'.[4] It was a landscape that placed the traveller in the vastness of nature. Far from cities or ruins of earlier civilizations, the sensation was bewildering and destabilizing.

During his 1699 voyage past 'these solitary rocks and mountains' where Mary Magdalene wept, Joseph Addison began to appreciate the sea in a manner that would help to shape the Romantic response to the dangerous yet inspiring ocean. He claimed that he could not look upon the sea 'without a very pleasing astonishment'.[5] To Addison, the ocean was no longer just a medium through which he travelled; it had begun to engage his emotions. Yet for most travellers in the south of France from the eighteenth century until the arrival of the railway in the mid-nineteenth, water remained largely a convenience. Journeys along the coast were often easiest by a ten-oared felucca, which was sizeable enough to transport an English travelling carriage.

In 1763, Giacomo Casanova – a pathfinder in this paradise made for pleasure – visited the region during his endless search for sexual gratification. Having found the women of Marseille 'undoubtedly the most profligate in France', he took up with a local girl called Rosalie – who first was not, then claimed to be, and then again declared she was no virgin. It was of no consequence to Casanova, as she allowed him 'to gaze on all those charms' of which his 'hands and lips disputed the possession'. Rosalie 'was only fifteen, but with her figure, her well-formed breasts... would have been taken for twenty'. Casanova fitted her with a wardrobe, took her for a mistress, and told her that his servants would respect her as if she were his wife. Moving on to Antibes, they found a felucca to transport them to Genoa. The journey would take 2–3 days, and the passengers were grouped aft under a protective awning while the oarsmen – packed in the prow under hot skies – powered the craft.

With the journey under way, the sea became rough. 'Rosalie being mortally afraid', Casanova had the felucca put into Villefranche where the bad weather delayed them for three days. A carriage then drove them to Nice, which Casanova found 'a terribly dull place'. The couple played faro in a café and – aided by Casanova's experience as a gambler – Rosalie won a little money. She would, Casanova hoped, be the one with whom he could spend his days, so that he should not 'be forced to fly from one lady to another'. But, as he recounts this episode in the early chapters of volume four of his six-volume memoir, 'inexorable fate' obviously 'ordained it otherwise'. In Genoa, Casanova met Veronique...[6]

In 1745, the French art critic l'Abbé Le Blanc explained the burgeoning English passion for going abroad – they 'look on their isle as a prison; and the first use they make of their love of liberty is to get out of it'.[7] Their unlikely trailblazer in the south of France was the Scotsman Tobias Smollett. Maligned for having waved his wand of woe over Nice, Smollett actually delighted in the natural qualities of the region. While the swelling catalogue of Grand Tour tales publicized the treasures of Italy, Smollett promoted the south of France. Among sickly Britons, there was a grand appetite for his enthusiasm for a potentially life-saving destination. Smollett's *Travels Through France and Italy* was an instant success – its 1766 first edition swiftly sold out. There were several reprintings, the inevitable pirated Irish editions, extracts in English periodicals, a German translation, and an abridged Swedish edition.[8] In the wake of such success, it was the jocular Laurence Sterne who, in 1768, nicknamed Smollett 'Smelfungus' and – in an act of self-promotion – accented Smollett's misanthropy. 'The learned SMELFUNGUS travelled from Boulogne to Paris – from Paris to Rome – and so on – but he set out with the spleen and jaundice, and every object he pass'd by was discoloured or distorted – He wrote an account of them, but 'twas nothing but the account of his miserable feelings.'[9]

In the same year, Philip Thicknesse likewise suggested that Smollett's *Travels* should rather be called 'QUARRELS through France and Italy'.[10] A decade later, Thicknesse relented. 'Poor man! He was ill; and meeting with, what every stranger must expect to meet, at most French inns, want of cleanliness, imposition and incivility, he was so much disturbed.'[11]

Smollett was not only ill but feeling ill-used. 'Traduced by malice, persecuted by faction, abandoned by false patrons and overwhelmed' by the death of his beloved and only daughter, he set out for the south of France, where he 'hoped the mildness of the climate would prove favourable to the weak state' of his lungs. Early on in his *Travels*, it is clear that Smollett had no especial argument with the French. Indeed, even before crossing the Channel, he imagined that everyone, from publicans to port officials, was out to fleece him.[12] There were, almost inevitably, frequent upsets en route. Smollett's travelling library – detained by customs – took a good six weeks to be recovered. He caught a cold soon after his arrival in France and 'was seized with a violent cough' and fever. He then faced the difficult choice of the best method of transportation south, and the problem of obtaining the fairest rates. At times, he had better fortune than many. Crossing the Esterel, 'formerly frequented by… desperate banditti', he found the route 'very good'.[13] Thomas Nugent, in *The Grand Tour*, had described the atrocious roads between Antibes and Nice 'through rugged mountains bordered with precipices'.[14] Instead, Smollett found a gentle coastal road with 'neither precipice nor mountain'. He speculated that if only there were a bridge across the River Var and a post road from Nice to Genoa, then visitors to Italy would forsake the difficult trip across the Alps in favour of this 'infinitely more safe, commodious, and agreeable' route. Once arrived, Smollett had much good to say about Nice and its environs.[15] Why else would he have stayed two years? How else would he have persuaded so many ailing Englishmen to follow in his footsteps?

Smollett found Nice to be a 'little town, hardly a mile in circumference'.[16] Despite the extortionate rates, he rented the 'large, lofty, and commodious' ground floor of a house with two small gardens offering an abundance of salad and citrus fruit.[17] He delighted in the countryside with its modest traces of antiquity. Standing on the ramparts and surveying the scene, Smollett was enchanted. The 'plain presents nothing but gardens, full of green trees, loaded with oranges, lemons, citrons and bergamots... The hills are shaded to the tops with olive-trees, which are always green; and those hills are over-topped by more distant mountains, covered with snow. When I turn myself towards the sea, the view is bounded by the horizon...'. Such 'is the serenity of the air, that you see nothing above your head... but a charming blue expanse'.[18] Smollett listed the many fish available and celebrated a veritable cornucopia of fruits and vegetables. He discovered 'sorbettes' – an 'iced froth made with juice of oranges, apricots or peaches; very agreeable to the palette, and so extremely cold' that he was 'afraid to swallow them in this hot country', until he found 'from information and experience, that they may be taken in moderation, without any bad consequence'.[19] A long-time advocate of hydrotherapy, Smollett bathed in the sea and helped establish the custom.[20] When 'it was perceived that I grew better in consequence of the bath, some... Swiss officers tried the same experiment'. Within a matter of days, 'our example was followed by several inhabitants of Nice'.[21]

Describing the poorer locals, Smollett despaired. Their diet was basic – unsold leftovers from the garden, coarse bread and polenta. Their animals fared worse, being 'so meagre, as to excite compassion'. Overall, he found the population 'quiet and orderly' and drunkenness all but unknown. He did, however, lament the quality of the artisans – 'very lazy, very needy, very awkward and void of all ingenuity'.[22] There was, it seems, a want of those very talents that nourished Italian art and architecture. In response to a question on 'the state of the arts and sciences at Nice', Smollett replied, 'almost a total blank'. The town seemed to be 'consecrated to the reign of dullness'; it was 'very surprising, to see a people established between two enlightened nations, so devoid of taste and literature... the very ornaments of the churches are wretchedly conceived, and worse executed'.[23] Sentiments echoed by the Swiss scientist Johann Georg Sulzer, who a decade later confirmed that Nice 'has no public edifice worth mentioning'.[24]

Bugbears for Smollett included lizards, scorpions, 'flies, fleas and... gnats' – all intolerable. It was 'impossible to keep the flies out of your mouth, nostrils, eyes and ears. They crowd into your milk, tea, chocolate, soup, wine and water; they soil your sugar, contaminate your victuals, and devour your fruit.'[25] But any climate, however blissful, carries with it disadvantages. Taken all in all, Smollett made no more complaints or negative observations than the average traveller who rails against dirt and cost. Eighteenth-century visitors in France found porters a rough and rowdy lot. They were often served watered-down wine, overcharged for accommodation, and were cheated in the way that modern tourists imagine they might be in more exotic places.

About two years after Smollett left the south coast, love or lust sped the twenty-eight-year-old Duke of York – brother of George III – to a liaison in Genoa. In August 1767, a ball was given in his honour at Toulon, where the duke danced so much that he sweated heavily. The following night, he returned from the theatre with a chill. Deciding to proceed to Genoa on land, he stopped in Monaco, where Prince Honoré III invited him to rest before continuing on his journey. Stood out in the hot sun during a welcome salute, York became feverish and took to his bed. Two days later, he was dead. George III rewarded Honoré handsomely for his kindnesses towards the extravagant brother for whom he had shown little care. He sent Honoré two of the duke's racehorses and invited him to visit England. Sadly for Monaco, none of the diplomatic possibilities that such an invitation promised would materialize.[26]

Nice was also beginning to find favour with royalty. In 1775, the Duke of Gloucester – another brother of George III – came south with his wife, Maria, the illegitimate daughter of Sir Edward Walpole. After the death of Maria's first husband, Lord Waldegrave, in 1763, Gloucester – scarcely twenty years old, short-sighted and awkward – started to court her. Although decorum required that she rebuff him, he persisted. In September 1766, three and a half years after Waldegrave's death, Maria and Gloucester were married by her private chaplain at her house in Pall Mall. The match was supposed to remain secret, but it became common knowledge and an embarrassment to the court. Frequently snubbed, Gloucester became ill and decided to take Maria and their two children to the south of France. Although one child died of smallpox before they set off in July 1775, the rest of the family travelled south in four handsomely appointed carriages. Gloucester spent two winters in Nice, 'astonishing the people with the splendour of his mode of living and contributing materially to the gaiety of the place'.[27]

While Savoy acknowledged the growing importance of Nice, the dominant city on the south coast remained – as it had been since antiquity – Marseille. Travelling on the eve of the French Revolution, Jean-Pierre Bérenger, professor of eloquence at the Collège Royal at Orléans, commented that 'Marseille is for Provence and its neighbouring provinces what Paris is for France… it attracts youth, distracts the bored and is a trap for the imprudent'. As Bérenger describes it, Marseille is abuzz with big-city life, attractive to those who 'are fed up with the calm and uniformity' of the provinces. There are over 15 million transactions a month. The port is a forest of masts, and the odour of alluring drugs and elixirs emanates from the shops. Products from all corners of the earth and exotic clothes dazzle the eye. Nonetheless, Bérenger also delves into the dark side of a city in which great numbers perished in obscurity and misery. Unlike so many writers of the day, who delighted in the easy virtue of the southern women, there is no voyeurism in his vision of Marseille, which, 'like a rotting corpse teeming with worms', is a place that exploits and devours 'lost girls'.[28]

Bérenger advises the traveller to expect no kindness in the nearby countryside. The peasants will allow a stranger to follow a dangerous path, then laugh at his idiocy. If a traveller snatches a grape of theirs which is overhanging the road, they take a shot at him or unleash their hounds.[29] At the same time, Bérenger is not impervious to the charms of rural tradition, and writes with affection about the Provençal celebration of Christmas, when people would feast on the local delicacies that are still prized by tourists today: 'Figs, raisins – fresh or dried – Brignoles prunes covered in laced paper, pyramids of oranges at times crowned by a bouquet from the same tree… nougat with hazel nuts, pine nuts, pistachios and Narbonne honey.' The festive dining room he describes is fragrant with the scent of fruits and flowers, and 'neither carcases of animals nor those irritating drugs that are served in the middle of a meal to revive the satiated palette' are to be seen.[30]

One of the first Americans to visit the south of France was Thomas Jefferson, who became the third president of the United States. He travelled along the Riviera in the spring of 1787, during the time that he was a minister to the court of Louis XVI. Interested by the shallow ponds for refining salt on the shore at Hyères, he found, in the countryside around, 'delicious and extensive plains'. The people, 'generally well clothed' and with plenty to eat, were perhaps overworked – 'the excess of the rent required by the landlord obliging them to too many hours of labour'. Jefferson conducted his research thoroughly: 'You must be absolutely incognito, you must ferret the people out of their hovels as I have done, look into their kettles, eat their bread, loll on their beds under the pretence of resting yourself, but in fact to find if they are soft.'[31] From Hyères, Jefferson travelled along the coast to Fréjus, Antibes, Nice, Monaco, Menton, and on into Italy. Interestingly, as a visitor coming from a country that had freed itself from the British yoke, he described the 'gay and dissipated' Nice as an 'English colony'.[32]

In the year of the Revolution, Arthur Young – an economist and England's great authority on agricultural matters – travelled throughout the south. As Jefferson and Smollett had done, he found the lowlands near Hyères 'richly cultivated, and planted with olives and vines'.[33] Impinging on this rural idyll were the many villas being constructed to house winter residents.[34] The proximity of Hyères to Marseille made it one of the first towns selected by those seeking a cure in the warmth of the south. When Arthur Young wanted to get to Nice so as to travel on into Italy, he found it incredible that, in 1789, for a journey from 'Marseilles with 100,000 souls' to Nice, there was no diligence. That lumbering long-distance stagecoach, seating six in its stifling interior and several more outside, fore and aft, was an uncomfortable but efficient mode of transport. The southern roads, however, were inadequate for such a vehicle, and Young concluded with that familiar observation: 'the whole coast of Provence is nearly the same desert'.[35] For the French and Sardinian locals, the coast provided ports for trade and fishing villages which fed the local population. There was some agriculture on the generally poor soil. Otherwise, there was nothing.

Dr Edward Rigby was, like Arthur Young, interested in agricultural experiment. As he left Marseille to head east, he encountered the first rough roads he had found in a thousand miles of travelling through France. Yet his Romantic fascination with the wilderness went some way to dispelling his discomfort. The landscape was eerie. The road wound between rocks which were 'absolutely perpendicular' – some 'split down… from their tops to their very bases'. Others formed arches or opened into 'caverns, which seemed to lead to dreadful abodes'.[36]

While usually trusting the peasants of Provence, the French antiquary and naturalist Aubin-Louis Millin cautioned travellers heading eastwards, describing how the locals would hide 'in the depths of the Esterel, wait for the traveller, begin by thieving and end with murder'.[37] Neither was the road from Fréjus to Nice or Nice to Genoa free from robbers preying on the affluent travellers making for Florence, Rome and Naples. During the time of Napoleon's empire, thieves robbed the Marchioness of Bute near Menton, but were quickly apprehended after they fell into a slumber induced by the opium they had stolen from their victim. Almost everybody in the gang was identified, and 'it was learnt with astonishment' that many belonged to or had connections with the noble families of Nice. When three of the gang were condemned to death, their partners in crime fled to other parts of France. Years passed, and the son and daughter-in-law of one of these thieves returned to Nice. At a ball, the daughter was seen wearing some 'scintillating jewels and the intelligence was that they were the diamonds' belonging to the Marchioness of Bute.[38]

Rigby, Young and Millin were pathfinders in what engraver and landscape painter Albanis Beaumont called a 'wild and tremendous region of the globe'. Writing in 1795, he observed that 'even in this enlightened age, the region was neglected... scarcely noted by the naturalist, or frequented by the traveller'.[39] Yet in art, Neoclassicism – that offspring of the Enlightenment – was being rattled by a new, raw energy. This can be seen by comparing two portraits painted by that champion of the Grand Manner, Jacques-Louis David. His subject: a man just beginning to make a mark when Albanis Beaumont was writing – Napoleon Buonaparte. In *Napoleon in His Study*, which hangs in the National Gallery of Art in Washington, David celebrates the orderly, diligent Napoleon. In another vision, *Napoleon Crossing the Alps* – a piece of stirring mythmaking which hangs in the Château de Malmaison in Paris – David acknowledges classical poise but shows Napoleon confronted by difficult terrain and challenging weather, which both reflect and spur the leader's energy, power and determination. The Alps were the very landscape through which Albanis Beaumont had travelled, and had presciently written that those 'awful and tremendous' mountains would 'no doubt, soon become to the philosophic traveller a subject of astonishment and admiration'.[40]

With its violent juxtaposition of mountains that could satisfy the Romantic search for danger, and sea and clear skies promising infinity, the Riviera was coming into its own. Yet the region was still difficult to access – Napoleon did not cross the Alps on David's stallion, but on a mule.

❖

The Revolution was in its infancy when Rigby reached the south. At Toulon – one of Louis XVI's most important naval bases – he saw 'no cockades... nor any marks of rejoicing'. Rigby's party was the first to cross the Var after the cataclysm of July 1789, and the commandant at the frontier did not recognize their new passports. He asked to keep one, plastered the visitors with questions about the clashes in Paris, provided new documents and let them proceed.[41]

In Nice that summer, the Revolution seemed remote. At the *table d'hôte* of his hotel, Arthur Young found that the French were predominantly pro, the Italians against. Used to buying into the nobility, Italian merchants could obtain a French title for the equivalent of three or four hundred pounds. Smollett mentioned 'a count at Villefranche, whose father sold macaroni in the streets'.[42] The Italians loved titles, observed the writer Mme Ratazzi: 'A simple monsieur one day, becomes "Monsieur de"... ; then six months later "Monsieur le Baron"; then "Monsieur le Comte"; then, the following year, he will be "Monsieur le Marquis".'[43] More importantly, most Italians opposed the revolution because a good number of them were beginning to rely on visitors for their livelihood. The political volatility of France would discourage English families from wintering in the south.

After the Savoyard soldiers guarding the Var frontier withdrew, a ragged French army entered Nice on 30 September 1792. Among them was a lieutenant-colonel born in the city – André Masséna. Rising to the rank of Maréchal d'Empire, Masséna – whom Napoleon would dub 'the Spoilt Child of Victory' – enjoyed a spectacular military career until he was defeated by the Duke of Wellington in Spain. After the French arrived, the Comté de Nice was absorbed into the department of Alpes-Maritimes. Teaching would be in French. Dechristianization was underway. Monaco was seized and the palace pillaged. The principality was renamed 'Hercule' – in line with its original name, Heracles Monoikos. Prince Honoré III and his family were imprisoned in France. By April 1794, the Alpes-Maritimes – except for small pockets of resistance in the backcountry – was in French hands.

Toulon had been recaptured from the English after they destroyed the dockyard and fleet on behalf of French royalists. On 16 December 1793, a range of batteries placed secretly by the Republicans bombarded the English for thirty-six hours. Consolidated by an attack, the winning strategy had been devised by an ambitious twenty-four-year-old artillery captain, Napoleon Buonaparte. Early in 1794, he was in Nice, appointed Inspector of the Coast. Two years later, he was named Commander-in-Chief of the French Army of Italy. He addressed that ragged band in a manner that heralded the shape of things to come: 'Soldiers! You are naked and ill-fed: the Government owes you much but can do nothing for you. Your patience and the courage you display... are admirable; but they procure you no glory... I wish to lead you into the most fertile plains in the world. Rich provinces, great cities will be in your power.' The rest is history.

Between the outbreak of the French Revolution in 1789 and Waterloo in 1815, Nice – understandably – did not fare well with foreigners. Revolutionary uncertainty, war and the 'continual motion' of troops resulted in an unstable environment. When, in 1799, an epidemic carried off one-sixth of the town,[44] it was clear that Nice had become no place for ailing northerners. The short-lived Treaty of Amiens of March 1802 briefly suspended hostilities between England and France, but Napoleon was soon on the march again, with his desire to redraw the map of Europe. His empire – which lasted from 1799 to 1814 – proved a sorry time for Nice. Writing midway through the period, in 1807, John Bunnell Davis recorded that 'the rage of the revolution, carried to an almost inconceivable excess, has scarcely left any hotel or mansion of grandeur without marks of degradation'.[45] The streets of the old part of town – so laid out to keep pedestrians shadowed from the hot sun – were 'so narrow and dirty' that few foreigners set foot in them. 'Foul air' emanated from stairwells, and the rooms in the houses were dark. When windows were glassed, the gloom was deepened by dust and fly dung on the exterior and by the yellow residue of smoke inside.[46]

One ecological method of enriching the poor soil around Nice added to the nasal discomfort of the visitor. Tobias Smollett, writing in the 1760s, and Aubin-Louis Millin, in 1807, describe the procedure in almost identical terms. Smollett noted that agricultural land required 'something highly impregnated with nitre and vegetable salts'. The locals used pigeon dung and other ordure on vegetables and around the trunks of young orange trees. Thus, miserable soil offered produce in profusion – 'peas and beans grow promiscuously together in the midst of winter' and there were 'vast quantities' of cereal crops.[47]

To secure this level of production, gardens were often fitted with a ditch, and opening onto it was a hole in the wall which invited passers-by, who felt the need, to use it as a toilet. There was also, in each house, a pit where the excrement of the entire family was collected. Smollett records that, as a result of their respective diets, the production 'of a protestant family… bears a much higher price' than that of a Catholic family. The dietary privations caused by Catholic observances resulted in an uneven production. Smollett and Millin – who seems to offer nothing but a translation of the earlier writer's text – both give an account of the procedure and the surprising manner of collection: 'The peasant comes with his asses and casks to carry it off before day, and pays for it according to its quality, which he examines and investigates, by the taste and flavour.'[48] Half a century later, the Yale professor Benjamin Silliman had his carriage followed by children who collected horse droppings, which they scooped into baskets that they then carried on their heads. Later still, the role of *décrotteur* – 'dung scooper' – was restricted to those over the age of sixteen and authorized by the *mairie* of Nice, who also provided a badge of office.[49]

If the war meant that foreigners were scarce, French and Italian society was abundant. Napoleon's sister, Pauline Borghese, stayed in the Villa Carlone surrounded by a small group of admirers – including the sculptor Antonio Canova, who immortalized her as Venus and pursued her with ardent love letters.[50] It was rumoured that she even posed naked for the sculptor – scandalous for a person of rank at that time. Their association reflects not only the first stirrings of the amorous excesses of society on the Riviera, but also a predilection for luxury. Canova, who became the darling of fashionable Europe, sought to consolidate his position by making his erotic art so anodyne, so luxurious, that it reached what the novelist Michael Dibdin called the 'nadir of ghastly good taste'.[51] It is rumoured that Rolls-Royce, desiring a luxurious finish for the body of their motor cars, sought a depth of lustre that emulated a Canova sculpture.

Pauline Borghese also counted the young violinist Niccolò Paganini among her lovers. Later, after his astonishing international career, Paganini – on the run from the French police after the collapse of a casino he had set up in Paris – died in Nice in May 1840. When a priest arrived to hear his absolution, he asked the violinist what there was in his instrument that allowed him to obtain such wonderful sounds. Raising himself up, riddled with pain, Paganini snapped back, 'The Devil!' Although he was confronting death and resentful of ecclesiastical intrusion, Paganini's remark was more than a flash of anger. He had once intimated to the poet Heinrich Heine that the devil guided his hand.

The celebrity was embalmed and put on show in a glass-topped coffin for three days. 'Poor Paganini!' wrote the author of an 1869 guide to Nice. 'His corpse used for an exhibition for the English like a stuffed crocodile or a lizard.'[52] Even after its unseemly display, the corpse had a hectic life. Catholics in Nice and Genoa refused Paganini a Christian burial. The body spent a year in an oil vat belonging to the Comte de Cessole, leader of the Nice Senate. At length, there was a burial in the grounds of Paganini's villa in Parma, until – in 1876 – Pope Pius IX absolved the violinist and the body was transferred to the town's cemetery.

In 1814, with the apparent end of the Napoleonic adventure, the French were forced to leave Italy and the King of Sardinia repossessed Nice. The Imperial School was shut, Jesuit colleges were re-established, and teaching reverted to Italian. Napoleon – captured and exiled – felt he was far from finished. Escaping from the island of Elba, where he had been smouldering in prison, he landed at Golfe-Juan on 1 March 1815 with eleven-hundred followers. He made one of those emotional, self-serving declarations that touched a nerve with his sympathizers: 'Frenchmen, in my exile, I heard your complaints and your wishes.' Initially, however, things did not go well. Antibes resisted and imprisoned those soldiers and officers Napoleon despatched to sound out the town. Still undeterred, the ex-emperor pitched camp outside Cannes. The following day, his armed band struck north through Grasse and marched fifty kilometres before nightfall. As the days passed, they attracted great support. On 20 March, Napoleon arrived in Paris at the head of many of the troops that had been sent to oppose him. The tricolour supplanted the white flag of the Bourbons. Shops replaced their *fleurs-de-lys* with Napoleonic eagles, and the ever-popular Bonaparte marched north to Waterloo.[53]

The Second Treaty of Paris, signed in November 1815, placed Monaco under the protection of Sardinia, which also annexed the Republic of Genoa. This was bad news for Nice. The recent deepening of the port by 800 galley slaves condemned for smuggling or desertion had, by the end of the eighteenth century, 'wonderfully enlarged' the commerce of the town.[54] Yet while Genoa secured its place as the major port of the Piedmont, Nice began to scent its destiny. In the mid-1780s, a significant number of English and French northerners had begun to pass the winter in the city. In 1784–5, there were 300 English people staying in the new Croix de Marbre district, with its neat streets and fine houses. Important additions to the city reflected the new attraction of the sea. Arthur Young commented on the building of a row of low houses a quarter of a mile long, with flat roofs covered with stucco forming a gracious terrace. This Galerie des Ponchettes overlooked the sea and was 'raised above the dirt and annoyance' of the street.[55] When, during the winter of 1821–22, a severe frost increased unemployment to a dangerous level, the English vicar in Nice raised funds to put the jobless to work building what became the Promenade des Anglais – a walkway conceived to satisfy the English fondness for strolling by the sea.

Although the Revolution had interrupted the fledgling habits of winter visitors, by 1827 there was a guidebook for foreigners on sale. A new bridge was constructed over the unruly River Paillon, which divided old Nice from the new town. The river had long been a problem. People quipped that the Paillon was a river in which the washerwomen of Nice dried their laundry. Often no more than a rivulet, it could – in a trice – become 'an impetuous torrent' that 'sweeps away houses and stables, ruins crops and tumbles furiously into the sea'.[56] In April 1744, during the War of the Austrian Succession, countless French soldiers drowned in a flash flood caused by the Paillon waterfalling down the mountains into Nice.[57] A flood warning system, in the form of a trumpeting sentry, was sited upstream.[58] Much later, in the 1880s, as tourism became of prime importance, the river was culverted and paved over.

Created in 1832, the Consiglio d'Ornato – a commission overseeing the amelioration and embellishment of Nice – originated plans for the impressive Place Masséna. This huge square was named after Nice's Napoleonic Maréchal, who had switched allegiance to the Bourbons after Waterloo. The Consiglio also extended the beach path started by the English, thus creating the Promenade des Anglais. In 1834, that novelty the steamship docked in Nice's Lympia port.[59] Exotic visitors started to arrive. After the French invasion of Algiers in June 1830, Hussein-Bey, the defeated Dey of Algiers, was received at a banker's villa in Cimiez, where he spent his days – according to the mid-century guide writer Léon Watripon – 'languishing under the spell of opium' with 'his most supple and devoted courtesans spread at his feet'.[60] For the previous 2,500 years, the region had been prey to strangers. Now it would start to welcome them.

If pulmonary disorders sent northerners in search of the sun, then it was an epidemic that changed the fortunes of the tiny fishing village of Cannes. Before the Revolution, Johann Georg Sulzer had been surprised 'that among the English who go to Italy for the bad season', no one had thought of stopping in Cannes, 'where the winter must also be relatively mild'.[61] For Smollett, his own discovery of Cannes came too late. It was on his return journey to Britain that he suggested he would rather have lived in Cannes 'for the sake of the mild climate, than either at Antibes or Nice'.[62]

By 1830, cholera, first observed in the Ganges delta of British India in 1817, had become a European pandemic. By 1834, it had reached the south of France. The Comte de Cessole – in his capacity as president of the Council of Health in the Comté de Nice – decided to close the frontier with France. On 18 December that same year, a Scottish lord who had helped terminate the slave trade, promoted primary and secondary education, given funds towards the creation of London University, and exposed the brutality of flogging in the army, was travelling to Genoa. He was stopped by the closure of the Var frontier. Used to getting his own way, Henry, Lord Brougham, was furious. Then he looked about him.

3

'Bathing in Sunshine'
1835–60

etween branches of umbrella pines swept against the sea, sunspots shock the water's surface, flashing silver-white. As the ripples calm, emerald, turquoise and sapphire are feathered by dark green foliage.

People from brick confines, shrouded in phlegmy-yellow fog, began to value this coast. Those who lumbered across the arid plains of Provence treasured its clear sea and cloudless air. They breathed and bathed in the infinite benefits of blue. Yet, even in 1839 on the shores of Golfe-Juan, an observant writer could mistake the place for a wilderness. Victor Hugo thought the gulf 'a small bay, melancholy and charming'. Surveying the scene ashore, the novelist saw no trace of human beings. Once again, 'Everywhere was deserted.'[1] Only one year earlier, returning by boat from Italy, Stendhal had remarked that the southern coast of France was 'bare and barren'.[2]

By contrast, George Sand found Eden in 'the very heart of immensity'. The endless ocean stood before her to the south; and behind her, 'fantastic palaces of eternal snow cut their brilliant summits in the pure blue sky'.[3] The region was newly prized. It was 'the true garden of Provence', a region covered with the thick, evergreen leaves of olive trees. Indeed, as the perception of 'wilderness' gave way to visions of paradise, a tradition grew that Adam and Eve, expelled from Eden, had found heaven on earth in the south of France. Even the olive trees, native to the Holy Land, were seen to give this coast a 'Scriptural character'.[4]

Not long before Lord Brougham discovered Cannes, the spirits of the French Romantic composer Hector Berlioz were revivified by a brief but important sojourn on the unspoilt coast. Its landscape and climate soothed the overheated imagination of the young Berlioz, who was contemplating an operatic, but all too real, murder. Arriving in Nice from Rome in the spring of 1831, the composer was en route to Paris – where he intended to do away with his ex-fiancée, Marie Moke. Berlioz had won the prestigious Prix de Rome and, while he was working in Italy, his betrothed treacherously married the heir to the Parisian firm of piano makers, Camille Pleyel. Berlioz plotted to disguise himself and kill Marie, her husband, her mother and – for his crimes – himself.

His journey from Rome was agitated. In Florence, he found a dressmaker to supply his disguise – the outfit of a lady's maid, with a hat and 'green veil'. Such attention to theatrical detail must have done something to allay the inflamed spirit of a man who spent the day 'raging up and down the streets… like a mad dog'. Upon reaching Genoa, Berlioz found that his costume had been mislaid. He obtained another and rehearsed his plans: 'Disguised as the Countess de M.'s lady's-maid, I would go to the house about nine o'clock with an important letter. While it was being read, I would pull out my double-barrelled pistols, kill number one and number two, seize number three by the hair and finish her off likewise', then 'turn the fourth barrel upon myself. Should it miss fire… I had a final resource in my little bottles.'[5]

Having planned his last act par excellence, upon his arrival in Nice, the calmness, vastness and beauty of the region began to work its magic on the young composer. The coast mollified him and he spent 'the twenty happiest days' of his life 'bathing in the sea, wandering through orange groves, and sleeping on the healthy slopes of the Villefranche hills'. The dramatic impact of the landscape prompted sketches for his *King Lear* overture. But such Romantic communion with nature roused the suspicion of the Kingdom of Sardinia's police. They reported that this so-called musician never went near a theatre but wandered 'alone on the hills, no doubt expecting a signal from some revolutionary vessel; he never dines at the *table d'hôte* in order to avoid spies; he is ingratiating himself with our officers in order to start negotiations with them in the name of Young Italy'. In the face of such suspicions, Berlioz was summoned to police headquarters. 'What are you doing here, sir?'

'I compose, I dream, I thank God for the glorious sun, the sea, the flower-clothed hillsides –'

'You are not an artist?'

'No.'

'Yet you wander about with a book in your hand. Are you making plans?'

'Yes, the plan of an overture to *King Lear* – at least the instrumentation is nearly finished, and I believe its reception will be tremendous.'

Asked who King Lear was, Berlioz explained.

'Sir, I know that you cannot possibly compose wandering about the beach with only a pencil and paper, and no piano, so tell me where you wish to go, and your passport shall be made out. You cannot remain here.'

'Then I will go back to Rome, and, by your leave, continue to compose without a piano.'[6]

The brief spell in Nice in the spring of 1831 had been decisive. At night, high up on the Corniche, 'the thunder of the waves upon the iron cliffs below, the stupendous majesty of Nature burst upon me with greater force than ever before'.[7] Berlioz decided that he was incredibly talented and should not throw away his life for a fickle eighteen-year-old. He returned to the Académie de France at the Villa Medici for an unhappy but stimulating stay.

Searching for solace – which Berlioz had unexpectedly found on the cliffs around Nice – Henry, Lord Brougham set out for Italy in late 1834 determined to restore his health, which had been 'ruined after 34 years of slavery'.[8] A potent choice of words. As the 'unofficial' leader of the Whigs during the 1820s, Brougham had been a tireless campaigner whose efforts resulted in the Emancipation Act of 1833, which improved on earlier, imperfect measures for the abolition of the slave trade. He struggled for legal and parliamentary reform and social amelioration. He championed education for working men and was involved in plans to create a university in London. In 1827, in the first book published by the Society for the Diffusion of Useful Knowledge, Brougham stated his belief in the joy of education: 'There is something positively agreeable to all men... in gaining knowledge for its own sake... The mere gratification of curiosity; the knowing more today than we knew yesterday...'[9] It was a credo that motivated his experiments and studies in the south of France.

The success of Brougham's career was counterpointed by a sad and chaotic private life. His marriage to Mary Ann Eden was no paradise. Having lost their first daughter in her infancy, Mary Ann was incapacitated by the birth of their unhealthy second child, Éléonore-Louise. Brougham suffered from bouts of hard drinking and depression. For a spell, he was blackmailed by Harriette Wilson – one of the most notorious London courtesans of the 1820s.[10]

Waspish and quick-witted, Brougham demonstrated his capacity for repartee in a famous exchange with the Duke of Wellington. When Wellington suggested that Brougham would only be remembered for the carriage he had designed, the retort was that Wellington would be remembered for a pair of boots. Although never losing his train of thought, Brougham was such a complex speechmaker that Charles Dickens once commented that he found himself 'falling into parenthesis within parenthesis, like Lord Brougham'.[11] On one occasion, Brougham spoke in Parliament on law reform for six hours, all the while sucking oranges to keep himself going.[12] Cannes was ideal for a man given to sustaining himself with citrus fruit. Bitter oranges had been introduced to Provence by the Crusaders. The sweet orange came later – brought to southern Europe from south China by the Portuguese during the Renaissance. At Cannes, the orange orchards were white with flowers in April and May – blossom used in the manufacture of *Eau de Cologne*.[13] As Brougham arrived in mid-December, the fruit was already ripening.

When Brougham – aged fifty-six – unexpectedly found himself stuck in Cannes, his sickly and beloved daughter, Éléonore-Louise, was with him. Apart from the arcadia spreading around him, Brougham delighted in a concoction many visitors found to be 'a broth of abominable things'. Of bouillabaisse, Charlotte

Dempster remarked, 'Every fisherman can cook it, but it is not every Englishman who can digest it'.[14] Brougham's pleasure in the dish was refreshing, and stood in contrast to Dr Rigby's relief in finding, in Nice, a dinner *'tout à l'Anglaise...* plain roast beef and boiled potatoes, with some special good draughts of porter'.[15] Brougham, with his appetite for bouillabaisse, was clearly made for the south.

The haven that Brougham came to know and love was extolled by a Welsh painter married to the German ambassador to Britain – Frances, Baroness Bunsen. Writing to her son, she basked in the scene: 'Here we are at Cannes, inhaling, swallowing, bathing in sunshine, in beauty, in purity of air!' The night sky 'could not be clearer... the stars more magnificent – Sirius and the entire constellation of the Dog high over the sea, Orion still higher, and Jupiter in zenith'.[16] Margaret Brewster noted that the moonlight could be so clear 'that one can easily read by it'.[17] A keen astronomer, Lord Brougham wrote that on the Mediterranean coast only three days out of 111 he was prevented from conducting experiments, whereas in England the ratio was reversed. Brougham's claim was somewhat inflated. Dr de Valcourt, a long-time practitioner in Cannes, 'studied the subject carefully' and rated 'the average over the whole Riviera at 51 wet days in the year'.[18]

Within weeks of being stranded by the cholera epidemic, Brougham bought a plot of land and commissioned a villa. It took over four years to build, by which time his daughter had died.

Lord Brougham and his friends on the terrace of his Cannes villa.

Stendhal – who much admired Brougham's progressive ideas – found the resultant Villa Éléonore-Louise 'so bourgeoise, so lacking in everything that speaks to the imagination'.[19]

Suffering from the loss of his second child, Brougham desperately needed the comfort and serenity of Cannes, where he could write for uninterrupted periods on the wide-ranging topics that absorbed him. He wondered if he ever wanted to return to Parliament. As he slowly overcame his grief, he began to enjoy the social whirl of Nice and Paris.[20] Furthermore, Cannes was becoming less secluded. Sir Herbert Taylor, bound for Italy with his own sickly daughter, passed through Cannes. Finding Brougham there, he decided to stay.[21] Another friend arrived. Finding he could bathe all through the winter, he also decided to settle. Many affluent Englishmen followed their example, bought land and set about building. They shipped turf from Britain – often annually – and so a process of genteel Anglicization began.

Although a diehard Republican, among Brougham's acquaintances in Parisian society was King Louis-Philippe, and it was this connection that enabled him to solicit nearly one million francs from the French government to build a proper port for the essentially English Cannes. By 1838, a protective jetty was finished. In 1843, the Hôtel Beau-Site opened and became famous for its seven hard tennis courts. The following year, there were twenty-five English families living in Cannes, a town protected from the fierce mistral wind by the hills to the north-west and shielded from the east winds by the hills above Antibes. The new development was blessed with a calm sea and sand, so bathers didn't have to bruise their feet on a pebble beach as they did at Nice. In 1851 – doubtlessly inspired by Nice's Promenade des Anglais – the mayor of Cannes decided to transform the seafront, which consisted of sand dunes, a few trees, rivulets and stagnant puddles, into a walkway. The resulting Boulevard de l'Impératrice, finished in 1866, soon became known as 'La Croisette' – derived from the Provençal word for a 'little cross', like the one that stood at its western end, marking the point of departure for the nearby island monastery of Saint-Honorat. Along this promenade, the most majestic hotels and villas were, one by one, constructed.

Cannes underwent such a dramatic transformation that, eight years before Brougham's death in 1868, a French epistolarian wrote to a friend, 'You have to visit its Babylonian villas to understand what the English can do with determination and money.'[22] Another Frenchman observed, 'One goes to Nice for the season, to Cannes to build a reproduction of Windsor and live forever.'[23] When he was buried in the cemetery at Cannes, Lord Brougham, founder of this new and elegant town, had reached the impressive age of eighty-nine. His calm life in Cannes had blessed the last three decades of his previously hectic political life.

As people started to come south in greater numbers, the tricks of travel and the pitfalls of the road were shared. Before the Revolution, Philip Thicknesse had advised travellers in France that 'when you make an agreement with an *Aubergiste* where you intend to lie, take care to include beds, rooms, &c. or he will charge separately for these articles'.[24] In the 1840s, John Murray's guidebook warned visitors not only to bargain but also to be skilled in negotiation – the innkeepers were past masters. Furthermore, he noted that the want of comfort and cleanliness rendered French inns vastly inferior to their German or Swiss counterparts. The common table, or *table d'hôte*, was a rowdy affair at which the English had to be wary lest they lose out in the general scramble for what was on offer. Added to that, ladies could suffer the indignity of hearing language that no Englishman would think of using in their presence.[25] It was a blessing, then, that the linguistic skills of the English left something to be desired. Henry Morford's *Short Trip Guide to Europe*, published for Americans later in the century, wisely advised travellers to focus on a range of enquiries and answers related to buying tickets, finding lodgings and making purchases. These 'may be committed to memory without much trouble and without the miserable affectation of supposing that this is "learning a language"'.[26] Published in 1874, Morford's guide was aimed at a more demotic range of voyagers. Murray's early handbooks were obviously pitched at the upper, educated class, as he left lengthy quotations from Latin authors untranslated.

In Murray's 1844 *Handbook of Travel-Talk: or Conversations in English, German, French and Italian* – which offers phrases to aid the traveller in an imaginative range of situations – the stiffness of the English gives insight into the quality of translation throughout. There are boasts tumbling from the lips of innkeepers that may surprise: 'Do not be afraid, Gentlemen: in our house the same sheets are never given to two persons.'[27] There are useful and reassuring exchanges for people who wish to rent: 'Are there any fleas here?' 'There are neither fleas nor bugs in my house.' There are imperious commands for frequently encountered travelling situations: 'Will you have this chest of drawers wiped out, it is quite dirty.' Resident chambermaids could be nothing if not thorough: 'You must first comb my hair well; it is all entangled. Take the open comb first; and then a fine one to clean my head... Do not press so hard, you hurt me.' 'I pressed rather hard to get out the scurf; but you have none, your head is quite clean.' There are soundings to be taken from fellow travellers: 'Is the road safe?' 'It is very safe, but still it is not prudent to travel after sunset.' And there is help for dealing with the complexities the traveller might encounter at the table: 'Sir, let me give you a wing or leg of chicken.' 'If you will allow me, I will eat a quail... it is neither too fat, nor too lean. I killed it myself the day before yesterday.'[28] To be linguistically forewarned was to be forearmed.

Between the months of May and November, visitors to the south were welcomed by 'a small gnat, with long legs and yellowish brown wings'. At its most dangerous, the mosquito came buzzing in the night. It moved closer for an attack effected 'by driving its proboscis like a lancet into the skin, extracting a drop of blood, and leaving behind, I fancy, a minute drop of poison or other cause of irritation'.[29] Murray noted that the 'pain inflicted by the bites is bad enough, but it is the air of triumph with which the enemy blows his trumpet, the tingling, agonising buzzing which fills the air, gradually advancing nearer and nearer, announcing the certainty of a fresh attack, which carries the irritation to the highest pitch'.[30]

Mosquitos were clearly an obsession. Margaret Brewster noted that 'in the middle of the gravest conversation, perhaps about the principles of the Peace Society, one hears a voice exclaim in savage glee, "I've killed him."' Brewster declared 10 November to be 'their day of doom'. Before that date, she counselled lemon juice as an effective antidote to their bites.[31]

In the late 1830s, there was still a rustic aspect to life in Nice. A goatherd milked on demand as he crammed his large trip into the houses of his customers.[32] Still under Sardinian rule, Nice was a colourful town. The Piémontaise soldiers, with their over-braided uniforms glinting and glittering, reminded the French epistolarian Antoine de Tourtoulon of the costumes at the Opéra-Comique.[33] Local dress was likewise a riot of colour, but of uniform cut. Fishermen wore the red Phrygian cap – a souvenir of their Greek ancestors – while the women imprisoned 'their beautiful and abundant hair in *crépines*' – silk nets of various colours under broad-brimmed, gently sloping straw hats or capelines. The flat tops of these were used to carry baskets full of olives, fruit or flowers. Léon Watripon noted the 'mischievous keen eye' of the local women, their relaxed Italian manner and 'teeth that could make milk seem black'.[34]

Fishermen and washerwomen at the eastern end of the Baie-des-Anges, Nice.

The town's population was musical, and delighted in the many festive days occupying the Catholic calendar. Albanis Beaumont, on his travels through the Maritime Alps, descended to Nice on a Sunday when the workers were at rest and dancing to the music of tambourines, flageolets and guitars.[35] The Rigbys – despite relishing English food – were delighted by the sights of what was, already, a vanishing world. One evening, Edward Rigby was charmed to see two women and a soldier dancing the courante on a pavement, while another soldier accompanied them on a mandolin.[36] In the poor villages around and above Nice, the inhabitants had no clocks, sundials or barometers. The time of night was judged by the position of the stars. During the day, they told time by the course of the sun.[37] Yet Nice itself was modernizing.

The census of 1838 revealed that most of Nice's population of 35,000 was, predictably, Catholic. The 322 Jews were fortunate enough to have a synagogue, while the 214 Protestants were obliged to worship in a private house behind high walls.[38] Permission had been granted by the King of Sardinia on condition that 'neither the exterior, nor the interior' would have the appearance of a church. Out on the streets, however, visiting Anglican clergymen were zealous. Watripon remarked that if you stopped to chat with English men of the cloth for just five minutes, they would slide a pamphlet into your hands entitled 'Go to Jesus'.[39] A place for prayer was of paramount importance for most British winter residents – rather like air conditioning, reliable Wi-Fi, and DEET are for the summer visitor today. In nearby Cannes – which in the first half of the nineteenth century was still in a different country from Nice – Brougham's friend, the wealthy Glasgow merchant Sir Thomas Woolfield, petitioned the French government for the right to build, on his property and at his own expense, an English church.[40] During its construction, the Sardinian position softened, and when Woolfield's church was finished, the architect proceeded to Nice to start work on a pseudo-gothic Protestant structure. A German Lutheran chapel followed. Then a modest Russian Orthodox church, funded by the imperial family. If Smollett and Brougham had prepared the way for colonies of ailing Englishmen, then it was the rigours of winter that sent the Russian aristocracy south.

As Russia's political climate was similarly harsh, embattled members of the intelligentsia fled to Europe and – for one reason or another – south to the Mediterranean. Among those who came to escape the repressive regime of Nicholas I were Mikhail Lermontov in 1840, Nikolai Gogol in 1843, and later, Ivan Turgenev, Alexander Herzen and Leo Tolstoy. Gogol and Turgenev came because of infatuation or amorous obsession; Herzen from political exhaustion and despair; Tolstoy to care for a tubercular brother.

It seems somewhat odd that Nikolai Gogol spent twelve years of his life abroad – much of that time in Italy. Gogol was the supreme conjurer of St Petersburg absurdity, the riotous divulger of Russian corruption who grew increasingly close to the Orthodox Church. Between November 1843 and March 1844 he was in Nice, nurturing his friendship with Alexandra Osipovna Smirnova – who had been a lady-in-waiting at the imperial court before marrying the landowner Nikolai Smirnov. Her Petersburg salon attracted literary figures such as Pushkin and Lermontov, and she interceded with Nicholas I to persuade the censor to pass Gogol's *Revizor* – or *The Government Inspector* – for performance. It was remarkable that such an audacious lampoon of provincial officials could be performed before a tsar obsessed with disciplining his unruly empire. At the premiere, etiquette dictated that no one could laugh aloud until the emperor himself was heard to do so. Nicholas laughed heartily and incessantly, guaranteeing a splendid evening for all.[41]

In Nice, Alexandra Smirnova and Nikolai Gogol became more intimate. He read her passages of his absurdist novel *Dead Souls*. Every day, they went for long walks, Gogol marvelling at the late-afternoon light playing on nearby mountains. Across slopes low enough to be covered with trees, he noted how the sun 'performs the most amazing miracles. These green mountains become crimson.'[42] As a late convert to Christianity, Gogol was fanatical and urged Alexandra to learn the psalms. She tried. Naturally, rumours started to circulate about the time they spent together, and friends in St

Petersburg warned Gogol that Alexandra should expect to be the target of gossip when she returned to the Russian capital in 1844.

The novelist Ivan Turgenev came south reeling from the physical eruption of a passion that had obsessed him for years. Pauline Viardot, the powerfully talented opera singer and composer, was singing in St Petersburg when Turgenev fell hopelessly in love with her. He followed her when she returned to Europe only to find many people similarly besotted. Of gypsy origin, Viardot had a remarkable range of three and a half octaves, and she occupied a prominent place in musical and literary circles. She enjoyed a sixty-year friendship with Clara Schumann, and when that notorious womanizer the poet Alfred de Musset went after her, she was protected by her long-time friend George Sand.

Viardot had a house at Courtavenel near Paris. Turgenev, like Alexander Herzen, was in the French capital to witness the revolutionary fervour of 1848 – unrest that was part of the pan-European republican revolt.

On 15 May, there was a mass demonstration in Paris in favour of Polish independence from Russia. Turgenev wandered among the crowds hoping for street-level solidarity, but instead found opportunist chocolate and cigar vendors moving through the masses – 'greedy, contented and indifferent'. The day before, the ever-reactionary Nicholas I had issued a manifesto proclaiming that it was the duty of every loyal Russian to oppose this new French revolution. Members of the Russian intelligentsia in Paris thought otherwise. They were, however, disappointed, as the overthrow of King Louis-Philippe in February was being compromised by the increasingly conservative Assembly of the Second Republic. When, on 23 June, the workers pushed hard to secure some semblance of liberty, both Turgenev and Herzen were at the barricades. Turgenev fled the violence; Herzen stayed, but became frustrated as mismanagement resulted in defeat.[43]

Turgenev spent the rest of the summer at Courtavenel, where he and Pauline became lovers. After years of trailing after Viardot like a devoted puppy, Turgenev was finally in the arms of his adored. Why he left Courtavenel abruptly at the beginning of October for Toulon and Hyères is not known, though one theory is that, although Viardot enjoyed Turgenev, she never loved him. From the south, Turgenev wrote effusive letters to her in German, as Pauline's husband did not understand the language. When it became clear that she was not going to join him, his letters degenerated into grumpy grouching about the weather – the thick fog seemed 'gloomy and grey'. Nevertheless, when Turgenev died in 1883, he left everything to his beloved musician.[44]

The philosopher, novelist and political agitator Alexander Herzen first came south in December 1847, delighting in this 'blessed area of Europe'. Despite the manifold social injustices to be found in France, Herzen was happy to be in a Europe seething with revolutionary intention. He had fled Russia after twice being arrested and exiled from its capital. As he crossed the Esterel for the first time – departing by moonlight and descending to the east as the sun was rising, he found that innumerable 'worries, sadnesses and above all, tiny irritations' were 'dispelled by such a morning'.[45] These moments in the sun offered Herzen a brief respite from his political unease. The tyranny of ideals and political abstractions were anathema to him. He understood that history was not logical, but rather evolved naturally in contempt of any desire to categorize it. Furthermore, he believed that to restrict freedom in the name of some future liberty was delusional – a mere excuse for authoritarianism. Each problem required individual and particular measures.[46]

Three years later, the south coast once again offered him relief. Shaken by the failed revolution of the liberal and radical movements, Herzen wrote that when he crossed the Var, he relaxed and 'breathed more freely'. He was, of course, no longer in France. It was 23 June 1850, two years to the day since Herzen had witnessed the revolutionary barricades going up on the Place Maubert in Paris during the 'June Days'. He agonized over that crushed uprising in which 10,000 workers were killed or injured. He understood that France was not ready to accept the dreams of the socialists and workers. 'Authority', he wrote, 'triumphed over liberty; the question that had agitated Europe since 1789 was resolved negatively.' To shelter and rest, Herzen chose Nice, 'not only for its soft air and sea' but also because it had no political, scientific or artistic meaning. 'I have less aversion for Nice than anywhere else and I'm happy. It's the peaceful monastery where I distance myself from the world... to which I bid goodbye. It has tormented me sufficiently and... I have neither the strength nor the desire to play a part in its cruel games.' He found the Sardinian town hot, calm, perfumed and deserted.[47]

Surveying the scene in France, Herzen beheld 'a tyranny without a tyrant'. It was an abstract and religious climate in which 'the fanaticism of ideas' went 'hand in hand with a lack of respect for persons'.[48] At the top, there was 'a limited company of political crooks and speculators who rely on social corruption, the sympathy of the bourgeoisie, the brutality of the police... and this company has, as its head, a chief police commissioner who received six million votes in memory of his uncle... who filled the plains of Europe with French corpses in order to make a Bourbon restoration possible!'[49] Under Napoleon III, that 'limited company' would behave exactly in the way that Herzen defined the state – 'a weapon wielded by the governing class to defend its own privileges'.[50] The irony of Herzen's chosen refuge was that the Second Empire under Napoleon III would define the social scene in Nice. Herzen would be forced to flee again from a haven which was fast becoming the playground of the aristocracy, a haunt of grand dukes, empresses and rich invalids.

The civilizational failure of 1848 was soon to be matched by personal tragedy. Herzen's wife, Natalia, began an affair with his friend, the German revolutionary poet Georg Herwegh. Devastated, Herzen suffered an emotional and intellectual paralysis although Natalia repented and remained with her husband. Then, in November 1851, the couple were waiting in Nice for Herzen's mother and their deaf-mute son, Kolya, to arrive by boat from Marseille. At 4 a.m. on the 16th, the modern paddlewheel steamboat *Ville de Grasse* collided with the *Ville de Marseille* west of the Île de Porquerolles. The larger boat had suddenly appeared from behind the rocks, ramming the *Ville de Grasse* which sunk at once, killing Kolya and his grandmother. To cap the personal tragedy, the following month, Louis-Napoléon Buonaparte – president since

1848 – proclaimed himself Emperor of France. The long-looked-for revolution was over. Natalia developed pleurisy and died in May 1852, after giving birth prematurely to a son who did not survive. Too numb to register her burial, Herzen would only remember the torchlit service in Nice, with 'a band of exiles, the moon, a warm sea beneath a mountain'.[51]

Leo Tolstoy passed the winter of 1860–1 in Hyères, 'for the simple reason that I am here, and it makes no difference where I live'. When his brother Nikolai was sent to Germany to cure his tuberculosis, he had decided to visit Europe with his sister and her children to study different systems of education. As the family toured the country, Nikolai's health deteriorated and the doctors prescribed rest on the south coast of France. Leo and his sister accompanied the invalid who – shortly after their arrival – died. Tolstoy wrote to his friend, the poet Afanasy Fet, 'nothing is worse than death. And, when one reflects well that it is the end of everything, then there is nothing worse than life either.' Moments before he died, Nikolai 'drowsed off but awoke and whispered with horror, "What is that?" That was when he saw it – the absorption of himself into Nothingness.'[52]

Deeply depressed by the early loss of such a wise and kind man, Tolstoy stayed on in Hyères trying to write. His diary confides how he had been 'torn' from life – his faith 'in the good in everything' shaken.[53] Nevertheless, he made visits to Marseille to pursue his enquiries into education. French schooling did not impress him, with its almost military discipline and incessant learning by rote. Although Germany was undoubtedly more progressive, Tolstoy discovered that everybody in Marseille had read Dumas and that 'each week, in the *cafés chantants*, at least one-fifth of the population received oral education, as the Greeks and Romans used to do'.[54]

Back in Hyères, Tolstoy started to write again. Aloof from the Russian community – despite the fact they had kindly arranged Nikolai's burial – he spent much time encouraging and teaching his sister's children. He arranged lengthy walks in the countryside, accompanied by a donkey carrying their food and wine. After a brief visit to Italy, Tolstoy went on to Paris and then to London, where he found Herzen – back in circulation and busy editing *Kolokol*, the revolutionary paper published for Russian exiles. For years, the death of his young brother continued to rankle Tolstoy. Two decades later, in *My Confessions*, he admitted that it 'showed me that the superstitious belief in progress is insufficient as a guide to life'.[55]

Members of the intelligentsia came south with emotional and intellectual baggage. The Russian nobility that started to arrive in the 1850s came with trunks full of luxury and left with a cargo of photographic albums containing souvenirs of the sun and light. In the winter of 1856, the widow of Nicholas I, Dowager Empress Alexandra Feodorovna, came to Nice to restore her fragile health. She settled in the Villa Aquaviva, owned by the future banker to the Russian community, Septime Avigdor. The local newspaper, *L'Avenir de Nice*, was justifiably excited that, once news of her presence spread abroad, a number of rulers would follow.

During the 1850–1 season, there had been fifty-two Russian families in Nice – a presence large enough to warrant fireworks celebrating the Russian New Year. By 1856–7, when the dowager empress arrived, there were 141 Russian families.[56] By 1860 – in the wake of Empress Alexandra's initiative and in the year of Nice's annexation by France – there were a significant number of Russians who, as Prosper Merimée noted, all seemed frightened by the imminent liberation of the serfs.[57]

After Russia's defeat in the Crimean War of 1853–6, the Russian fleet had been forbidden to pass through the Black Sea straits. Strategically, a Mediterranean port was desirable. Because the King of Sardinia-Piedmont, Victor Emmanuel II, was looking for an ally to free Italy from Austrian control, he offered Russia the use of the harbour at Villefranche. When Grand Duke Konstantin, second son of Nicholas I and Admiral-in-Chief of the Russian fleet, arrived with a small squadron on 1 March 1857, they were given the old penal colony to use as a coal depot. Trade between the two countries thrived. Russian wheat was imported; oil and fruits were sent to Moscow and St Petersburg. When the English protested that the facility at Villefranche provided a loophole for Russia to ignore the terms of the treaty that had ended the Crimean War, the southern press suggested it was an exaggerated response. There was, however, an alarming item in the *Journal de Nice* claiming that the Russians wanted to purchase the impoverished Principality of Monaco to use as a permanent Mediterranean base – but nothing more was heard of the idea until the early years of the twenty-first century.[58]

Russian naval officers, with their unfamiliar uniforms, cut a dash, while the influx of Russian aristocrats gave a vibrancy to the Riviera which the English valetudinarians did not. 'To give you a little gossip,' bubbled Prosper Merimée in a letter of December 1856, 'we have a Countess Apraxin who smokes, wears a round hat and keeps a goat in her salon that she has covered with herbs.'[59] The Apraksins were indeed a colourful family. Peter the Great had made the sea-fearing Fyodor Apraksin – a man credited with downing 180 glasses of wine in three days – an admiral.[60] In the early years of the twentieth century, another Apraksin who spent the winter in Cannes had a group of cellists playing night and day to soothe his nerves. When they failed to do so, a servant stood behind the count's chair ready to massage him and curtail his suicidal urges.

In the decade leading to the annexation of the Comté de Nice by France, there were French, German, Belgian, Danish, Polish and Russian visitors, but the majority remained English – 'reserved, a little proud, a little naive, but honest and reliable'.[61] Their dominance was clear from an encounter related by Alexandre Dumas *père*. Asked about the new arrivals, an innkeeper at the Hôtel d'York replied, '*Sono certi Inglesi, ma non saprai dire si son Francesi o Tedeschi*' – 'They are definitely English, but you can't tell if they are French or German.'[62] The preponderance of the British made them an obvious target for xenophobia. Their apparel appeared 'eccentric' and their attempts to speak French – according to Clément Balme – were ridiculous: '*Aoh! Comment vó appeler ce rue-ci. Oh! Yès, jé avé beaucoup de satisfécheunn de été venou môa dans cette beau pays. Il était aussi oun beau pays dans lé Angleterre.*' The British were distinguishable by their unmistakable wardrobe, their loftiness, their mispronunciation and their dining habits. When they ate, Balme noted, 'the most solemn silence reigns in the restaurants'. People seated at adjacent tables spent an entire season without developing an acquaintance initiated with a stiff 'good evening' on their very first day.[63] John Murray sprang to the defence of the English, explaining that their 'character is misunderstood by foreigners. The morose sullenness attributed by them to the Englishman is, in perhaps nine cases out of ten, nothing more than involuntary silence, arising from his ignorance of foreign languages.' The flipside of such restraint was a reputation for belligerence. Murray warns the traveller that Englishmen 'have a reputation for pugnacity in France: let them therefore be especially cautious not to make use of their fists... No French magistrate or judge will listen to any plea of provocation.'[64]

In 1860, Nice determined its destiny. The prolific French author Countess Drohojowska noted that 'if Nice is Italian by virtue of the supreme decision of the European governments, then by virtue of its manners, sympathies and habits it is French, or rather, with the aid of foreigners, it has become a cosmopolitan city'.[65] While the pro-French saw annexation as a return to their motherland, and argued that it would be in the best interests of local tradesmen, many Italians considered that France's proposed takeover would be achieved against the wishes of the people. At best, they saw it as a sad but necessary sacrifice in the cause of Italian unification.[66]

In February 1860, demonstrations for and against annexation disturbed theatrical presentations. At the Théâtre Royal, there were cries of '*Nice italienne*'; and at the Théâtre Tiranti, '*Vive la France, vive l'Empereur*'. At the Tiranti on 11 March, blows were exchanged in the stalls, and knives drawn, before soldiers arrived to restore order. On the streets, there was scuffling, and groups marched brandishing Italian flags. Despite the clashes, *L'Avenir de Nice* announced, on 23 March, that annexation was a fait accompli and that French troops would shortly arrive to maintain order. Two days later, the Tiranti was the scene of yet another demonstration, as pro-Italian spectators screamed, 'Down with France,' forcing the authorities to evacuate the theatre. A Piémontais regiment took possession of the offices of *L'Avenir*, demanding that the newspaper publish a rebuttal of their account of the incident. The author of the article – in hiding, since he had been challenged to a duel – published a retraction and apology at once.

To all intents and purposes, the annexation was a foregone conclusion, the result of bargaining between Napoleon III and Conte Camillo di Cavour, the prime minister of Piedmont-Sardinia. The French would help free Italy from the Austrian occupation of Lombardy and Venice. In return, they would obtain Savoy and the Comté de Nice – subject to a referendum. The results of municipal and provincial elections held on 15 and 22 January 1860 revealed a divided population. On 15–16 April, the referendum on the annexation saw an 85 per cent turnout. Voting was almost unanimously in favour of France, which promised a huge investment in transport that would aid the burgeoning travel industry. On 14 July 1860, the formal date of the handover, there was much rejoicing. At midday, the Sardinian flag was lowered on the governor's palace and replaced by the *tricolore*. It was, to a large extent, the moment when Nice became modern.[67]

During the 1850s and '60s, Napoleon III hoped that economic growth and cultural development would place France at the forefront of Europe. Paris was transformed by its prefect, that ruthless Alsatian bureaucrat Georges-Eugène Haussmann, who set the stage for the splendour of the Second Empire and created the backdrop for the Belle Époque. Haussmann vastly improved public health by channelling mains water and building underground sewers. He lit the city and commissioned useful buildings, including Les Halles, the extensive central market designed by Victor Baltard in 1847. A triumph of Second Empire architecture, the celebrated Paris Opéra – designed by the young Charles Garnier in 1861, though not completed until 1874 – was prompted by an Italian nationalist attempt to assassinate Napoleon III in the crowded street outside the old opera house. Garnier's building was sited on a separate, easily defendable city block – part of a plan for

Paris in which the new thoroughfares driven through old working-class neighbourhoods were deliberately made too wide to build insurrectionary barricades but straight enough for troops to move swiftly and fire on the disenfranchised who took to the streets.

Financiers – property speculators and railway barons such as the Pereires and the Rothschilds – accumulated vast wealth from the enormous building programme and expansion of transport under Napoleon III. The seductive and newly annexed Comté de Nice provided great investment potential. There were railways to construct, hotels to build, an infrastructure to improve. Charlotte Dempster noted that Napoleon III – in a forward-looking, ecological move – replanted the hills behind Nice, 'in the hope of rendering the climate less dry, and of preventing the dangerous floods'.[68] In Cannes alone, there were eleven hotels built in the 1860s, twenty-two in the 1870s and fourteen in the 1890s. Between 1860 and 1914, Nice became France's fastest-growing city, and as income depended on the spending of winter visitors, municipal projects were conceived with them in mind. Nice was shaped by outsiders. By 1862, palm trees and mimosas were planted along the Promenade des Anglais, and gas lighting had replaced the oil lamps. The city was becoming elegant and smart.

Hercule Trachel, *The Bay of Villefranche*, nineteenth century. Musée Masséna, Nice.

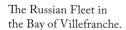

The Russian Fleet in the Bay of Villefranche.

The Les Ponchettes walkway above the *Cours* in central Nice. Henri Harpignies, 1887. Musée des Beaux-Arts de la Ville de Paris, Petit Palais.

The St Nicholas Orthodox
church, Nice, 1912.

The conservatory, Palais de
Masséna, Nice , 1898–1901.

Claude Monet, *Corniche near Monaco*, 1884. Rijksmuseum, Amsterdam.

Claude Monet, *Old Fort at Antibes*, 1888. Barberini Museum, Potsdam.

Paul Signac, *Saint-Tropez in a Storm*, 1895. Musée de l'Anonciade, Saint-Tropez.

Pierre Bonnard, *With Signac & Friends*, 1924. Kunsthaus, Zurich.

Henri Manguin,
The Siesta, 1905.
Villa Flora,
Winterthur.

Edvard Munch, *At the Roulette Table in Monte Carlo*, 1892. Munch Museet, Oslo.

Léon Bakst, set
design for Diaghilev's
Schéhérazade, 1910.

Georges Barbier, Paul
Poiret dresses, 1912.

French Art Deco book
plate, 1920s.

Le Train Bleu choreographed
by Nijinska for Diaghilev.
Costumes by Coco Chanel. Paris
Opera Production, 1992.

4

A Welcome to the World
1860–90

'How can France tolerate such a moral infection on its doorstep?' In 1865, Léon Pilatte asked how his countrymen could condone 'a princeling on a denuded rock' who 'braving universal condemnation, enriches his coffers with this shameful industry'.[1] The princeling was Charles III; the rock, Monaco; the shameful industry, gambling.

Charles was the latest in the long line of Grimaldis who ruled a principality that had never been more than a modest harbour. A suggested origin for the name 'Monaco' was *menouack*, meaning 'haven' or 'refuge'. It was also an allusion to the Phoenician god Melkarth Menouack.[2] Others link the name to Hercules, the divine hero who was venerated all along the southern coast of France. There were at least six and perhaps as many as forty-four exceptional warriors named Hercules. It is possible that one – named Monoecus, 'the solitary' – took refuge on the rock to which he gave his name: Monaco.[3] Around the time of Christ, the Greek geographer Strabo called the small haven 'Herculis Portus'. In the second century AD, Ptolemy wrote that the significance of the harbour was merely as a point of access to the Augustan Trophy of the Alps at La Turbie.[4]

On a January night in 1297, a Franciscan friar sought refuge in a castle built by the Genoese on that windswept rock. With armed supporters hiding outside, François Grimaldi threw off his religious disguise and the insurgents – including his nephew Rainier I, Lord of Cagnes – overpowered the castle's small garrison. The Grimaldis – one of the ruling families of Genoa during the Crusades – were shipowners and bankers who sided with the papist Guelphs. Forced into exile by the rival Doria and Spinola families – Ghibelline supporters of the Holy Roman Empire – the Grimaldis settled around Nice. François 'the Malicious' soon lost the rock to superior Genoese forces. Rainier I became the father of a dysfunctional but tenacious dynasty still ruling Monaco today.

Grimaldi coffers were replenished by trade and, in 1338, Charles Grimaldi purchased Monaco from Genoa. When he went off to fight for France in the Hundred Years' War, the small Monégasque population took to piracy. After serving ten years, Charles returned with a bounty that enabled him to add Roquebrune and Menton to his domain. Yet, once again, the Grimaldis were dispossessed by the wealthy Genoese. It wasn't until 1419 that they re-conquered the rock and held it.

Centuries of lethal family feuding followed. In the early sixteenth century, Lucien Grimaldi murdered his brother Jean II. Lucien was then killed – along with his brother Augustin – by their nephew François. In 1604, Lucien's grandson Hercule was slaughtered by a Monégasque mob whose daughters he had raped. The seven-year-old son of the rapist, Honoré II, was sequestered in Milan while his uncle ruled as regent. After ten years, during which Spanish troops were allowed to quarter in Monaco, Honoré II returned in 1615 and took the title of prince – thus transforming his modest territory into a principality. With Spanish troops encrusted on the rock and busy marrying Monégasque women, Honoré was powerless. He sought French help to evict the foreigners, but France's engagement in the Thirty Years' War meant that Monaco's problem was sacrificed to the wider European conflict. In September 1641, taking advantage of a freak storm, Honoré overpowered the Spanish. His accomplishment earned the respect of Louis XIII, and for the next 150 years the Grimaldis and their principality were tied to the convoluted, corrupt and often debauched French court.

When a member of the French nobility married a Prince of Monaco and was brought to the tiny rock, with its narrow streets and lacklustre palace, she invariably turned her back on it. Husbands proved all too ready to follow, as a pattern of aversion to the principality became the norm. The Grimaldis became prey to the intrigues of the French court. Such was the case with the match between Antoine Grimaldi and Marie de Lorraine in 1688, which was blistered by gossip. Jealous of the sexual adventures attributed to his wife, Antoine hung effigies of her lovers in the courtyard of his chateau. As new liaisons were whispered in his ear, effigies were added. When Marie visited, she was obliged to walk among these mute testimonies to her impropriety. Although Antoine was sexually free and easy, it was Marie who was forced to watch the images of her lovers burn on a huge bonfire of intrigue.

When the couple returned to the rock, the prince invited singers, dancers and musicians to enliven their tiny court, but want of money and the question of succession hung heavily. A dancer had given Antoine an illegitimate son, but Marie had given him daughters. A wealthy husband willing to become a Grimaldi had to be found. The only option was to plunge back into the libertine soap opera of the eighteenth-century French court, where Antoine found a husband for his daughter Louise-Hippolyte among the wealthy de Matignon family, who were prepared to cover Monaco's debts.

Increasingly, Monaco – all twenty-four square kilometres, including Roquebrune and Menton – depended on the protection of France, which by the mid-1780s was uncertain. Taxes were raised, and the small population, inspired by the stirrings of French malcontents, took to the streets. Once revolution flared in France, it erupted in the principality. Then, after more than 150 years of French protection, Monaco came under Sardinian domination.

Ill-advisedly, Honoré V returned Monaco to the old feudal system – the state becoming his private property and its inhabitants his serfs.[5] As an absentee landlord, he spent time in Paris while oppressing and plundering his principality. Throughout the five decades following Napoleon's defeat, Honoré V and his successor, Florestan, exploited Monaco's poor.[6] Visiting in 1840, Antoine de Tourtoulon found it a sad, lifeless town. He would only 'take away from Monaco the sweet hope of never returning'.[7]

Apart from the centuries of squabbling Grimaldis, the theme running through Monaco's dramatic history was the impoverishment of its ruling family. After Florestan died in Paris, his son Charles III – driven by his ambitious mother, Caroline – became the maker of modern Monaco. Impressed by the increasing success of Nice in attracting international visitors, and fascinated by the way in which the casino in Bad Homburg generated finances for the small, sovereign state of Hesse-Homburg, Caroline made plans to enrich the Grimaldis. Gambling houses in France – open, then shut, then open – had been closed once again by King Louis-Philippe on 1 January 1838.[8] Here was an opportunity for Monaco, and one with which other Riviera resorts could not compete.

In April 1856, a thirty-five-year concession to run a casino in return for a quarter of the profits was awarded to two Frenchmen, Léon Langlois and Albert Audet. An absolute disaster, their venture was abandoned two years later. An entrepreneur named Pierre-Auguste Daval took over and failed.[9] Théodore de Banville watched as the casino's bank was broken three times in a row, with a loss of 54,000 francs.[10]

In Bad Homburg, the casino was run by two brothers who had fled France, accused of the illegal telegraphic communication of insider stock-exchange information.[11] With a combination of audacity and publicity, the Blancs made a great success of Bad Homburg, relying on a lucrative clientele of German princes and Russian aristocrats. William Makepeace Thackeray, satirizing the set-up in *The Kickleburys on the Rhine* of 1850, called Bad Homburg 'Rougetnoirbourg' and François Blanc 'M. Lenoir'.[12]

After a spate of suicides forced the Bad Homburg casino to shut, François Blanc was on the lookout for new opportunities. Compared with the chic German spa town, Monaco appeared nothing if not unattractive – particularly in light of the failures of its recent gambles. When, in 1863, Caroline persuaded Blanc's arthritic wife that the Mediterranean climate would be of great benefit to her, Grimaldi lawyers found Blanc willing to try his hand. The concession would cost him – for a fifty-year hold on the Société des Bains de Mer et du Cercle des Étrangers – 1,700,000 francs. The Grimaldis would receive 10 per cent of the net profits, 50,000

Monaco at the very beginning of the mid-nineteenth century boom.

francs annually, plus a weekly private allowance of 2,000 francs.
Through James de Rothschild of the Paris–Lyon–Méditerranée
Railway, Blanc raised the capital to build a casino, hotels, villas and
roads.[13] Soil was brought in to cover the rock, and exotic vegetation
was planted as the new casino would be built on a hitherto deserted
plateau with the unwelcoming name of 'Spélugues'. This derived
from the Latin *spelunca* – 'cave' – which carried the connotation
of 'a low, disreputable haunt, a den of thieves'.[14] Providing obvious
ammunition for moralists, on 1 June 1866 Spélugues became Monte
Carlo, in honour of Charles III. Soon afterwards, the fortunes of
Monaco were changed by the arrival of Rothschild's railway.

Almost by accident, Romantics, botanists and determined
travellers had found Eden. Privileged people followed, with illnesses,
prejudices, and the general grumbling which filled the empty hours
of sunlit boredom. Difficult access protected their paradise. Then, in
mid-October 1866, the first rail passengers arrived on the Riviera
after a twenty-three-hour journey from Paris. It was a hissing,
rattling, rumbling method of transport, which replaced the bone-
breaking carriage, stubborn mule and pitching felucca.

When the British first started building in Cannes, the surrounding
countryside had remained undisturbed. With the arrival of the
railway, arcadia was ruffled. The projected route along the flat strip

of coastal plain was a threat to the peace and property of the early British. The line was planned to run right through Lord Thomas Woolfield's estate. Only after the intercession of Prosper Mérimée and Lord Brougham was the track diverted.[15]

Writing from Cannes to the great architect Eugène Viollet-le-Duc, Prosper Mérimée remarked that the 'English are established here as in a conquered land. They've built 50 villas or châteaux each more extraordinary than the last' and they 'deserve to be impaled for the architecture they imported'.[16] Mérimée persistently complained about British dominance. 'In two months', he fretted, he had 'hardly had the chance to speak French'. However, as the seasons went by, Mérimée came to enjoy the company of men like Brougham and Woolfield.[17] Universally 'liked and respected',[18] Woolfield made a great contribution to the style of life on the coast. He imported the Australian variety of eucalyptus, and there is no better testimony to the Riviera's astonishing climate than the success of that tree and the ornamental date palm. Elsewhere, they are only to be found several degrees further south.[19] Woolfield also introduced English sports to the Riviera. When Queen Victoria sent her eight-year-old son, Leopold, to Cannes in 1861 as a palliative for his haemophilia, Woolfield laid out a croquet lawn in the garden of his villa. Crown Prince Wilhelm – later Kaiser Wilhelm II – spent six months in Cannes in 1869 with his brother Henry. They likewise much enjoyed Woolfield's croquet lawn.[20] Five years later, when the craze had faded, the turf was converted into a lawn tennis court – the first on the Riviera. So much in demand, matches were booked to begin as early as eight in the gentle chill of a winter's morning.[21]

In 1864, the watercolourist and fabricator of nonsense rhymes Edward Lear made Nice his first choice for a winter base – describing it as 'odious to me in all respects' except for its magnificent climate. Lear took furnished lodgings on the Promenade des Anglais in which the carpets and wallpaper were full of 'large flights of red and blue and green parrots with roses and mustard pots interspersed'. So awful was the effect that Lear was obliged to buy plain material to cover them. For the next three years, Lear chose Cannes, where the villas were so widely spaced and the roads so dirty that without a carriage he felt somewhat stranded. Unlike Nice, there were no public amusements, so people made their own. Lear's neighbour during his first winter was the bisexual writer and scholar John Addington Symonds, who was in Cannes with his wife and his daughter, Janet. Only in his mid-twenties, Symonds was seriously affected by consumption yet his condition did not prevent him from enjoying lively exchanges with Lear, delighting particularly in their grumbling competitions. Lear entertained Janet with his nonsensical rhymes. He recited one originally written for the children of his patron, the Earl of Derby – 'The Owl and the Pussycat went to sea in a beautiful pea-green boat...' For Janet, Lear embellished his performance with drawings.

Lear's French neighbour was Prosper Mérimée, who did not like Lear's drawings and watercolours. Indeed, the paintings did not provoke much local interest. When he gave up Cannes and its 'barely aristocratic idiots' – Lear had sold only £30 worth of pictures during his final season.[22]

A yearly visitor to Cannes from 1856 until his death in 1870, Mérimée was well placed to observe its development. He noted that a plot of land bought by a local from Lord Brougham for 4,000 francs in 1840 was being sold in 1862 for 150,000. A plot bought from the state some years earlier for 300 francs was covered with houses and would be worth, if it were for sale, more than 500,000 francs.[23] Lord Woolfield purchased large swathes of terrain, constructed villas, and sold to the English who were flocking south. His gardener, John Taylor, became a banker, estate agent and wine merchant. He started *L'Indicateur de Cannes*, a publicity sheet dedicated to sales, rentals and the hiring of servants. He also brought English builders and engineers south, not only to work on private commissions but also to improve the local infrastructure. In 1884, Taylor became the first British Vice-Consul in Cannes, where down through the years his descendants have managed the prestigious John Taylor real estate firm – whose clients have included Queen Victoria's son Edward, Prince of Wales, Richard Burton, Gregory Peck, and the playboy and Fiat proprietor Gianni Agnelli.

During the eighteenth century, new initiatives in medicine led to experiments in seawater therapy. This drew people to Scarborough, Weymouth and Brighton. After that, British bathers tried northern France at Boulogne and Dieppe, while travellers on the Grand Tour were much impressed by the sight of Italians frolicking in the waves.[24] *Cook's Handbook* noted that, at Cannes, 'there is a beautiful sandy beach, gently sloping towards the sea, whose waters are warmer by ten to fourteen degrees than those of the Atlantic'. As there was little tide, cumbrous and ugly horse-drawn bathing machines in which to change were unnecessary. Small wooden huts were placed on the beach for that purpose, making Cannes 'one of the most attractive bathing resorts on the shores of the Mediterranean'. The handbook did, however, warn its readers to avoid parts of the beach 'which are situated near the outfall of the town drainage'.[25] Although much safer than the unruly surf on the English coast, ladies visiting Cannes were counselled to venture into the water with great caution, 'and never stoop without taking hold of a rope when a wave passes them'. To ignore such advice would be to 'run the risk of receding with a wave, which, on account of the rapid descent of the coast, retires with... celerity and strength'.[26] The littoral, formed by dramatic geological activity, created a narrow and precipitous continental shelf – the seabed became very deep very close to the shore.

An early and passionate advocate of sea bathing on the Riviera was one of the liveliest members of the Russian community – the 'remarkably clever, well-informed' Grand Duchess Helena, widow of the Grand Duke Mikhail, brother of Nicholas I. She had, wrote Margaret Brewster, 'rheumatic gout, like the whole winter population of Nice'[27] – a condition that encouraged her to experiment in the sea. To a Russian grand duchess used to a *banya* in which the sauna is followed by an icy plunge, naked bathing in the waters of the Mediterranean would hardly have proved challenging. As summer approached, Helena found the temperatures rising fast, but the soothing sea breezes argued that the resort could be kept open – at least until the end of June. Bathing in the summer might be a possibility, and the grand duchess was among the first to subscribe to a projected municipal winter and summer casino with gardens, lecture halls and sea bathing.[28]

Haunting the magnificent villas of Cannes, and dogging fashionable promenades taken in varnished boots, crinolines and conical crinolettes, was the spectre of chronic illness and death. Guy de Maupassant, who rented the Villa Montplaisir in 1884, observed that tuberculosis, 'the sickness that gnaws, burns and destroys thousands of people, seems to have chosen this coast to claim its victims'. He dubbed Cannes 'the flowery cemetery of aristocratic Europe'.[29] A doctor's recommendation for a patient to take a cure in the south of France was 'generally the first scene of the last act of the drama'. Charlotte Dempster rejoiced that 'sometimes, thanks to these fair skies, we see Death baulked of his conquest'.[30]

At a time when medical books came dosed with the wisdom of the ages, the Irish doctor Thomas More Madden celebrated the long tradition of recommending the benefits of convalescence away from home. The phrase 'a change of air' resonated down the ages, from Hippocrates to the Elizabethan Thomas Browne – who urged an escape from the 'malevolent places on earth, which single out our infirmities'.[31] During the nineteenth century, one of these was Dickens's London, with its 'fog too thick... mud and mire too deep' – a murky place where shops were 'lighted two hours before their time'. That is the baleful portrait of the British capital which Dickens offers in *Bleak House*, published in 1853.[32] Interestingly, his reaction to Marseille, which he visited in 1846 to board a steamer for Genoa, hardly painted a more salubrious picture. On the outskirts, he found 'dust, dust, dust everywhere'. The city itself was 'a dirty and disagreeable place', but from the fortified heights the view of the Mediterranean was 'delightful' and they provided a refuge from 'a compound of vile smells perpetually arising from a great harbour full of stagnant water, and befouled by the refuse of innumerable ships with all sorts of cargoes'. The city yields a truly Dickensian vision: 'In the very heart of all this stir and uproar, was the common madhouse... looking straight upon the street... where chattering madmen and madwomen were peeping out, through rusty bars… while the sun, darting fiercely aslant into their little cells, seemed to dry up their brains.'[33]

The Mediterranean was not all blue skies and balmy days. As a maritime region, the south-east coast was exposed to plague and yellow fever. As a frontier, it knew the contagious diseases that rifled the camps of troops on the move. In 1735, 3,000 people perished in Nice; and again, in 1799, fever was rampant. Even at its peak as a haven for convalescents, smallpox was reported in the town in the winter of 1878–9.[34] Nevertheless, the region's situation and climate increasingly attracted sickly people from the north. In every corner of industrialized England, with its soot-laden air, sufferers from pulmonary diseases were at great risk. About 75,000 people died of tubercular consumption in 1840.[35] Doctors urged those who could afford it to go south.

Despite the great number of medical treatises, Madden lamented that 'there is still a great deficiency of accurate information concerning the most frequented health resorts'.[36] Some publications merely copied information from advertisements, while others were not written by doctors but by people with a commercial interest in the locality they promoted. As for the people who haunted such places, Madden had little time for the wealthy, 'who, having no necessary occupation have become prematurely exhausted or "used-up", by the laborious idleness of modern fashionable life, and imagine themselves to be ailing when, in fact, they are merely blasé'. The increasingly fashionable escape from their 'condition' was 'to travel in pursuit of health', merely to provide them with something to do.[37] Their jaded attitude helped to explain how places like Nice – initially health resorts – became pleasure havens. If diversions were not disagreeable to the rich when they imagined they were ill – how much more fun it would all be when they found their health miraculously improved. Indeed, the 1879 *Cook's Handbook to the Health Resorts* suggested that Nice – inferior to 'Cannes, Hyères or Menton, as a winter residence for invalids' – was the centre of 'fashion and gaiety'.[38] Nine years later, high society had moved on. Without wishing 'to disparage the very pleasant society to be met with in Nice, it is universally admitted that the tide of the best

people has undoubtedly flowed towards Cannes'.[39] Nice prices were
no longer only affordable to the rich.

There were serious problems associated with a trip to the south.
Departure was frequently left too late, to a moment 'when every
remedy has been tried in vain' and a change of climate was the only
option left. Then there were the 'accidental difficulties on the road'
that 'invariably added to the patient's sufferings'.[40] One family,
having spent five weeks travelling, lost their sick daughter only
days after reaching Hyères.[41] Invalids found prices high in resorts
where hoteliers and shopkeepers were obliged to make their living
in only six months of each year. Repeated visits – often necessary
for a cure – were beyond the means of many, and recurring winter
absences played havoc with the career of anyone obliged to work.[42]
But for those who could and did afford several trips, the results
could be spectacular.

One function of the numerous guides and medical treatises
published in the last three decades of the nineteenth century was
to point the visitor to the microclimate best suited to their disease.
Jules Monod's 1902 *Nice, Monaco et Menton* records that, in Nice,
a Dr Salemi specified four distinct quarters that were advantageous
to different conditions. The seafront, with its dry air, was good for
tuberculosis, the old, the infirm and scrawny children. The hills,
including Cimiez, were good for people with catarrh, as well as
for diabetics and the aged. To the north of the port, upstream on
the Paillon, the Plaine de Riquier and the Vallon des Fleurs were
humid – good for gastric problems, skin diseases, nervous and
genitourinary conditions. The boulevards and avenues of the city,
exposed to salty breezes, were good for a variety of temperaments
in which nervous conditions did not predominate. This central area
was also suited to hypochondriacs, who would benefit from the
many distractions that Nice had to offer.[43] Those who were anxious
or irritable should clear out of Nice altogether, and seek refuge in
the surrounding countryside.

Invalids were advised to avoid the freshness of the early morning,
the evening dews in the hour after sunset, and to dress warmly and
use a parasol.[44] Opponents of gambling at Monte Carlo suggested

that great danger lay in leaving the closed, stuffy gambling rooms in a highly excited state and walking in the chill that settled after sunset. Most importantly, a patient should never consider returning north before the month of May.[45] If the worst should happen, those who accompanied the dying were advised to remove all precious items from the deceased, as there were people who thought that stealing from a dead body did not constitute theft.[46] The dead should ideally be buried within twenty-four hours because 'decomposition occurs rapidly' in the south. Representatives of the deceased were then responsible for any cost of 'making good any damage caused by the illness and death' and 'putting the bedroom into a proper sanitary condition' by repapering, whitewashing and renewing the curtains.[47]

The two towns most associated with cure and convalescence were at opposite ends of the Riviera – Hyères and Menton. Hyères was well sheltered from the mistral, the wind that blew mercilessly for two or three days at a time. At full force, the mistral was capable of total disruption. Dempster complained that 'cypress hedges are bent down... as for the dust, *that* is everywhere! It is in your eyes... in your dress, in your ink-bottle, and between the leaves of your books.'[48] At its best, when blowing gently, the mistral – accompanied by steel-blue skies – had the effect of purifying the air and dispersing epidemic diseases.[49]

A host of French doctors who had reservations about 'cold, damp and windy' Nice heartily recommended Hyères. Yet the town was found wanting in hygiene. Dr Madden advised visitors to avoid the 'water of the wells... dug dangerously near to the cesspool or manure heaps' and instead drink the subterranean water found to the south-east of the town.[50] Drainage – as elsewhere along the Riviera – was also a problem, with open sewers running down the centre of the steep streets of the old town,[51] diffusing 'pestilential odours'[52] and generating typhus spread by the bacteria-filled faeces of parasites. The wife of the Scottish writer Robert Louis Stevenson wrote to John Addington Symonds in January 1883 about the victims of a typhus outbreak – 'all day the death-bells rang, and we could hear the chanting whilst the wretched villagers carried about their dead lying bare to the sun on their coffin-lids, so spreading the contagion through the streets... During the night a peasant-man died in a house in our garden, and in the morning the corpse, hideously swollen in the stomach, was lying on its coffin-lid at our gates.'[53]

Robert Louis Stevenson – on the cusp of success when he arrived on the Riviera – was suffering from ophthalmia, rheumatism and sciatica. After a spell outside Marseille and a stay in Nice where his health improved, he and his ailing wife, Fanny, tried Hyères. From March 1883 to July 1884, they rented La Solitude, a 'cramped' Swiss-styled cottage with a small garden. Stevenson considered the early days at Hyères 'the happiest time of my life'.[54] He was writing *Penny Whistles* – a working title for what became the *Child's Garden of Verses*. He wrote ecstatically to his parents, 'There has been offered for *Treasure Island* – how much do you suppose?... A hundred pounds, all alive, O! A hundred jingling, tingling, golden, minted quid. Is not this wonderful?... The weather... continues vomitable; and Fanny is quite out of sorts... it does look as if I should support myself without much trouble in the future... It is dreadful to be a great, big man, and not be able to buy bread.'[55] In excellent spirits, Stevenson had 'crushed through a financial crisis' and was able to work between four and five hours a day. Amidst this euphoria, he was forced to leave Hyères penniless to consult a doctor in Nice – the money for *Treasure Island* had not yet come through.[56]

Early January 1884 saw Stevenson lying 'at death's door' in Nice with 'an acute congestion of the internal organs'. He returned to La Solitude a few weeks later to profit from the effects of 'a beneficent, loud-talking, antiseptic mistral'.[57] His remission was short-lived. In May 1884, 'violent haemorrhages from the lung' forced him to leave Hyères, where cholera broke out shortly afterwards. Yet his sojourn had secured Stevenson ten more years. The decade until his death in 1894 on Samoa was prolific and adventurous.

In 1874, the Polish sailor and English writer Joseph Conrad spent time on the Giens Peninsula, south of Hyères, before shipping out from Marseille. After three years at sea, Conrad returned in March 1877 when a painful abscess kept him ashore longer than he intended. He tried a little smuggling. Successful at first, he was then caught and barred from serving as a French seaman. With borrowed money, he took himself to Villefranche to try his luck with the American squadron. Unsuccessful, he moved on to Monte Carlo and gambled away the rest of the money he had scrounged. When he managed to get back to Marseille, he attempted to shoot himself.[58] Abscess, self-inflicted wound and gambling apart, Conrad was not in the region to cure disease or luxuriate. He was there to ship out.

At the other end of the Riviera from Hyères was Menton. Sheltered from fierce winds from the north by high mountains covered on their lower slopes with pine forests and olive, orange and lemon trees,[59] Menton was celebrated as 'the queen of the winter resorts' – although access was difficult. Before the early years of the nineteenth century, the town could only be reached 'by sea, on foot or on muleback'.[60] Even when transport improved and the railway arrived in the early 1870s, Menton – encircled by mountains – still remained remote from the world. For those seeking rest, its isolation was a powerful aid to recovery.

As with Hyères, visitors found that the residents had 'very dirty habits' and were 'sadly wanting in nasal sensibility'. One writer, 'on attempting to advance through one of the narrow side streets dividing the pretty villas' was 'obliged to beat a hasty retreat; and this was not the only pretty lane so vilely misused'.[61] The Promenade du Midi fronting the port was messy and the beach was sometimes made inaccessible by the piles of clothes spread out to dry.[62] Washing was a perennial problem. Go 'where one might, women were washing clothes, and that in a manner most disgusting and repulsive to English notions. Instead of washing them in some rural part with pure hot water and soap... these women will walk to any spot where a drop of water can be had, no matter how foul, or whence it comes... they haunt the rivulets, which are full of olive juice sent down from the olive mills' along with 'mud, and other dirt'.[63]

The reputation of Menton as a health resort was largely secured by Henry J. Bennet's *Winter and Spring on the Shores of the Mediterranean*, first published in 1861, translated into German in 1863 and published in New York in 1870. Dr Bennet had arrived in Menton in October 1859, worn down by decades of hard work in London and suffering from tuberculosis. Soon finding his condition improved, he adopted Menton 'as a permanent winter professional residence'[64] and set out to promote its medical benefits. After the arrival of the railway in 1869, Bennet enthused that a 'traveller may leave the London Bridge station at 7.40 on Monday morning, by mail train for Paris, and be at Mentone for supper at 9.45 p.m. the following day'.[65] To promote his medical practice, Bennet observed that sufferers from asthma and bronchitis also benefitted from the climate and boasted that 'after ten winters passed at Mentone, I am surrounded by a phalanx of cured or arrested consumption cases'.[66]

In the early days, invalids outnumbered visitors and 'society' could scarcely be said to exist. In the period between New Year and carnival, the municipality gave balls and – 'with great kindness and cordiality' – invited foreigners. Residents who had visited in previous winters knew better than to send clothes to the wash during carnival, as laundresses would think nothing of loaning garments for disguises.[67] Menton's carnival celebration was shabbier than its Nice counterpart, and somewhat terrifying to people unfamiliar with the liberties it afforded. English families were obliged to lock their doors to prevent revellers from bursting in upon them. One unsuspecting lady answered her doorbell and was frightened to find 'four hideous masks with long bird's beaks at the door'. The intruders 'took advantage of her surprise to fly past her into the drawing room' and startled everyone 'by perching themselves on the armchairs and sofa, and by chattering together in shrill bird's language for some time'.[68] Then they dropped their disguises and revealed themselves to be the family's dressmaker and her friends. The Mardi Gras parade that formed the climax to carnival, when the 'huge Menton man' was set ablaze, was again less spectacular than at Nice but no less frightening. The concluding rowdiness was the ball for the workers, which continued until dawn to the loud cries of 'Another polka!' 'One more waltz!' – their last chance for a little fun before the deprivations of Lent.[69]

Between Holy Thursday and Easter Sunday, the church clock was stopped and time was kept by shaking boxes full of bones – a tradition known as 'rattling the bones of Judas'.

Easter Sunday was a moment of jubilation and release for locals, but for the winter residents – many of whom were sad to face their return home – it marked the beginning of the end.[70] Although a good number left in a much better condition, there were – increasingly – questions raised about the suitability of the coast for certain ailments. By the late 1880s, physicians were observing that sanatoria in the mountains were more suited to consumptives. There had always been misgivings, and it was observed that the locals – believing a dry climate better for chest infections – sent their consumptives away from the coast to avoid the irritation caused by the evaporation of salt water. Dr Thomas More Madden, having considered the opinion of various medical authorities, came to the conclusion that he could not 'share the opinion of those who consider Mentone the Utopia for invalids generally, and the climate *par excellence* for pulmonary sufferers in particular'.[71] Although, over the years, many people benefitted from cures in the south, the growing scepticism of the medical establishment led to the Riviera realigning itself to leisure and pleasure.

In Menton, one perfectly healthy and illustrious visitor was Queen Victoria, staying for the first time on the French Riviera. In 1879, she had holidayed on the shores of Lake Maggiore at the eclectic, neo-Gothic villa owned by the railway engineer and Renaissance art collector Charles Henfrey. Three years later, she accepted Henfrey's offer to use his Swiss-styled Châlet des Rosiers at Menton, 'prettily situated, out of the town… near a fine valley covered with olive woods'.[72] Her Majesty toured the gardens at nearby La Mortola, which had been created by the Quaker silk and tea merchant Sir Thomas Hanbury with the aid of the German botanist and landscape gardener Ludwig Winter.

The queen travelled through France incognito, posing as the Countess of Balmoral. Xavier Paoli, the French special commissary detailed to protect foreign royalty on French soil, suggested that it was a disguise 'to which she attached great importance' but which 'did not deceive a soul'.[73] The royal train comprised seven coaches – two of them, the queen's private property. One of these was Victoria's saloon-carriage, which Paoli noted was 'padded throughout in blue silk' and 'presented, in its somewhat antiquated splendour, the exact appearance of an old-fashioned apartment in a provincial town'.[74] Victoria's Scottish doctor, Sir James Reid, recalled the journey. They travelled at thirty-five miles per hour during the day and twenty-five at night. They stopped every morning for the queen to dress and for the gentlemen to shave. The train also paused for meals. While excellent French menus were enjoyed by many who were travelling, the queen dined on food brought from Windsor, including an Irish stew which was kept lukewarm in red flannel pouches hung from the carriages – an unappetising practice that persisted on the queen's subsequent visits to the south.[75]

Somewhat spoiling Victoria's delight in Menton was the knowledge that her abrupt, short-tempered companion, John Brown, disliked the town.[76] Anxious about a spurious threat from Irish revolutionaries, he despaired of the attention his kilt provoked among the locals. His surliness was exacerbated by his sufferings from the disease that would kill him the following year.[77] Victoria's trip was short. Leaving for home on 12 April, she was sad yet 'grateful to have been permitted to spend four weeks in that lovely and far famed Riviera'.[78]

The queen's visit clearly contributed to the rising status of Menton as a fashionable resort for the British. Everywhere you looked, signs were in English. Pharmacies displayed jars of monumental proportions bearing English coats of arms. Shops were full of British beer, wines that were dear to the English, York ham and breast of smoked goose. English routines mapped out the day: breakfast and a promenade, then letter-writing at the hotel, lunch, another promenade, tea, then dinner followed by shows or games. There was sport. A cricket pitch had been laid out. The English pastor was William Webb Ellis – the man credited with the invention of rugby football.[79]

If Victoria's visit promoted Menton for the British, the Russian royal family drew their own countrymen. Nicholas II's aunt, Grand Duchess Anastasia, founded the Russian Orthodox Association of Saint-Anastasia in 1880 so that poor-ish young Russians with pulmonary troubles could benefit from a rest home in Menton. She also built an Orthodox church and a Russian farm with a restaurant attached. If the English church at Menton would not have been out of place in Hertfordshire, the Russian church would not have seemed odd in Pavlovsk.

The invention of Monte Carlo and the arrival of the train changed Nice. Year by year, it became less suited to convalescence, burnishing its appeal for increasingly healthy and urbane visitors. People came for pleasure and for playing baccarat in the clubs on the Promenade des Anglais. On arriving at the station, W. Cope Devereux found a scene 'far more doubtful and mixed than at Cannes, where you feel pretty sure of everyone'. Shop windows of stationers teemed 'with books professing to teach the secrets of roulette' or 'how to win at Monte Carlo', and the general riff-raff included 'many wretched desperadoes from the gaming-tables'.[80] Nonetheless, Nice looked more splendid by the year. Each winter, while people trembled with cold in Paris and noses froze in St Petersburg, Nice flowered.[81]

Alphonse Karr – novelist, editor of *Le Figaro*, horticulturalist and fervent Republican – decided to flee Paris for Italy as soon as Louis-Napoléon declared himself emperor in 1852. Karr settled in the easy-going atmosphere of Sardinian Nice, where he noticed that people – content to enjoy the wildflowers growing in the countryside – would send their orders to Genoa when they needed a formal bouquet. So, in 1857, he opened the Maison Alphonse Karr – and, with it, established the city as a great flower market. He imported roses and bushes from the north to extend his stock and, as his reputation grew, his firm sent flowers to all corners of France and subsequently to Berlin, Vienna, London and St Petersburg. As Karr wrote in June 1875, 'I brought flowers to Nice and founded and left behind me an industry that has made a fortune for several and provided a living for a good hundred people.'[82]

By the 1870s, the Promenade des Anglais was three kilometres long, twenty-seven metres wide and flourishing. A walkway raised three metres above sea level, there was no other easily accessible esplanade in the world that afforded such an impressive vista.[83] Bands played daily, and the Battle of the Flowers during the carnival celebrations was first 'fought' in 1876. This parade of floral floats – from which, and at which, people would pelt one another with flowers – would so delight Queen Victoria whenever she visited. People owning or renting grand villas along or just off the Promenade were royal, rich and larger than life, with dramatic destinies. Sometimes even the villas themselves suffered disturbing fates. The Villa Louvaroff was lost in one night's play at Monte Carlo.[84] One of the most striking and beautiful mansions was the English-styled Château de Valrose, built in the late 1860s by the Russian railway magnate Baron Pavel von Derwies. He adored music. Having begun his life as a modest piano teacher, he was introduced to stocks and shares by a pupil. Derwies found he had a talent for investment and was soon the owner of railway tracks – some of which would become part of the great Trans-Siberian Railway. By 1866, he had become so rich that – aged forty-five – he retired from business and acquired the estate in Nice. Derwies imported an entire wooden Russian *izba* from the Kiev region to place in the garden, and set about organizing performances in his magnificent concert hall.

In 1868, horse racing was added to the list of amusements that Nice had to offer. The sport – along with pigeon shooting – opened the winter season in the second week of January.[85] Six years later, racing came under the control of the all-important Cercle Masséna. *Cercles* were an important element in the social structure of Nice.[86] Families – sponsored by a club member – could subscribe and gain access to entertainments and facilities. On offer were reading, conversation, conference and gaming rooms, a *table d'hôte*, an art gallery, a gymnasium, billiards and shooting. Some – like the Cercle de la Méditerranée, with its magnificent *salle des fêtes* – were

Carnival celebrations in the *cours*. Visconti's library on the extreme left.

joint-stock companies with shareholders exercising more or less power depending on the size of their stake.[87] The English Club in the Place Masséna was 'frequented by the upper class' but, in his 1878 guide, Murray warned his readership that it had 'become a gambling club; high play; ought to be avoided'.[88]

Benoît Visconti had opened his 'polyglot' library for visitors at the end of the 1830s. It was well located opposite the terrace of Les Ponchettes, on the other side of the *cours* which, at that time, was the commercial centre of Nice. Apart from a wide range of non-fiction in languages that included English, Italian, Spanish, Greek and Latin, Visconti's stocked a prodigious list of newspapers and periodicals from across Europe and the United States. By 1855, it had a collection of 12,000 works, which increased to 30,000 by 1885. With a bureau where books and papers could be ordered from abroad, its elegant premises became the intellectual hub of Nice. Celebrated visitors included musicians such as Paganini and Charles Gounod, and writers such as Mérimée, Maupassant and Turgenev.[89] Other subscription libraries sprang up to satisfy the increasing influx of visitors. The English established the Nice Book

Club in the early 1860s and, on the Quai Masséna, there was Galignani's Reading Room and Subscription Library – an offshoot of the celebrated Parisian institution.

One of the most fascinating aspects of borrowing from a lending library was the chance encounter with a mysterious or sentimental message tucked into a text. Sometimes, they made for better reading than the book itself. 'One day,' wrote Léon Watripon, 'flicking through a book chez Visconti, my eyes alighted on a pretty, trembling handwritten note' – 'I can't go to you tonight... I fell into a deep reverie' – perhaps a message to a secret lover framed in the style of the Romantic novel the sensitive young gentleman or lady had been reading.[90]

Nice boasted two large theatres. There was the 2,000-seat Théâtre Français, which offered works by Molière, Eugène Scribe, Dumas *fils* and the prolific Victorien Sardou.[91] There was also the Italian Opera, founded in 1770, which had a chequered history. During the winter season of 1855–6, its director had gone bankrupt and left without paying his cast. Refurbished and reopened in the style of an elaborate chocolate box, it presented the operas of Verdi, Bellini and Rossini until disaster struck on 23 March 1881.[92] There was a full house that night for the nine o'clock performance of Donizetti's *Lucia di Lammermoor*. Throughout the day, theatre staff had been worried by the smell of gas, yet after consulting the municipal council, it was decided to proceed with the performance. A gala night, numerous candles lit each box. As the spectators installed themselves in the radiant auditorium and the singers waited in the wings for the curtain to go up, an explosion ripped through the theatre, sending debris flying and smoke billowing. Those in the boxes and stalls had a ready escape. Up in the gods, people who had scrimped and saved for a seat could only crush down one narrow staircase, which rapidly blackened with thick smoke, suffocating those trying to flee. Below, in the auditorium, burning beams started to collapse, trapping those who hadn't yet made the street. As rescuers worked through the night in the hope of finding survivors, the victims were carried to the nearby church of Saint-François-de-Paule. At first count, there were sixty-five dead and hundreds more wounded, many of whom died in the following days.[93] Nice was left with only the Théâtre Français and the smaller Opéra Comique until a new opera house was built. The city's first head engineer, François Aune, designed a building using the modern techniques employed by Charles Garnier in Paris and at Monte Carlo, where the opera house had opened in 1879.

From the late 1860s, shops were becoming better stocked and commercial endeavours more enterprising. Paul Lavit started a service for order-in – 'Dinners at your House'. An innovative entrepreneur, Lavit also opened a resort at Bollène outside Nice, offering recreational packages with excursions, hydrotherapy, and amusements such as billiards, boules and shooting. Feeling the necessity of attracting customers familiar with Paris, shops were obliged to show the latest novelties in lace and lingerie. There were ribbons, corsets and crinolines to be found in Victoire Cohen's Au Paradis des Dames. The refrain running through the adverts for such establishments was '*à des prix très modérés*' – 'very moderately priced' – as if shoppers expected to be fleeced at every turn.[94]

Services flourished. Language teachers offering French, Italian, English and German were easily found.[95] Dentists were competitive, and anxious to declare their qualifications. M. Ninck of Nice had a 'diploma' – reassuring – and proceeded to boast that he was the only dentist in the provinces who had been 'awarded a distinction' at the 1867 Exposition Universelle in Paris. Oustric Père et Fils in nearby Cannes were the proud possessors of a *certificat de capacité* – a guarantee of 'ability' – and traded on the facts that they were 'the ex-Dental Surgeons to Lord Brougham' and spoke English.[96] That was a useful skill, as the British continued to dominate the coast through the second half of the nineteenth century – 'the force of the English character, and still more of the English money, bearing down and upon the native population'.[97] In Nice, you could find 'an English Shop' run by a Mr Weeks, an 'English Warehouse' and an 'English Butcher'. Pierre Bessi made 'English Bread'. In Hyères, the 'English Bakery' – the Boulangerie des Palmiers – hedged its bets, not only selling English loaves and hot-cross buns, but also

Viennese and Russian breads. Shops sold Guinness stout, Dublin whiskey, English biscuits, cornflour, jams, pickles and calf's foot jelly. Tinned Australian meat was obviously popular, as many shops kept it in stock. However, these items – subject to import duty and transport charges – were expensive. One writer pointed out that olive oil and local fruits and vegetables were not only excellent but also comparatively cheap – even though many shopkeepers raised their prices when dealing with foreigners.[98]

Adolphe Smith suggested that, with their 'stiff, haughty, unbending behaviour' towards shopkeepers, the English invited extortion. In France, 'the tradesman, the workman, the peasant expect, and are generally treated with the same deference as a lord or plutocrat' – something that British visitors found difficult to grasp. British customers entered a shop, ignored 'other and perhaps more modest customers, who being first come, have the right to be first served'.[99] The English thus became obvious targets for disgruntled traders who relied on their local customers throughout the year. Dr Thomas More Madden, commenting that no people travelled so widely and so well as the English, tried to fathom why 'no tourists seem to be less popular on the Continent'.[100] He attributed it to the fact that the English were largely incapable of realizing that they were guests when abroad. Instead, 'the majority of our travelling compatriots… indulge in incessant depreciation of all the manners and institutions of foreign lands, or in invidious comparisons with something they think much better at home'.[101] It is telling that Adolphe Smith, like Thomas Jefferson, used the phrase 'English colony' when describing Nice. Though for Britain, after centuries of invading and trading, the appropriation of this foreign coast was achieved by renting and recuperating rather than by force. The English were used to riding roughshod over countries – a veranda in a civil station of British India and a terrace occupied by the English in Nice hosted similar attitudes.

Léon Watripon observed English men sitting in the sun, devouring English newspapers, oblivious to everything around them.[102] Charlotte Dempster thought that France was unknown to her fellow countrymen, who really couldn't care about it. They preferred to 'meet English people and to read English books, and to talk of their ailments, hotel bills, and lawn-tennis parties'. They seemed incapable of surmounting two great stumbling-blocks – 'a foreign language and a different Church'.[103]

All the nationalities who came to the Riviera packed manners and customs in their luggage. Pedantic German patients and pastors came south – among them, flocks of lepidopterists fluttering along the coast with their butterfly nets. A Russian duke, used to delivering brutal punishments at home, had to be restrained by the mayor of Cannes from flogging a porter at the railway station. The Americans – like the British – had to be urged, by one of their early guidebooks, to throw overboard the idea that everything was done better back home.[104] The opulent classes of many countries, with their tremendous spending power and their expectation of having things their own way, jolted a region that was *dolce far niente* and used to living on a pittance. Some foreigners shopping must have resembled shrieking C-list celebrities going nuclear because their limo is two minutes late – a spectacle for the Riviera to endure in the future.

With the two visits of the Dowager Empress Alexandra Feodorovna and the circle that surrounded Grand Duchess Helena, the Russians are rightly credited with making the Riviera a prime resort for European royalty long before Queen Victoria. Four years after the final visit of the ailing empress, and just days after the railway line reached Nice, her son Alexander II arrived with his wife in a downpour at 5 p.m. on 21 October 1864. Despite the rain, crowds lined the streets to witness what was to have been a low-key arrival.[105] A week later, Napoleon III arrived incognito, followed several days later by the future Léopold II of the Belgians.

The tsar's ten-day visit, with its punishing schedule, was particularly trying for his wife, Empress Marie Alexandrovna, who was concerned for the health of their son, the tsarevich. When the royal couple attended a performance of a Sardou comedy at the Théâtre Français, there were spontaneous outbreaks of the Russian national anthem. On Sunday 23rd, they heard mass at the small

The magnificent *Villa Peillon* with its magical landscaped gardens.

Orthodox church on the rue Longchamp, then visited the Russian ships which had arrived in Villefranche a few days earlier. That evening, the royal couple attended a performance of *La Traviata* at the opera.

In his second visit to Nice since annexation, Napoleon III met with officials in the town and with Alexander II at the magnificent Villa Peillon, with its magical landscaped gardens – the scene of a glittering dinner given in the French emperor's honour on 28 October. After the banquet, the royals went again to the opera house, which had been filled with flowers from Alphonse Karr's shop. Napoleon met the widow of Grand Duke Konstantin, who wanted to travel to Genoa with her grand piano but refused to take the steamer with the commoners. Napoleon obligingly arranged for a French frigate. When the ship arrived in Genoa, it was found that the piano would have to be taken ashore in a skiff. Resolutely refusing to endanger her instrument, the widow stayed aboard the frigate for two weeks until a temporary pier was constructed.[106]

Alexander II visited Monaco before leaving Nice by train on the 31st. The empress remained behind to tend the tsarevich who

The memorial chapel to the tsarevich, Nicholas Alexandrovich.

– after a tour of Europe – came to rest in Nice. Four years earlier, having fallen from his horse and crushed his spine, the seventeen-year-old Nicholas Alexandrovich had developed cerebrospinal meningitis.[107] During the first months of the new year, there was a rapid deterioration in his health, and he died in his mother's arms on 24 April. The next in line – the future Alexander III – arrived from Petersburg. The funeral procession – watched by residents and winter visitors alike – included the emperor and empress, along with their children and members of the Russian nobility. After the service, a solemn march to the sounds of psalms, bells and a gun salute conveyed the coffin to Villefranche.[108] Placed on board the *Alexander Nevsky*, bound for St Petersburg, it would be taken to the resting place of the Romanovs in the Peter and Paul Cathedral.

Alexander II purchased the Villa Bermond, where work began, in March 1867, on a Byzantine-style garden memorial chapel to his son. It was a modest structure covering just seventy square metres and standing twenty metres high. In the early years of the twentieth century, it would be dwarfed by a greater memorial to Nicholas – the dazzling Russian Orthodox Cathedral of Nice.

The gilded but embattled Second Empire played out against a significant evolution in the European balance of power. Otto von Bismarck engineered the rise of Prussia and attempted to forge a united Germany by provoking France. Supporting a Hohenzollern candidate to the vacant Spanish throne in 1868, he succeeded in scaring the French. Rashly declaring war on Germany, an ill-prepared French army suffered a humiliating defeat at Sedan at the beginning of September 1870. German forces advanced on Paris and, by 20 September, encircled the French capital. Bismarck had some justification for his actions. For two centuries, French aggression had disturbed the peace of Europe. Germany was obliged to prepare to protect itself in the future.

After the armistice was signed on 28 January 1871, France ceded Alsace and Lorraine to Prussia and paid an indemnity of five billion francs. Elections resulted in a National Assembly with a conservative and pro-peace majority, headed by Adolphe Thiers. Paris, with its revolutionary tradition stretching back a hundred years, felt alienated and formed an alternative government. The determination of the Paris Commune and the severity of its repression in May 1871 reflected the chasm between a progressive, socialist initiative and the deeply conservative elements of France's Third Republic. After twenty years of realignment and reconstruction, the ashes of the Second Empire would be resurrected as the Belle Époque.

German visitors in the south were welcomed for the revenue they brought, but after the Franco-Prussian War they were suspected and blamed – as they would be again after 1914 and 1945. In the late 1870s, Laurent Germain was travelling from Toulon to Fréjus in the company of three Germans – 'Bad, really bad fellow travellers, no?' Although they turned out to be relatively quiet, Germain couldn't help observing that 'the German "jah" always grated on the nerves of the French'.[109] Titled Germans visiting the coast were, to an extent, insulated against the political fallout from the Franco-Prussian War. The numerous dukes, duchesses, princes and princesses from a plethora of German states were too exalted to be slighted. A good number of them were married into the royal families of England and Russia. Of Queen Victoria's nine children, six married Germans and one a Russian. The queen herself was of the House of Hanover and her mother was Princess Victoria of Saxe-Coburg-Saalfeld. Tracing bloodlines is a terrifying tutorial on inbreeding.

After the crumbling of Napoleon III's empire in 1870, France became a more attractive refuge for Russian anarchists and nihilists. When, in 1879, Empress Marie Alexandrovna visited Cannes, there was considerable anxiety over the anarchist threat. The mounting revolutionary tension in St Petersburg, which would climax in March 1881 with the assassination of Alexander II, was cause for concern on the coast. Anxiety was heightened by the arrival of the future Alexander III and his wife. While Alexander enjoyed the freedom of being away from the Russian capital – roaming the streets of Cannes and visiting the potteries at Vallauris – the police filed daily reports for the Minister of the Interior. Of particular concern during the empress's visit to Cannes was a shadowy nihilist by the name of Pierre Alissov, who had turned up at Nice's Librairie Visconti and asked them to publish a pamphlet. Prior to that, a certain 'Vassilof' approached a printer in Menton about publishing a brochure ostensibly welcoming the empress. It was, in fact, a diatribe against Alexander II. Finally, the Garibaldi Press in San Remo agreed to publish the attack under the title *His Majesty Alexander II, 'the Liberator' – A Biographical Study*. After smuggling a number of copies into France, one reached the empress in Cannes and its impact accelerated her rapid decline.

Local police were rightly concerned that Alissov's presence would attract other revolutionaries to the area. One such was Frédéric Stackelberg, who had been traumatized – aged twelve – by the brutal flogging of a peasant. Having fled Russia, then Germany, he found himself in Marseille in October 1879 at a workers' congress which saw the creation of France's socialist Parti des Travailleurs.[110] When Alissov contributed to Stackelberg's short-lived socialist paper *Le Réveil des Travailleurs* and was exiled for his anti-tsarist articles, a sympathetic Parisian revue, *La Lanterne*, noted that Alissov was merely a Russian citizen expressing his views. The real crime was perpetrated by the Republic of France, whose police force had been transformed into agents in service to the tsar.[111] Stackelberg, who became head of the Groupes Anarchistes de Nice, Cannes et Menton, remained under continued surveillance for decades.

While the Riviera was coping with aristocratic Russian excess and revolutionary threat, a Russian girl arrived in Nice – precocious, talented, vivacious and moody. A vivid and candid diarist and a promising young painter, the young Marie Bashkirtseff would live her short life to the full. Whimsical, she adored Nice yet was capable of denouncing it as an 'execrable' town – a 'hole'.[112] Facing the prospect of summer in Nice, she wrote, 'With winter, *le monde* will come, and with *le monde* gaiety. It will no longer be Nice but a little Paris.' Despite her eagerness for drawing lessons, as the hot weather approached, she felt 'incapable of working. Summers in Nice kill me and there's nobody.'[113] However, as she grew up, Marie exhibited increasing affection for the town which gave her 'health and new colours'.[114] Absences from Nice upset her. After a trip to Russia, she rejoiced in the pure air and translucent sky of the south. In May – that enchanting month on the Riviera – she adored prowling in the garden of her family's villa by moonlight, listening to the croaking of the frogs and the murmuring of the waves lapping on the pebbles.[115] From Rome, she wrote on New Year's Day 1876, 'O Nice, Nice, is there, after Paris, a more beautiful city in the world? Paris and Nice, Nice and Paris!... Is it possible to live in any city but Nice?'[116] Yet, as an art student, she needed Paris – where she enrolled at the private Académie Julian. Progressive, inasmuch as it accepted women students at a time when the *École des Beaux-Arts* did not, during the years that Bashkirtseff was there it had not yet become a springboard to modernity as it would be a decade later, when its students included

Marie Bashkirtseff, *Self Portrait with Palette*, 1880.

the Nabis – Pierre Bonnard, Maurice Denis and Édouard Vuillard. In Paris, Marie railed against her lack of freedom as a woman – the constant need of a chaperone, which prevented her from seeing the streets at night, visiting museums and sitting on park benches alone. Her painting showed great promise but tuberculosis would take her life while she was still a student.

Marie was always romantically involved. Studying in Rome, aged seventeen, she refused proposals from no less than one Englishman and two Italian counts. In Nice, she developed a great pash for her neighbour, the English dandy the Duke of Hamilton. who had an Italian mistress in tow.[117] Marie wrote amorous letters to Guy de Maupassant in nearby Cannes, signing them 'Miss Hastings'. She was very beautiful, and her intelligence shone. When the editor of her letters, François Coppée, met her a month before her death in 1884, he remarked on her 'sombre eyes… burnt by thought'.[118]

Just as maverick figures like Marie Bashkirtseff and Alexander Herzen were egregious Russians on the Riviera, the philosopher Friedrich Nietzsche was an exceptional visitor. Almost unique amongst the great nineteenth-century writers and philosophers who came to the south, he worked rather than rested in Nice – where he spent the winters between 1883 and 1888, overwhelmed by the landscape and climate. It was in Nice that he wrote part of what many consider to be his masterpiece, *Thus Spake Zarathustra*.[119] The largely clear skies and occasionally blustery weather suited his temperament, as did the old part of town where, twenty-three years after annexation, locals still called their city 'Nizza' and spoke Italian.

When he first arrived in December 1883, Nietzsche could not have found a less suitable *pension*. He wrote to his mother and sister, describing the guests at the *table d'hôte* – a Prussian general and his daughter, the wife of an Indian prince and her daughter, along with the predictable Russian and English contingent. As eating with strangers upset Nietzsche's delicate digestion, he moved to a quiet villa where the German landlady cooked him familiar dishes. By 18 January 1884, he surprised his publisher with the news that part three of *Zarathustra* had been completed. The whole work had been achieved in a year – or, more precisely, in three two-week periods. The writing of the second and third parts in Nice were, Nietzsche claimed, the happiest weeks of his life. To have written a work which he described as 'a dance, a game of symmetries'[120] in six weeks was indeed remarkable. In boasting about the speed of composition, Nietzsche was ignoring the hundreds of pages of notebook preparation. As he himself said, 'artists promote themselves by disguising perspiration as inspiration'.[121]

There was a lack of good libraries and music in Nice – otherwise Nietzsche had pinpointed an ideal winter residence. Looking out on the Square des Phocéens, he realized that the ancient Greeks had once occupied the site – and he felt 'victorious and super-European'. He noted that to sojourn in a city established in antiquity 'gives me confidence and tells me: you have your place here'. His health was good – only adversely affected by rare cloudy skies which were blown away by windy interludes. Nietzsche is possibly one of a very select few who have written lines of admiration for the mistral: it was a 'strong cloud chaser', a 'sky-brush sweeper' – above all, a 'sorrow-strangler'.[122]

In Nice, Nietzsche could be alone but not lonely. Friends and colleagues visited and rekindled his hopes of forming a circle of like-minded thinkers. A friend of a friend, Resa von Schirnhofer, a twenty-nine-year-old philosophy student at the University of Zurich, journeyed south with trepidation to meet the great Friedrich Nietzsche. She found him disarming, mild-mannered and 'professorial'.[123] For ten days, Nietzsche showed her much kindness. They climbed the windy Mont Boron, where he became steadily more exulted with each gust. He took Resa to a local 'bullfight' – a farce compared to the drama of a Spanish *corrida*. The tame spectacle left them laughing heartily, particularly when the pompous blasts of Bizet's *Carmen* fanfared between each dismal encounter. Nietzsche showed Resa a speck on the horizon, asserting that it was a mountaintop on Corsica – a sight that has been hotly claimed or contested by innumerable people for the last 200 years. For Nietzsche, a glimpse of Corsica elicited a eulogy on Napoleon, whom he placed somewhere between a man of his times and a 'superman'.[124]

In November 1884, on the recommendation of a friend in Zurich, Nietzsche tried Menton.[125] Too protected from the wind and with a cultural scene more restrained than that of Nice, he left for the larger town and his usual Pension Genève. January 1885 saw rare sub-zero temperatures, a heavy snowfall and a three-day storm – the worst in fifty years. By contrast, on Christmas Day that year, Nietzsche was driven to the tip of Cap Ferrat, 'drank three quite large glasses of a sweet local wine', told the breaking waves to shut up, and walked halfway back to his *pension* in warm sunlight.[126]

While in Nice, Nietzsche discovered Dostoevsky, whose *Notes from the Underground* he bought in French. He read more works by the Russian and was particularly impressed by the account of Dostoevsky's exile in Siberia, *The House of the Dead*.[127] Deeply aware that European pessimism had contributed to nihilism and anarchism, Nietzsche was proud to boast the Polish origin of his name was *niszczyciel*, which means 'destroyer'. Nonetheless, he insisted that his generation were the 'gift-encumbered but also lavishly duty-bound heirs of thousands of years of European culture'. Although – like the composer Richard Wagner – Nietzsche was later co-opted by the National Socialists, he clearly stated that Germans 'were too much descended from an ancient mixture and intermingling of races to be prepared, as "modern men", to indulge in "racial self-admiration"'.[128]

Nietzsche's final and most dramatic sojourn in Nice began with him visiting no less than forty different boarding houses, before settling on a sunny, south-facing room on the rue des Ponchettes. Two weeks later, he visited Monte Carlo to hear a local orchestra play the *vorspiel* to Wagner's *Parsifal*.[129] He noted that Wagner had never been finer, though his disappointment with the rest of Wagner's final opera is well known. It was in the year that Nietzsche had first come to Nice that Wagner suffered a heart attack in his hotel on the Grand Canal in Venice on 13 February and died in his wife's arms. The news sent the philosopher to bed for several days. He confessed that it had been 'extraordinarily hard for six long years to be the opponent of someone whom he honoured and loved', yet he felt insulted by Wagner's 'creep back to Christianity and the Church' which had resulted in that singular last opera.[130]

On 23 February 1887, Nietzsche felt the earth tremble. There were three short quakes. The first and most severe was at 6.10 in the morning and lasted fifty seconds. The second, fifteen minutes later, lasted only twenty seconds. The third, at 8.15, was a shudder that did no harm. The epicentre of the earthquake was thirty-two kilometres out to sea to the east of Menton. The worst damage was done in the Valley of San Remo where Diano Marina and Diano Castello were completely destroyed.[131] Menton was so badly hit that refugee tents sprouted under the olive trees. Fifty kilometres to the west, two houses were destroyed in Grasse. At the Hôtel Esterel in Cannes, the Prince of Wales refused to leave his bed during the thunderous tremor and postponed his scheduled departure by five days in order to forestall the panicked exodus.[132] In Monte Carlo, on the morning of the earthquake, the Place du Casino 'was one mass of people, some in night clothes, others in fancy dress, but all in hysterics'.[133] The only buildings harmed were churches – the Bon Voyage chapel on the Menton road was ruined. The Casino was untouched.[134]

In Nice, a number of buildings were damaged, including the *pension* in which Nietzsche was staying. The self-styled 'fearless' man strolled through the city to survey the pandemonium. Dogs were howling, and Nietzsche found acquaintances from his lodgings 'stretched out under green trees, well towelled and blanketed… thinking with every tiny tremor that the end of the world had come'.[135] As he wrote to a friend, he watched as the streets filled with 'horrified, half-dressed figures and unhinged nervous systems'.[136] Of course, many of the winter residents had permanently shattered nerves.

That evening, the *table d'hôte* in the Pension Genève was deserted. By the third week in March, all but six of its guests had left, and the room in which Nietzsche had written two books had to be demolished because of structural damage.[137] The season was cut short. Those who relied on an income from winter visitors sought help from the authorities in the form of loans or mortgages, but government aid did not completely compensate their loss.[138]

Later in the year, the train between Milan and Genoa on which Nietzsche was travelling became stuck in a long, dark tunnel and gave the philosopher a series of terrible headaches. Nevertheless, he claimed December 1887 to March 1888 as happy months. Refusing coffee and alcohol and taking long walks eased his head.[139] By March – the sun too bright – Nietzsche left for Switzerland, seeking out new places of inspiration. His peripatetic life was an attempt to secure a 'permanent, mild winter' climate.[140]

Nietzsche had little time for the hordes of English and Russians. Neither did he remark upon the new nationality beginning to be seen in Nice – the Americans who, from the mid-1860s, registered an increased presence. The end of their long and bloody Civil War coincided with improvements in shipping across the Atlantic and the railway connection from Paris to Nice and Monte Carlo. America emerged from that conflict into an era of expansion marked by the amassing of astonishing fortunes by the men who drove America's industrial growth. Their great wealth secured a gilt-edged existence for their offspring. Nice and Monte Carlo, along with Baron Haussmann's elegantly refashioned Paris, became popular destinations. So many American visitors came in search of luxury that Henry Morford's guide was a little out of step when the writer enthused that in 'dirty and picturesque' Marseille – a 'centre' of trade in human hair – might be found a 'sublime of squalor and misery'.[141] American visitors had their sights set on the Promenade des Anglais and the tables in Monte Carlo.

In 1840, the Canadian Samuel Cunard launched the first regular Atlantic steam crossing and spawned a circle of competitors. It was, however, the introduction of the screw propeller in the mid-1850s that significantly cut the time of the trip. By the 1870s, a typical crossing took one week but was not altogether comfortable. Morford advised Europe-bound travellers to avoid 'attempting to read much, at sea... There is a motion and jar of the vessel, making the letters swim, damaging head and optic-nerves' in such a way that they took days to recover. In order not to be shamed by ripely cultured Europeans, he advised Americans 'to freshen up in English, Scottish and Irish history'. French history – 'especially that of Napoleon and the Revolution' – would also prove useful. Travellers to England were urged to brush up their Shakespeare. At the same time, in order to field questions from people whose knowledge of the re-United States was somewhat hazy, Morford instructed his readers to mug up on America.[142]

Statistics from 1879 register 137 American families wintering in the south of France, a figure lower than that of the Russians, Germans, French and the overwhelming English. It was, however, a significant increase on the previous year, when there had been only 67 families logged. By the early 1880s, the British Stores at 15 rue Masséna were stocking 'American produce'. An Anglo-American oyster bar advertised that it stayed 'open after the theatres'. In the harbour at Villefranche, a warship from the United States Navy lay at anchor during winter months.[143]

The arrival of the railways in the south had dramatically increased the winter population. There were ambitious plans for trains to push on into Italy with ten tunnels to be blasted between Nice and the frontier. There would be sustaining sea walls and

viaducts built. The estimated cost – 800,000 francs per kilometre –
was twice the average elsewhere in France. With such a direct and
speedy route, it was doubted that the Corniche road – improved
under Napoleon – would be much used.[144] Sinclair Tousey, one of
the early American visitors and founder of the American News
Company, disagreed. Tousey claimed that a carriage trip along the
Corniche 'is one of "the things" to do'.[145] Ninety years earlier, in
her 1782 epistolary novel, *Adèle et Théodore*, Mme de Genlis had
revealed her terrified delight in the danger of the pre-Napoleonic
road. Running 500 metres above the shoreline, the Corniche – she
suggests – was aptly named. It was 'a veritable ledge… so narrow
in many places that even a single person can hardly pass'. Above it,
an enormous mountain wall reached to the sky, and below the sea
pounded on the rocks, creating a sound 'as sad as it is terrifying'.[146]
Tousey was doubtlessly exhilarated by the bracing air of the high
coastal road after enduring a Christmas Eve rail journey from
Marseille to Nice, lumbering along in what he called a 'monstrous
crawling creature' and crushed between 'fashion-birds from the
north and invalids from everywhere'.[147]

The early days of train travel were not without incident. In
January 1872 – the very month that the line was extended as far
as the Italian frontier at Ventimiglia – a bridge collapsed between
Antibes and Nice. After sixteen days of heavy rain, the usually
modest River Brague became a lake swelling against the railway
embankment. On the sea side, huge waves dumped quantities of
pebbles, damming its mouth. The stationmaster at Antibes tried
to telegraph Nice to stop the train, but the storm had fouled
communications. He despatched a rider, who likewise found himself
powerless against the storm. From Antibes, the station staff kept
their eyes fixed on the lights of the train as it approached. The
rain blurred the scene until they lost the engine lamps. The train
had plunged through the bridge, and two carriages heaped on top
of the locomotive. A coupling snapped and the carriages behind
toppled seawards.

The following day, the infantry from Antibes secured themselves
with ropes and battled the waves in an attempt to recover bodies.

Charlotte Dempster had a German friend on board the train who survived. Visiting her in the makeshift hospital, what struck Dempster was the squalor. The place was 'filthy beyond description' – riddled with fleas. She was disgusted, not only by the evil-looking couple who made money 'showing to visitors the surgeons' basin, and other ghastly tokens of the wreck', but also by the sight of an amputated human hand left lying 'in one of those shallow baskets which are used for keeping lemons'.[148]

In 1876, the first *wagon-lits* ran between Paris and Menton on the *Rapide*, which left Paris just after 7 p.m. and arrived twenty-four hours later.[149] By 1881, the journey time had been reduced. Paris–Cannes took twenty hours, Nice twenty-one, and Monaco or Menton twenty-two. The trains were fairly simple affairs and, unless you booked the whole compartment of four places, there was a lack of privacy. The first restaurant cars were running Paris–Nice in 1882, and the following year, the Calais–Nice–Rome Express came into operation. Initially intended for the British, it did not stop in Paris.

Slow on the property uptake in Cannes, the wealthy French under Napoleon III were the new invaders from the north. Baron Haussmann, the man who brutally but beautifully restructured Paris, had a villa in the heights above Nice, and bought the empty, rocky land in front to secure his sea view.[150] Henri Germain, the banker who founded Crédit Lyonnais, made Cimiez fashionable by building Villa Orangini at the end of the 1870s.[151] When Guy de Maupassant published 'Fin de Saison' in 1885, he observed that 'true Parisians are never in Paris. Or rather, they spend three months there a year – April, May and June. In July and August, they take the waters in the Pyrenees, the Auvergne or in Germany. From September to November they hunt on their lands and then, passing through Paris to buy a winter wardrobe, leave rapidly for the Mediterranean.'[152] As the French became a larger presence in the south, the occupying forces of foreign winter residents began to study their modes and manners. The Russian satirist Mikhail Saltykov-Shchedrin was lodging at the Pension Russe in Nice for a year from April 1875. He was reworking his most celebrated novel, *A Family of Noblemen: The Gentlemen Golovliov*, in which he observed, 'In France, hypocrisy is a result of education; it constitutes, so to say, a part of "good manners".'[153]

Business on the Riviera was booming. A 'thick and mediocre'[154] book about the area, published in 1887 by Stéphen Liégeard – a lawyer and poet who spent his winters at his villa in Cannes – carried the title *La Côte d'Azur*. Awarded a prize by the Académie Française, the following year, the title – if not the text – was suited to the age of promotion. It made a splash, and the Côte d'Azur captured the public's imagination.

Around 1800, 'tourist' had been a straight synonym for 'traveller', but towards the end of the nineteenth century it was fast becoming pejorative. Tourists were beginning to arrive in droves. Different resorts specialized in different kinds of visitor. While Cannes was awash with Russian grand dukes and their butlers, valets, chefs, coachmen, doctors, major-domos and aides-de-camp, Nice was making a pitch to tourists. In 1888, Nice's pleasure pier, the Jetée-Promenade – which had burned down in 1883 – reopened. It had remained an unsightly, burnt-out ruin 'in the midst of the very centre of the gay life of Nice for some years'.[155]

Business was so good in Monte Carlo that, in February 1869, Charles III – at François Blanc's behest – scrapped income, property and construction tax. The creation of luxurious hotels and restaurants, as well as the spreading fame of the Casino, had swelled the coffers of the Société des Bains de Mer (SBM). The Russians were the high-rollers in the early days, and delighted in the relaxed and reckless atmosphere of the ostentatious resort.[156] Sinclair Tousey was not impressed. Looking down from the Corniche onto a territory about 'as big as a piece of chalk', Tousey thought that Monaco looked like 'some little one's play-table, covered with toy-houses'.[157] If the children had been playing Monopoly, then Tousey was looking down on houses and hotels placed on squares that were dark blue or green in a principality – not driven by the wheels of industry, but by François Blanc's roulette wheel in a casino where *rouge ou noir – c'est blanc qui gagne*, 'red or black – it's white who wins'. The money pouring into this tiny, tax-free principality led to a building spree. Driven by 'the wages of sin', Monte Carlo was fast becoming the richest resort on the Riviera.

Its crowning glory was the construction of Charles Garnier's vast new casino building. After his successful career in Paris, Garnier had fled the Commune and decided to build himself a villa at Bordighera – just over the Italian frontier. In nearby Monte Carlo, Blanc advanced the French government nearly five million francs at 6 per cent interest so that they – impoverished by the Franco-Prussian War – could complete the Paris Opéra. His financial involvement led to the announcement, several years later, that a new concert hall would be built as an extension to the Monte Carlo Casino by 'that most talented of architects, Charles Garnier'. Begun in May 1878, the exterior masonry of the concert hall was completed by 15 October – 400 workers, mainly Italian, had laboured day and night.[158]

The Monte Carlo opera house was on a smaller scale, with an auditorium seating only a quarter of its Parisian counterpart. Its front of house was similarly decorated with caryatids, frescoes and exuberant candelabra. To prepare for the inauguration of the concert hall on 25 January 1879, an orchestra rehearsed against the construction noise in the Casino's garden. There was a specially written prologue performed by Sarah Bernhardt, who had lost money in the Casino before her appearance and added to her losses afterwards.[159]

Contemporary architectural critics were not altogether pleased with the building. It was too reminiscent of the Paris Opéra, where audiences were invited to be as entertained by the decorative flourishes in the foyer as what was presented onstage. Was the Monte Carlo clone right for the 'modern age'? There was a similar reaction to Garnier's designs for the Trente-Quarante room in the Casino, where the lavish use of gold reminded critics of the court of Louis XIV.[160]

One surprising visitor to the principality was Karl Marx. He had recovered from the worst of pleurisy in the dryness of Algeria, but lingering illness forced him into the enemy's camp as he arrived in Monaco to consult a German doctor. Noticing the title 'Dr' on his patient's card, the physician was relieved that he was not treating the revolutionary Karl Marx. The specialist confirmed that the pleurisy had come back in the weaker form of chronic bronchitis, so Marx was obliged to stay on at the Hôtel de Russie for the month of May 1882, not daring to speak to anyone about that 'absolute tyrant, Charles III'. He compared the principality to the fanciful Duchy of Gerolstein in Jacques Offenbach's 1867 light opera and left the 'haunt of thieves' in early June. He wrote to Friedrich Engels from Cannes that, in Monte Carlo, there was no trace of the 'masses' except domestics and the staff of hotels and cafés who formed an underclass devoid of class consciousness. The place was a 'lair of idleness and adventurers... a hole'.[161]

Charlotte Dempster wrote that 'the Casino is the thing that all Europe, Asia and America talk of, that all moralists decry, and that all pleasure-seekers declare to be a paradise'. It was the Casino alone 'that causes a dozen trains to stop daily... that keeps up the palace, the army, the roads, the opera-house, and the Hôtel de Paris. It is the green table that keeps the gardens green and the violins in tune.'[162] It also attracted many hundreds of prostitutes and anti-social elements, and kept Monaco's prince – fearful of indignation, suicides and scandals – away. Laurent Germain, returning from his excursion to Italy, stopped in Monte Carlo hoping to recoup the money spent on his trip. Entering the gaming rooms, sweat and despair made him think twice. He took the next train for Nice and warned his readers to see the splendour of Monte Carlo without leaving their money there.[163]

Pan-European disdain vilified Monte Carlo. *Cook's Handbook* noted that the faces of people at the tables wore an expression that 'can only be compared to that caused by the pangs of physical hunger'.[164] The Norwegian painter Edvard Munch became transfixed by the scene, the intensity of his experience captured in his 1892 painting *At the Roulette Table in Monte Carlo*. John Addington Symonds saw Monte Carlo as a 'large house of sin, blazing with gas lamps by night... flaming and shining by the shore like Pandemonium'.[165] W. Cope Devereux, in *Fair Italy, the Riviera and Monte Carlo*, exposed the 'deadly evils of the plague-spot of this paradise' where 'the demon "Play" has fixed his abode… in the very pathway of invalids', the 'happiness of homes is wrecked' and suicides were frequently 'found at early dawn in the charming gardens surrounding the Casino'. It was 'indeed a little paradise; but alas! Paradise *after the fall*'. Devereux recorded that, on 10 March 1884, the *Daily Telegraph* reported 'another suicide, occasioned by losses at the gaming-table'.[166] A local newspaper noted that in the previous three months, nineteen similar suicides had occurred, all the victims 'ruined by play'. There were questions in the House of Commons. Petitions urging the closing of the Casino were presented to the French Senate, which endorsed them and passed them on to the Minister of Foreign Affairs.

The English historian J. R. Green, who lived at Hyères and died in Menton, took a less 'Victorian' attitude. The gambling rooms were surrounded by beautiful gardens with statues and tropical plants. Their doors stood 'hospitably open, and strangers may wander without a question from hall to reading-room, or listen in the concert-room to an excellent band which plays twice a day'. The gambling room itself was far from a 'terrible "Hell"' – rather 'a pleasant room, gaily painted'. Green saw no signs of frenzy or despair, finding the games 'dull and uninteresting'. The gamblers 'sit round the table with the vacant solemnity of undertakers. The general air of the company is that of a number of well-to-do people bored out of their lives… Everybody looks tired, absent, inattentive.' Summing it all up, Green surmised that 'at Monaco, as elsewhere, there is the usual aristocratic fringe – the Russian prince who flings away an estate at a sitting, the half-blind countess from the Faubourg St Germain, the Polish dancer with a score of titles… But the bulk of the players have the look and air of people who have made their money in trade' – a perception sufficient, in Green's day, to compromise the Casino's attraction for aristocratic gamblers.[167]

Outrageous or tempting, Monte Carlo was about to play a starring role in the splendour of the Belle Époque. Its hotels and restaurants would be fêted as among the best in the world. Its abundance would bewitch.

5

The Belle Époque
1890–1914

Not since the days of panthers, sabre-toothed tigers and jaguars had such exotic creatures been seen on this coast. The conspicuous consumers of Second Empire fashion were adorned with ruches, flounces and furbelows, and concealed by greedy crinolines capable of squandering up to one hundred metres of silk. As the chorus of one comedy had it,

> So much material crimped and compressed
> That nothing remains to cover the breast![1]

Hips were rounded out while the waist was strangled to within an inch of its life by cruel corsets that scrunched a modest bosom into a perfumed offering. The bustle was big, and in the 1880s – making a comeback – became even bigger. A decade later, puffed sleeves were fashionable and grew so enormous that the Baroness de Stoeckl had to travel alone to a soirée in a brougham while her husband – equerry to Grand Duke Michael of Russia – followed in a hansom. Ladies fussed with ostrich head-dresses, feather boas and flirted with fans. They draped themselves in cloth of gold, georgette, and bead embroidery on rich velvet. They swathed their bodies in fabrics of brocaded silk or were lapped by diaphanous fabrics, waves of sea greens and blues that submerged them in a mysterious realm untouched by the uglier aspects of industrialized life.

On the Riviera – preserve of the privileged – the Second Empire glided gracefully into the Belle Époque. There was no need for that slow reflorescence of the beleaguered old order, as in the north of

France. Growth in the sun-drenched south was perennial. Sea coasts and alpine passes were no longer a source of anxiety. Art Nouveau was born of a new interest in a tamed nature. As scientists probed and recorded microcosms, jewellers and dressmakers exploited the sinuous, twisting forms observed in microscopes. Designers created a new world of narcotic motion. As people were increasingly disturbed by mechanization and urban hubbub, couturiers and artists looked to the soothing arabesques of plants and waves.

Dressmakers became a little too zealous in their lust for the exotic and – in the absence of restrictive legislation – societies were formed to warn ladies that in pluming themselves they were threatening 'birds of paradise, herons, gulls, terns and a host of other beautiful and useful birds'. The anti-plumage movement urged them to wear only the feathers of birds killed to eat.[2] Yet the fashion persisted for hand-painted feathers applied to silks and brocades, their tips often beaded with glass.[3] In 1911, an incredible 300 million birds a year were slaughtered to feed the fashion industry.[4]

The second half of the nineteenth century witnessed the flourishing of the French middle classes, which emerged triumphantly from the revolutions of 1830, 1848 and 1871. While the masses struggled to consolidate minute gains and voice industrial discontent, entrepreneurs made huge profits developing infrastructure. Often enmeshed in financial scandals, they were troubled by instability as political unrest escalated. President Sadi Carnot was assassinated in Lyon in 1894 by an Italian anarchist revenging the execution of a French terrorist. In 1898, Empress Elisabeth of Austria was wantonly stabbed to death in Geneva by Luigi Lucheni, another Italian anarchist who had been planning to assassinate the Comte de Paris, pretender to the French throne. Unable to find his target, he drove a four-inch industrial needle deep into the thorax of the empress, who was travelling incognito. In 1900, Umberto I of Italy was assassinated. The Shah of Persia narrowly escaped an attempt on his life in Paris, and the anarchist Jean-Baptiste Sipido fired a revolver through the window of a railway carriage carrying the Prince and Princess of Wales across Brussels. Intended as a retaliation for the suffering caused by the Boer War, Sipido's bullet missed its mark.[5] The Belle Époque was not all champagne at Maxim's and Monte Carlo. Danger lurked in the exotic, as barriers of the acceptable were broken down. The masturbating faun in Nijinsky's groundbreaking ballet *L'Après-Midi d'un Faune* shocked 1912 Parisian audiences. Seven years later, in a poster designed by Mario Simon for Paul Poiret's perfume, Antinéa, a naked woman was seen languorously caressing herself.

The privileges and wealth of the aristocracy and upper-middle classes gave them a licence to spend and misbehave. *Fin-de-siècle* decadence, with its world-weariness, brought people south to the Riviera to enjoy and forget. The French – through fashion and lifestyle and newly armed with their own name for the place, *la Côte d'Azur* – began to impose themselves. The genteel hospital for ailing northerners was replaced by the brio of French *ooh-la-la*.

With the consolidation of an *haute bourgeoisie* emulating the aristocracy, a new market opened for couturiers, jewellers and perfume manufacturers. As Parisian fashion houses became established in the first years of the Second Empire, it was the son of a ne'er-do-well Lincolnshire solicitor, Charles Frederick Worth, who drove the industry. After a spell as an apprentice in London, Worth joined Maison Gagelin, a fashion house famous for making and selling material. During his twelve years there, Worth sophisticated the art of cutting out by following the run of the cloth. Consequently, material could accommodate itself to the motion of a woman's body, responding to a desire for increased freedom and flexibility.

In 1857, Worth set up on his own in the undeveloped rue de la Paix, where Empress Eugénie, court ladies and the wives of wealthy entrepreneurs became his devoted customers. Worth dressed the court, the *monde* and *demi-monde*, yet set no trends and pushed no particular style, because he considered each client an individual with particular desires.[6] Consuelo Vanderbilt, daughter of the American railroad millionaire, remembered being fitted by Worth. There was an evening dress 'of sea-blue satin with a long train, whose length was trimmed with white ostrich feathers. Another creation was a rich pink velvet with sables.'[7] The fashion industry grew as the list of wealthy clients lengthened. By his death in 1895, Worth employed

1,200 dressmakers producing between 6,000 and 7,000 gowns and 2,000 to 4,000 cloaks every year. By 1901, 60,000 people were employed in the Parisian garment trade. The city's glove industry employed a staggering 70,000 people in 1906, and by 1909 there were 3,000 embroidery shops in the French capital.[8]

By the second decade of the twentieth century, over twenty new fashion houses had opened in Paris.[9] Many were run by women – among them Jeanne Paquin, whose clientele included the mistresses of the Prince of Wales, the rival *demi-mondaines*, Liane de Pougy and La Belle Otero, along with the queens of Belgium, Portugal and Spain.[10] There were spring and summer fashion shows, where any dress presented could cost more than a seamstress earned in a year. For the ritual of daily life, society women needed a number of outfits. Travelling could involve up to twenty trunks packed with a vast array of morning dresses, tennis outfits, afternoon frocks for visits and excursions, cocktail dresses, evening gowns, theatre and concert creations, plus indoor robes and a trove of extravagant accessories.[11] It is a wonder that a Belle Époque woman had time for anything other than her *toilette*.

The *Paris Herald* was generous in giving flattering fashion advice to its female readership, many of whom were callow American travellers. The paper urged women to tell their shoemaker to make their boots 'long and narrow', to 'give the foot the effect of length and not width'.[12] It advised women to 'take a good look ahead when buying pretty lingerie… the necessary washing, the caprices of fashion, which changes novelties to antiques almost before one is aware of it, and the dyer's bills, all swell the monthly budget for the *toilette* to the point of bankruptcy'.[13] At a time when a glimpse of stocking was certainly shocking, one of the big hits of turn-of-the-century France was the song 'Frou-Frou', celebrating how the swishing of a lady's petticoat drove gentlemen crazy.

In 1908, the *Herald* introduced a fictitious American visitor, 'Fluffy Ruffles', who was agog at fashionable France. An amusing chronicler of Parisian chic, she found that she couldn't quite master French style: 'I walk too brusquely, my hat is worn too far back and I'm too boyish.' Her brother William, who was too tall and wore shoes that were too yellow, was simply not allowed to escort Fluffy anywhere.[14]

Of all the cruel distortions of fashion, the corset was the most brutal. Hardly allowing a woman to breathe, fans became a life-saving necessity. When the *Herald*'s Sunday supplement for 7 July 1901 devoted its second page to dress at the seaside, it reported that to wear the mid-calf bathing dresses of the day, 'it is indispensable to have a waistband corset of strong linen, very slightly stiffened which supports the back and gives a curve to the loins'.[15] Corsets seemed to be tenacious, but there was rescue on its way in the form of a plump, theatrically dressed man with bulging eyes.[16] Paul Poiret – influenced by the paintings of Ingres and by classical antiquity – threw out the tight, S-shaped corset in favour of a straight girdle.[17] He was to become the couturier who dictated fashion in the second, more daring phase of the Belle Époque.

If the landscape embracing the Côte d'Azur appeared somewhat forbidding, the nineteenth-century French travel writer Adolphe Joanne observed that mountain slopes, hills and coastline in close proximity offered a thousand species of plants within a small compass. The reason was that vegetation changed with altitude. Above 2,300 metres, there were magnificent pastures and fragrant flowers. Just below, there were pine forests; and between 1,800 and 1,200 metres, beech trees and firs. Below them, oaks and chestnuts stood, and potatoes, apples, pears, cereals and hemp grew. Then, below 700 metres, the glorious Mediterranean climate produced citrus fruits – 40 million lemons were harvested around Menton in 1900 – as wells as figs, aloes, almonds, olives, vines and eucalyptus.[18]

Such diversity was reflected in the assortment of nationalities visiting the coast. In 1898, the young Aga Khan – descended from the Prophet Muhammad and leader of the Ismaili sect of the Shia Muslim community – came to the south of France. He experienced great difficulty in finding accommodation because, as he later recalled, 'a considerable proportion of the Royalty, nobility, and gentry of Europe was concentrated along this strip of coastline'. He eventually found himself a room at the Excelsior Hôtel Regina in

Statue of Queen Victoria in Cimiez with the Hôtel Regina behind.

Cimiez, where Queen Victoria was staying. 'Of pretty small account I was in the vast, glittering, aristocratic, and opulent company gathered for the Riviera season... The young man from Bombay was dazzled and awed.' Shop windows presented him with 'great, sparkling diamonds, pearls, rubies, emeralds, and sapphires winking and gleaming in the bright winter sun'. He was not, however, over-awed by everything. Watching Queen Victoria helped into a landau by her Indian domestics, the Aga Khan and his attendants concluded that they were 'distinctly second-class servants, of the kind you find around hotels and restaurants'.[19]

Despite the medley of mediocre Indian domestics and the curious spectacle of her Scottish companions in their Highland dress, Victoria's seven visits during the 1890s consolidated the prestige of the Riviera resorts, lending a sense of stability to a capricious coast. Amid the slew of aristocratic reprobates – her son and heir included – she lent a sense of regal respectability. For the ageing queen, the Riviera was a tonic – a maid-in-waiting noted that in the south 'she enjoys everything as if she were 17 instead of 72'. The short, apparently dour monarch who – it seemed to onlookers – owned only one black dress, was energized, even liberated by the south. The seventy-two-year-old fulfilled diplomatic and familial obligations. The seventeen-year-old had fun.[20]

Having delighted in the Hanbury gardens at La Mortola in 1882, one of the principal reasons for visiting Grasse in 1891 was to view the meticulously planned garden which Alice, Baronness Rothschild laid out over 333 acres on either side of the road leading north from the town. The baroness employed ninety terrified gardeners who were charged with maintaining its perfection. Rumour has it she upbraided the queen when she inadvertently trod on a flower bed and crushed several plants.[21]

There were flowers everywhere around Grasse. In February – mimosas; March – violets; April – daffodils; May – roses and orange flowers. From June to September, there was the tuberose; and from August to October, jasmine. These blooms sustained the fifty-odd perfumeries for which Grasse was famous. During May, the principal period of distillation, the town consumed 45,000 kilos of roses and 15,000 kilos of orange flowers a day.[22] After the queen's visit to the *parfumerie*, the March violets were re-baptized the *violette Victoria*.[23] During the town's carnivalesque Battle of the Flowers, Her Majesty much enjoyed pelting the masquerading crowd from the balcony of her hotel. When she ran out of flowers and craved more, enterprising servants gathered those flung down onto the street and returned them to their sovereign.[24]

For the courtiers who often found the weather at Balmoral 'deplorable', a trip to the south of France was welcome. But at Grasse in the spring of 1891, the weather was unkind. The wind was sharp, yet Victoria still insisted on her daily drive in an open carriage. Marie Mallet recorded that while the mistral was raging, 'we drove for two hours… along a dusty road and returned as white as millers!'[25] Victoria succumbed to a bad cold, her doctor suffered from a sore throat, the cook had diphtheria. Meanwhile, there was an outbreak of smallpox in the town and, at the queen's command, the royal entourage was vaccinated.[26] To cap it all, Elizabeth, the queen's personal housemaid, died of blood poisoning.[27]

Death was never very distant during Victoria's visits to the south. Marie Mallet wrote from Grasse on 10 April, 'It is very curious to see how the Queen takes the keenest interest in death and all its horrors, our whole talk has been of coffins and winding sheets.'[28] Three days later, Mallet wrote, 'Today being bitterly cold the Queen elected to drive to Cannes cemetery and visit the tombs of various friends. We started soon after 3.30 and were not home till ten to seven!'[29] Victoria's previous visit to the Riviera, in 1887, had been to Cannes to see the Church of St George built in memory of her son Leopold – the haemophiliac and mild epileptic – who died there in 1884. The queen's 1892 trip to Hyères was tainted by her mourning for her eldest grandchild and heir presumptive, Prince Albert Victor. Premature at birth, slow at study, this shadowy figure known as 'Prince Eddy' has attracted a multitude of rumours. He was linked to the Cleveland Street male brothel scandal and the death of a suicidal chorus girl who swallowed carbolic acid. He has even – with a convoluted set of coincidences that would be the envy of any conspiracy theorist – been proposed as a possible Jack the Ripper, who murdered and mutilated five – or possibly eight – women in London's East End during the autumn of 1888.

When Victoria and Lord Salisbury were both on the Riviera, they met regularly. The eccentric, bearded politician owned an Italianate villa at Beaulieu and rode around the Cap Ferrat peninsula on a tricycle. Serving as Foreign Secretary during his premiership, the conversations that the queen and her first minister shared while they holidayed on the Riviera dealt with important international issues. Foremost among them was the tension caused by a botched attempt to overthrow President Kruger of the South African Republic and the massive influx of British gold-diggers to the Transvaal – events that would eventually trigger the Second Boer War of 1899–1902.

The issue that absorbed monarch and minister towards the end of March 1896 was the French and Russian opposition to British initiatives in Egypt and Sudan, and their planned railway from Port

Said to Cape Town that would enable trade, troop movement and further colonization. To counter Russian hostility to the British in Egypt, when Dowager Empress Maria Feodorovna visited the queen, Victoria merely asked her to mention the matter to Tsar Nicholas II. However, disagreement between France and England almost erupted into war two years later, with the 1898 Fashoda Incident in which the French sought to take control of the Upper Nile and block British access to Sudan. This, along with the queen's sympathy for the 'martyr' Alfred Dreyfus – the Jewish scapegoat accused of passing French military secrets to the Germans – incensed the French. Her Majesty's opinions on the subject – relayed by a coded telegram to her embassy in Paris in October 1898 – were leaked to the press. The hostility that ensued threatened Victoria's 1899 visit to Cimiez, although the trip did go ahead. In fact, she enjoyed herself so much that she prolonged her stay until the beginning of May – a total of fifty-one nights.[30]

Victoria would visit Maria Feodorovna at the Villa des Terraces in La Turbie. She also called on her old friend Empress Eugénie at the Villa Cyrnos on Cap Martin.[31] Unlike Victoria, the widow of Napoleon III 'hated flowers and beat them down with her walking stick' as she moved about the Cap.[32] Next door to her was the holiday home of Franz Joseph, Emperor of Austria, and his wife, Empress Elisabeth – 'Sisi'. The couple travelled as the Count and Countess Nohenembs, and with such a large retinue that security chief Xavier Paoli was obliged to send to Paris for police reinforcements in order to protect them.[33] There was so much royalty and so many politicians visiting, that the Riviera was like a club or court providing informal diplomatic access. Unmarried royals mixed with members of the small pool in which they might find suitable partners. A Teck married a Saxe-Coburg. A Romanov married a Saxe-Coburg. Another Romanov married a Saxe-Coburg-Gotha. A Schleswig-Holstein married a Saxe-Coburg. The reprobate Léopold II of the Belgians married and divorced a Saxe-Coburg-Gotha. Add to all this royal inbreeding, all the liaisons, mistresses and *grandes horizontales*, and you have, on the tiny Côte d'Azur, a pan-European aristocratic clusterfuck.

Away from the court and diplomatic meetings, Victoria delighted in the life of Nice. She was always welcomed, early in a visit, by the market women who came bearing flowers. When in 1899 they arrived 'with vast bouquets for the Queen and Duchess of York, the latter had to submit to a smacking kiss on either cheek from the fattest and most "garlicky" of the worthy fish-wives', who also insisted on embracing the equerry Colonel Carrington and the queen's doctor, Sir James Reid. Victoria gave generously to local beggars, well aware that, at times, she was being taken for a ride – 'I prefer to make a mistake in giving than to make a mistake in not giving'. During a drive to Villefranche, Marie Mallet noted that the 'beggars were the chief excitement'. The queen 'was delighted to recognise old friends and they were equally charmed' to know that her generosity showed no signs of abating. She was regularly so generous to a one-legged pauper pulled around Nice by two dogs that the man took the liberty of inscribing his cart 'By Special Appointment to her Majesty'. After he obliged the queen by removing the inscription, Her Majesty continued to give.[34]

Anti-royalist and anarchist rumblings caused extra anxiety for the security services. While the people of Nice had very warm feelings for Queen Victoria, it was a city with a 'fluctuating and cosmopolitan population' that 'could easily contain disorderly elements'. When the queen visited, there were usually two or three English men o' war anchored in the bay of Villefranche along with fifteen ships of the French Mediterranean Squadron.[35] When Victoria occupied an entire wing of the newly constructed Excelsior Hôtel Régina from 1897, she had a private entrance which needed protecting without a demonstrable show of force. Xavier Paoli commented that never 'was the police service around an illustrious personage organized with greater reserve and discretion'. For Victoria's long country drives, Paoli sent detectives disguised as tourists to cover the planned route.[36]

On 1 May 1899, Queen Victoria lamented going north – every year she was growing fonder of Cimiez. Intending to visit again in 1890, strong feelings stirred by stories of the brutality of the Boer War led to a cancellation. There were anti-British music hall sketches. In satirical revues, Victoria was depicted bent over Kruger's knee being whipped by two Boers.[37] In shops along the Riviera, signs saying 'English Spoken' were replaced by 'American Spoken' as the conflict took its toll. The local *Anglo-American Gazette* reminded its readers that 'whilst sons and lovers are over the seas defending our empire... the large leisured class for whom the winter sun of the Riviera has become a necessity, will return to its accustomed haunts'. Nonetheless, it declared that it would be a sad Christmas and reported that, even at Monte Carlo, all the talk was of the war, putting a damper on festivities. The season, it concluded, would be 'a dismal failure'.[38]

Over two decades, Victoria spent nearly a year on the Riviera. When she left on 2 May 1899, she would never return to the 'beautiful country'[39] which she loved and admired. Four days after the queen's death on 22 January 1901, the *Menton and Monte Carlo News* published a tribute: '"Victoria the Good", the Queen-mother of the countless millions of our mighty Empire is mourned by more sorrowing subjects than any monarch that ever existed. Her pure-souled and glorious career, the astounding growth of our mighty empire, and her sweet personality and wondrous tact will be by-words till the end of time... The millions of her coloured subjects were wont to call her the great White Mother: and they were right for never was a whiter soul in this world!'[40]

For Nice, Victoria's visits had prompted improvements to the infrastructure. In 1895, an electric tram connected the centre with Cimiez. There were drains with automatic flushers, improved street gullies, and the securing of an 'immense water supply' – all, according to the British consul, 'superior to anything of the kind I have seen in England' and certainly not to be found in 'other towns on the French Riviera'. By 1892, the main avenue leading to the Nice railway station was lit by electricity. By the last year of the century, the Promenade des Anglais was longer by half a mile and wider by two metres. The *Anglo-American Gazette* reminded its readers that the Bureau d'Hygiène carried out its compulsory 'hygienic disinfection of houses, villas etc... free of charge'. The city was cleaner, but the influx of confidence tricksters and the ubiquity of professional beggars – one gentleman was accosted by eight in as many minutes – were considerable problems.[41]

Edward, as Prince of Wales, had visited the Riviera before his mother. He made his first visit to Cannes in 1872 with his wife, and frequently returned alone to indulge in gambling, women and gluttony. In April 1877, Xavier Paoli was at the railway station in Nice when his attention was directed to 'a powerfully-built, broad-shouldered man, with an expansive face tapering into a short fair beard'. When he was told that it was the Prince of Wales, Paoli moved to help but was restrained – 'Don't do that. Your display of zeal would annoy him. Besides, he knows everybody at Nice and everybody adores him.' Later, Paoli went so far as to call Edward 'the King of the *Côte-d'Azur*'.[42] Even when the Russians started to dominate Cannes, Edward took precedence over the leading light of the Russian community, Grand Duke Michael, who was merely a grandson of Nicholas I and – to boot – out of favour with Nicholas II.

When they were both on the Riviera, if Victoria was in Nice then Edward would stay in Cannes or Monte Carlo. According to the editor and writer Frank Harris, Victoria considered Edward 'loose, if not dissolute'; for the queen, laxity of morals was 'a sin that could never be forgotten'. For the last twenty years of her life, Victoria was a bastion of the established order, revering traditional rules of conduct. Such propriety was shared by her 'beloved grandson' Kaiser Wilhelm II, who 'regarded Prince Edward as a fat elderly person who sacrificed the dignity and serious purposes of manhood to the vices and amusements of youth'.[43] Edward was consequently delighted when he found out that the Kaiser wasn't above a little philandering – consorting with a Venetian countess and also with that great courtesan La Belle Otero, whose lovers included the lecherous Italian poet Gabriele D'Annunzio, the 2nd Duke of Westminster, King Alfonso XIII of Spain, and Tsar Nicholas II of Russia. Otero was invited to join Westminster on a cruise given by the duke's friend, Kaiser Wilhelm. After the duke left, Otero stayed on with the 'hard' and 'unsympathetic' Kaiser.[44]

Edward also dallied with La Belle Otero. In Paris, he would arrange for her to dance for him after supper at Voisin's or the

Edward, Prince of Wales for whom women were an obsession like hunting, smoking and eating.

Café Anglais. The prince made her a gift of a hunting lodge outside the capital, so they could easily meet. As he watched Otero dance, Edward would draw a clock on his napkin showing the hour at which he would like to visit.[45] In the little black book of memoirs which she kept, Otero noted that Edward was 'an admirable' lover.[46]

The marriage that had been arranged for the Prince of Wales while he was shooting crocodiles in Egypt took place in March 1863. He was deeply in love with his bride, Alexandra[47] – daughter of the King of Denmark and sister of Dagmar, who became Maria Feodorovna, wife of Tsar Alexander III. Alexandra was, according to Consuelo Vanderbilt, 'a beautiful woman... her breasts and arms seemed specially fashioned for a fabulous display of glittering jewels'.[48] She was, of course, under no illusions about Edward – she knew that for the prince, women were an obsession like hunting, smoking and eating. Edward consumed enormous quantities of food, often finishing the day with a plate of grilled oysters. He became so large that, in 1890, a *siège d'amour* or 'love chair' was built for his visits to the Chabanais brothel in Paris so he could enjoy sex with several partners without crushing them.

The prince journeyed to the Riviera for the society and sport. He preferred cards to conversation and 'only talked freely when he went to the opera'.[49] In Cannes, he played tennis in the early eighties, adding to the prestige of the game. From 1894 until 1897 – sailing his yacht *Britannia* – the prince often won the local regattas against increasing international competition. As the century drew to its close, Edward began to play golf, 'determined not to be behind the times'.[50] Cannes profited from a course with well-kept greens, sand bunkers, a sumptuous clubhouse, and a membership list that suggested it was the most fashionable course on the continent.[51] Cannes became Edward's Riviera base, and its Cercle Nautique his favourite club.[52] The membership charge of £100 and the annual subscription of £25 ensured exclusivity. The prince played baccarat. He liked to drink a traditional whisky and soda. Meanwhile the barman introduced transatlantic novelties like the Bronx cocktail and served that study in viscosity, an after-dinner *pousse-café*, with the liqueurs chosen to match the colour of the gowns worn by the ladies who ordered them.[53]

Edward enjoyed the company of Americans. In Cannes in 1883, travelling as Baron Renfrew, he pursued a heavily chaperoned young American lady from Cleveland, Ohio – Miss Chamberlayne, whom the long-suffering Princess Alexandra referred to as 'Chamberpots'. It was reported that Miss Chamberlayne's breakfast consisted of 'two eggs, a fried sole, a beefsteak and plenty of potatoes', leaving her well prepared to take on the hearty appetites of the incognito philanderer. Renfrew peppered dignified and aristocratic Cannes with the spice of scandal, and even appeared as the devil on a carnival float.[54] The *Paris Herald* reported that Edward was particularly fond of the Goelets – 'old New York' and worth $50 million. Edward enjoyed their household, 'in which the arrangements and appointments exactly fit his royal taste. The English on the Riviera are a very rag-and-bobtail lot, impecunious to a degree, very undesirable associates for the First Gentleman of Europe... The Goelets have the best house on the Mediterranean. Mrs Goelet is very charming and full of tact... She entertains divinely, has the best cook, and being an American, is quite removed from any suspicion of courting royalty for the sake of what royalty can do for her.'[55]

Edward enjoyed Monte Carlo more for its sociability than for its gambling. Paoli recorded that the Prince 'spoke little', had an exceptional memory and was 'very clever at making others speak'. He had a 'loud, jovial laugh'.[56] Any risqué story was permitted, as long as it was sufficiently funny.[57] When he was introduced to Frank Harris in the Casino, the prince asked Harris to place his bets for him as the writer was having a streak of good luck. Harris continued to do well for the prince and augmented the winnings with a couple of naughty stories. Delighted, Edward asked for more, so Harris told the story of the ex-cook and wife of the 'hanging judge', Sir Henry Hawkins. She had a shaky grasp on refined English. Complimented on an oriental rug in her sitting room, she replied, 'I don't know how many men have copulated me upon that carpet.'[58] The prince roared and asked for more and more.

The Irish-American Frank Harris had become editor of the London *Evening News* at twenty-seven and then became proprietor and editor of the *Saturday Review*. He migrated to the south of France when England was no longer hospitable. Apart from opposing the British government by supporting the Boers, he backed Oscar Wilde, who had been forced to quit the British Isles in shame. While his *Importance of Being Earnest* was enjoying a huge success in 1895, Wilde sued the pugilist the Marquess of Queensberry for criminal libel. He was forced to drop the suit, which led to his own arrest and prosecution for gross indecency. Sentenced to two years' hard labour in 1895, Wilde was moved from gaol to gaol, weakened by illness. Upon release, he left for France in May 1897 and never returned. He had paid the price for following his maxim that 'the only way to get rid of a temptation is to yield to it',[59] and he would continue yielding on the continent, where such things were possible. Travelling incognito as Sebastian Melmoth, Wilde visited northern France, Naples and, at the end of 1898, spent three months with Harris near Cannes in La Napoule.

His former sparkle lost, Wilde still had grand appetites. Merely having done what many of the people who turned their back on him did, the rouged, destitute and dissolute scapegoat lived on drink and drugs and whatever rough trade he could lay his hands on. Naples was obviously delightful – Théophile Gautier had observed that the English 'go to Italy to satisfy their taste for pederasty which is punishable by hanging in their own pleasant island'.[60] Arriving in La Napoule, Wilde was happy to find that 'the fishing population of the Riviera have the same freedom from morals as the Neapolitans'.[61] But life was fraught. Harris recalled an incident at the Café La Regence in Nice where he was dining with Wilde. An Englishman came in with a lady and loudly declared, 'Do you know who that is... fancy his showing himself in public.' As Harris was about to threaten the man, the manager arrived and asked the couple to leave. A bewildered Wilde was left 'trembling from head to foot'. 'Good God, Frank, how dreadful; why do they hate me so. What have I ever done to them?'[62] There were, however, some pleasant moments. Wilde was on the Promenade des Anglais when the Prince of Wales drove past. Wilde raised his hat. When Edward was informed of the man's identity, he instructed his driver to turn his carriage. Drawing abreast of Wilde, the prince raised his hat and bent low in a sweeping bow. Princess Alice of Monaco invited him to her celebrated salon. Wilde also had a warm meeting with Sarah Bernhardt. For the most part, however, an outcast and increasingly ill, Wilde was left to eke out an existence until his death in Paris in November 1900.

A year before Wilde was in Nice, the Russian playwright and short story writer Anton Chekhov was wintering at the Pension Russe 'spitting blood'.[63] A haemorrhage kept him indoors after three in the afternoon, and in a letter to the wife of his editor, he complained, 'I don't drink anything, don't eat hot foods, don't walk fast, in short, I am not living.' Chekhov was reduced to studying the Russian ladies staying at the pension – 'the self-indulgent sort, and I am afraid of resembling them'.[64] A badly managed tooth extraction led to an 'infectious periostitis' developing in his upper jaw. 'Typhoid fever set in. An operation was performed.'[65] Even when the weather became magnificent, Chekhov remained disgruntled: 'I am more than ever firmly convinced that a Russian can't work and be his own self unless the weather is wretched.'[66]

While nature on the Riviera appeared 'alien' to him, Chekhov wrote that 'I passionately love warmth, I love culture.' Presumably referring to fashion, furnishings and the arts of the table, he added, 'here culture juts out of every shop window'.[67] Above all, what captured his attention was that travesty of justice, the Dreyfus case. If the Wilde conviction laid bare the sexual hypocrisy of British society, then the Dreyfus case revealed the antisemitism that festered in France. Like Queen Victoria, Chekhov was convinced that Captain Dreyfus was innocent.

French antisemitism was bolstered by the perceived 'strangeness' of the Jewish community, which remained exclusive and inward-looking – 'a nation within a nation'. Animosity was aggravated by the successful publication of Édouard Drumont's 1,200-page *La France Juive* in 1886, and by the influx of Jews fleeing persecution and pogrom in Russia, Poland and Romania. Jews were appropriating prestigious professional positions in Catholic France. The Jewish captain Alfred Dreyfus, accused of selling military intelligence to a German diplomat, became a scapegoat. The memorandum leaked to the German army offered low-grade information, yet Dreyfus was arrested and kept in solitary confinement. A military tribunal unanimously found him guilty and sentenced him to incarceration on Devil's Island, a former leper-colony on the coast of French Guiana.

On 4 January 1898, Chekhov wrote to the French scholar, Fyodor Batyushkov, 'All the talk here is about Zola and Dreyfus. The overwhelming majority of the intelligentsia is on the side of Zola and believe in the innocence of Dreyfus.'[68] The French novelist Émile Zola had entered the fray with an article published in *Le Figaro* a month earlier: 'We have seen the gutter press on heat, minting money with its unhealthy curiosity, upsetting the masses to sell its newsprint... we have seen the press, the squalid press, continuing to defend a French officer who has insulted the army and spat on the nation.'[69] Zola was referring to Ferdinand Esterhazy, the real culprit in the so-called Dreyfus case. Convinced that Esterhazy would be acquitted by his fellow officers, Zola wrote his celebrated tract, 'J'Accuse...!' Published in the 13 January 1898 issue of *L'Aurore*, it was a sensation that resulted in the trial of Zola himself. He was sentenced to a year in jail – a judgement happily quashed by the Court of Appeal.[70] Dreyfus was repatriated, to face retrial. The military judges again found the captain guilty and sentenced him to ten years in gaol. With the 1900 Exposition Universelle looming, this ruling proved so profoundly embarrassing to the government that Dreyfus was given a presidential pardon. The upshot of this seemingly endless antisemitic farce was that Germany had further proof of French military incompetence and bigotry. In its pavilion at the Exposition, the Germans vaunted the technical expertise and military might that had given them victory in the Franco-Prussian War thirty years earlier and would devastate Europe during the first half of the new century.[71]

Salons were an important aspect of Belle Époque life. They were centres of artistic patronage, providing occasions for private concerts which presented new works by contemporary composers. The Jewish novelist Marcel Proust cherished his access to these salons, which enabled him to observe the high society he excoriated in his long novel *À la Recherche du Temps Perdu*. He extolled the countesses and duchesses of the Faubourg Saint-Germain until the Dreyfus case opened his eyes and revealed the heartlessness of their world. Catholic and nationalist, Proust's beloved duchesses were anti-Dreyfus, and his ultimate disillusionment with the society he most revered reflected the intellectual movement of the age.

Dreyfus – after the pardon – absurdly received the paltry compensation of rehabilitation followed by a *Légion d'honneur* in 1906. Chekhov did not survive to witness the end of the saga. He died in 1904, aged forty-four. His repeated trips to Nice had been necessary for his health and he had, from time to time, managed a little work. December 1900 found him making last-minute adjustments to *Three Sisters* before sending them off to the rehearsals underway at the Moscow Art Theatre, where the play opened to a mixed reception in the new year.

❖

A decade earlier, Chekhov had visited Monte Carlo convinced he had invented a winning system for the tables. Starting with 500 francs, 'on the first stake I won a couple of gold pieces, then more and more; my vest pockets were weighed down with gold; I handled French coins dated as early as 1808, and coins from Belgium, Italy, Greece, Austria. Never before did I see so much gold and silver. I began to play at five, and by ten I didn't have a franc in my pocket and I only had one thing left: satisfaction at the thought I had already bought a return ticket to Nice.'[72]

The procedure for someone who lost all their money at the tables was complicated. If they told the Casino they had been cleaned out and swore that they had squandered over a certain sum – £300 in 1900 – then officials would march them round the rooms so the croupiers could verify their story. If they did, two directors signed a document, photographed the loser and presented them to the doorkeepers, who were instructed to never admit that person again. After that, the unfortunate would sign a promissory note for the travelling expenses, and a second-class ticket would be handed over by a Casino employee at the railway station.[73]

The English novelist Arnold Bennett was also foiled by a system. Making very modest plays, Arnold tried a tactic that initially worked in his favour. After winning a small amount, he went to have tea at the Restaurant de Paris. 'In the falling twilight, with the incomparable mountain landscape in front of us, and the most *chic* and decadent Parisianism around us, we talked roulette.' The Russian grand duke who had recently won several thousand pounds in a few minutes sat at the next table. In that moment, flushed by his gambling success, Arnold felt that 'the art of literature seemed a very little thing'.[74] He superstitiously returned to the table where he had won, but his system no longer worked in his favour.

In a highly successful and singular book, *Ten Days at Monte Carlo at the Bank's Expense*, Victor Bethell relates how he and his friend Frank Curzon financed their trip to the south by playing a system at the tables. *The World* called the book 'a compendium of useful and semi-forbidden knowledge'. The *Pall Mall Gazette* noted that it was 'a little guide-book for gambling cyclists'. Curiously,

Bethell offered an odd mixture of gaming strategy and itineraries for cycling trips – none 'beyond the powers of even the average lady cyclist'. Not only did the book aim to demonstrate the importance of proceeding very slowly at the tables, it urged readers – when luck was against them – to stop. Bethell presented cycling as an alternative to the limited and unhealthy routine adopted by most gamblers, who would rise late, lunch heavily at Ciro's until 2 p.m., and then gamble till 6.30, when they returned to their hotels and dressed for dinner at the Grand Hôtel or the *Restaurant de Paris*. After an ample feast they would then go back to the tables to gamble until the Casino closed. They never ventured out to explore the natural wonders of the Riviera.

The crux of Bethell and Curzon's system was that once they began to show a small profit on the day, they would stop. They were well aware of the passion that seized most players. If someone 'commences by losing, he is in too much of a hurry to get his money back. If he wins, at first, he stays at the tables too long and exhausts his good luck.' Their system was cunningly restrained, and therefore sufficiently profitable to allow them to enjoy Monte Carlo, an exhilarating cycling holiday, and return home with their capital intact.[75]

A native of St Petersburg, the senator and historian Alexander Polovtsov had a villa on the border between Monaco and France, and spent two years perfecting a system to beat the Casino bank. Consulted by the Russian Minister of Agriculture about which trees should be planted to establish a Russian Riviera on the Black Sea coast, Polovtsov replied, 'Plant a roulette... then everything will grow.'[76] Sometimes Polovtsov's system worked wonderfully and he won extravagantly. After one such windfall – his winnings stashed in a metal box – Polovtsov awoke to find an intruder strangling him. Wrestling free, he told the man to get out and take the money with him. The robber was from a prominent Russian family, who poisoned him in jail to prevent a 'trial and disgrace'.[77]

The story of the theft and poisoning never got out – the Casino was adept at concealing adverse publicity – but Consuelo Vanderbilt had it from the victim's son, General Pierre Polovtsov, who became president of the International Sporting Club and thus had a privileged insight into Monte Carlo gambling. Often opinionated, certainly hidebound, General Polovtsov was observant and amused by people's peccadilloes. He noted that gaming 'may be wicked; it is certainly very stupid, but it happens to be an innate characteristic of mankind'. People, he observed, gamble, 'for the sake of the sensation it gives them'. On one occasion, J. Pierpont Morgan asked to raise the maximum stake of 12,000 francs. The Casino refused, and so Morgan hardly played. He obviously got no thrill from 'playing with… "chicken feed"'. Polovtsov enjoyed life's inconsistencies. He watched rich men emerge from the Casino – pockets stuffed with cash – then quibble over five francs with a taxi driver.[78]

Obsessive gamblers became sick if they spent days away from the Casino. Others became absurdly superstitious. Polovtsov watched two Dutchmen winning handsomely at roulette by placing bets on 17 on certain tables at certain times. But superstition was no system. As Arnold Bennett observed, if you flip a coin six times and it comes up tails each time, there is no reason to suppose that it will come up heads next time. Big losers spawned pawnbrokers, while the Casino fought to stifle bad publicity by bribing papers not to report scandals and suicides. Victor Bethell believed 'that one of the most prominent of the Paris "dailies" drew a big sum annually on these conditions'. The paper was also paid to insert a paragraph on their front page whenever 'the weather was particularly rotten in Paris, stating how sunny it was in Monte Carlo'. To exploit the Casino's anxieties, one enterprising band of hucksters erected a hoarding in the centre of Nice on which they depicted the ills of Monte Carlo. They hired people to distribute handbills listing recent scandals, and then invited the Casino to pay them 100,000 francs to cut the adverse publicity. The Casino refused and the blackmailers went bankrupt.[79]

When a player broke the Casino's bank, it sparked good publicity promising visions of the sudden untold wealth captured in Fred Gilbert's 1891 popular music-hall song:

Has I walk erlong the Bor de Berlong with an independent air,
You should 'ear the girls declare: 'He must be a millionaire.'

You should 'ear them sigh and wish to die
And see them wink the other eye
At the man who broke the bank at Monte Carlo.[80]

According to Pierre Polovtsov, Charles De Ville Wells – the probable inspiration for the song – was 'a coarse, unlikeable fellow' who first came to Monte Carlo in the summer of 1891. He played from the opening to the closing of the Casino – eleven hours at a stretch. He employed a system that was not new but which obviously worked in his favour. 'He doubled steadily up to the maximum when in luck, always playing maximums when there was a run in his favour. When he had won three times running, he withdrew.' In December 1892, Wells was aboard his yacht in Le Havre when French police intercepted him. Handed over to the British authorities, he was jailed for inveigling investors to back the development of spurious inventions.[81] On 25 March 1899, the *Menton and Monte Carlo News* reported, 'Wells is out of prison. Wells has come back to break the bank. Wells is at Monte Carlo. Wells is playing maximums and winning!'[82] The success of Fred Gilbert's song was worth in free publicity much more than the Casino lost when Wells or anybody else was on a winning streak. Breaking the bank was not as infrequent or rewarding as the song implied. The father of the British art historian Sir Kenneth Clark broke the bank several times during the Belle Époque, when people played with gold and silver coins and not the counters that were used after the First World War.[83]

It was certain – and it has proved true to this day – that the rapid circulation of vast sums of money in Monte Carlo attracted criminals. Despite a staff of eighty detectives of various nationalities deployed to keep the rooms free of crime, there were 'lady-grabbers' at the tables who arrived early to obtain prime positions from which they would scoop up the winnings of careless players. Similarly, men – 'often French or Belgian' – were 'pretty quick to spot their prey, usually some nervous English girl or tongue-tied Englishman'.[84] At the end of the nineteenth century, Victor Bethell warned visitors 'to be most careful about making acquaintances, either at the tables, in

The Monte Carlo Casino.

the hotels, or in the railway travelling on the Riviera'.[85] The *Anglo-American Gazette* warned its readers to shun confidence tricksters in cafés and to 'avoid money changers as you would the plague'.[86] Queen Victoria, who considered the Casino to be most harmful, noted that while 'Monte Carlo is a very clean looking place... One saw very nasty disreputable looking people walking about.'[87]

The cleanliness was likewise noted by the American writer Willa Cather. She found Monte Carlo anodyne and unreal – too good to be true. The 'sea was too blue to be wet, the casino too white to be anything but pasteboard'. In keeping with someone from the solitudes of the American Great Plains, Cather was more at home in Le Lavandou, 'a fishing village of less than a hundred souls' near Hyères. She chose to visit simply because she 'could not find anyone who had ever been'. Indeed, 'Paris people seemed never to have heard of the place'. It did not exist 'on the ordinary map of France'. 'No books have ever been written about Lavandou, no music or pictures ever came from' there, 'but I know well enough that I shall yearn for it long after I have forgotten London and Paris.'[88] Cather couldn't know it, but during the preceding decade, some exciting young painters from the north of France had begun to work along that untouched part of the coast.

Villages like Le Lavandou were an age away from the hotels and restaurants of Monte Carlo, where Chekhov noticed something 'hovering in the air' that 'insults your decency'. Having described his unsuccessful attempt at the tables, Chekhov considered what he called 'another sort of roulette – the restaurants. They fleece you frightfully and feed you magnificently. There isn't a serving that isn't a complete composition before which one must genuflect in reverence... Every morsel is over-rich with artichokes, truffles, all kinds of nightingale tongues. – And, O Lord my God, how utterly contemptible and abominable this life is...'[89]

Around 1900, the best hotels along the coast were offering twelve-course luncheon and fourteen-course dinner menus in two-hour sittings – a surely insufficient time to enjoy such a cornucopia. Dining was becoming a lost art. Baron Alphonse de Rothschild's chef was outraged that people devoured fifteen courses in forty minutes. The chef of the Baron de Hirsch pined for the old days when '10 pounds of beef, a capon, four partridges and half a ham were cheerfully sacrificed to make a sauce'.[90] Monte Carlo was a haven of excess, but the urge to move on to the gambling tables clearly triumphed over haute cuisine. Among the gargantuan menus on offer, it is curious to observe the lack of interest in local fare. A typical Christmas dinner made no acknowledgement of Provençal dishes or produce – the salmon came from Holland, the pheasant from Périgueux, the asparagus from Argenteuil. After-dinner nougat from Montélimar was as close as the chef came to the south coast.

Tipping was not just cursory; it reflected the skill and panache of the service. The maître d'hôtel of the English-owned Grand Hôtel cut up a 'duck in the twinkling of an eye' and popped 'the carcass into a press for the juice to be squeezed out'.[91] For such skill, he deserved a generous gratuity. As waiters often paid the hotel as much as ten francs a day for the privilege of being allowed to work, they relied on generous tips. A customer who did not reward adequately would receive diminishing attention over subsequent visits.[92] When the *Paris Herald* ran a questionnaire asking which nationalities were the most opposed to tipping, hotel proprietors replied, 'The Russians and then the English and the French.'[93]

Born between Nice and Antibes, the great chef and petty fraudster Auguste Escoffier opened a restaurant in Cannes in the late 1870s before moving on to Monte Carlo, where he was employed by César Ritz at the Grand. In 1890, both were invited to take charge of London's Savoy, where they cooked the books and served much the same clientele as they had done in Monte Carlo. Typically, at the Grand, you would 'be surrounded by London society – the Duke of Cambridge, a socialite entertaining the Grand Duke Michael and the Countess Torby, the Prince of Wales with Lord and Lady St. Oswald, Sir Arthur Sullivan, the Duke and Duchess of Marlborough and some people from elsewhere such as James Gordon Bennett or Princess Daisy of Pless'.[94] Among Escoffier's talents was the ability to exploit celebrity. For the Australian opera singer Dame Nellie Melba he created '*Pêche Melba*',[95] and for the *demi-mondaine* Cora Pearl, '*Noisettes d'Agneau Cora*'.[96] To create a special dish for a courtesan was a demonstration of the celebrated position these *grandes horizontales* occupied in Second Empire and Belle Époque France.

Arriving in Monte Carlo on her first honeymoon in the winter of 1896, the American heiress Consuelo Vanderbilt dined at the Hôtel de Paris. She was told that, as a meal 'is the only pleasure one can count on having three times a day every day of one's life, a well-ordered meal is of prime importance'. She added somewhat acidly that the maître d'hôtel had therefore become the person 'to whom at meals most of my husband's conversation was addressed'. Dining amid 'beautiful women and elegant men', she asked her husband, the 9th Duke of Marlborough, who they all were. He became evasive and forbade her to look at them. She pursued the subject until, at length, she learned that many were 'ladies of easy virtue whose beauty and charm had their price'. The situation became more absurd when she was told that she could not acknowledge the men who were with them. Only months before, she protested, some of them had counted among her suitors.[97]

Consuelo Vanderbilt was learning the strange etiquette that mingled and divided the *monde* and *demi-monde*. She learned that the courtesans of 'the *demi-monde* vied in beauty, in elegance, in wit and charm with the greatest ladies of the *Faubourg*'.[98] Indeed, the world of the *demi-mondaine* mirrored high society, so that a courtesan's 'protector' could be seen with her at the restaurant, the races and the theatre.[99] Often ex-dancers blessed with grace of movement, courtesans had the charm to allure and the ability to play the perfect lady, thus camouflaging the sexual favours they were selling. The *demi-mondaine* did not solicit, she did not receive money in return for sex in the hard transactional manner revealed by Édouard Manet in his shocking and celebrated 1865 painting *Olympia*, which starkly revealed the merchandizing of sex in the Second Empire. She did, however, receive priceless jewels, property and a sufficient allowance for luxurious indulgence.[100] Courtesans often entertained an easy-come, easy-go attitude, and – as their charms tarnished – they often became poor. Such was the case with the inspiration for Escoffier's *Noisettes d'Agneau Cora*.

Born in Plymouth, Eliza Emma Crouch changed her name to Cora Pearl after she ran off to France and aspired to the life of a *demi-mondaine*. Attracting a string of increasingly powerful protectors, she was dressed by Worth and became famous for using a face powder tinted with silver and pearls that added lustre to her skin. Consuelo Vanderbilt noted how society women were forbidden from such strategies – 'no well-bred woman could afford to look seductive, at least not in public'.[101] Living a life of extravagance and exhibitionism, Cora Pearl gave a dinner at which she was carried into the dining room on a silver platter – naked but for the parsley. Her guests were invited to tuck in.

Pearl's ascent was stopped abruptly at the age of thirty-seven. Alexandre Duval – ten years her junior – had squandered his fortune on her. When she wanted rid of him, Duval decided to kill her. On 19 December 1872, as he was en route to her apartment, the gun he was carrying discharged accidentally and critically wounded him. For her role in the drama, Pearl was deported, and fled to London and then Monte Carlo. She lost 70,000 francs on the tables. She owed 700 francs to her hotel and – after having her luggage impounded – was obliged to borrow from the management in order to travel.[102] A big spender, she died impoverished, working as a prostitute.

Monte Carlo was a place of licence. Socialite Daisy Fürstin von Pless was quite philosophical about what the men got up to. One night, she remembered, they sent the ladies home 'and stayed at Monte till five, and got home here at six'. They 'went to a ball... or so they said'.[103] In a town rife with courtesans, one of the most notorious was Agustina de Carmen Otero. Born to an unknown father and Carmen Otero in Puente Valga in Spain, she was raped at twelve, ran away from home, and was seduced by a Catalan who taught her to sing and dance. By her early twenties, adding 'Belle' to her name, Otero's opening night at the Cirque d'Été in Paris was a sensation.[104] *Le Figaro* gushed about her 'eyes that flame' and her body – slim but rounded-out – that was as 'supple as a panther'. The gyration of Otero's hips drove audiences wild. For her debut at the Folies Bergère in 1893, *Le Figaro* praised her 'blood-red lips' and her 'raven black hair'.[105]

In the Casino, during an early visit to Monte Carlo with a dissolute Italian count, Otero placed two gold coins on red and – not really understanding how it all worked – wandered off. By the time she returned she was 50,000 francs richer. Red had come up twenty-eight times. Later that night, she caught the Italian count in her hotel room, a maid escaping through the window. Although the count absconded with her money, such winnings were a beguiling introduction to gambling. Thenceforth, Otero would be in Monte Carlo for only a matter of minutes before she hit the tables.[106]

La Belle Otero became one of the Belle Époque's most successful courtesans. Apart from Edward, Prince of Wales and his gift of the hunting lodge, there was another Englishman who bought her an apartment on the Champs-Élysée.[107] As her life became tempestuous and fraught with scandal, it only added to her fame. The Vicomte de Chênedollé spent a fortune on her. When his money was exhausted and he could no longer buy Otero's favours, he blew his brains out. A jealous mistress of one of her protectors tried to assassinate Otero onstage, but an observant electrician diverted the shot.[108]

190 ▭MONTE-CARLO. — Le Casino. — La Nouvelle Salle de Jeux. — Les Grâces Florentines.
The Casino. — The new Gambling-Rooms. — The Florentine Graces. — LL.

SELECTA

A painting in the new gambling rooms of the Casino. The figures are said to be La Belle Otero flanked by Lianne de Pougy and Cléo de Merode.

Otero dazzled St Petersburg, where Grand Duke Pierre introduced her to the future tsar Nicholas II. In the culinary tradition of Cora Pearl, she was served naked on a silver platter by members of the Imperial Guard. She danced. Grand dukes knelt before her and she added jewels to her magnificent collection.[109]

At 2 a.m. on 5 November 1898, two shots woke guests at the Hôtel de Paris in Monte Carlo. Security staff entered room 211, where La Belle Otero had just fired at an officer on the general staff of the Russian Ministry of War. Worse for wear, having celebrated her birthday on a date Otero thought might be appropriate, the couple were in thrall to a passionate romance. Perhaps for professional reasons, Otero had decided to end it. The guards officer protested, incensing his mistress, and was nearly killed. He didn't, however, press charges, and Otero was merely asked to leave the principality – temporarily.[110]

Otero had an intermittent relationship with Prince Albert I of Monaco over a period of years. She had an affair with the eleven-times leader of the French government Aristide Briand, who visited her regularly while she was performing in Monte Carlo.[111] In her little black book of memoirs, which was peppered with exclamation marks, Otero noted the sexual behaviour of her lovers. The Emperor of Japan 'would caress me for hours and then sleep. That was his pleasure – and what a rest for me!' Of Léopold II of Belgium she wrote, 'He was very good but exhausting! After his departure I needed several days rest!'[112] The French novelist Colette noted that Otero in her forties was 'still slim above a rump that was her especial pride'. She appeared, wrote Colette, 'like a caryatid, carved in the fashion of the period', adding that you can't get close to a caryatid – you can only look at it.[113]

Otero's great rival, Liane de Pougy, a courtesan and a lesbian, was renowned for her grace. If the breasts of La Belle Otero were cited – bafflingly and unflatteringly – as the model for the cupolas of the Carlton Hôtel in Cannes, then de Pougy was renowned for her

One of the two cupolas of the Carlton Hôtel in Cannes, said to have been inspired by the breasts of La Belle Otero.

flawless skin, perfect proportions and features. Both women were proud of the fabulous jewels that had been showered upon them, and the tale of the celebrated occasion at which they attempted to upstage and outshine each other exists in several versions. It occurred – people claimed – at Maxim's in Paris, at the Grand Hôtel in Deauville, but Albert Flament in his 1946 *Le Bal du Pré-Catelan* was precise – 'Saturday 6th February 1897, Monte-Carlo. In the atrium of the Casino around 10 o'clock'. This was the climax of contests in which Otero and de Pougy would attempt to outdo the stylish attire that the other wore on the previous evening – a dress more *décolletée*, accessories a little more ostentatious, a flamboyant gem. On 6 February, the glittering crowd noticed that Otero had added her collection of fabulous emeralds to her usual array of jewellery. After a long interval of hushed expectation, Liane de Pougy appeared, dressed simply in diaphanous white mousseline. She wore no jewels, merely a single rose placed at her breast.[114] In another version of the tale, the rose is missing but de Pougy's maid followed her covered in jewels that out-dazzled those worn by Otero.[115] In another version, de Pougy was followed by a diamond-draped poodle.[116] In yet another, by a bejewelled fox terrier.[117] Dogs were not allowed in the Casino, but in the case of notorious *grandes horizontales* with their capacity for publicity, they were tolerated. What is strange is that such wealthy courtesans appeared reluctant to pay those who supplied them. In 1900, Liane de Pougy was sued by the Parisian department store Le Bon Marché for an alleged debt of 858 francs for articles supplied eleven years earlier. Otero was worse. 'She is as well-known at the Palais de Justice as she is at the Folies Bergère,' wrote the *Herald*. 'A few days ago, she was sued by her groom and yesterday by her milliner.'[118]

By 1900, love between women had become an undercurrent of life in Belle-Époque Paris. One figure who promoted and practised it was the American heiress Natalie Barney, daughter of the manufacturer who supplied railroad carriages to the Pullman Sleeping Car Company. When her father died, he left Natalie $2.5 million with which she was able to fund her Académie des Femmes, where afternoon entertainments included poetry readings, along with *tableaux vivants* and other visual spectacles. On one occasion, Barney's lover, Colette, drifted naked through her wooded garden on the Left Bank, while Sapphic nymphs danced in rounds like figures encircling Grecian urns.

As with the fashionable restaurants on the Riviera, the Bois de Boulogne in Paris was a realm where the *monde* and *demi-monde* mixed. It was in that park that Natalie Barney met Liane de Pougy. In the early stages of their relationship, Barney used the pseudonym 'Florence Temple-Bradford' to forestall society rumours and newspaper gossip.[119] It was under that name that Barney appeared in de Pougy's bestselling 1901 novel, *Idylle Saphique*, which tackled a subject that was taboo, if not illegal, at a time when conservative attitudes to gender were hindering the emancipation of women. Double standards were blatant. If a husband found his wife in flagrante delicto, he could kill her, knowing the courts would excuse his 'crime of passion'. If a woman acted likewise, she would be convicted of murder. Inequality and lack of educational opportunity meant that many women were condemned to low-paid work, which resulted in the need to subsidize their income through casual prostitution. While society women flirted with the erotic thrill of same-sex caressing, prostitutes sought comfort in one another's arms.[120]

Idylle Saphique is candid, tender and emotional. The heroine, fed-up with the high life of a *demi-mondaine* – its social round, its lace and stays – asks her maid to lay out an old pink flannel dressing gown in which to lounge at home. De Pougy creates a sentimental rather than titivating vision of life with Florence Temple-Bradford, though the two women do bathe together and the narrator delights in slapping the bottom of her new friend.[121] Liane de Pougy's comfort in her sexuality is clear when she writes of 'the voluptuousness of these female hugs, the ardour of these lesbian caresses, the languid softness of these forbidden kisses'.[122] Natalie Barney sought to free Liane de Pougy from what was ultimately the economic servitude of the *demi-mondaine*. In the event, Liane betrayed Natalie with the wife of an Italian count for whom she was a courtesan. For many years, Liane de Pougy had a villa, La

Perle Blanche, at Menton, where she was surrounded by other villas occupied by courtesans. She married Prince Georges Ghika of Moldavia in 1910 and lived quietly and happily until his death in 1937, when she entered a convent of Dominicans in Lausanne – where she died a nun in December 1950.[123]

In sleepy Menton – only ten kilometres away from Monte Carlo – the new local paper reported the excitements of the upper classes. The purpose of the weekly, as with other anglophone publications along the coast, was to announce who had arrived for the season and – when the time came – who was departing. In between, it kept winter visitors up to date on what was organized for their amusement and what amenities had been added. Readers of the first issue of the *Menton and Monte Carlo News* would have been pleased to learn that 'the lethal chamber by which dogs can be put to death has been introduced at the Abattoir'.[124] A week later, there was information on 'Walking backwards as cure for headache'.[125] Readers of early issues would have been hooked into a serialized story, 'Martyr or Murderer?', which reached its gory conclusion on 11 December 1897 – 'An awful muffled sound gurgled from her lips... the eyes that had undone so many protruding from their sockets...'[126]

The paper offered a forum for English grumpiness: 'Whoever made arrangements for supplying programmes at the Charity Ball, is responsible for a great many sad disappointments. No pencils were provided... and ladies found themselves sometimes with two partners for one dance and none for the next.'[127] After the fashion clashes of La Belle Otero and Liane de Pougy and the constant parade of haute couture in Cannes, Nice and Monte Carlo, Menton appeared rather muted. The *Thé Dansant* at the International Club on 24 December 1898 saw Miss Glover 'looking very attractive and beautifully dressed in white; Mrs Cochrane especially charming in blue and black; the two Miss Crowes, two handsome Irish girls, dressed in black; Miss Kennedy from Nice looking very well in brown...'[128] The club Fancy Dress Ball to end carnival offered something a little more varied: 'Madame Ebner looking lovely in a beautiful Marie Antoinette costume of strawberry coloured moiré, a perfect picture... The Comtesse d'Oultrement magnificently dressed as a Dame of the Directoire period.' Miss Stern 'in white and barefoot as a Druidess, Mrs Worsdell as a Norwegian peasant... Miss Walton as Perdita in "Winter's Tale", a lovely costume. Mrs Cléricy as a Spanish dancer, Miss Muntz as an Egyptian water girl, the Hon. Miss Bigge dressed as twilight...' On 26 February 1898, announcing that carnival was over, the paper registered 'a rather flat feeling. Looking back on the days and nights of wild frivolity, one is surprised at the delightful way in which everyone' made 'up their minds to forget all worries and go raving mad'.[129]

On 2 April 1898, the paper reported the death of one of Menton's winter residents, the revolutionary English illustrator Aubrey Beardsley – 'Whatever you may think of his art, there can be no doubt that it created more discussion than any other school since Mr Whistler began to startle the world.'[130] James Abbott McNeill Whistler – raising the curtain on modern art – had declared, 'To say to the painter, that Nature is to be taken as She is, is to say to the player, that he may sit on the piano.'[131] His dreamy, almost abstract evening paintings, or 'nocturnes', were reviled. When John Ruskin saw his evocation of a firework display, he famously accused Whistler of 'flinging a pot of paint in the public's face'.[132] Whistler found the work of the young Beardsley 'wonderful' and judged the artist to be 'already a master'.[133] It was a compliment Beardsley took to heart, as he sensed he had not long to live. In just six years of activity, his macabre decadence and overt – often pornographic – eroticism helped define the *fin-de-siècle* aesthetic. His sure, sweeping line looked forward to the significant simplifications of dress designers at the outset of the stripped-down twentieth century.

March 1897 found Beardsley in Bournemouth, tended by a doctor for attacks of 'blood spitting'. With the English resort 'so cold and wintry', it was suggested that Beardsley went south – not to be cured, but to arrest the development of the disease. Under the threat of death, he was received into the Catholic Church at the end of that month, and the prospect of being in France was welcome.[134] He was financially stable. Leonard Smithers – his publisher, who specialized in 'decadent' literature – was commissioning work. Beardsley was also benefitting from a generous quarterly allowance from the champion of male love that transcended physical desire, fellow Catholic Marc-André Raffalovich.

Beardsley reached Menton on 20 November 1897. In a letter to Smithers, he confessed that while the 'journey nearly did for me... Menton is less loathsome than I expected'. He wrote to Raffalovich that the 'air is lovely and there is so much sun. I do hope I may get a little better.' Two weeks later, benefitting from the mountain air around his hotel, Beardsley was 'throwing off... languor and depression'. Everyone in the town, he wrote, 'is on a bicycle and bursting with health. I believe I am the only invalid in the place.' The 'strong English contingent here furnishes me with quite a number of people to talk to. There is a famous Egyptologist... who looks like a corpse, has looked like one for fourteen years, who is much worse than I am, and yet lives on and does things. My spirits have gone up immensely since I have known him.' Beardsley was feeling well enough to work on his illustrations for Ben Jonson's *Volpone*.

LYSISTRATA.

Aubrey Beardsley, *The Lysistrata of Aristophanes*, 1896.

The festive season proved difficult. A 'horrid pseudo-Christmas gaiety spread over this French town, that has depressed me utterly'. Christmas Day itself was 'wet and beastly' and Beardsley did not leave his room all day. In the middle of February, he 'had a vile attack of congestion of the lungs, and spent three weeks in bed'. It left him unable to work. In a panic on 7 March, he instructed Smithers to destroy all copies of *Lysistrata* and 'by all that is holy *all* obscene drawings'. On the 16th, it was all over. Beardsley had not dressed or left his room since late January. Diagnosed with tuberculosis aged seven, he was dead by twenty-five – the fatal illness having charged his short working life with urgency.[135]

If Beardsley's work explored the dark sexual undercurrents of his time, then Léopold II of Belgium, who owned villas in Beaulieu and Cap Ferrat, lived them. The king bankrolled his building on the Riviera by what Joseph Conrad called 'robbery with violence, aggravated murder on a grand scale' – the spoliation of the Congo.[136] A sexual predator, Léopold's selfishness and immorality saturated his personal and political life, providing a grotesque example of how to finance a paradise. Visiting the Riviera on his yacht in the mid-1890s, he found the climate so agreeable that he started to buy up land.[137] He would 'bully, threaten and intimidate' until he got the plot he wanted.[138] Among his purchases was an Italian-style, stuccoed villa at Beaulieu, next door to La Bastide, owned by Lord Salisbury, a politician who detested Léopold's regime in the Congo.

The Belgian king's project for colonization was presented at the 1876 Conférence de Géographie in Brussels as a philanthropic, humanitarian initiative to bring civilization to a backward people. When the new independent Congo Free State was proclaimed in February 1885, it was clear that Léopold had duped diplomats and politicians. By the early 1890s, ivory for piano keys, cutlery, fans, false teeth and billiard balls, along with rubber for bicycles and car wheels, was highly profitable.[139] Other African countries had a degree of freedom in selling those commodities, but in the Congo Free State hunters and producers were tied to the Belgian king whose

Léopold II of Belgium
whose Congo regime
'became a byword
for exploitation and
genocide'.

La Trique, Brussel, 25 februari 1906.

regime 'became a byword for exploitation and genocide'.[140] Not
only did Léopold stifle private initiative, his brutality in stimulating
production levels was notorious. Slavery, sexual abuse and murder
were the order of the day, and inhabitants were sometimes shot
if they did not agree to produce rubber. An English businessman
witnessed 'brutalities and mutilation'. Others reported hangings.
Men, women and children were punished with the *chicotte* – a
hippopotamus-hide whip whose strands were cut to the sharpness
of a knife blade.[141] Sir Roger Casement – diplomat and, later, Irish
revolutionary – had known the Congo as a flourishing territory in
its pre-Free State days. Under the new order, he saw women – some
pregnant, some with their babies – chained together in detention
until their husbands produced sufficient rubber to set them free.[142]
Casement met with Joseph Conrad, who had spent six months in
the Congo as a captain of a riverboat and who, in 1899, wrote
Heart of Darkness. Casement was shown the limbs of children
that had been amputated to punish their parents for not achieving
their official quota. It was not as if the British, or the French or the
Americans, were blameless in their dealings with colonial countries,

but they all protested against the horrors of Léopold's Congo – which the king treated as his personal possession.

Meanwhile, Léopold was sunning himself on the Riviera, tucking his white beard into a rubber pouch when he went swimming and generally upsetting people. Xavier Paoli found him as 'uncommunicative as it was possible to be'[143] and observed his 'excessive egotism or supreme indifference' at close quarters. At a luncheon at Léopold's 'huge, ugly villa at Cap Ferrat', Princess Daisy von Pless watched her host peel grapes with his abnormally long fingernails. She felt there was 'a look of satisfied cruelty on his face as if he were gleefully skinning alive the President and all the members of the Aborigines Protection Society'.[144] Léopold's cousin Queen Victoria found him disagreeable. Edward, Prince of Wales did not like him. Theodore Roosevelt, the American president, forbade the 'dissolute old rake' from attending the St Louis World's Fair. When Léopold was received by Victoria at Balmoral in 1897, Marie Mallet observed the 'unctuous old monster' believed 'a visit to the Queen might give him a fresh coat of whitewash'.[145]

Two years earlier, when the *Pall Mall Gazette* exposed child prostitution in the British capital, a former servant of a brothel testified that Léopold paid a standing order of £800 a month to maintain a constant supply of young virgins aged 10–15.[146] This predator was also frequently mocked for his endless array of mistresses. He followed the famous courtesan Cléo de Merode all over Europe. On one occasion, Kaiser Wilhelm II – not known for his wit – said, 'I don't see Cléopold.' Émilienne d'Alençon, a famous courtesan and lover of Liane de Pougy, was another of Léopold's indulgences. Otherwise, 'the Old Excursionist' was caricatured with common prostitutes with names like 'Miss Beaunichon' (Miss Pretty Tits), '*La Belle en Cuisses*' (Beautiful Thighs) and '*Nini Pattes en l'Air*' (Nini, Legs in the Air). Then, in 1900, Léopold met a vulgar, busty sixteen-year-old, Blanche Lacroix. He was sixty-five and the girl already 'had a past'.[147] After the death of the king's consort in 1902, Blanche visited the Riviera frequently. She became pregnant, was given the title of Baronne Vaughan, and was installed in Victorien Sardou's old villa in Nice, where she bore Léopold a

second son.[148] The baronne
and the king remained
together, even marrying
five days before he died in
1909, the year in which –
after much international
pressure – the Congo was
opened up to free trade.[149]

Among Léopold's neigh-
bours on Cap Ferrat
was the daughter of the
director of the Banque
de France, Béatrice de
Rothschild. Separated from
her husband, the Austro-
Hungarian banker Maurice
Ephrussi, in 1904 and using
a substantial inheritance
from her father, Baroness
Ephrussi de Rothschild
secured seventeen acres
of land on the Cap in the
face of Léopold's rapacity.
Over the next seven years,
with the aid of thirteen

Léopold 'the Old Excursionist' was
caricatured with the names of common
prostitutes.

architects, Béatrice created an estate of nine gardens inspired by
different horticultural traditions to surround her pink Villa Île-de-
France.[150] Her occupancy of the sumptuous and well-sited house
was short-lived. During the First World War, the baroness went to
live in Monaco – where, in the Casino, the designer Erté observed
her scattering 'chips all over the table... more chips on the table
than any win could possibly pay off'.[151]

   In nearby Beaulieu, a French Hellenist and polymath, Théodore
Reinach, built a house based on a second-century BC dwelling on the
island of Delos – birthplace of the twin gods Apollo and Artemis. He

purchased terrain surrounded on three sides by water and named his villa 'Kerylos' – Greek for 'halcyon', the mythical bird that nested on the sea, charming wind and wave into submission. Reinach's villa was all mod-cons – astutely concealed by the decoration and furniture, which were exact replicas of classical originals. It was Reinach's building of the Villa Kerylos that prompted Baroness de Rothschild to build the *Île-de-France* on Cap Ferrat. Reinach's bequest of his villa to the Institut de France in 1928 perhaps inspired Béatrice Ephrussi to leave hers, along with its collection of paintings, tapestries and antiques, to the institute when she died six years later.

At the beginning of the 1870s, Beaulieu – at the gateway to Cap Ferrat – had a population of 300. Three decades later, it was one of the most fashionable resorts on the Riviera. Its new status was secured by the English furniture magnate and MP John Blundell Maple, who constructed the 300-bed Hôtel Bristol which opened on 1 January 1899 – 'specifically built to English requirements and appointed in the most luxurious manner'. Its restaurant, La Rotonde, was inaugurated by the Prince of Wales. On the seafront, La Réserve de Beaulieu – with its own oyster beds, fish tanks and a wine cellar cut into the rocks – was already a popular restaurant with winter residents.[152] To consolidate Beaulieu's sudden success, the town council placed an advert to assure visitors that hotels would refuse consumptives lest their other guests 'would be upset by the early morning coughing'.[153] It was a sure indication that the *raison d'être* of the Riviera had changed.

The wealthiest enclaves on the coast attracted fantasists, the spoilt and the self-indulgent. The most eccentric and striking inhabitant of Beaulieu was the American newspaper proprietor James Gordon Bennett, who built his Villa Naouma in the part of the town where bananas grew – Petite Afrique. The tall, blue-eyed Bennett had been obliged to quit New York in 1877 after committing a social transgression at the home of his rich fiancée. Notorious for being unable to hold his liquor, Bennett arrived drunk and proceeded to urinate – there are two versions – into a fireplace or onto the grand piano. The girl's brother clobbered Bennett, who responded by challenging him to a duel. The upshot was that Bennett became

Beaulieu – La Rotonde with a corner of the Hôtel Bristol behind.

a pariah in New York, departed for Paris and remained in France for forty years. In exile, he launched the Paris-based edition of the *New York Herald*. Son and heir to the paper's founder, Bennett Jr ruled his new roost in the best Citizen Kane manner – 'I want you gentlemen to remember that I am the only reader of this paper. If I want the columns to be turned upside down, they must be turned upside down.'[154] Eccentricity ruled as Bennett printed the same letter to the editor every day for nineteen years. From an 'Old Philadelphia Lady' living in Paris, it enquired how to convert Fahrenheit to centigrade and vice versa.[155] Method in his madness, the editor's reply would have been perennially useful for American visitors to France.

An adept and flamboyant newspaper man, Bennett made the *Herald* the 'most serious of frivolous newspapers', read by kings and leaders. Technologically advanced, it was the first to use radio to receive news. Enterprisingly, Bennett sent Henry Morton Stanley to Africa to find the lost British missionary Dr David Livingstone. The mission's success was reported in the *Herald* with Stanley's phrase 'Dr. Livingstone, I presume'.[156] The weekly explored new sports exploiting new equipment. Top couturiers such as Worth and Poiret were happy to grant exclusive interviews, as the paper was a barometer of the preoccupations and habits of the affluent classes in Paris and on the Riviera.

Impetuous, Bennett was known to throw rolls of banknotes into open fires and to pass between the tables of a restaurant and swipe the cloths from underneath plates and glasses in protest against slow service. When he arrived at a Monte Carlo restaurant which he prized for their mutton chops and found all tables occupied, he bought the establishment for $40,000. When his favourite waiter, Ciro, arrived with his chops, he gave him the restaurant as a tip.[157] As with the Belle Otero/Liane de Pougy jewel contest, there are other versions of this incident. Ciro – variously an Egyptian pastry cook or a Neapolitan who had worked at New York's fashionable Delmonico's – was Bennett's favourite waiter at the Café Riche, where he liked to eat on the terrace.[158] Arriving one day, Bennett found all the tables cleared away and so he bought the restaurant, gave the deeds to Ciro and told him that, as the new owner, he could put the tables back on the terrace and serve him a mutton chop. More tamely, Polovtsov claimed that Bennett merely liked Ciro's pastries and encouraged him to set up a restaurant of his own, promising free publicity in the *Herald*.[159]

Gordon Bennett kept his yacht *Lysistrata* anchored off the coast. It boasted a suite of rooms on each of the three decks, a Turkish bath, a crew of a hundred, and an Alderney cow – presumably for fresh milk.[160] One evening, Bennett invited some American society ladies to dine with him on board. In the middle of dinner, he retired to his cabin as the yacht put out to sea. When the Mediterranean became choppy, the ladies pleaded with the captain to return to port. 'I have Mr Bennett's order to proceed to Egypt,' he replied. No entreaty would sway him, and Bennett was locked in his cabin. The following morning, the host saw reason and ordered the *Lysistrata* to return to France. The furious guests were put ashore in evening dress. Embarrassing – if not compromising – only generous presents and extravagant apologies restored relations.[161]

As the new century got underway, the *Herald* did its bit to make it an American century. The oil king John D. Rockefeller had – the paper claimed in a front-page story of 17 November 1905 – an annual income of '$30,000,000. Nearly Equal to Those of All Europe's Crowned Heads Combined'.[162] The following year, it registered a record 331,453 Americans visiting Europe, up dramatically from nearly 262,000 in 1905.[163] Some seemed too uptight to negotiate European playfulness. On their outward voyages, certain American ladies recoiled from the solicitude of Cunard officers. The *Herald* reported complaints of flirting.[164]

During the heat wave of September 1906, the paper noted that the 'flower of French, Spanish and Russian nobility are all drinking American cocktails with long thin straws'.[165] The perception that all things American were modern and efficient meant that even in the Hôtel d'Angleterre in Nice, the new lift was advertised as 'running on the American system'. Along the Riviera, real-estate agencies and pharmacies hedged their bets by calling themselves not 'English' but 'Anglo-American'. Identity was all hooey – of the 'many so-called English pharmacies' in Nice, there was only one actually owned and run by an Englishman holding a diploma from the Royal Pharmaceutical Society.[166]

Nice, Baie-des-Anges with the neo-Moorish Jetée-Promenade.

Somewhat eclipsed by Monte Carlo during the Belle-Époque, Nice opened a second casino on the neo-Moorish Jetée-Promenade. On this pier, there were also popular afternoon concerts and evening plays.[167] An entertainment hub for winter visitors, many locals disliked the structure, which broke the gentle and extensive sweep of the Baie des Anges. The city had indeed become a mixed blessing.

New structures rose – beautiful oddities intruding on a city that had developed graciously since annexation. The most singular – built between 1903 and 1912 – was the Russian Orthodox Cathedral of St Nicholas. There was also the Hôtel Negresco – designed by the Dutch architect Édouard-Jean Niermans, who had been responsible for the Moulin Rouge in Paris. His spectacular hotel crowning the Promenade des Anglais was opened in 1913 by Negresco, a former baker's boy from Bucharest.[168] With its pink mansard roof and cupola laced with acid green, it immediately became a landmark – its mixture of the elegant and the extrovert so characteristic of the Belle Époque. One of the city's most curious new structures was the kiosk of the seafront Restaurant de la Réserve, where diners could stroll and then walk the plank to reach the deck of a small sailboat perched on a rock above the waves. Among the increasingly bumptious villas was one based on the palaces of the maharajas of Rajasthan. Robert Smith, a civil engineer and colonel in the British Army, had bought land on Mont Boron in 1856 and constructed a souvenir to his time in India. To cap such follies, there were the annual excesses and grotesqueries of the carnival. In 1903, Madame Carnival appeared as a courtesan riding a lobster. With a population swollen to 150,000, in the years leading up to the war Nice was less grand, less focused, than Monte Carlo. It astounded a young Jean Cocteau with its 'sordid ostentation' – it was an 'Italian comic-opera set', a 'theatre of illusions'.[169]

At the outset of the twentieth century – excluding festivals – traditional costume was limited to the *marché des fleurs et légumes*, where it was worn largely for the benefit of visitors. Certain charming local customs persisted, such as the *festin des reproches* in Cimiez on the first Sunday of Lent. Couples would confess misdeeds

Restaurant de la Réserve, where diners could stroll and then walk the plank to reach the deck of a small sailboat perched on a rock above the waves.

305   NICE. — Bataille de Fleurs Automobile. — LL.

The parade of the 'Battle of the Flowers'.

committed during carnival, scold one another, go to church, kiss in reconciliation and break the traditional *pan bagnat* – stale bread wetted and stuffed with salad.[170] Although hardly seen on the menus of fashionable hotels and restaurants, local delicacies included *socca* – a baked galette of chickpea flour, very thin and eaten with black pepper. There was *tourta-cauda* – a purée of herbs between two sheets of thin, brittle pastry; *la trocia* – an omelette of chopped leek; and *pissaladière* – a bready base topped with chopped onion soaked in white wine, anchovies and black olives.

In contrast to Nice, Cannes retained its dignity and exclusivity, but it was the Russians, led by Grand Duke Michael, grandson of Nicholas I, who became the driving force behind the Casino and the founding of the Carlton Hôtel. A weekly broadsheet in Cyrillic appeared on the Riviera. When the Cannes Lawn Tennis Club came into existence in February 1908, it was under the presidency of Her Imperial and Royal Highness the Grand Duchess Anastasia. Protocol remained strict in the Russian community. A coachman would wear his cockaded hat sideways and use white reins if he was driving a grand duke or duchess.[171]

One major change to Côte d'Azur society took place in 1901, when the fun-loving Prince of Wales became Edward VII and gave up the Riviera habit. He told Xavier Paoli that 'you meet too many princes... I should be obliged to spend all my time in paying and receiving visits, whereas I come to the continent to rest.' Edward chose Biarritz.

Reigning during the first decade of the century, his court more cosmopolitan and less stuffy than that of his mother, Edward made a significant impact on foreign policy.[172] Despite sounding German – as his mother had done – with guttural pronunciation and rolled r's,[173] he pleased his Liberal opponents in the British government by preferring Republican France to imperialistic Germany. As Pierre Polovtsov observed, the secret of Edward's popularity 'lay in his *bonhomie*. His tact and good nature did much to ease the European situation and promote the *Entente Cordiale*'.[174] After the strained relations between England and France in the wake of the Fashoda Incident, Edward's state visit to Paris in May 1903 and the return visit made by President Loubet two months later led to negotiations that resolved such touchy issues as the Suez Canal and African frontiers, and laid the foundation for the Triple Entente between France, Russia and Britain. Such an accord had already become more likely after an important visit made by the Russian navy to Toulon in the early 1890s, during which its fleet was grandly fêted.[175] If newly industrialized Germany and its allies, Austro-Hungary and Italy, became aggressive, there would be a strong triple alliance to strike back.

Monaco also had a new leader during the Belle Époque. Albert I had acceded to the throne in 1889. Although he felt uncomfortable deriving income from gambling, he needed the revenue to fund his oceanographic expeditions. He secured a new contract with the charming and chubby Camille Blanc, somewhat improving the image of the Casino by creating a Sporting Club that would count among its members the cream of English, French and American society, along with the Emperor of Brazil, the Prince of Nepal and the Russian grand dukes – Alexis, Serge, Paul, Peter, Nicholas, and Michael the compulsive gambler.[176] In Monte Carlo, they found themselves among newly rich industrialists such as Renault, Michelin and Vanderbilt.[177]

Born to wealthy French-German Jewish bankers in New Orleans, and married to the Duc de Richelieu at the age of seventeen, Alice Heine presided over a celebrated salon at her home in Paris. Nearly a decade after her husband's early death, she married Prince Albert in the year he came to power. Her circle started to frequent Monte Carlo as Alice began to transform the principality's cultural scene. Between 1898 and 1904, there was extensive remodelling of Garnier's casino theatre. The orchestra stalls were inclined for better visibility, the prince's box was refurbished and equipment and lighting were overhauled.[178] But – in between the acts of an opera – members of the audience would hit the tables.[179] Alice sought to establish a new seriousness by securing the services of a thirty-seven-year-old Romanian impresario, Raoul Gunsbourg, who – as soon as he arrived in Monte Carlo for the 1892–3 season – began presenting top performers such as Dame Nellie Melba and

Sarah Bernhardt. Gunsbourg also scheduled the second opera by the London-born Isidore Cohen. Small, with outsized shoulders and a hunchback, Cohen had an appealing face. His first opera, *The Light of Asia*, was performed at Covent Garden in 1893, by which time he had renamed himself Isidore de Lara. His second opera, *Amy Robsart*, was not well received in Monte Carlo, but Alice fell under his charm and arranged a six-year contract. While Albert was off on his scientific expeditions, Alice and de Lara became lovers until – in the spring of 1902 – as Albert and Alice were climbing the stairs to the royal box to attend the premiere of *Le Jongleur de Notre-Dame* by Jules Massenet, de Lara snatched a few whispered words with the princess. Albert lost control, slapped Alice's face in public and left. She froze, then continued up the stairs to watch the opera.[180] In May 1902, an official separation was secured, and the princess went off to London to live at Claridge's – as did de Lara. She left behind her an artistic crucible that turned Monte Carlo into a melting pot for modernism.

Bronislava Nijinska, having resigned from the Imperial Ballet, left St Petersburg by train in early March of the 'blisteringly cold' winter of 1910–11. Among the other dancers travelling with her was a red-haired nineteen-year-old, Olga Khokhlova, who – seven years later – would marry Pablo Picasso. After three days, they arrived in Monte Carlo. Bronislava's brother, Vaslav Nijinsky, was already there, as were the designer Léon Bakst and the daring impresario Sergei Diaghilev. A self-confessed unscrupulous and charming charlatan, Diaghilev was, above all, a great visionary. Leading ballerinas Tamara Karsavina and Olga Preobrajenska would join later that March to complete the Ballets Russes, a company formed by dancers – not only from the Imperial Ballet, but from all over Russia and Poland.

Nijinska noted in her diary that 'to get from the railway station to our hotel in Beausoleil, we had to walk across most of the city in our Russian fur coats, our warm hats and overboots'. Fortunately, it was early morning so there weren't many people 'in their Parisian spring fashions' out and about to mock or marvel at the sight.

The company immediately began a demanding schedule of classes with Enrico Cecchetti, and rehearsed with Mikhail Fokine from early morning till after midnight, only catching sight of the Riviera sunshine when they returned to their hotel for lunch and dinner.[181]

Their Monte Carlo season – from 9 to 30 April 1911 – included *Schéhérazade* with its exotic costumes by Bakst, *Le Spectre de la Rose* with Karsavina and Nijinsky dancing, and *Les Sylphides*. It was the first time the Riviera had played host to artistic events of such consequence. On 11 April, the *Menton and Monte Carlo News* reported that Diaghilev's troop was 'unique and, although some of their ballets may not please everyone, their dancing is something so new, so different to anything seen before'.[182] Diaghilev was out to astound and shock and, by collaborating with the most exciting artists and innovative composers, he would change the course of ballet and become pivotal in the development of modern art and fashion. Dance was, Misia Sert observed, 'dying in Europe, imprisoned in an academic rigidity'.[183] Diaghilev and his dancers, choreographers, composers and painters set it free. The Aga Khan was often present at conferences between Diaghilev and his collaborators, likening them to councils of war at which the impresario 'was the supreme commander' turning 'a mass of brilliant objects into an ordered and coherent work of art... and the final result, far more often than not, was a masterpiece'.[184]

For Nijinska, who was to grow into one of the ballet's most innovative choreographers, this first Monte Carlo season was made memorable by her romantic flutter for the great Russian bass, Feodor Chaliapin. One night, after a performance of *Schéhérazade*, she was passing the Café de Paris with members of the company when they were stopped by Chaliapin. Highly excited by Nijinska's performance, he accompanied the dancers up the hill to the Hôtel Français and invited them to visit Nice the next day. In the event, Nijinska was called for rehearsal. Chaliapin and her friends went to the theatre to wait until she was released and then they all drove off to Nice by motor car. They took tea at fashionable Rumpelmayer's – which, at the time, found it worthwhile to advertise in English, French and Russian. Its interior was a testimony to how the elegant

Belle Époque could be rather uncomfortable. It was a time when fashionable ladies were condemned to sit on metal terrace chairs, straw-seated wooden café chairs and straight-backed, un-cushioned seats.

After tea, the Russians drove along the high Corniche at sunset to dine in La Turbie. Nijinska found herself infatuated. Bass and ballerina began to spend a good deal of time together, until Nijinska's older brother, Vaslav, intervened to alert her to Chaliapin's reputation as a womanizer. She protested that the singer was behaving with honour and much kindness. After Nijinsky's failed attempt, Karsavina was sent to warn Bronislava about Chaliapin's philandering. Nijinska confessed she was in love but assured Karsavina that it was platonic.

Shortly afterwards, Chaliapin absented himself, but soon reappeared, confessing he was unable to pull himself away from his 'pure angel'. He had praised her work in conversation with Diaghilev who had, indeed, begun to take notice of her. Nijinska was grateful and smitten. Then, one day, walking towards the Casino, the warnings were confirmed. Chaliapin was out with two 'rather overdressed women'. He dropped them and rushed to Nijinska, calling himself 'guilty' and 'wicked' and explaining away his gaudy companions as business related '*prima donnas* from New York'. Her enchantment faded.[185]

During the following Monte Carlo season, in the spring of 1912, Nijinsky and Nijinska were seen together in Igor Stravinsky's *Petrushka*. Preparing to dance the role originally created by Karsavina and knowing they were worlds apart as dancers, Nijinska approached the role in a novel manner. Stravinsky congratulated her on the interpretation, and Diaghilev decided that – as they offered such contrasting readings of the part – the two dancers should alternate performances.

It had been in Cannes in the spring of 1866 that Stéphane Mallarmé had a revelation about the purpose of his poetry. He went on to Nice where, in May, he took up his poem *L'Après-Midi d'un Faune* once again. It would inspire Debussy's *Prélude* in 1894, music which – according to Mallarmé – captured the nostalgia and the light of his poem. The *Prélude* would, in turn, inspire Nijinsky to choreograph. If Pierre Boulez considered Debussy's score to be the beginning of modern music, then Nijinsky's first work – premiered to boos in Paris and given shortly afterwards in Monte Carlo – was one of the first modern ballets. All through the winter of 1912 in St Petersburg, and then in Monto Carlo that spring, Nijinsky developed his first attempt at choreography. *L'Après-Midi d'un Faune* was a completely new way of working in which every movement of every part of the body was predetermined. The dancers of the day – used to a modicum of self-expression – felt constrained. Negative reports came in from all quarters. Diaghilev became unusually jittery and was only persuaded to persist with the project by Léon Bakst, who had not only designed the sets and costumes but also helped rehearse the short work.[186] Then – after all the tortuous rehearsals and Diaghilev's hesitation – the project was nearly quashed by an heir of Stéphane Mallarmé. The idea of

Nijinsky dancing the faun.

a faun masturbating with a nymph's veil onstage was too much for Mallarmé's estate. Diaghilev rallied support from art-world luminaries such as the sculptor Auguste Rodin – himself a maker of erotic art. At the Paris premiere, the audience was primed to be scandalized. *Le Figaro* came up with that mindless attack on adventurous art – that people were being had. They found the faun's 'movements of erotic bestiality… emphasized in a shameless manner'.[187] But the ballet stayed in the repertoire – the following April, Nijinsky was dancing the faun in Monte Carlo.

Deny it as he might, Paul Poiret – the man who filled Paris, Nice and Monte Carlo with glamorous creatures – was inspired by Bakst and Diaghilev and their colourful ballets. Bakst used shock tactics in his designs – peacock greens and blues with complementary rose pinks and coral reds. These stimulated Poiret. Indeed, the designer had been thinking along similar lines. In the first years of the century, he was already producing richly embroidered mandarin coats and, from 1904 to the outbreak of the First World War, Paul Poiret dominated fashion.[188]

His first great innovation had been to banish the corset, the second was his 'Oriental period'. To advertise his immersion in the East, Poiret organized 'The One Thousand and Second Night Party' in January 1911. The painters Raoul Dufy and Dunoyer de Segonzac were in charge of the decoration, and after the party – struck by Poiret's extravagant role and flamboyant dress – Jean Cocteau dubbed him 'The Sultan'. Benefitting from the vogue for fancy-dress balls, Poiret's sense of extravagance captured the imagination of rich clients who bombarded him with orders for all things Eastern. Next, Poiret threw a mythologically themed party at which Isadora Duncan danced and the 300 guests downed 900 bottles of champagne. Poiret was dressed as Zeus and, as dawn broke the night's revelry, a breakfast of lobster, foie gras, melon and ice cream was served to refresh jaded palates.[189]

Rather in the manner of Diaghilev, Poiret was skilled at discovering talent. Over the early decades of the twentieth century, he commissioned artists such as Sonia Delaunay, Mariano Fortuny

The designer Erté in costume. From a long line of Russian admirals, someone not quite suited to the Russian navy.

and Raoul Dufy.[190] He alerted Lucien Vogel, editor of France's top fashion magazine *Gazette du Bon Ton* to the dress designs of Erté, the rogue son from a long line of Russian admirals. When Poiret employed Erté, the artist – too young to sign his own contract – relied on the approval of a disapproving father. Poiret also kick-started the luxury goods industry when he became the first couturier to start a perfume line in 1911 with Rosine – named after one of his daughters. It was made in Cannes-la-Bocca by a subsidiary of the celebrated Chiris perfumery in Grasse. Again catering to the fashion for the exotic, one of Poiret's perfumes was called Nuit de Chine. Another was called Aladin. Another, Maharadjah. Then came a romantic scent, Pierrot, and a dangerous one, Borgia. In all, Poiret produced thirty fragrances between 1910 and 1923.[191]

While he had freed women from the corset, Poiret trapped them in the hobble skirt.[192] There is footage of French suffragettes struggling to move efficiently as they are, once more, hampered by that tyranny against women – fashion. As Erté put it, 'the feminine body is, to the designer, essentially a malleable entity which fashion moulds'.[193] It would be left to the post-war couturiers, headed by Coco Chanel, to begin to give women a measure of freedom.

Monte Carlo, in the years leading up to the war, was a thicket of plumed turbans, a dance of dazzling tiaras, diamond dog-collars and precious stones draped across powdered breasts. Between December and March, the principality was quite simply the hub of high society – a profusion of aristocracy. Daisy von Pless – the Welsh Mary Cornwallis-West who married Prince Hans Heinrich of Pless – lists but a few: 'Jennie, my sister in law (Lady Randolph Churchill)', Lady Adèle Essex, the Duke of Marlborough, the Duchess of Coburg, Prince Arthur of Connaught, the Duchess of Edinburgh who was born Grand Duchesse Marie of Russia, 'the mother of Queen Marie of Romania, the Grand Duchess Kyrill, the Infanta Béatrice of Bourbon d'Orléans'.[194]

The pre-war hit song 'Sur la Riviera' helped promote a region already hyped by the enterprising Camille Blanc with novelties such as parasol competitions, beauty pageants, dog shows, and automobile, bike and boat races. The Tir aux Pigeons – which would so horrify John le Carré when he visited Monte Carlo as a young man in tow to his snazzy dad Ronnie – was, ironically, started by Blanc to attract the 'right kind of people'.[195] Unless you enjoyed the sponsorship of two Sporting Club committee members, you had to be a member of the Hurlingham or Gun Club in London, or similar establishments in France or Belgium, to join in the massacre of half-crazed birds rendered helpless by the plucking of their tails and wings.[196] As for the lyrics of 'Sur la Riviera', they proceed from joy to sorrow, reminding the listener that words of love can whisper something cruel – that promises will not always pan out.

In Nice, an aristocratic crowd played tennis in a club situated in the heart of the city with 'hot and cold showers, reading rooms and a comfortable lounge'. At Hyères, a very popular golf course made a great appeal to Englishmen who came south for the winter expressly to play.[197] But the motivation behind sport was changing. French defeat in the Franco-Prussian War and the introduction of games and contests from England, along with the technological innovations responsible for bicycles, cars, yachts and aircraft, led to an increased interest in physical prowess. With Germany seen as an increasing military threat, the French and English were keen for their youth to develop strength and stamina.[198] The Nice horse races attracted international competitors, as did the polo played at Cannes from 1908. Car races, regattas and competitions in the air trimmed the frills and furbelows of Belle Époque fashion. 'Sporting tastes have so invaded modern society,' observed the *Herald* in 1902, 'that a fashion paper dealing exclusively with sporting costumes might sustain the interest of its weekly readers from one end of the year to the other.'[199]

While Belle Époque Monte Carlo and Nice were pictured in the frothy and gaudy advertisements of Jules Cheret, the 'Tiepolo of poster art', a new age was twisting its way along the treacherous roads of the coast, throttling the air. As early as 1899, the *Anglo-American Gazette* remarked that with 'erratic automobiles, furious cyclists, and devil-may-care cab drivers, the streets of Nice are not at any time a Paradise for the nervous or sensitive pedestrian'.[200] Eight years later, Marie Mallet noted that automobiles 'make driving here a hideous nightmare and kill at least three people a week'.[201] Out for an excursion in 1904, Daisy von Pless found the approaching motors like wild beasts with 'big round eyes and a roaring voice'.[202] Cars brought with them not only a nuisance for pedestrians but new types of crime. On 20 April 1912, the *Menton and Monte Carlo News* reported the presence of 'motor bandits' along the Riviera.[203]

Initially, cars were rare and cars were elegant. They allowed Belle Époque people to travel with unprecedented freedom – but always in style. Each 'person had his special car made to his taste' noted the photographer Henri Lartigue. The details were luxurious – created from tortoiseshell, ivory, mother-of-pearl, gold, leather and mahogany. Nonetheless, the Aga Khan remembered – among the fashionable landaus and victorias – seeing two motor cars 'as curiosities in front of the Hôtel de Paris at Monte Carlo'. He remarked 'how elegant was the disdain with which the fashionable crowd regarded these noisy, smelly toys'.[204]

The year 1898 had seen the first Concours d'Élégance de Monte Carlo, which took place in front of the Café de Paris. It involved a display of sumptuous motor cars and models brought from

Paris and dressed by the big names in fashion. There was Worth, Jacques Doucet, Poiret and Jeanne Paquin. There were Daimlers, Rolls-Royces, Austins, Napiers, Wolseleys, Argylls, Packards and Pierces. The previous year, the first automobile race in France had been organized between Marseille and Monte Carlo. Forty-three vehicles and twenty-five motorcycles participated in a race won by the Comte de Chasseloup-Laubat in seven hours and forty-five minutes. Édouard Michelin – co-director of the tyre company – didn't do so well. Losing control of his motor, he crashed into the Café de Paris. Monte Carlo passed legislation to control the circulation.

Daisy von Pless remembered watching the third Henri de Rothschild Cup race in 1904, when – as his car achieved a speed of 100 kilometres an hour – the winner broke a world record. Two years later, the Automobile Club de France and the International Sporting Club organized the first Paris–Monte Carlo–Paris race with contestants averaging a speed of fifty-five kilometres per hour.[205] Emil Jellinek, a financier who summered in Baden-Baden and wintered in Nice, owned the Villa Mercedes on the Promenade des Anglais. Unhappy with the Daimler he bought in 1897 and attending a race in March 1900 in which a Daimler Phoenix killed two spectators at the first bend, Jellinek proposed lowering the car's centre of gravity. Gottlieb Daimler implemented the idea and a car – the Mercedes, named, like the villa, after Jellinek's daughter – was delivered in 1901. With its 'tilted wheel, long bonnet, low-slung chassis spring suspension' and water-cooled brakes, it marked the birth of the modern car.[206]

In the years before the outbreak of war, as Russian grand dukes enjoyed Cannes and gambled in Monte Carlo, the social and political situation in Russia deteriorated. The humiliating annihilation of Russia's Second Pacific Squadron by the Japanese in the Strait of Tsushima in May 1905 occurred against a backdrop of revolutionary activity and industrial unrest at home. While there was a good deal of complacency among aristocrats, the confrontations of 1905 – the 'Bloody Sunday' march of the workers to petition the tsar for improved conditions, the riots, and the increasing anarchy – sent ripples through the expatriate community on the Riviera.

The organizer of the Bloody Sunday protest which ended in the massacre of hundreds of participants was a vain and disturbed Orthodox priest who had both compassion for the poor and the charisma to control them. Shortly after his tragic attempt to lead the workers, Father Gapon fled Russia to Switzerland to make contact with exiled revolutionaries. Finding himself a celebrity, their endless debates and devotion to Karl Marx proved tedious, so he moved on to Paris and London. He dined out on stories of Bloody Sunday and signed a book deal with an impressive advance.[207] In Monte Carlo, disguised as a Romanian bishop and sitting at the same gaming table as a grand duke, Gapon placed sizeable bets. Unstable, he returned to St Petersburg and cooperated with the secret police. Shortly afterwards, he was found strung up in a *dacha* outside the capital – murdered, most probably, by socialist revolutionaries.

Anxiety among the Russian community on the Côte d'Azur was somewhat mollified by Nicholas II's mendacious 1905 October Manifesto and his subsequent reassertion of faith in autocracy. The Russians continued to behave outrageously and with aristocratic hubris. Polovtsov recalled that when the wealthy Count Vorontsov was treated discourteously in the Casino, he called 'Banco' and bet against the large sum in the bank. Winning, he turned to a nearby waiter and said, '*Domestique, pour vous.*' The count left as the banker handed over a small fortune to a man who had merely been standing near the disgruntled winner.[208] When Princess Suvorov won a fabulous sum at roulette and wanted to throw a magnificent party, she couldn't find anyone who wished to rent out their villa, so she bought one for the occasion.

Shadowing this privileged community were the agents of change. In Monte Carlo, Feodor Chaliapin was attacked by Russian revolutionaries who discovered that onstage – following the example of the rest of the cast – the singer had kneeled for the tsarist national anthem. The socialists felt betrayed by a performer who had been humbly born. Chaliapin was outraged. 'Those revolutionary heroes, they sit here on the Riviera, and assert their revolutionary ideas by attacking me… Good thing I had a walking stick with a solid silver handle, so I could fight them off.'[209]

Among the revolutionaries who visited Nice was Vladimir Ilyich Lenin, who came down from Switzerland in 1909, 1911 and 1913. He stayed at the Pension Russe as Chekhov had done, made contact with local radicals, enjoyed the sun and sea air, and made pilgrimages to the grave of Alexander Herzen.

Meanwhile, locals – newly exposed to the events of the greater world – began to react as workers were doing everywhere. Employees in the Grasse perfume plants were miserably paid and initiated a series of strikes in the first years of the century. The potters in Vallauris, producing 200 casseroles a day for biscuit firing, were paid five francs. They protested at this hardly decent wage.[210] In April 1910, 600 poor Monégasques marched on the palace to signal their economic plight. As foreigners were employed in the Casino and hotels, they had no work. From nearby Villefranche, British sailors hastened to protect British residents. Guns to suppress a rebellion were stashed in the wine cellars of the Hôtel de Paris. French troops in Marseille were put on alert. The protest did not turn violent but it did force Albert to create a municipal council of Monégasques – and led, two years later, to improvements in education and health care.[211]

The Belle Époque was the apogee of the luxury and privilege of the preceding decades, and the beginning of a grand spring clean. From 1900 until the outbreak of the First World War, fashion and art underwent a tremendous change. Young artists engaged with non-European artefacts, making no attempt to demonstrate the kind of panache found in fashionable paintings by Second Empire artists such as the portraitist and court-flatterer Franz Xaver Winterhalter. African and South-East Asian sculptures were a blunt attempt to cut to the quick by ignoring surface realism and revealing the emotional impact of a subject. European painters began to adopt visceral techniques to challenge and aggress society. The violence of the First World War – that conflict between the conservative and the progressive – was, in a sense, already manifest in the art made in the years before hostilities began. If the 1890s seemed like the beginning of the last act of a grand opera, then – as the drama swept towards the final curtain – the old stage set of a gilded society was being torn down.

In the first years of the twentieth century, sensibilities were shocked into a new way of seeing and being. There were challenging artworks like Matisse's *Woman with a Hat*. The 'ugliest smear of paint I've ever seen', declared Leo Stein, who – on the advice of his sister Sarah – proceeded to buy it.[212] There was Fauvism, Cubism, Expressionism. There were developments in theatre and in the new medium of film. A studio opened on a seventeen-acre lot outside Nice where, in 1900, the Prince d'Esling had built a villa in homage to his aunt Victorine.

During the Belle Époque, the Côte d'Azur strived to maintain the social order of a disappearing age. Among the winter residents were many unprepared to embrace modernism. Ballets Russes composer Igor Stravinsky wrote the music for *Petrushka* in Beaulieu. The score caused some members of Monte Carlo's Russian colony to protest to the president of the local music society, asking for it to be banned. The nostalgic melodies of its opening scene gave way to something too modern for their ears. Stravinsky's score for *The Rite of Spring*, which rocked Paris audiences in 1913, was almost drowned out by the catcalls of the audience on opening night. Then there was its story. No ballet audience minded seeing a swan die, or someone like Giselle, deranged by class pressure. But the indiscriminate sacrifice of a young virgin for no reason other than that she was in the wrong place at the wrong time – that they found unacceptable. *The Rite of Spring* was presented when everybody's head was buzzing with the possibility or even the inevitability of a war to end all wars. Maybe they felt, uncomfortably, that they were in the wrong place at the wrong time. Facing carnage, people looked back with affection and regret on a dying age. Even as the Riviera was a-twinkle with new-fangled electrical illumination, the lights were about to go out all over Europe.

6

Painting the Warmth of the Sun

Most visiting nineteenth-century writers, having opened the eyes of the public to the beauty of the region, made no substantial contribution to the cultural identity of the Riviera. The painters who recorded Nice in its various stages of evolution made little impact in the world at large. It wasn't until the twentieth century that writers and painters offered the Côte d'Azur – reimagined – to the world.

Over the centuries, there had been artists born in Nice, but the political volatility of the borderlands meant that no substantial school evolved. Painters gravitated to rich and reasonably secure Genoa. During the Renaissance, Ludovico Brea – the foremost member of a family of painters – produced some of the best works in churches at Cimiez, Nice, Monaco and Menton. Later, the importance placed by the Counter-Reformation on the power of visual art resulted in much undistinguished church decoration in Nice during the Baroque period. Journeymen employed by churches with large spaces to fill produced mediocre scenes of well-worn subjects.

At the outset of the eighteenth century, Carle van Loo was born in Nice. He would become the most successful painter in a family of artists of Dutch descent. His work, however, had nothing to do with the south. In 1762, he was named First Painter to Louis XV, and that kept him at the French court. In Paris, one of his pupils was a promising young painter born in Grasse in 1732, Jean-Honoré Fragonard. The career of this theatrical, Rococo painter was centred on the French capital, although he left a small legacy in his native town.

The *Menton and Monte Carlo News* reported on 21 January 1899 that the large Fragonard panels *The Progress of Love in the*

Heart of a Young Girl – commissioned by Madame du Barry, aka Jeanne Bécu, retired prostitute and mistress to the king – were on show at Agnews Gallery in London.[1] Unable to pay for them when Louis XV died, du Barry had never taken possession. When Fragonard fled Paris at the time of the Revolution, he shipped the panels back to Grasse, where they stayed in the family of a close friend. In the second half of the nineteenth century, people tried to buy the paintings, but even when a would-be purchaser arrived with 800,000 francs in cash, he was refused.[2] During Queen Victoria's stay in Grasse in 1891, her daughter Princess Louise took Britain's ambassador to France, Lord Lytton, to see the panels. The owner was a Republican who pointedly kept his hat on and remained seated in the presence of the princess. His house – according to Marie Mallet, who accompanied them – was 'a curious mixture of squalor and magnificence'. It contained the 'very finest Louis XV furniture' but 'covered in thick dust' and embellished with 'the vulgarest antimacassars'.[3] At the end of the 1890s, the owner was persuaded to sell the panels to a Charles Wertheimer of Norfolk Street, London, for £50,000, on condition that the purchaser gave him time to have them copied. They were large, and Wertheimer, having 'miscalculated the dimensions' of the walls in his Mayfair house, was obliged to sell them on to Agnews for a slight profit.[4]

Landscape painting had long been part of the Dutch tradition. Only since the Romantic period had artists outside the Netherlands shown much interest in landscape for its own sake. Inspired by the example of John Constable, painters in northern France began to go out into nature to work. Of those who went south, Camille Corot presented enchanting views – but concentrated on the Italian countryside. Then, in the mid-1850s, Gustave Courbet confronted the Mediterranean in a series of paintings that asserted the power of the sea and revealed the wildness of its shore. The association between solitude in nature and freedom was an important notion for Courbet, who used the desolate southern coast to explore the theme.

Gustave Courbet, *The Edge of the Sea at Palavas*, 1854.

When rail travel made the south more accessible, painters began to visit. In December 1883, Pierre-Auguste Renoir and Claude Monet travelled together along the Riviera from Marseille through Hyères and Saint-Raphaël to Monte Carlo, Menton and on into Italy – in only two weeks. The following year, Monet returned to Bordighera to paint. During his stay, he began to make an important contribution to how we see the Riviera.

Used to the delicate atmosphere around Paris and the freshness of the Channel coast, Monet complained about the difficulty of capturing the clarity of vibrant light at Bordighera. Palm trees and exotic vegetation entranced the artist, but after two weeks searching, he wrote that 'general views are rare. It's too thickly wooded – it's all fragments with many details, a confused mass of foliage which is terribly difficult to render.'[5] He visited sites recommended by that celebrated local resident, Charles Garnier, in his *Les Motifs Artistiques de Bordighera*, but remained disgruntled. Monet was used – in his own carefully cultivated and well-ordered garden at Giverny – to defined areas that he himself had composed. At Bordighera, nature was rampant. Setting out on his journey home, Monet stopped in Menton and made paintings of the Corniche du Littoral. In Monte Carlo, he admired 'the sweeping lines of the mountains'. Motifs were 'more complete, more like paintings and therefore easier to execute'.[6]

In his 1848 guidebook to Provence, John Murray warned visitors against delusional visions of courtly love, troubadours, silks and perfumes. In Provence, the terrain was arid and there was 'a sombre, melancholy sternness in the landscape'.[7] In early 1888, searching for the radiance of Japan as it appeared in cheap reproductions of Japanese woodblocks, Vincent van Gogh went south to Arles. One month after his arrival, he wrote to the painter Émile Bernard about the 'clarity of atmosphere and gay colour effects. Water forms patches of lovely emerald or rich blue in the landscape, just as we see in the crêpe-prints. The pale orange of the sunsets makes the fields appear blue.'[8] Van Gogh's volatile imagination was stimulated. The resulting canvases, with their saturated colouring and heightened response to the landscape, made Provence appear exotic.

That same year, Claude Monet was back on the Riviera at Antibes, where he found 'superb' motifs. He became transfixed by the 'magical light'[9] of the Mediterranean, which he rendered in blues and pinks. He wrote, in a letter of 12 February 1888, that it is 'so bright, so luminous! One swims in the blue air and it is frightening.' Yet after three months of hard work, he returned home 'in despair'. Although he felt many of the canvases were 'inadequate', ten were taken by Theo van Gogh, the art dealer at Boussod & Valadon, and put on show in June. It was the first exhibition of paintings by Monet that had been made in one place.[10] All views from the eastern shore of Cap d'Antibes, the exhibition included two pictures painted from exactly the same position in different lights. To Émile Bernard, Vincent van Gogh wrote that 'my brother is having an exhibition of Claude Monet. I'd like to see it. Among others, Guy de Maupassant came to have a look and from now on he says he'll be a frequent visitor' to the gallery.[11] Maupassant was perhaps as much attracted by Monet's subject as by his style. Moreover, some critics were not impressed. Félix Fénéon wrote that the paintings demonstrated Monet's 'brilliant vulgarity'.[12]

In 1895, Renoir was ordered to go south to ease his rheumatism. He tried Beaulieu, Le Cannet and Nice. Then – refusing to cut down the 900-year-old olive trees on the plot of land he bought on the slopes above Cagnes-sur-Mer – he completed his house Les Collettes in 1908. There, Renoir painted from a wheelchair, his brush strapped to arthritic hands that echoed the gnarled roots of the olive trees that filled his garden. In many canvases from these last years of Renoir's life, blood red predominated – a wizened man keen to celebrate vitality.

A native of Aix-en-Provence, Paul Cézanne enjoyed painting in the south because the vegetation did not change – olive and pine trees kept their leaves. His favourite landscapes were those around his native Aix, which he attempted to paint time and time again. He found, in the Montagne Sainte-Victoire which dominates the town, an anchor for his 'aesthetic researches'. Happiest roaming the hills, working relentlessly and independently, Cézanne declared, 'I go ahead very slowly, as nature appears very complex to me... one cannot be too scrupulous, too sincere or too humble'. His career had taken the artist from the demise of Romanticism, through Realism, Impressionism, Post-Impressionism, and on into Proto-Cubism in the first years of the twentieth century. On 8 September 1906, a month and a half before his death, he shared his feeling of failure with his son: 'for me the realization of my sensations is always painful. I cannot reach the intensity which appears to my senses. I have not the magnificent richness of colour that animates nature.'[13]

Over the years, when he needed an escape from the countryside immediately around Aix, Cézanne would cross the hills to L'Estaque on the Mediterranean coast near Marseille. Kenneth Silver poetically suggests that when Cézanne painted at L'Estaque, his views looked above the chimneys and bare hills 'towards the Riviera, and the future of modern art'.[14] With no tradition of painting this coast, the Riviera was a blank canvas for artists with a fresh vision.

✧

The Neo-Impressionists, or Divisionists, applied unmixed pigment to their canvases in tiny strokes or dots – which, when seen from a certain distance, were fused by the eye of the spectator into areas of intense colour. Their scientifically driven method had limited degrees of success, as it tended to result in uniformity and monotony.[15] Its chief exponent was Georges Seurat, who worked in the north. Another important Divisionist was Paul Signac, who went south on the advice of the painter Henri-Edmond Cross. Having wintered in Saint-Tropez, Cross – who had changed his name from Delacroix on the advice of an art teacher – suggested that the fishing village would be a wonderful place to paint.

During the mid-nineteenth century, this town of 3,400 inhabitants was rarely visited by travellers. The only public transport was a steamboat from Saint-Raphaël and an old stagecoach. Seen from the gulf, the colourful houses, the white walls of the citadel's bastions, and the draped sails of the tartanes made the village appear attractive.[16] Sailing from Antibes in his boat *Bel Ami* in the spring of 1888, Guy de Maupassant found the small port of Saint-Tropez smelling of fish, burning tar and brine. Myriads of tiny sardine scales were scattered – like pearls – over the cobblestoned streets.[17] On the eve of the Belle Époque, when Nice and Monte Carlo were aglow, Maupassant found a region, 'as deserted as the American solitudes… unexplored country remote from the world'.[18] Signac settled there in 1892, convinced that the village, coast and countryside around would give him enough work for a lifetime. Deserted and sparkling, it proved a suitable place for innovative artists to evoke Arcadia.

Most towns and villages along the Côte d'Azur face south. The café terraces of Saint-Tropez, looking north across a protected gulf, are bathed in a warm, afternoon light that gives way to the rich sunsets found in the paintings of Signac, Matisse and Bonnard. 'Furious sunsets' as Colette called them.[19] The transformation of Saint-Tropez from fishing village to resort was not the initiative nor the result of foreigners. The earliest promoters were not Smolletts or Broughams but rather Maupassants and Signacs. Saint-Tropez – exceptional among the resorts of the south coast – was a French creation. This tiny port in the wilderness of southern France stimulated the Divisionists and Fauvists of the Parisian avant-garde, who thrust it – reimagined in audacious colour – onto the international stage.

Signac invited other Divisionists and some younger painters. By 1905, these newcomers were perplexing critics sufficiently for Louis Vauxcelles to suggest that the paintings of their informal ringleader, Henri Matisse, would suffer the same fate as 'a Christian virgin cast before the wild beasts' in ancient Rome.[20] The name stuck, and a loose group of painters – most of whom had been trained in the studio of the Symbolist Gustave Moreau at the *École des Beaux-Arts* – became known as '*les Fauves*' – 'the wild beasts'.[21] The core of this loose group comprised Henri Matisse, Henri Manguin, Charles Camoin, Albert Marquet, Maurice de Vlaminck and André Derain. All of them – except Vlaminck – came south, to where the food was good and life cheap. With fresh fish, fruit and local wine all for two *sous*, these painters found paradise.

Signac invited Matisse and his family to Saint-Tropez in July 1904. There, Matisse painted using heightened colour and – at times – a loosely Divisionist technique. The short, broken stroke worked best in his oil sketches, which captured the energy of the coast. In finished canvases, the technique was not so successful. Most overtly Divisionist was *Luxe, Calme et Volupté*, a title taken from Baudelaire's poem, *L'Invitation au Voyage*:

> Là, tout n'est qu'ordre et beauté
> Luxe, calme et volupté.

'Down there, all is order, beauty, luxury, peace and well-being' – or in the translation of Edna St Vincent Millay: 'There, restraint and order bless luxury and voluptuousness.' While the poem conjures the kind of landscape found in the south, it is Matisse's painting which places the spectator firmly in a Mediterranean Arcadia.

While making the painting, Matisse had in mind Signac's 1895 *Au Temps d'Harmonie*, which presents an imagined golden age on the Riviera in an image so ordered and didactic that it fractures the leisured harmony it sets out to evoke. Uncomfortable with Divisionism, Matisses's *Luxe, Calme et Volupté* suffers from a jerkiness unsuited to its title. The painting dazzles but the short strokes do not fuse. It was not the ideal way to evoke Baudelaire's lines – Richard Wilbur's translation suggests 'grace and measure, richness, quietness, and pleasure'.

Matisse introduced a contemporary clothed figure into this vision of Arcadia, presumably to suggest – in line with what Cross and Signac felt – that the golden age was upon them in remote parts of the Riviera, away from the brouhaha of the Belle Époque. Matisse abandoned Divisionism in his highly decorative *Bonheur de Vivre*. Its band of blue and mauve evoking the Mediterranean, its arabesquing trees and bodies, and its presentation of a joyous, southern dance offer a playful utopian vision. Indeed, the painter called the work 'my Arcadia'.[22] It was made over the winter of 1905–6, after the great breakthrough that occurred during the summer of 1905 – not on the Riviera – but at the far western end of the Mediterranean coast, at Collioure, a busy fishing village near the Spanish border.

Matisse had left Saint-Tropez, skint, in 1904.[23] To spend the summer of 1905 in Collioure, he was obliged to borrow money from Manguin and Camoin. Inviting André Derain to join him, both painters worked in a state of high excitation. Throwing off all but the residue of Divisionism, they applied broadly painted strokes using strong, often unrealistic colours – pure vermilion, cobalt blue and emerald, offset by softer pinks, mauves, yellows and pale greens. As Derain later said, 'Colours became sticks of dynamite.' There was no traditional underpainting and no overt demonstration of technique. They skilfully proclaimed a lack of skill, and their apparent lack of sophistication suited the scenes they painted. The unremitting light which threw the scene into stark contrast sharpened the vision in a manner suited to the brashness of the new century. By attacking with strong, imaginative and expressive colour, they were overcoming what Monet had found so testing – the problem of rendering sparkling and brilliant light. Working where the sun was so strong that it bleached colour, they found a contradictory way to express their joy in the south by using an intense range of colour and simplified, distorted or blurred forms. Matisse, Derain, Manguin, Marquet and the other painters flocking south were rendering the coast in a way that would impact on the poster design and the marketing of the Riviera in the first decades of the twentieth century. At a time when backwaters along the south coast were beginning to yield to villas, hotels, and roads with motor cars – even Signac acquired a Peugeot – the Fauves were asserting a new arcadia. The aggravating details of everyday life were lost in an impassioned, affectionate vision of a coast that was – at one and the same time – ancient and modern. They were painting the warmth of the sun, while rupturing people's notion of what was meant by art. By 1906, the Fauves were attracting a good deal of attention in Parisian commercial galleries as well as at the progressive Salon d'Automne and Salon des Indépendants. It was becoming clear that they were part of a larger, international tendency in art. As Matisse remarked, before nature 'we let our temperaments speak'. Their subjective and heightened response was expressionist – a reaction, as Roger Cardinal put it, that does not 'think things through' but rather 'feels, guesses and gambles'.[24]

Most visitors to the Côte d'Azur during the Belle Époque had little interest in engaging with the locals and their world. They expropriated the coast for their own pursuits and lifestyle. Those who came for the season brought their world with them, merely seeking sunshine to burnish familiar routines. They ignored the untouched villages and rough hills that tumbled down to their thin strip of imported civilization. By contrast, the Fauves engaged with the work and customs of the locals. Visiting unspoilt, obscure places such as Saint-Tropez, Cassis and La Ciotat, they were able to rediscover a coast known to eighteenth- and early-nineteenth-century travellers – before Brougham and Woolfield imported English turf and the Grimaldis charged their coffers with the profits of a gambling den. Fauvist paintings recreated the sun-drenched simplicity of the Mediterranean fishing village with a freshness that only became more appealing as the coast developed.

Charles Camoin and Henri Manguin were based in Marseille and Nice between 1904 and 1906. Manguin was still under the influence of Impressionism, though, increasingly, he used heightened colours to create intimate and restful images of the coast. He painted the figure in idyllic settings – a quietly erotic vision of his wife Jeanne on a deckchair, or sunbathing naked on the rocks at Cavalière. Camoin, often more timid in his use of the Fauvist vision, could, on occasion, explode in a riot of saturated colour. Georges Braque, better known for his Cubism, spent time in L'Estaque and La Ciotat during the winter of 1906–7, painting the landscape in purples, ochres and pinks. He was often in the company of Émile Othon Friesz, who painted coves, inlets and woods in saturated yet acidic colours. Pierre Bonnard was in Saint-Tropez and experienced the place as if it inhabited the world of *One Thousand and One Nights*. By the spring and summer of 1908, when Braque was painting with Raoul Dufy at L'Estaque, Derain was in Cassis, already moving away from the Fauvist style. Following the example of Cézanne, his painting became progressively Cubist. As the mantle of shocking modernity passed from Matisse to Picasso, the first glorious engagement of painters with the Mediterranean coast was ending. But many of these artists would be back – some to settle. Matisse lived in Cimiez until his death. Bonnard chose Le Cannet above Cannes and stayed there seasonally till he died. Raoul Dufy went to Vence after the First World War and became known for his brightly coloured, playful paintings of sport and society in Cannes and Nice. Fernand Léger and the painters of the *École de Paris* visited – as did Picasso before he moved to the Riviera after the Second World War. The Russian Jewish exile Marc Chagall settled in the sun. Local artists formed the mid-twentieth-century *École de Nice*. The newly established tradition of painting in the south would survive two world wars. In 1914, the radiance of the Impressionist, Divisionist and Fauvist years which had bathed the coast in joyous colour was – temporarily – subdued by a world turned suddenly grey.

7

The First World War

1914–18

On the eve of the conflict, the fashion designer Erté, having contracted scarlet fever, was sent south to convalesce. As trains were detailed for military use and many people had been urged to leave Paris, the journey was trying. After two days trapped in a compartment by the clog of refugees in the corridor, Erté arrived.[1] The lights were going out all over Europe – except in Monte Carlo.

Hedging his bets, Albert I declared Monaco neutral against any outcome, although the prince and most visitors stood firmly on the side of the Allies.[2] There were initiatives to aid the war effort and to care for combat victims, while the authorities attempted to maintain some semblance of gaiety – the economy of the principality depended on a functioning Casino and happy-go-lucky visitors. 'Monte-Carlo may be tempered with the shadow of the war,' observed the *Menton and Monte-Carlo News*, 'but certainly this happy Principality offers more amusement than any other winter resort.'[3] Hotels and restaurants welcomed guests. The gaming rooms and the Sporting Club were open from early until late. Theatres performed three times a week. Indeed, life seemed so utterly normal that one reader even wrote to the *News* to complain about the programming in the cinemas: 'charming girls do not appreciate too much of "Charlot" slipping on banana skins, or covering other people's faces with ice cream... a little of Charlie Chaplin goes a long way'.[4]

If people thought Monte Carlo immoral in the past, this cocoon of pleasure now seemed even more difficult to countenance. While people need diversion and refreshment in time of war, there was something unsettling – even obscene – about this opulent haven. Its spa – 'a splendid bathing establishment' offering 'waters from all the springs of France… Turkish Baths and Russian baths and all sorts of electric cures' – sat uneasily beside the burnt and blistered wounded who began to arrive in the first weeks of the war. Its 'first class doctor in attendance'[5] would have proved more useful in the impromptu hospitals springing up along the coast.

The Great War spread epidemically from the two shots that killed Archduke Franz Ferdinand – heir presumptive of the Austro-Hungarian throne – and his wife, Sophie, on 28 June 1914. Their assassination in Sarajevo gave Austria–Hungary a pretext for declaring war on Serbia one month later. On 1 August, Germany declared war on Russia – two days later, on France. German troops entered Belgium on 4 August, and Britain declared war on Germany. The conflict that would stifle Europe for nearly half a decade had already encompassed the continent.

It was a dead time in Nice. Hotels and shops were closed-up until the beginning of the 1914–15 season in late autumn. Behind shuttered windows, there was guarded excitement, rumour and then relief when nearby Italy decided to remain neutral. Spies were cause for concern given the number of German hoteliers and tradesmen scattered along the coast. The *Journal de Nice* went so far as to claim that German 'infiltration, slow, continuous and methodic gave to our worst enemies, all spies, a part of our hotel and flower industry'. Some Germans took Swiss nationality so they could continue to trade. Others were rounded up and repatriated, held in central France or incarcerated on the Île Sainte-Marguerite – their hotels, shops, boats and villas confiscated. In the streets, anti-German sentiment ran high. People from the east of France were mistaken for the enemy, simply because they were tall and blond. A Danish journalist was similarly targeted. Lynchings of pale-skinned, flaxen-haired people were plotted, but happily forestalled by the swift intervention of the authorities. Eau de Cologne became Eau de Louvain. German Shepherds became Alsatian Wolf Dogs. German beer, Prussian blue and landaus were forbidden or renamed.[6] Four months into the war, a hotel in Menton was attacked for proposing, as a Christmas dessert, 'Bombe-Sedan' – a tactless, if not provocative, evocation of the French defeat in the Franco-Prussian War.[7]

Nice city council ruled that the price of bread should not increase by more than five centimes a kilo, and a local paper published lists of 'patriotic' bakers who sold at normal prices. Locals stockpiled goods, fearing price increases and scarcities, while vendors who rushed to exploit the situation were met with intolerance. A shopkeeper who raised his prices unreasonably so angered customers that they threw his produce into the River Paillon. Dishonest butchers tricked peasants into selling livestock cheaply by predicting that prices would fall. One man – caught making a 400 per cent profit – was jailed for five years yet acquitted on appeal.[8] Such knavery appeared pathetic against the plight of the broken new arrivals. At daybreak on 3 September, the first wounded soldiers reached Nice – 62 victims of a war that would turn northern France into a wasteland. At 10 p.m., there were a further 316. Another 250 at midnight.[9] Once again, the Riviera was to become a hospital.

During the first months of the war, a good number of wounded were lodged in the casino of the Jetée-Promenade, while the French army began to requisition hotels to serve as hospitals and nursing homes. With unfortunate timing, two of Nice's grandest hotels – the Ruhl and the Negresco – had opened in 1913 and were packed with Germans who accounted for nearly half of all foreign visitors. Just over a year later, 400 beds were commandeered at the Negresco, 300 at the Ruhl. Up in Cimiez, the Hôtel Majestic lost 500 beds in the first year, and at the Grand Hôtel, 500 beds were taken from the outbreak of war until January 1919.[10] After three operating theatres and a radiography unit were installed, the most critically wounded were taken to the Grand.

On Cap d'Antibes in early 1914, Antoine Sella had begun to prepare for a trial summer season by dynamiting a seawater pool into the rocks by the Hôtel du Cap.[11] His forward-looking plans were interrupted by the war, and the hotel was turned into a hospital. In Cannes, part of the Carlton Hôtel was transformed into a military hospital under the direction of the mayor's wife, Madame Capron.[12] Later, it became a convalescent home and – after the war – lost a good number of its habitués to the fallout from the Russian Revolution.

In complete contrast to the selfishness of his uncle Léopold II, Albert I of Belgium put his villas at Beaulieu and on Cap Ferrat at the disposal of wounded Belgian soldiers. When in April 1915 the Germans first used gas, at Ypres, these villas welcomed the burnt, suppurating victims, many of whom would be buried there. On Cap Ferrat, the Hôtel du Parc and the Villa Sicard were turned into a home for Serbian refugees and a clearing centre for war orphans. The children arrived by train with their identity papers pinned to their clothes. The youngest among one group of arrivals had a second paper attached: 'I am going to the summer-camp of the orphans of the war and have been entrusted to the care of the other travellers.' As with similar centres at Cannes and Juan-les-Pins, schools were hastily set up for the children who were awaiting adoption, and their free time was filled with singing, walks and costume parties. The women who eventually took them in were often war widows briefed that no child should ever go to bed without being cuddled, hugged and tucked up.[13]

War orphans taken for a walk on Cap Ferrat.

For over half a century, Nice had been split between its rich seasonal visitors and its poorer local community. From August 1914, the arrival of a heterogeneous mix changed all that. Apart from the wounded of all ranks, some civilians came south to escape the violence or to convalesce. The Ukrainian sculptor Alexander Archipenko arrived with his wife soon after war was declared. Deprived by wartime shortages of the materials necessary for sculpture, Archipenko produced his celebrated reliefs such as the *Bather* of 1915, for which he used oil and pencil on metal, wood and paper. His wife set about knitting sweaters for friends in the army.[14]

On 11 September, French and Belgian refugees began to arrive. Most were grateful to be lodged in homes and hotels, but some were bitter and bewildered. After the grey, war-torn coalfields of the north, they found the ostentation and ease abhorrent. Some merely found the place too hot. Others – like the orphans from the north and the east – were enchanted by the balm, beauty and comfort of the coast.[15] Regaining consciousness on a bed set up under the chandeliers in the ballroom of a sumptuous villa, twisting gently to gaze out at palm and lemon trees framing the deep blue sea, a wounded soldier might have thought himself dead and woken

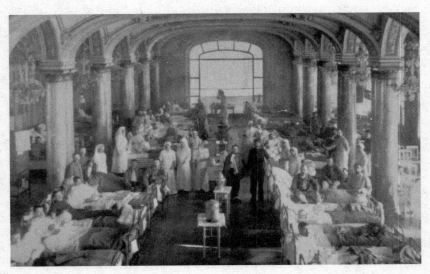

The wounded in a temporary hospital ward set up in the Hôtel Ruhl.

up in paradise. The contemporary writer Renée d'Ulmès observed that, for the ashen-faced arrivals who were washed, bandaged, and placed in clean sheets, it was a 'resurrection'. When a tactless visitor remarked that these victims were spoilt, the writer retorted, 'Madame, without them you wouldn't be alive.'[16]

For officers who were not in a critical condition, convalescence on the Côte d'Azur was almost as congenial as a peacetime visit. Yet the prospect of death overhung all merriment. Ford Madox Ford later remembered that a 'peeress of untellable wealth and of inexhaustible benevolence' took those with congested lungs to the Hôtel Cap Martin. 'We ate *Tournedos Meyerbeer* and drank *Château Pavie* 1906.' Yet 'one looked round and remembered for a second that we were all being fattened for slaughter'.[17]

As trainloads of casualties from the Marne, Arras and Ypres arrived, Renée d'Ulmès observed that a great sense of community grew up between these victims and the often grand ladies who volunteered to care for them. Days spent in nursing were strictly organized and full of emotional tumult. There was a happy hour for the nurse's *toilette*. 'A sad hour attending to dressing wounds. A comforting hour for lunch. A joyous hour for cards. An anxious hour taking temperatures followed by the hour for doctors doing their rounds.' An elderly socialite from Nice spent many nights with a delirious soldier, dismissing her attentiveness – 'At my age you don't need much sleep.' To watch her at work, no one would have guessed that she was wealthy. Only through her generosity, as she arrived each day with gifts of chocolate, fine wine and biscuits for the patients, was it apparent.

A group of eight wounded soldiers had been trapped for days in a tight space ripe with the putrefaction of dead comrades. At first, they ate stale bread. When that was gone, they were forced to chomp on fabric. For men who survived that, to watch a countess who, most probably, had never done the dishes in her entire life, appear in the makeshift ward with a tray of apples that she herself had baked, forged strong arcs across the chasm of the social divide. If the rich buggers had got them into this mess, their wives were doing everything in their power to ameliorate the misery.[18]

December 1914 arrived with no resolution of the war that 'would be over by Christmas'. In Nice, 700 soldiers were invited to eat with local families, but the authorities refused to sanction it, fearing that it might fatigue the men.[19] On the 24th, Renée d'Ulmès was at the Grand Hôtel serving dinner when the head surgeon came in to announce that, during the night, 150 casualties were expected. They began to arrive just before twelve, some almost petrified in swollen uniforms full of mud, blood and pus. It was Christmas night. The sight of the open wounds reminded her of Golgotha.[20]

The requisitioning of eighteen hotels made an impact on Nice's 1914–15 season, and it is remarkable that visitor numbers were only down by a third. The figures were indeed impressive considering the competition from neutral Spain, where summer casino resorts like San Sebastián launched winter seasons. The casino on the Jetée-Promenade reverted to its normal function at the end of January, and cinemas and theatres reopened to present charity galas with top performers. Nonetheless, Nice – a city of pleasure – had become solemn. Any Englishman who arrived was obliged to have his passport stamped at his consulate and obtain a *permis de séjour* from the police. To travel outside the city – even to adjacent Villefranche – required a pass from the authorities. The Russians found it difficult to obtain funds from their motherland, and their consulate offered to repatriate them. With men departed for the front, Boy Scouts on bicycles replaced despatch riders, and sumptuous Belle Époque motor cars were commandeered for official use. Trams were adapted to carry stretchers. Recuperating soldiers – free to visit museums and cinemas – became a presence on the streets.[21] A city once dazzled by the splendid uniforms of strutting Sardinian and Russian officers, or by the top brass of Second Empire France, was now haunted by unsteady, bandaged men in sombre khaki or drab blue kit. For them, a promenade was a difficult blessing, not a social rite.

In Monte Carlo, profiteers and victims walked side by side in a stark reminder of the relation of capital to carnage. Victims ghosted among those who, wittingly or unwittingly, were complicit in the preparations for the war – the industrial competition, brinkmanship, and the huffing and puffing of the jingoistic press that had made the conflict almost inevitable. By 1914, different European powers had claimed – or claimed and lost – most of the globe. They could now only take from one another. Thus the fratricidal slaughter, the mindless wasting of the land. Billed as the 'war to end all wars', 1914–18 would not be the last time the Riviera welcomed arms profiteers.

Up to 3,000 soldiers passed through the tiny principality in each year of the war. Residents both temporary and permanent rushed to help. When a lady complained to the *Menton and Monte Carlo News* about a new fifty-centime levy for the use of the cloakroom at the Casino, she was tartly informed that it was being collected on behalf of the war charities. Women set up the Orphelins de la Guerre so that children of the poorer Monégasques killed in action would be adopted as 'godchildren... by benevolent ladies', who would look after them and help them towards a career.[22]

La Belle Otero spent much of the war at the Hôtel de Paris. At the Casino, Erté noticed her jewellery piled on 'with such abandon that the final impact was utterly tasteless – in keeping with the vulgarity of her manners'. He had once seen her 'whistle through her fingers like a ruffian to attract the attention of a friend'. Apart from adopting and schooling an orphaned boy, Otero did much for the victims of the war by performing at Nice and Monte Carlo charity galas.[23]

On 23 May 1915, Italy entered the war on the side of the Allies. Given the proximity of the frontier and the strong historical ties, towns and villages along the Riviera were full of Italian flags and song – particularly in Old Nice and around the port, where many Italian families were living. In September, the Negresco, the Ruhl, the Winter Palace and the Riviera Palace reverted to their normal activity, and there was optimism for the 1915–16 season.[24]

The journey from England was difficult but not impossible, and tubercular patients still managed to convalesce on the coast. When the twenty-seven-year-old short-story writer Katherine Mansfield was told by her doctor to go south, she later admitted, 'I would not have swapped my lung with any man alive.' She arrived in Marseille in November 1915 with her future husband, the prolific writer John Middleton Murry. After a few days, they went on to Cassis – where a fierce mistral blew, only easing when the sun went down. They moved to the Hôtel Beau Rivage in Bandol where – nine days after her first haemorrhage – Mansfield finished her celebrated short story 'Bliss'. During the month of December, the couple settled at the Villa Pauline, though Murry's work forced him to return to London. Mansfield was left alone to write her short story 'Prelude' and to revel in a land that reminded her of her native New Zealand. She wrote to Murry, 'I wish you could see the winds playing on the dark blue sea today... the clouds are like swans... the air tastes like fruit!'[25]

Mansfield found herself alone at Bandol only a matter of months after her brother died in a training accident in the Ypres Salient. The loss, compounded with the atmosphere on the coast, acted as a catalyst for her finest work. Memories were brought to life by an environment that chimed with what she had known young, and loved. She was eating heartily – 'vin blanc and grilled sardines and carottes à la crême and saucisses pommes parmentier and oranges'. She was walking healthily. On 22 December, she wrote to Murry, 'if you were here, we could walk to Sanary – watch the fishermen pull in their nets, have coffee at the café on the quay, and come back by train, carrying a big bunch of yellow roses'. When he returned in the new year, they shared three blissful months at Villa Pauline, getting up early, sitting down to work by 8.30 and continually interrogating one another, while he wrote his study of Dostoevsky and she fictionalized her New Zealand childhood.[26]

In that new year of 1916, four German 77-millimetre guns – captured in the Champagne offensive and now on a national tour – drew crowds to the Promenade des Anglais, where they were on show.[27] For most inhabitants of the Riviera, the war 'stayed a mystery, a huge drama that took place a long way away'. Renée d'Ulmès observed that 'unlike people in the north and east, we haven't seen our houses destroyed and our town devastated'.[28] The duty of locals and winter residents alike was to welcome refugees and invalids with kindness, resilience and love. It was a terrifying task – a battle in its own right. As the Riviera struggled to overcome the shortfall in its economy, volunteers fought to appease the desperately altered expectations of the wounded. Among the blind soldiers received by a Monte Carlo hospital, one man remembered that, when it happened, there was no pain but 'all of a sudden, it was night'. Those who with infinite kindness tended the men, knew the horror of war. They organized outings, taking small groups of patients on excursions or to luncheon at a good hotel. These tireless volunteers – like the men they nursed – had been thrown with scant training into a world that was strange and frightening. What can anyone say when a soldier clutches his blanket up about his neck and confides that 'both legs are marmalade'.[29] On the part of the soldiers, there was understandable bitterness but, more often than not, a bewildered gratitude. In a new world where Eau de Louvain mixed with disinfectant – a place as strange to them as the trenches – they found love.

Patients were haunted by what they had seen – Germans ransacking villages, bayonetting children, shooting the infirm.[30] The ladies on night duty presided over wards shattered by nightmares and troubled by the endless groaning of those desperate for morphine. When relatives managed the difficult journey to visit those in peril, the nurse in charge would whisper to them as they entered the room where men were about to die, 'Go in gently.'[31]

During the afternoon of 12 February, there was an event that signalled that the Riviera's isolation from the direct ravages of war might be threatened. Captain Valentine of the Royal Flying Corps was seen over Nice, testing a new three-engine, three-propeller plane built in Italy and purchased by the British government. There was considerable astonishment that he flew from Milan to Antibes in 'only three hours'.[32] A new kind of warfare was in the air – yet, in the fashion world, there was a surprising throwback to the style of the Second Empire. Such nostalgia doubtless reflected a need to feel secure and powerful and shun the daring and haphazard modernity that had preceded the conflict. In Paris 'the new fashions' had 'gone back to the early days of the Empress Eugénie, slightly modernized'. 'Elegant tissues with printed flowers... and crinolines' were in vogue. Yet, just as cycling along the coast had been replaced by motoring, the *News* reporter wondered whether 'after this war, motoring will in turn go out of fashion in favour of flying'. He mused that 'the fashions Paris is trying to bring in now, of inflated skirts and crinolines, will be of no use, when every smart and extravagant woman has her own flying machine'. Unable to miss the chance for a swipe at the enemy, he continued, 'Let us hope that we shall never allow hordes of German tourists to descend upon us... in excursion Zeppelins. The cruel and dangerous Boches will never be forgotten or forgiven to that extent.'[33] Promoting a popular venue the following week, the *News* peppered its article with more anti-German sentiment: 'There is no place pleasanter for lunches and teas and dinners this season than the Sporting-Club. Far away seem the days when "le Sporting" was so overrun by Germans that English and French visitors alike seemed crowded out by insolent Teuton officers with their plain faces scarred by ugly cuts... and their loudly-dressed and loud-voiced lady companions.'[34] At a conference in Menton, German 'Hymns of Hate' were recited to reveal the savagery of the enemy.[35] Of course, the Germans would be roundly welcomed once their currency recovered from its post-war tribulations.

What was blatantly absent from the pages of local papers during the war were reports of the festivities surrounding that peacetime highlight of the season: carnival. Likewise, Epiphany was a damp squib. The festival's traditional *galettes des rois* 'were certainly not plentiful. The confectioners' windows made but a poor show.'[36] The wealthy, however, still managed to celebrate. A Mr and Mrs Branch gave a dinner at the Sporting Club for Mr Branch's birthday. 'The cake,' reported the *News*, 'with its fifty-two candles was much admired.'[37]

❖

Senegalese soldiers enjoyed their time in Menton. The writer Baroness Orczy, who spent time in neutral Monte Carlo during the war, recalled that there was a 'bevy of young Mentonese beauties who hung about round their quarters and walked out and flirted with them to the loudly expressed disapproval, not to say horror, of the American visitors'. She went on to add – through typically rose-tinted spectacles – 'in France, of course, there is no such thing as differentiation between white and coloured races'. 'Black or yellow or white', the children of France 'are all alike in the eyes of Frenchmen and, seemingly, of Frenchwomen also'.[38] Some of these Senegalese soldiers were on leave and others were wounded, but all were gone by 1916. Only two hospitals remained in Menton – one was a Red Cross Auxiliary Hospital installed by Lady Dudley at the Hôtel Mont Fleuri. Apart from welcoming many English officers and their wives, it included a dispensary which supplied hospitals along the Riviera with free material shipped from England – bandages, dressings, cotton-wool vests against pneumonia, slippers and loose shoes for wounded feet.[39] There were concerts by the sea every morning, and although the Casino had been boarded up, there were more visitors to the principality than in the previous season. Hotels remained very full at the end of March. The *News* hoped that 'with the bad weather in the North and the difficulties of getting to England now, many will stay the summer through' and 'learn how beautiful that season is here'.[40]

Cannes, where the eighty-two-year-old John Taylor was still vice-consul, was similarly full of visitors – golf, croquet and tennis remaining popular. In Nice, when the season ended in April, it was – under the circumstances – declared a success. Forty heavily censored comedies had been presented at the theatres. There had been daytime concerts and charity shows featuring the likes of Mistinguett, Réjane and La Belle Otero. In the absence of an opera house kept shut by insufficient funding, *Aïda*, *William Tell* and *Rigoletto* were given at the Château Valrose.[41] There were tennis matches in aid of charity, featuring players like the up-and-coming local girl Suzanne Lenglen.

Nice had also taken on a somewhat unexpected role as the provisional capital of Serbia. The government had been chased from Belgrade to establish a short-lived wartime capital in Niš. Forced again to flee, the politicians escaped across the Adriatic to Brindisi, moved on to Rome and then to Nice, where a room was put at their disposal in the town hall. The influx of Serbian troops and the large number of wounded arriving during the summer – victims of the futile Somme offensive which began on 1 July – were stark reminders of the difficulties shadowing any attempt at normality.[42]

A reduced police presence combined with the early closure of taverns and bars meant that gangs were out on the streets of Nice along with 'almost undressed' prostitutes. Soldiers entering and leaving their barracks were besieged, while men returning from the theatre were harangued if they ignored the whores. Crooks ran fake subscriptions for clothes to donate to the wounded. Swindlers would pose as friends of a soldier and solicit clothing and money on his behalf. There was a traffic in transit visas. French deserters could escape over the frontier to Italy by purchasing the necessary travel documents from Italians who had arrived in France. With many apartments and villas uninhabited, burglaries were commonplace. Vandalism and theft committed by children as young as ten increased throughout 1916. Gangster films were blamed, and the city authorities invited cinemas to cut scenes that might incite violence. The source of the problem was the war – fathers at the front and mothers working. Out of 38,000 children enrolled in school, 4,000 were not attending, while many teachers were away serving in the army.[43]

Over the winter, life became more austere. In Nice, municipal lighting was cut to a minimum and shops shut at 6 p.m. At the beginning of 1917, with its unusual weather – rain, 'continuous cold and gloom' – coal and oil became scarce. Items such as matches and paper would periodically become unavailable. Paper money was badly deteriorating, so Nice's *École des Arts Décoratifs* designed and printed currency on the only material available – paper so thin that sweaty palms made the notes disintegrate. Furthermore, the lack of sophisticated printing techniques meant that thieves were not slow to counterfeit. Consumption of cocaine, opium and morphine was on the rise. Roughly a third of those in prison were between sixteen and eighteen years old and, in Menton – when the English Book Club was 'wantonly damaged' – three boys, aged thirteen, were arrested.[44]

During the 1916 opera season – when hats were, at last, banned in Monte Carlo theatres – Raoul Gunsbourg had miraculously secured singers from the Russian Imperial Opera to present Tchaikovsky's *Eugene Onegin*, Glinka's *A Life for the Tsar* and Rubinstein's *The Demon*.[45] It was no mean feat, given the conflict. For the 1917 season, Gunsbourg did even better – he secured the world premiere of a Puccini opera. Originally commissioned for Vienna's Carltheater, the war intervened and neutral Monaco seemed a suitable alternative, particularly as the opera's third act was set on the Riviera.

At the premiere of *La Rondine* on 27 March 1917, Puccini joined Prince Albert in the royal box. The *News* reviewer found the orchestration fine, but the story 'most uninteresting and banal, ridiculous even in places… The self-sacrifice of the *demi-mondaine* in giving up her poverty-stricken lover' was hardly interesting at a time marked by 'innumerable acts of noble self-sacrifice'.[46] Although melodically enchanting and fresh in its use of contemporary dance rhythms, the reception was warm rather than rapturous. *La Rondine* was consigned to semi-oblivion as one of Puccini's minor operas – until, in recent decades, the increasing frequency of fine productions and good recordings argued its merits.

As the war dragged on through 1917, a sense of vulnerability began to undermine resolve. The Ventimiglia–Marseille railway line – carrying troops, munitions and equipment from Italy – was kept under constant surveillance against sabotage. On 21 October, Nice was blacked out for fear of a Zeppelin raid. There was concern over possible attacks against hydroelectric installations and factories. Villagers in the backcountry reported clandestine signalling across the hills in the hours of darkness, but investigation could not substantiate their claims. Meanwhile, the police were monitoring a threat from a different quarter – the *Féderation Communiste Révolutionnaire du Sud-Est*, inspired by the pacifist and revolutionary Frédéric Stackelberg, who believed that the war was being fought 'to slaughter the proletariat'.[47] Members of his revolutionary group were eager to obtain news about what was happening in Russia, where the trouble brewing would profoundly affect the ambiance of the Côte d'Azur.

Weariness with the war and shortages of food in the Russian capital were accelerating demand for change. By the end of February 1917, protest had taken on the dimension of a general strike and the students came out in support. Socialist propaganda was aided by subversive German agents. Then, after America entered the war, an anxious Germany deployed a secret weapon to disrupt the Russian military effort – they sped Lenin and thirty Bolshevik comrades across their territory in a sealed train to reach a Russia primed for revolution.

On 25 October, at about eight o'clock on a raw morning, the cruiser *Aurora* anchored in St Petersburg's River Neva – its crew sympathetic to the Bolsheviks. The following day, delegates from the revolutionary committee arrived at the Winter Palace to demand the surrender of the provisional government. As there was no reply, a blank was fired from the deck of the *Aurora* to trigger the Russian Revolution. In a speech reproduced in *L'Éclaireur de Nice*, Frédéric Stackelberg appeared delighted by the way things were going: 'It is a population coming to life!... Bureaucracy has been defeated; tsarism expires.' On the Côte d'Azur, the first problem posed by the events of October 1917 and the subsequent civil war was the arrival of suddenly impoverished refugees who remained loyal to the tsar.[48] If they had property in the south of France, Russians descended on Nice in the knowledge that they had a villa to live in, or – if times got hard – sell. Rather as French Royalists had fled to England after their Revolution, noble Russians came to the Riviera to await the day when their country would welcome them back. The outlook was not bright. Marxists met at cafés in central Nice in the dead of night to gloat.[49]

❖

The end of 1917 was a period of great distress. Mutiny had become chronic in the French army. There were air raids on Paris and huge civilian discontent. The British offensive at Passchendaele had won five miles of Flanders quagmire at a cost of a quarter of a million British and Commonwealth lives. It was the Somme all over again. There was a massed tank attack at Cambrai in late November. After two weeks and 75,000 Allied casualties, the Germans prevailed. To counteract hopelessness and disarray, that same month, Georges Clemenceau became prime minister and war minister of France. His ascendancy combined with America entering the war raised morale. On the Riviera, the mayor of Nice renamed the Quai du Midi the 'Quai des États-Unis' out of gratitude for the American intervention. Mrs Edward Tuck, wife of the American financier and philanthropist responsible for restoring the Trophy of the Alps at La Turbie, was awarded the *Légion d'honneur* for her charitable work. Hotels were almost full. On the Jetée-Promenade in Nice, Mistinguett and Maurice Chevalier performed, the Comédie-Française appeared, and a festival of the music of Gabriel Fauré took place.[50] Then, on Christmas Day, a singular visitor arrived who would continue – during the following decades – to help forge the cultural identity of the Côte d'Azur.

The colourful window scenes Matisse painted at Collioure and Saint-Tropez in 1904–7 had been replaced, in 1914, by a singular image – the ominous blank rectangle of a window at night. After that bleak and immediate response, Matisse remained severely depressed by a war that was devastating the landscape of his childhood and threatening Paris. Intending to stay only a few days, he took a spartan room at the Hôtel Beau Rivage. Nice was cold and deserted. On the last day of the year – his birthday – it snowed. On New Year's Day, it poured and he thought he would soon leave. However, by mid-January, the mistral had blown away the bad weather and Matisse stayed, hooked once again by 'the luminosity' of the Côte d'Azur.[51]

In early 1918, despite the difficulties of travelling locally, Matisse took to visiting Renoir at Les Collettes – although the older painter didn't much like the work that Matisse brought with him.[52] Otherwise, Matisse lived an austere life, drawing at the art school in the afternoons and, most nights, going to bed by 8.30. His palette had become subdued, his paint applied thinly. At least for the moment, the coast had taken on a wistful, subdued aspect – gone was the splendour and jubilant rage of the Fauve years. His new motif was empty rooms, which eventually became – as he collected North African bric-a-brac over the years – an exotic setting for his odalisques. In the spring of 1918, when he moved to lodgings on Mont Boron and found himself surrounded by the tents of Moroccan soldiers, the excellent views across the Baie des Anges lifted his spirits.

From mid-January to mid-March 1918, Katherine Mansfield was back at the Hôtel Beau Rivage in Bandol. Spitting blood and excited by her work, she slept fitfully. Although sad to be separated from Murry once again, as she contemplated a 'sea like quilted silk' there was the compensation of her new New Zealand. However, towards the end of February, the rough sea – which often gave her pleasure – became threatening. It was 'like a bombardment'. Its roaring screamed, 'Danger! Danger!'[53]

The war was coming closer to this isolated coast. The German UC-67 was a powerful minelaying submarine that penetrated the security channel at Marseille to place devices that sunk the cargo ship *Drôme* and the trawler and minesweeper *Ker-Bihan* in January 1918. Eight months earlier, UC-67 had sunk the British hospital ship the *Dover Castle* in the Mediterranean. It was the fifth strike against British medical ships within two months. With German U-boats doing their worst, some decommissioned French submarines abandoned in the arsenal at Toulon were used as target practice for the squadron of bombers from the air base at Saint-Raphaël.[54]

There were rumours of Zeppelins attacking Italy. Should they stray in the direction of Nice, church bells and warning sirens would be sounded. Cellars were fortified and stocked against potential raids, at a time when there was confusion relating to the official measures for rationing. The bread card obliged customers to attach themselves to a single baker. When Nice found itself without water for ten days, the two teams of fifty men sent up to the hills to restore a collapsed aqueduct were delayed because they 'were unable to obtain bread and other food, as their ration cards were of no use outside Nice'.[55]

Food inspectors disturbed winter visitors. The *News* reported that two guests at an English hotel in Cimiez were taking luncheon in their rooms and were in the process of buttering their toast when there was a knock at the door and 'several strange men' entered 'and instantly seized the butter'. The proprietress of the establishment was to be summoned and fined unless the judges could excuse her on the grounds of knowing insufficient French.[56] Prices continued to rise. There were beggars everywhere. Marie Bashkirtseff's mother, who never washed but rather splashed her face with Eau de Louvain, was approached by some American soldiers who thought her a beggar and gave her some coins. She rose from the bench on which she was sitting, turned and pointed to her splendid villa on the far side of the Promenade des Anglais. 'That, sir, is my house.'

Spanish flu – brought to Nice in mid-May by a soldier on leave – spiralled and peaked in the autumn. The return to school was pushed back to mid-November. Theatres and cinemas were shut and religious ceremonies were conducted outside churches. With the arrival of the Americans, the incidence of venereal disease increased as dollar-hungry women resorted to casual prostitution.[57]

There was, however, a promise of economic salvation. In April 1918, the *News* reported that hotels which should have been on the point of closing, 'remain full and people still arrive. In fact, one of the dreams of peace time – a summer season – will become this year a reality.'[58] Remarkably, the hotels were still open in June and July and, all along the beach, people were out in the sun – some completely naked, provoking a new order from the mayor forbidding nude swimming and playing on the beach.

The season was simply better and longer because of the Americans. A deal was struck between the US authorities and the hotel keepers' syndicate to offer lodging at the inclusive price of two dollars a head. For the many who came on leave, a Franco-American bureau was set up in Nice to offer advice and deal with complaints. English-speaking staff were employed by the larger shops, while military police were kept busy trying to divert privates away from cheap, seedy bars in the remote quarters of the city.[59]

The war ended on 11 November 1918 and made way for the 1918–19 season, in which 65,000 Americans arrived to enjoy the balm of the Riviera. Erté was still in Monte Carlo where the American General of the Armies, John J. Pershing, was resting. Loving solitude, Erté enjoyed the hot summer months and 'sunbathed long before it was considered "chic" to be tanned'. He found inspiration for his drawings 'during long, solitary walks along the seashore to Cap Martin, into the mountains towards La Turbie and on the Moyenne Corniche'. He often exchanged small talk with a bearded man, stripped to the waist and walking briskly. He later found out this 'vaguely familiar' figure was George Bernard Shaw. Erté had been commissioned by the editor of *Harper's Bazaar* to pen a monthly newsletter full of 'observations and impressions of life in what had become the most fashionable resort in the world'. On Armistice night, he described how an English lady 'appeared in the Casino wearing a huge hat studded with long hat pins flying the flags of all the Allied Nations'. There were spectacular celebratory fireworks – doubtless straining at the nerves of recuperating soldiers.[60]

After the initial euphoria, people came face-to-face with a difficult future. Soldiers lay wounded – some irrevocably. Others – shell-shocked – would suffer lives unravelled by combat stress, unable to share the inexplicable horror of war with those in front-room parlours back home. In and around Nice, refugees arrived until well into 1919. Then, in 1920, hotels that had been requisitioned found that they received in compensation only a quarter of the value of their damaged property. For poor and middle-income families, there was financial hardship. Commodities like milk and potatoes were three to four times more expensive than they had been before the war.

Monte Carlo was in full swing. Convalescing in nearby Menton, Katherine Mansfield found Monaco's gambling rooms to be 'the devil's headquarters'. Up and down the carpeted steps passed 'a continual procession of *whores*, pimps... ancient men stiff and greyish'. While the Casino offered a vision of hell, the Hermitage rest home in which she was staying presented a kind of purgatory: 'It's not that these people are ill. They look exactly as though they were risen from the dead... They are still sexless, and blow their noses in a neuter fashion.' The home proved too noisy and Mansfield's cousin welcomed her at the Villa Isola Bella, where – armed with a £40 advance for a collection of short stories – she was busy writing and clearly content: 'If I don't get well here, I'll never get well.' She would not, as so many others had done, die in Menton, but in Fontainebleau in January 1923, aged thirty-four.[61]

On his winter visits to Nice, where he found a city 'untouched by the war', Henri Matisse encountered Sergei Shchukin, the Moscow collector who had bought many canvasses and commissioned two of his greatest paintings, *Dance* and *Music*. Shchukin had fled Russia when his house was seized and opened as a Soviet museum – at least, until the Revolution turned against modern art as an expression of 'bourgeois individualism'. Shchukin had a winter retreat on the Riviera, and Matisse took him to visit Renoir shortly before that artist died.[62]

Towards the end of the Great War, there had been a death that signalled the end of an era. On 9 March 1918, the *Menton and Monte Carlo News* reported that James Gordon Bennett Jr – that larger-than-life eccentric who had done so much to colour existence on the Côte d'Azur – was 'lying seriously ill at his villa in Beaulieu'. Two months later, he was dead.[63] The bells had been tolling for the Belle Époque since the summer of 1914. The war – a disjuncture between the old order and a new vision – primed this precious coast for new glories. The verve of Bennett's young compatriots was about to make the Riviera jive to the rhythms of the Jazz Age.

8

'The British-American Riviera Colony'

1922–9

I n this post-war world, there were American cocktails, American money, American dancers and bands, yet the most significant Americans to inhabit the coast – the 'lost generation' – weren't found until the mid-twenties. Even then, they didn't make much impact beyond the confines of their circle. Elsa Maxwell – socialite and party organizer to the rich and famous – thought the 'lost generation' were 'the dreariest bunch' of 'half-baked mediocrities'. She met the novelist F. Scott Fitzgerald several times and found 'he was never sober enough to carry on a coherent conversation with anyone' – what else was new? One evening, Ernest Hemingway taunted Fitzgerald about not holding his liquor. He didn't realize that Scott had been drinking all day and the pre-dinner cocktail was just a swig too far.[1] As for Hemingway, Maxwell suggested that 'the gentleman protests too shrilly his virility'.[2]

In the mid-twenties, the columns of the *Menton and Monte Carlo News* were full of book reviews of works by now-forgotten writers. The sole mention of Fitzgerald was a March 1926 Nice hotel registration – 'Mr. Scott Fitzgerald of New York has arrived at the Hotel O'Connor'.

The 'lost generation' were busy becoming a cultural phenomenon – the 'first real' generation, claimed Malcolm Cowley, 'in the history of American letters'. Yet, on the Côte d'Azur, they were not the people who made the news, although the stories of their private lives began to redefine the Riviera as they grew 'rapidly... into legends'.[3]

Throughout the twenties, British and American habits and customs vied for the soul of the coast. At the outset of the decade, British winter visitors who had known and loved the Riviera before the war slumped back into Belle Époque modes and manners. When the politician Duff Cooper stayed at the Carlton in Cannes in March 1921, he attended a gala dinner 'prettily done under the auspices of Poiret'.[4]

After a short post-war revival, the creations of the exotic 'Sultan' of haute couture started to lose popularity. Poiret was forced to reinvent himself as a party decorator as his once opulent fashion house edged towards liquidation. Post-war popular entertainment largely consisted of Belle Époque kitsch or pretentious items inspired by modern ballet. For the Fête de la Mer at the Negresco, 'Little Wanda, the tiny child dancer... emerged from a gigantic oyster shell'. At the Carlton in Monte Carlo, La Belle Samya, 'a beautiful vision in a silver frock', danced 'while gazing at her own beauty in a silver mirror' as her partner – 'in skin tight clothes' – danced 'Death' in their new act, 'Une Danse Macabre'.[5] Costume balls were held, as before the war, but themes had changed. Gone were the abstract evocations of 'Twilight', as participants largely focused on stereotypes and clichés. At the Ambassadeurs in Monte Carlo, the prizewinners included 'Mrs. Hutchins in a remarkable get-up as "Bridget", the maid of all-work. Miss Stewart as a resplendent Chinese... Mr Simon as a picturesque sheik.' Among those who didn't win were the Comtesse de Buat as 'Poupée', Mr French as 'an Apache' and Mrs Pollit as a 'Bohemian artist'.[6]

Society still met on the Riviera to replicate 'the whirl of the London season', but there was something not quite right. The stylish veneer of the Belle Époque was cracked. Lords and ladies filled the columns of the local press, but the British upper crust seemed uncomfortable with a new class visiting the coast. Exclusivity appeared at risk. Winston Churchill's wife, Clementine, wrote from the Hôtel Bristol in Beaulieu, 'Here I am feeling rather lonely in this vast hotel full of middle-class English people...'[7] Discomfort was exacerbated by her uneasy relationship with the most prevalent form of amusement on the coast. She was not fond of gambling, and often worried about her mother's and her husband's enthusiasm. When she did indulge in a flutter, she had a 'disastrous' time. In Monte Carlo, Clemmie left two gold coins on the gambling table to accumulate. They were stolen. 'Being somewhat inexperienced I did not protest loud or long enough for justice to be done – so shaking the dust from my feet I proceeded to the more select atmosphere of the Sporting Club where I lost all the money I had made.'[8]

The 1922 New Year's dinner at Ciro's included the American ambassador and the American philanthropists Mr and Mrs Tuck. The up-and-coming designer Coco Chanel dined with her current lover, Grand Duke Dmitri Pavlovich – first cousin of the ousted Nicholas II. At the Café de Paris, Consuelo and Jacques Balsan entertained Lady Essex and Winston Churchill,[9] who returned the hospitality several days later by giving them a dinner at Ciro's where they were joined by Clemmie's mother, Lady Blanche. Although Churchill had given her a handsome sum to enable her to live comfortably, Blanche persisted in staying at a modest hotel in Monte Carlo to gamble. 'She goes from 3 to 7,' Clemmie lamented. 'She won 7,000 francs laboriously & then flung it away in 10 minutes. I cannot understand such folly...' However, after the dinner at Ciro's, Lady Blanche won 400 francs at the Sporting Club, while Churchill, preoccupied with the peace conference about to take place in Cannes, went off to stay at the Negresco with the Canadian-British newspaperman and politician Lord Beaverbrook.

The conference had been convened to fathom how to reconstruct the battered economy of Europe. The leader of the British delegation, Prime Minister David Lloyd George, wished to include Germany in the negotiations. France was opposed, fearing a consequent weakening of the terms of the 1919 Treaty of Versailles with its heavy demands for reparations. The British, however, had come to believe that massive penalties were undermining chances of a pan-European recovery, as Germany, somewhat mendaciously, claimed it could not honour the repayment schedule. The French argued that if the Germans were treated too lightly, it would speed their recovery and threaten the stability of Europe. The 'eyes of the whole world'[10] were fixed on Cannes, where the meetings proved tortuous and achieved little. The follow-up conference in Genoa a few months later ended in stalemate, with France threatening to invade Germany unilaterally if Germany defaulted on its reparations.

If the British government was tending towards appeasement, privileged English visitors to the Riviera – with their lingering hatred for Germany – were suspicious that local casinos were turning a blind eye to German gamblers returning to enjoy themselves. In March 1924, an editorial in the *News* was provoked by sightings of the unwelcome visitors playing in the casino at Menton: 'We trust that the French authorities will do all they can to prevent this district from being again invaded by the Boche... the English have made the Riviera their winter home and they will not stand the German whether it be in the hotels or Casinos.'[11] The British, with their innate sense of entitlement, were trying to preserve an era that had already passed.

For Cannes, the peace conference was good. The French delegation stayed at the Carlton, the Germans at the Hôtel du Parc and Lloyd George at the Villa Valetta on the seafront. There was Pathé news footage of the French prime minister, Aristide Briand, strolling along La Croisette, and of delegates emerging from the gracious entrances to elegant hotels. They were men, all men with overcoats and hats, yet – as they left the Cercle Nautique – the egregious figure of a woman in a full-length fur was visible. She was a photographer. The post-war world was beginning to change.[12]

Many people from the British delegation would return to holiday in Cannes. In the following winter of 1922–3, Churchill rented the Villa Rêve d'Or in Cannes, played polo and gambled at the Casino. Clemmie played tennis.[13] By 1924, although you could travel back and forth between England and the Riviera by ship, there was so much traffic crossing the Channel that – in an attempt to aid industry and reduce the high level of unemployment – it was argued that building a tunnel would prove useful.[14] The *Menton and Monte Carlo News* expanded as its lists of visitors lengthened and advertising increased. 'Slowly but surely,' the paper declared, 'the charm of the Riviera in summer is getting known.' In 1923, 'Monte

Carlo had a wonderful summer season, to which the Mussolini ban against gambling in Italy largely contributed'.[15] In 1925, the summer season in Cannes was up on the previous year, and 1926 surpassed all expectations.[16] Two years later, the *News* predicted that the summer season would 'be a bumper one as many thousands of Americans' intended 'to come to the Riviera'.[17]

In 1923, an enterprising lady opened a boarding school for English and American girls in Menton.[18] Anglo-American clubs were popular. By 1924, the *News* was referring to 'the British-American Riviera colony'[19] – both cultures visible to Sir Frederick Treves as he motored along a coast where some café placards advertised 'afternoon teas' and others 'American drinks'.[20] For a newly empowered America, it was a cocktail colonization, as the 'invaders' imported habits, spent money and were enchanted by French life. Erté noticed 'it became the fashion to dance during one's meal. It was a strange custom. Between each course one would dance either the one-step, the foxtrot, the tango, the pasadoble or the shimmy. Sometimes one let one's dinner get cold.'[21] Quinto's restaurant in Monte Carlo reacted against American habits. They advertised 'food – no music' – 'no negro jazzbands... to annoy the lovers of the gastronomic art'. Quinto's thrived.[22]

Edith Wharton's association with the Riviera bridged the nineteenth and twentieth centuries. She had spent six years in Europe as a child, and another two on the eve of maturity in the early 1880s when her father died in Cannes. Wharton and her husband often motored along the Riviera and, in 1907, were accompanied by the novelist Henry James. She loved the coast around Hyères and was susceptible to what so many others had experienced – the echo of an Arcadian 'golden age'. During the Great War – exhausted from setting up sewing workshops, providing food and clothing for refugees, and campaigning for the United States to join the fight – Wharton came south to recuperate. After her marriage and the war ended, she returned with her long-time friend Robert Norton, rented a villa in Hyères and added the finishing touches to her celebrated novel *The Age of Innocence*. Walking with Norton one

The courtyard of Edith Wharton's house in Hyères.

day in 1919, they found an abandoned convent of the Order of St Claire standing on a hill in the old part of town.[23]

Wharton first rented the convent before buying it in 1927. From then until her death ten years later, she spent summers in Paris and winters in the south, where she would write in bed until eleven o'clock, then walk and picnic. Sir Kenneth Clark observed that Wharton, like all Victorians, felt a 'mysterious urge to go on picnics, which were preceded by endless fuss and usually went badly'.[24] Gardening was difficult on the stony soil around the convent,[25] but the result was so successful that Consuelo Vanderbilt wondered whether 'the warmth' of Wharton's 'nature had found its only blossoming in her garden'. This conjecture was modified when she read Wharton's memoirs. It was, perhaps, rather 'shyness that made her so inaccessible'.[26] Clark found Wharton 'fidgety' and unfathomably pessimistic beneath 'a perfectly conventional surface'. Inviting local dignitaries to luncheon, she dutifully listened 'with icy contempt to the endless stream of platitudes'.[27] The Riviera figures in several of Wharton's works, but there is a withering evaluation of its society in the 1905 novel *The House of Mirth* that perhaps best expresses her detachment. It is a place where 'conspicuousness passed for distinction, and the society column had become the roll of fame'. Monte Carlo – where the square before the Casino was 'set in an exotic coquetry of architecture' – was 'of all places, the one where the human bond is least close'.[28]

Edith Wharton was 'old New York' – gracious in a pre-war, European sort of way. There were other Americans who arrived in Europe and spiked it with American energy and acuity. Consuelo Vanderbilt was one – initially married to the Duke of Marlborough, before happily marrying the French aviator and manufacturer Jacques Balsan and settling on the Riviera. Another was the Princesse de Polignac, born Winnaretta Singer, daughter of the sewing-machine magnate Isaac Singer – a man who twice paid a dowry of $2 million to secure titles – *duchesse* then *princesse* – for his daughter Winnaretta,[29] who was, in fact, a lesbian. She enjoyed 'discreet and alternating' affairs with the Baronne de Meyer, the composer Dame Ethel Smyth and the painter Romaine Brooks, and a four-year liaison with the writer Violet Trefusis, daughter of Edward VII's mistress, Mrs Keppel. Nonetheless, Winnaretta became a *duchesse* through her brief first alliance, before making a lavender marriage with Prince Edmond de Polignac, who died in 1901. Injecting France with American cash, Winnaretta threw her energy and resources into support for modern composers. There is a story of a whingeing aristocrat protesting that her own title was as good as that of a Polignac. Winnaretta rounded on her – 'Not on the bottom of a cheque.' The Princesse de Polignac supported composers such as Ravel, Debussy and Satie, many of whose compositions were first heard at her salon. Her generosity and commitment to modernity continued after the war, when new works by composers such as Darius Milhaud and Stravinsky were promoted. The Diaghilev ballets *Renard* and *Les Noces* were first tried out at Winnaretta's musical soirées.

There were yet other Americans – energized by the wealth of parents who had made fortunes during America's 'gilded age'. Riches often aroused excess and self-indulgence – characteristics embodied by two larger-than-life figures who left their mark on the Riviera. The first was Henry Clews Jr – son of a wealthy member of the New York Stock Exchange – who made of the ruined Château de la Napoule a fantasy medieval realm in which to indulge his artistic talents and keep the modern world at bay. The other was Frank Jay Gould, the litigious son of a blacksmith's bookkeeper who had built up a huge railway empire. Gould brought American vigour and money to the development of Juan-les-Pins and the magnificent and ill-fated Art-Deco Palais de la Méditerranée in Nice.

The sculptor Henry Clews was working in Montparnasse during the war, when the shells of Big Bertha landing in Paris rattled his windows and persuaded him and his wife to seek refuge in the south. From a rich Philadelphia banking family, Elsie Whelen – renamed Marie by Clews – had first been espoused to the immensely wealthy heir and businessman Robert Goelet, older brother to the friend of Edward VII, Ogden Goelet. It was an unhappy marriage, with Goelet despising Marie's attraction to the arts. After their divorce in 1914, Marie married Clews. As a wedding present, he gave her his life-affirming sculpture *The God of Humormystics*. When they began to search for a substantial property in the south, they were shown the derelict Château de la Napoule by an honest estate agent who admitted that no one wanted it. Attracted by its two Saracen towers, they rented the property with an option to buy. Once it was theirs, they rebuilt the structure, adding medieval features such as crenellations, while discreetly installing modern conveniences. Creating a truly enchanting environment, Clews carved 'Once Upon a Time' in the lintel over the entrance. As visitors arrived, they were encouraged to turn their backs on the twentieth century.[30]

In the 130-page introduction to his 1923 play *Mumbo Jumbo* – with its cast of over thirty plus 'Orchestra, porters, lackeys' – Clews gives heated indications of where he stood in relation to modernity and the Riviera. It is an extended and confused rant in which the author drifts from target to target. Laying ultimate blame on 'James Watt, with his devilish invention of the automatic power machine, destined to uninvent civilization', Clews fears that 'Beelzebub, enthroned on his steam-roller of machine science and communism, is at our garden gate'. Looking out along the Riviera, he rails against the 'comfort-crazed... epoch of super-palace hotel... "Elite Toilet Paper"' and the 'ultra-modern chic, cosmopolitanized, Carltonized, Ciro-ized, trans-atlanticized, social columnized'. Clews attacks newspaper gossip for causing the destruction of trees, and finds America 'dangerous' because it is 'the most mechanized, unspiritual country in the world'. After his extended diatribe, Clews takes sixty pages to describe his cast of thirty-three – one of which is a wooden statue. *Mumbo Jumbo* then begins in the most prosaic way but soon builds to a tirade about urinals, which gives momentary relief from the leaden dialogue.[31] At least the author chose an apt title.

As for his sculptures, visitors were bemused by the mix of jest, the erotic, the grotesque and the fantastic. In the courtyard stood Clew's large wedding present, *The God of Humormystics*. Although appearing somewhat anguished, the figure smiles sadly and offers the mystic rose of earthly and heavenly love. With one foot, the god crushes a toad representing evil, and beneath his raised foot is the head of an inspirational smiling woman. Not only given as a wedding present, the sculpture was dedicated to his wife, whom Clews considered a collaborator.

Gravestone of Henry Clews at the Château de la Napoule.

Proclaiming his intention to banish science and restore mirth and mystery, Clews had the money to be mirthful and mysterious. With the resources to allow him to turn his back on the art world, his oeuvre was displayed in the Château de la Napoule, which Clews named 'La Mancha'. Styling himself as Don Quixote, whose 'romantic idealism' he admired, he called his servant Sancho. Henry and Marie dined in medieval costume with minstrels in the gallery. Their huge Senegalese butler wore 'baggy violet trousers, a waistcoat of Chinese embroidery and a tall hat that accentuated his height'. A temporary neighbour was the German diarist Count Harry Graf Kessler. Interested in sculpture, Kessler visited – and later remembered enjoying a medieval feast on a stone table with the moon shining on the sea through a Gothic loggia.[32]

The American eccentric Frank Jay Gould helped drive the modernization of the Riviera. A gourmet and a whisky drinker who danced two hours a day for exercise, Gould married a half-French San Franciscan divorcée whom he spotted at the Folies Bergère. There was nearly twenty years between them and they had an open marriage, conveniently enjoying two homes in the south – the Villa Sémiranis in Cannes and La Vigie in Juan-les-Pins, a town in which Gould invested heavily.[33] He bought a considerable amount of land and built, among other things, the Hôtel Provençal. After Juan-les-Pins, Gould poured money into the Palais de la Méditerranée in Nice. The prodigious project was jointly bankrolled by Gould, the promoter and hotelier Joseph Aletti and the casino owner Édouard Baudoin. It took 30 million francs and 350 workmen one year to build the 5,000-square-metre reinforced concrete structure cladded in marble from the old Roman quarry at Nîmes.[34] When it was opened in 1928, the *Cannes News* hailed it as 'probably the most luxurious building the world has ever known, designed, erected and conceived for the gratification of the pleasureloving public'. Upon entering, the first impression was of 'space, dignity and still more space'.[35] Its atrium with its marble floor, its sweeping grand staircase leading to gaming rooms overlooking the sea, and the *bas-reliefs* on the façade are a triumph of elegant Art Deco.

The façade of the Palais de la Méditerranée, Nice. A triumph of Art Deco architecture.

While there is an important American component in the show, the fantasy of what being on the Riviera in the 1920s meant to the British is captured in Sandy Wilson's 1954 musical, *The Boy Friend*. For Wilson, seaside resorts promised a world of continental naughtiness and decadence. His show *Valmouth* might be set in an English watering hole, but its flexible morals and the shady pasts of its characters are far more fitted to the Riviera, with its cocktail of illicit relationships and questionable conduct. Its sexual suggestiveness goes far beyond the innuendo of *The Boy Friend*, which is set in Nice and celebrates romance among the 'bright young things' who are sent to the Riviera to polish their social graces. Act I takes place in 'the drawing room of the Villa Caprice' and 'Mme Dubonnet's Finishing School'. Act II, *sur la plage*. In the third act, the simple love story resolves itself under a mirror ball and silver tinsel, as Pierrot finds his Pierrette at that evening's costume party. However, while the show presents a predominantly British Riviera, the character of the American Bobby Van Husen – who sings 'Won't You Charleston With Me?' – acknowledges a new cultural input. *The Boy Friend* owed something to the 1924

Vincent Youmans musical *No, No, Nanette*, which was set in the American seaside resort of Atlantic City. After successful runs in Chicago, London, New York and Paris, *No, No, Nanette* was performed in Monte Carlo in December 1927. A month earlier, *Rose-Marie*, Broadway's longest running show of the early 1920s, was presented.[36] There was clearly an audience for that new American form – the musical.

One of the giants of American musical theatre summered on the Riviera before that became popular and before he became famous. The rich Yale graduate from Peru, Indiana, was six years shy of a Broadway hit show when he first went to Antibes. In post-war Paris, Cole Porter was thoroughly enjoying the homosexual party scene, which did not stop him from marrying the divorced socialite Linda Lee Thomas in 1919. They honeymooned in the south of France during its winter season and went on to Italy, where Venice became a favourite haunt for their extravagant celebrations. Two years later, on the advice of the Scottish American opera singer Mary Garden, the Porters rented a villa for the summer at La Garoupe on Cap d'Antibes. Garden, who created one of the title roles in Debussy's opera *Pelléas et Mélisande*, and who often sung at the Monte Carlo Opera during the winter, was considered most eccentric for staying on to rest in the deserted calm of the summer. The Porters so enjoyed the Riviera, they returned the following year.[37]

An old friend of Porter's from Yale, the shy but stylish Gerald Murphy was living one of the sweetest and most elegant love stories. Although cruelly challenged, the romance would flourish throughout the couple's studied and generous lives. Sara Wiborg, Gerald's childhood friend five years his senior, had travelled in Europe as a young lady and been presented at court. She had studied painting intermittently – with William Merritt Chase in New York and at the Académie Julian in Paris. She saw *Le Sacre du Printemps* in London before the war, and was absorbing the cultural flurry to which the diffident and repressed Gerald Murphy would soon become attracted. When Gerald invited Sara to the Yale prom, she was a golden-haired beauty with deep-set and searching eyes. Both from affluent backgrounds, they grew into the artistic milieu they would so lovingly inhabit. After years of mounting affection, Sara wrote to Gerald, 'You are in my inmost heart & mind & soul – where I never thought I'd let anyone go.' They married in 1916 when Sara was thirty-two, and both were sexually inexperienced. Gerald – as he would throughout his life – agonized over an incident which had occurred when he was fifteen and made him aware that he might be homosexual.

At first, Gerald worked in the family business, though Sara's annuity facilitated their evolving desire to live and work together. 'What husbands and wives can do this?' asked Gerald, whose great gift was to embellish the tiniest gesture with panache – the lighting of a candle, the striking of a pose, the mixing of a cocktail.[38] When he arrived in Paris with his wife and three young children in the summer of 1921, Gerald became – through Diaghilev's Ballet Russes – drawn into the creative vortex of early 1920s France. When he spotted paintings by Braque, Picasso and Juan Gris in the window of the Rosenberg gallery in the rue la Boétie, it stimulated his brief but important artistic career.[39] Painting for only seven out of his seventy-six years, Murphy made few paintings – of which only eight have survived. His intensely personal, yet cool and detached canvases reflected the order sought by the French Purist painters in the aftermath of the Great War. Amédée Ozenfant and Charles-Edouard Jeanneret – aka Le Corbusier – initiated a way of thinking and painting that was, after the ambiguities of Cubism, both clear and objective. If the Purists were painterly, Murphy's surfaces were slick like posters.

In the context of American art, Murphy's small oeuvre was significant – identified with the Precisionists such as Charles Demuth and Charles Sheeler who, at the time, were composing sanitized paintings of unlikely industrial scenes. Murphy's work introduced the kind of luxury items made by Mark Cross, the company his emotionally taut father had taken over in the late nineteenth century and with which Gerald continued an association until the mid-1950s. Such ingredients meant that Murphy's work, along with certain canvases by the Precisionist Stuart Davis, anticipated the commercial subject matter of late 1950s and '60s Pop Art.

In the autumn of 1921, Murphy set up a Paris studio and worked through until the following summer, when the family went off to holiday on the Channel coast. The weather was cold and the children very young and vulnerable, so – when the Porters invited them to come to Cap d'Antibes – they hurried south. When the Murphys found a tiny beach at La Garoupe covered with seaweed over a metre deep, they cleared a corner. They 'bathed there and sat in the sun', delighting in the crystalline water which Gerald noted was 'that wonderful jade-and-amethyst colour'.[40] It was idyllic and deserted.

As if in anticipation of the stimulating environment that the Murphys would create for writers and artists on Cap d'Antibes, there was a hotel which had begun life as the Villa Soleil – a haven for novelists and poets who had lost their inspiration. Set-up by Hippolyte de Villemessant who had resuscitated *Le Figaro*, the idea never took hold and the Piedmontais Antoine Sella opened the Hôtel du Cap in 1887. Despite its fabulous location which would make it – as the Hôtel du Cap-Eden-Roc – the favoured haven of celebrities, in the first months Sella's only guests were two English matrons.[41]

The photographer Jacques Lartigue, who has left such a poetic and glamorous record of life on the Côte d'Azur in the twenties and thirties, wrote in his diary of May 1920, 'a restaurant has just opened in our little pavilion at Eden Roc... So now we lunch there every day, virtually in the middle of the sea and all alone, far away from the dreadful clientele in the hotel's hideous dining room. Straight after our swim, we have only to climb back up from our improvised changing room to reach our dazzling little table set between great windows looking out over the bay.'[42] One of Lartigue's most celebrated pictures, so evocative of the civility of life on the coast, was taken of his wife, Bibi, lunching at Eden Roc in 1920.

Antoine Sella – dreaming of a summer season since before the war – was persuaded to try his luck in 1923 with a minimal staff – a cook, a waiter and a chambermaid. Bad weather in the north made Sella optimistic but his guests were few. On 3 July, Gerald and Sara

Murphy, the three children and their nanny Mlle Géron arrived. Then Pablo Picasso – who had enjoyed Juan-les-Pins in 1920 – appeared with his wife, Olga, and his mother, Doña Maria, who had come to France to meet her grandchild, Paulo. Otherwise, there was only a Chinese family. The resulting seclusion appealed to people who had spent the previous months in the hectic Parisian art world.[43]

During that winter, Murphy had exhibited four works in the Salon des Indépendants. The two oil paintings – *Engine Room* and *Pressure* – owed debts to the Russian Natalia Goncharova, with whom he was studying, and also to a French artist who would become a good friend of the family – Fernand Léger. It was Goncharova who roped Murphy into painting sets for Diaghilev's 1923 ballet *Les Noces*. Léger was already at work, and Murphy enlisted further help from the young American writer John Dos Passos. Bronislava Nijinska's staccato choreography, Stravinsky's percussive score and Goncharova's austere sets were highly praised when the ballet opened in Paris in June 1923. On 17 June, the Sunday following the opening, the Murphys hosted an all-night party on a barge on the Seine to celebrate its success.[44] The guests included the cream of Paris's international avant-garde.

While Fernand Léger was helping Diaghilev, he was also designing sets for Diaghilev's rival, the short-lived Ballets Suédois. Its director, Rolf de Maré, told Léger that he wanted to do an American ballet. Léger suggested that Murphy could concoct a story – and he, in turn, recommended Cole Porter to compose the music. The result – *Within the Quota* – was written at the Palazzo Barbaro, which Porter rented in Venice in the summer of 1923.

Over the previous thirty years, about 13 million immigrants had entered the United States. Of the multitude who came through New York's Ellis Island were the families of Porter's contemporaries Irving Berlin and George and Ira Gershwin. Seeking to control the mass influx, Congress passed the Emergency Quota Act in 1921 to limit numbers. Murphy's story focuses on a silent-movie land of opportunity. A gauche Swede arrives and encounters a sequence of American archetypes based on figures from the movies such as Charlie Chaplin, 'the immigrant'; Tom Mix, 'the cowboy'; Mary

Within the Quota.

Pickford, 'the sweetheart of the world'; and Gloria Swanson, 'the American heiress'. Sara Murphy did some costume designs and probably modelled the heiress on her hoity-toity sister Hoytie. Gerald Murphy's sets were striking and had artistic repercussions both in literature and on the stage.[45] The characters appeared against a backdrop designed to recreate the front page of a newspaper. Its headline, 'UNKNOWN BANKER BUYS ATLANTIC', sat beside an upended ocean liner measured against a New York skyscraper. The message was unequivocal – American money was all-powerful and was about to conquer Europe by taking possession of the ocean that kept the continents apart. In Cannes, American-sounding places such as Palm Beach or the gallicized La Californie were attracting the admiration of visitors, not the old statues of Lord Brougham and Queen Victoria. A poster for the Paris–Lyon–Méditerranée railway presented a luxurious car parked on the waterfront under palm trees. There are two yachts moored. One has the French flag. The other, American.

Murphy's use of headlines for the backdrop obviously impressed John Dos Passos, who made extensive use of newspaper extracts in his landmark 1925 novel *Manhattan Transfer* and his magnificent 1930s trilogy *U.S.A.* – both towering and accessible contributions to American modernism. In the theatre, *Within the Quota* may have inspired Irving Berlin's 1930s revue, *As Thousands Cheer*, in which each of the twenty-one scenes is prompted by a newspaper headline. It is probable that Berlin saw or heard about *Within the Quota*, successfully presented in New York in November 1925 after its rapturous opening the previous month in Paris. The score by the still-unknown Cole Porter was much praised. Cole's ambitious wife, Linda, had wanted him to study with Stravinsky. That didn't happen, but there are flashes of Stravinsky, ragtime and jazz in the score of *Within the Quota*. Above all, the now lost work – a nexus of influences and possibilities – was rightly celebrated as the first American ballet. The next involvement of the Murphys with the dance world would see them as inspiration – a reflection of their style and life on the Riviera – for Diaghilev's 1925 *Le Train Bleu*.

Before 1914, there were deluxe trains running from St Petersburg, through Warsaw, Vienna and Milan, to Nice. A train ran from Berlin via Munich, another via Frankfurt where it hooked up with the service from Amsterdam. Above all, there was the Calais–Paris–Méditerranée Express. On 8 December 1922, this service was revamped with new steel blue carriages flecked with touches of gold. Each train comprised a restaurant car, a baggage wagon and five *wagon-lit* carriages each accommodating sixteen passengers – eight in single, eight in double compartments.[46] On this infamous train, people – if they wished – had direct access to their neighbour's compartment. Colette noted in *Ces Plaisirs* that 'Sapphos' met by chance on the Blue Train.[47] Clandestine relationships en route prepared voyagers for the notorious immorality of the Riviera.

Although the blue carriages were made of metal, the interiors were done in mahogany, making for a quieter overnight trip. Peggy Guggenheim was a regular traveller on the Blue Train after she bought a house at Canadel between Le Lavandou and Saint-Tropez.

Churchill delighted in the service. Cole and Linda Porter booked an entire carriage for themselves. Fashion giant Coco Chanel travelled on it regularly. From 1925, the Paris departure was fixed at 7.40 p.m., and the arrival at Nice 11.50 the following morning – in good time for lunch.[48] Or maybe breakfast. Lartigue noted that on the Riviera 'eight in the morning is too early, life is four hours behind'.[49]

The scene that greeted the passengers was promised in a poster for the Blue Train – 'Summer on the French Riviera'. While the actual track ran close to the coast beside expensive villas and through built-up areas, this image shows the train isolated, high up on a viaduct. Between its arches, the scene is untroubled by industrial intrusion. Holidaymakers relax on the beach, bathe and sail. The red-gold rocks of the Esterel meet the blue bands of an unruffled sea. There are only scattered traces of habitation. Taking the Blue Train made this an easily accessible, get-away-from-it-all paradise. Even if E. Phillips Oppenheim reminded the reader of his 1938 novel *The Colossus of Arcadia* that 'it came to its final standstill with a clanking of couplings and a succession of convulsive jerks', throwing off-balance 'most of the passengers who were standing in the corridors hanging out of the windows eager to attract the notice of a porter', the Blue Train was all about glamour. As the *Menton and Monte Carlo News* noted on 8 November 1924, it 'involved a little gentle snobbishness'[50] – everybody who took it wanted their friends to know how they came south. A few weeks later, there was a notice of new items to be presented by the Ballets Russes in Monte Carlo during 1925 – among them *Le Train Bleu*.[51] The ballet had nothing to do with a train and everything to do with the beaches to which the Blue Train travelled.

Gerald Murphy credited Diaghilev's company as 'the focal centre of the whole modern movement in the arts'.[52] Diaghilev brought unlikely people together, sparking incredible results. As he said, 'My tastes are simple. The best is good enough for me.'[53] For his new and playful twenty-three-minute ballet, Diaghilev had a story by Jean Cocteau, music by Darius Milhaud, a curtain by Picasso, sets by Henri Laurens and costumes by Chanel. After the high seriousness of *Les Noces*, there was sauciness in Bronislava

Nijinska's choreography for the affectations of the amorous intriguers and *les sportifs* playing on a Riviera beach. The ballet is a skilful combination of *joie de vivre* and a caustic observation of the uptight tantrums and narcissism of the age. The solos for a female tennis champion – loosely based on local star player Suzanne Lenglen – and a male golfer – any English *poseur* – are perceptive and witty. It is a delightful exploration of male vanity and female coquettishness, considerably aided by Chanel's liberating costumes. With the soft, easy-going cubism of Laurens's decor, the ballet captures the pulse of the 1920s on the Riviera.

The brilliant caricature of the tennis player was danced by Nijinska herself. There were two English dancers in the cast. Lydia Sokolova – born Hilda Munnings in Wanstead – who played the 'Beautiful Bather', and Anton Dolin – born Patrick Healey-Kay in Slinford, Sussex – who played the acrobatic Beautiful Beach Boy. It was Dolin's backstage gymnastics that had given Cocteau the idea for the ballet. Choreographed athleticism led to challenges for Chanel, who needed flexible fabrics in her designs. The overall look owed something to Gerald Murphy's choice of simple yet elegant beachwear – the blue-and-white-striped mariner's shirts that he found in Marseille – light and made of cotton. Even the celebration of fitness in the ballet owes something to Murphy's beach regime.

During the nineteenth century, people had gone to great lengths to protect themselves from the sun and keep their skin pale. By the mid-1920s, people began to pack beaches at the hottest times of the day. After the grim years of the war, there seemed something marvellously restorative about sunbathing. Gerald Murphy swam a lot, did calisthenics with his children and danced on the beach, striking poses that amused whoever happened to be watching. He did yoga and played tennis and golf.[54] Even Henri Laurens's fabric changing-cabins in his set for *Le Train Bleu* acknowledged the novel contraptions which the Murphys used on the beach at La Garoupe. Picasso's giant curtain showed two statuesque women running on the beach.[55]

Sara always sought to include Picasso's young son, Paulo, in beach parties that she organized for her children. The Murphys concocted delightful activities – treasure hunts with pirates' maps, and children's art competitions – *les salons de la jeunesse*, sometimes judged by Picasso himself. The artist, who enjoyed Sara's company very much, did many drawings of her – some in the nude. She never posed, but Picasso couldn't help imagining beneath her beach robes and drawing a naked figure with a string of pearls – an accessory Sara habitually draped over her bare shoulders on the beach.

Was Gerald becoming more perplexed about his latent homosexuality, more diffident about sex, or was it the sheer seductive power of Picasso with his intense, excoriating eyes that led to a possible but brief affair between Sara and the painter? Picasso's biographer John Richardson thought a physical relationship between them highly likely. Many men – including F. Scott Fitzgerald and Ernest Hemingway – developed crushes on Sara Murphy. Yet as she cherished a profound love for Gerald and adored her children, perhaps she was merely delightfully flirtatious and Picasso misread the situation. In the 1923 painting *Pipes of Pan*, now in the Musée Picasso in Paris, the figure standing on the left is probably Gerald Murphy. Infrared photography has revealed that there were originally two other figures in the painting – perhaps Sara as Venus and Picasso as Mars. Painting them out could suggest that Picasso had been rebuffed. The relationship between the Picassos and the Murphys did start to cool.[56]

Le Train Bleu opened in Paris in June 1924. It enjoyed a short season in London and then played Monte Carlo. Comfortable on home ground, where every bit of satire would be appreciated, Coco Chanel's colourful and free costumes helped consolidate the Riviera vogue for sportswear.

Hugh Grosvenor, Duke of Westminster, was nicknamed 'Bendor' after his grandfather's Derby winner of 1880 and the coat of arms which had been lost to the Scrope family in 1389 – 'azure with a bend or'. Over Christmas 1923, the duke was cruising around the Mediterranean in his yacht *Flying Cloud*, when he put into Monte Carlo and dined at the Hôtel de Paris. He spotted his friend Vera Arkwright eating with a slender, green-eyed lady who, as Cocteau put it, 'had the head of a little black swan'. Bendor joined them, loved the evening and invited them both to dinner on *Flying Cloud*. Arkwright, a beautiful and industrious Parisian socialite, was a personal and professional advisor to her dinner companion, Gabrielle 'Coco' Chanel.

At the time they met, the Duke of Westminster was forty-four and Chanel was forty.[57] A year earlier, she had launched Chanel No. 5 after Grand Duke Dmitri Pavlovich introduced her to the Russian-French perfumer Ernest Beaux, son of a *parfumier* to the tsarist court.[58] Hitherto, perfume had exploited an identifiable scent such as rose or jasmine. Chanel, with her great talent for innovation, asked Beaux for something concocted, crafted like a dress. It would be a scent identified not with the flowers of the field, but with the fashion house of Chanel. Beaux's complex and never-changing formula made the perfume perennially popular. In 1952, Marilyn Monroe revealed that in bed she wore only Chanel No. 5 – just five drops.[59]

With the determination of someone who had to fight from her earliest years, Chanel had grown into a woman of acumen, wit and great allure. By 1919, having opened boutiques in Deauville and Biarritz, she established her *maison de couture* at 31 rue Cambon in the heart of fashionable Paris. She had been enjoying an affair with Captain Arthur 'Boy' Capel, who financed some of her early endeavours and whose style of dress influenced her designs. In the spring of 1918, he married the widowed Diana Wyndham. After Diana resumed her affair with Duff Cooper, Boy resumed his with Chanel. Their time together was short. While Capel was serving as British Liaison Officer at the Paris Peace Conference in Versailles, he had a blow-out driving on the Riviera. His car rolled, burst into flames and he was killed. Among his bequests, he left Chanel £40,000.

The designer made her name by creating a workable look for the modern woman who wished to be seen as relaxed yet energetic. Chanel believed that simplicity was the essence of elegance, and her designs were a reaction against all the fussy and cumbrous fashions of the Second Empire and Belle Époque. She also opposed the idea that fashion was the preserve of the ultra-rich. While she carried on the couturier tradition – showing around 400 dresses a year in two collections – Chanel also created affordable designs. In the mid-twenties, she produced a suit with a collarless jacket and fitted skirt. She made black chic, showing how good the colour looked when she designed her famous 'little black dress'.[60] After she took up with the Duke of Westminster, Chanel determined to place her career first and resolved to remain financially independent. Meanwhile she danced to Ambrose's orchestra at the Embassy Club, fished on Bendor's Scottish estates, and resisted his offers of marriage which entailed giving up work. 'When I had to choose between the man I loved and dresses, I always chose the dresses.'[61]

Coco Chanel made simplicity and black chic.

If, in their unassertive way, the Murphys were influencing style and fashion on the Riviera, their influence went so much deeper than that. Through their welcoming generosity – complemented by Gertrude Stein's intellectual input in Paris – they became midwives to the 'lost generation'. Stein helped critically; the Murphys helped emotionally and materially. The writer Archibald MacLeish recalled that, 'There was a shine to life wherever they were: not a decorative added value but a kind of revelation of inherent loveliness'.[62] Fellow writer Donald Ogden Stewart noted that Gerald Murphy was 'intelligent, perceptive, gracious, and one of the most attractive men I have ever known. His wife Sara was the perfect complement to these virtues. If this sounds like a child's fable beginning "Once upon a time there was a prince and princess…" that's exactly how a description of the Murphys should begin.' When, in 1924, Stewart and Dos Passos were invited south by the Murphys, they found them installed at the Hôtel du Cap 'in solitary grandeur'.[63] Among the others the Murphys tempted south that year were Scott and Zelda Fitzgerald. While Scott worked hard on the novel that was shaping into *The Great Gatsby*, the 'excitement eater' Zelda became bored and restless.[64]

A Southern belle gone rogue, Zelda smoked at a time when it was unacceptable for women, swigged corn liquor with the boys, and enjoyed necking. Fitzgerald met her at a country club dance in July 1918, just weeks before her eighteenth birthday. Her zest for life matched his own. She needed to be the centre of attention and would do anything – cartwheels or a Highland fling – to liven up a dance.[65] In September 1919, when Scribner's accepted Fitzgerald's *This Side of Paradise*, the young novelist's desire to enjoy the best of two worlds was already apparent. He wanted to be a serious writer and to make a great deal of money. By the time the couple were married in April 1920, the novel was already in a second printing and Fitzgerald was publishing financially rewarding magazine stories. He was the incarnation of the American Dream – handsome, and minting money with his early success. The cost was drink.

During the Fitzgeralds' first trip to Paris in 1921, their hotel room became a chaos of overflowing ashtrays, books, papers, and half-filled wine glasses morning-aftering. They were eventually asked to leave after Zelda took the habit of trapping the lift with her belt so it would be on hand when she finished dressing for dinner.[66] For their first trip to the Côte d'Azur in 1924, after dismissing Hyères as 'picturesque' and having sampled hotels in Nice and Monte Carlo, they settled at the Villa Marie in Valescure.[67]

During their summers in the south, their drink-fuelled behaviour became notorious. Arriving drunk then drinking more, on one occasion the Fitzgeralds 'crawled among the vegetables on all fours tossing an occasional tomato' at the Murphys' guests.[68] When they left the party, they staggered down to Eden Roc at the tip of Cap d'Antibes, where Zelda slipped out of her evening dress and dived off the rocks that stood twelve metres above the sea.[69] Bored at the casino in Juan-les-Pins one evening, Zelda raised her skirt above her waist and danced around the room. Driving along the twisty coastal road, Zelda asked Scott for a cigarette. Obliging, Scott took both hands off the wheel to light one.

While Fitzgerald was busy with *Gatsby*, he wrote to his editor Max Perkins, 'I think my novel is about the best American novel ever written. It is rough stuff in places, runs only to about 50,000 words… It's been a fair summer. I've been unhappy but my work hasn't suffered from it.'[70] The unhappiness could well have been Scott's slow realization that while he was writing, Zelda had been carrying on with a glamorous young airman from the local air base. Edouard Jozan was thrilled to meet such crazy people and took to swimming, driving and dancing with Zelda while Scott was hard at work. Jozan would even fly low over the Fitzgeralds' villa to 'say hello' to Zelda.[71] Years later, he denied having had an affair, claiming Zelda flirted with him to grab Scott's attention. Some critics, however, assert that he did. In a sense, it isn't important. The relationship between the couple was bumpy at the best of times, and Scott got mileage from her dalliance when he created the character of Tommy Barban in his Riviera novel, *Tender is the Night*.[72]

If the Fitzgeralds were a handful, then British socialites and social climbers could be outrageous too. As the Americans divided their European life between Paris and the Côte d'Azur, British sagas played out in Chelsea and on the Riviera. Larger-than-life in more ways than one, the glutton, temperamental philanderer and newspaper columnist Viscount Valentine Castlerosse was known as 'Elephant and Castlerosse' after his size and a London Tube station near which he probably never set foot.

In 1922, Castlerosse went on holiday to the Riviera with Max Beaverbrook. To amuse themselves, they both wrote stories about Monte Carlo. Deciding his friend had written a good piece, Beaverbrook sent it to his *Sunday Express* and thus launched Castlerosse's journalistic career. Beaverbrook would often pick up the viscount's debts. Even when he won at the tables, Castlerosse could not keep solvent. Once, when a lucky streak won him £5,000, a prostitute picked him up on the steps of the Monte Carlo Casino and together they shot his winnings in less than a week.

Despite their tempestuous relationship, Beaverbrook thought that Castlerosse had the qualities of a great journalist, and in April 1926 announced the 'Londoner's Log'. The man who was seldom out of the gossip sheets himself produced a sizzling and controversial column for a nation eager to pry into the naughtiness of self-indulgent high society.[73] Frequently satirizing his peers, his features were full of quips such as: 'Played golf with Fruity Metcalfe. He went round the course in 20,000 words.'[74] Fruity – later a member of the British Union of Fascists and then equerry to the Prince of Wales – was part of a class that consisted of people with names such as Chips and Purity, Tufty and Zita, Baby and Baba, and Nana and Noo.

Meanwhile, a Streatham girl of minor aristocratic French descent was introduced to London society through her friend, the actress Gertrude Lawrence. Doris Delevingne thus gathered a circle of fashionable and notable friends – Duff and Diana Cooper, Tallulah Bankhead and Noël Coward among them.[75] With sex appeal, she was working her way up London society, enjoying the company of rich men and looking for a husband. She was frank and open about her lifestyle, which exemplified a new kind of woman determined 'to live her life in the way she chose'. She was held to be the inspiration for Iris Storm, heroine of Michael Arlen's bestselling novel *The Green Hat*.[76] Storm became the symbol of the 1920s woman with her revelation that 'I have given myself in disdain, in desire, with disgust, with delight, but I have kept that silly, childish boast of mine' – that she had only told one man she loved him.[77]

While Delevingne was stirring up London society, society's chronicler, Viscount Castlerosse, was becoming obsessed with her. Destined to become the 6th Earl of Kenmare, he offered her status and security bound up in one imposing figure. But she was flighty and he was an indebted, womanizing gambler with a flaming temper. There were early skirmishes – he bruising her, she sinking her teeth into his shins. Friends of both parties warned them off making a life together, but Castlerosse was captivated and a marriage notice was posted at Hammersmith Register Office. Lady Kenmare, the viscount's mother, asked Beaverbrook to intervene. The newspaperman invited Castlerosse to Cannes – leaving early on the day appointed for the wedding. Their stay on the Riviera was enjoyable and Beaverbrook was happy to have saved his protégé. Then the hotel bill came. Each day, a bottle of champagne had been charged to Castlerosse's room. Delevingne had followed them to Cannes.[78]

'One of the delights of the Riviera,' wrote Leslie Richardson in 1924, 'is the entire absence of anything in the nature of the squalid conditions of factory life. The staple industry of the Riviera is hotel-keeping and the allied arts of shopkeeping and ministering to winter visitors.'[79] Indeed, the Riviera was a place where rich industrialists could forget, for a season, how they made their fortunes. In other parts of the Alpes-Maritimes, however, there were strikes and agitation. The conference of the Parti Communiste Français in Nice saw the creation of cells, and a group of young Communists formed in the pottery town of Vallauris. The fragility of the French economy led to unrest, and in the wealthy orbit of the Côte d'Azur opportunist crime was on the increase. Fraudsters frequently passed dud cheques.[80] Hotel robberies were rife. The Villa Glovana in Roquebrune was burgled while its occupants lay asleep. Highway hold-ups were common. Two young ladies were driving down the winding road from Sospel when they were surprised by bandits. With great pluck, they accelerated round hairpin bends, escaped the robbers twice, and sped to safety. One week earlier, an English seaman, James Fogarty of HMS *Thunderer*, was shot and killed after an argument with an Italian.[81] Whether from scandal, ruin at the tables, or a broken heart, an Englishman was found dead in April 1925 on the beach of Roquebrune. He had 'killed himself by exploding a cartridge of dynamite in his mouth'. The *News* noted that it was one of the latest ways of committing suicide. In the dead man's pocket, a newspaper article was found reporting a case of suicide by the same method.[82]

Sir Frederick Treves wrote in 1921 that the Grande Corniche 'passes through a land which is a Vanity Fair to the frivolous, a paradise to the philanderer, and a garden of peace to all who would escape the turmoil of the world'.[83] But the number of cars and the wild lives of many drivers meant that was changing. In February 1926, the *News* reported that 'accident follows accident along the lower Corniche road from Monaco to Nice and Cannes'.[84] The paper also complained about the 'Advertising Hoarding Curse'. The placing of billboards along the roads of the coast had bothered people before the war, when the 'hideous excrescences' were taxed. The sitings had increased, and the *News* urged its readers to support the *préfet* in his attempt to urge landowners to get rid of them.[85] While the ruin of the Riviera's unblemished vistas was clearly a sin, in certain quarters the billboard was celebrated as a stimulating fact of modern life. Gerald Murphy's friend Fernand Léger was thrilled by speed and billboards. Both were aspects of the contemporary experience that was changing painting. 'When one crosses a landscape by automobile or an express train, it becomes fragmented,' Léger wrote. 'A modern man registers a hundred times more sensory impressions than an eighteenth-century artist; so much so that our language... is full of diminutives and abbreviations. The compression of the modern picture, its variety, its breaking up of forms, are the result of all this.'[86] The English novelist Virginia Woolf visited Cassis several times between 1925 and 1929. On the later trips, she had the first glimpses of ideas that would surface in her 1931 novel *The Waves*. In that book, she asks the question that expresses what contemporary artists were seeking: '"Like" and "Like" and "Like" – but what is the thing that lies beneath the semblance of the thing?'[87]

Léger claimed that 'the advertisement hoarding... that brutally cuts across a landscape... is one of the things that has most infuriated men of so-called good taste' yet 'that yellow or red billboard, shouting in a timid landscape, is the finest of possible reasons for the new painting; it knocks head over heels the whole sentimental and literary conception of art'.[88] Happily, the hoardings disappeared from the roadsides of the Côte d'Azur, while modernism transformed galleries and museums.

During the winter of 1924, Gerald Murphy caused a sensation at the Salon des Indépendants by exhibiting a six-by-four-metre painting of a boat deck in a Precisionist style. *Boatdeck* dwarfed the other American paintings hanging in the rotunda, and resulted in the temporary resignation of the president of the salon, the Divisionist Paul Signac. As Murphy cheekily told a reporter from the *New York Herald*, 'If they think my picture is too big, I think the other pictures are too small. After all this is the Grand Palais.'[89] While he offended the older generation, he had the support of Léger, who considered Murphy the only American painter in Paris of any consequence. Above all, Léger proved a great friend to the Murphys and particularly to their oldest son, Patrick, whom he sensed had considerable potential as an artist.

By July 1925, the modest house that the Murphys bought on Cap d'Antibes overlooking Golfe-Juan had been transformed by two American architects into an Art Deco villa. The roof had been turned into a sun deck, the floors were of black waxed tile, the modern aluminium tube furniture supported black satin seats and back rests, and there were electric fans and mirrors everywhere. On the rear terrace, Gerald painted the iron café chairs silver. American screen doors were added, which their cook left open – swearing that they trapped flies and mosquitoes inside the house. There were outbuildings including a *vacherie* for two cows so the children would have fresh milk, as well as a herb garden and Sara's corn patch. They called the house 'Villa America', Gerald painting a name board which – with its Pop Art look – remains one of his best-known works.[90]

The Murphys would dignify life ritualistically, yet with an apparent informality that lent a freshness to any event. Gerald was – noted his wild compatriot, the poet, publisher and sun worshipper Harry Crosby – 'very serious about trivialities'. 'Spontaneous' picnics were carefully planned, and Gerald made a ritual of mixing drinks. His ordered painting *Cocktail* reveals an attitude to drinking that was a world away from the desperate consumption of the Fitzgeralds, who came south again in 1925 – Zelda puzzled by Gerald Murphy's 'emotional need for his friends to behave well',[91] and Scott bathing in success. *The Great Gatsby* had been well-received. T. S. Eliot read it three times and 'thought it was the first step forward American fiction had taken since Henry James'.[92] Edith Wharton thought some passages 'masterly', but wondered if a short backstory would have lifted the final 'tragedy' above the level of a mere incident for the morning papers. When Wharton invited Fitzgerald to tea – true to form – he arrived drunk and insultingly screamed at his host, 'You don't know anything about life.' He attempted to shock her guests with a story of how he'd been obliged to stay in a bordello with Zelda. Wharton pleaded, 'Mr Fitzgerald – you haven't told us what they did in the bordello.' The young man cowered.[93]

Dos Passos said that 'Scott, with his capacity for hero worship, began to worship Gerald and Sara. The golden couple that he and Zelda dreamed of becoming actually existed.'[94] Nonetheless, Fitzgerald's behaviour continued to be unruly. On one occasion, after he smashed Sara's Venetian wine glasses, he was banned from Villa America for three weeks. In August 1925, when the Fitzgeralds were dining with the Murphys in Saint-Paul-de-Vence, Gerald pointed out the legendary dancer Isadora Duncan. Scott rushed over and knelt before her, gushed, flirted, and Duncan – perhaps seeking advice about writing her memoirs – told Scott that he could visit her that night. This was too much for Zelda, who got up and threw herself down a ten-step flight of stone stairs. People thought she might be dead until she re-emerged with blood streaming from her knees. As Zelda wrote to a friend, 'We went to Antibes to recuperate but all we recooped was drinking hours.'[95] When the Fitzgeralds returned to Paris, Gerald Murphy wrote with typical generosity that 'we do love you two'.[96]

In 1924, Scott Fitzgerald had written to tell Maxwell Perkins 'about a man named Ernest Hemingway who lives in Paris (an American)' and 'has a brilliant future... I'd look him up right away. He's the real thing.'[97] According to Dos Passos, Fitzgerald – who was 'selflessly generous about other men's writing' – 'had one of his literary crushes on Hem, the sportsman stylist, the pugilist storyteller'.[98] In May 1926, the Fitzgeralds let the Hemingways take over their Villa Paquita in Juan-les-Pins. Everyone seemed to be helping – as Zelda put it – that 'professional he man', that 'pansy with hair on his chest'.[99] Hemingway's desperate machismo, like Gerald's reserve, was a cover for unease and confusion. His childhood had been difficult, with a depressive father who eventually – like his son – killed himself. Hemingway's 'androgynous' mother made him particularly wary in front of women who were unstable and strong-willed like Zelda. Dos Passos claimed that 'Hem was the only man I ever knew who really hated his mother'. He was 'a moody kind of fellow... Sorry for himself' – bothered about never having been to college.[100]

The American writers coming to France in the mid-twenties brought American vitality to a continent ravaged by war. They brought jazz – its black performers welcomed in a way they were not at home. There was – despite the Murphys' cherished formality – a new nonchalance. Consuelo Vanderbilt had noted the 'slow and weighty phrases' of eminent Americans in Europe in the 1890s.[101] Gertrude Stein suggested this lingered – 'America is the mother of twentieth century civilization, but she is now early Victorian'.[102] Escape to Europe meant liberation. From Juan-les-Pins, where life was free and easy, Fitzgerald wrote, 'I'm happier than I've been for years. It's one of those strange, precious and all too transitory moments when everything in one's life seems to be going well.'[103]

While the Americans and British were 'doing the Riviera', Colette bought a house in the lush countryside outside the unspoilt and very French village of Saint-Tropez. Suspicious of the phoniness of the Anglo-Saxon resorts along the coast, she found Saint-Tropez to be 'another world'. In August, figs were 'already bursting' and the grapes sweet. As a vine circled her well, she called her four-room peasant house 'La Treille Muscate'. Reconnecting with her rural childhood, she delighted in nature, gardening and becoming 'something of a cook'.[104] From Menton – where Colette had been performing – she drove with her husband Maurice Goudeket to La Treille Muscate to enjoy Christmas 1926. En route, they stopped for a night in a hotel at Valescure just outside Saint-Raphaël. As they were the only guests, the sisters who ran the establishment spent the evening talking about their niece, whose marriage had astounded the *demi-monde*. Colette listened intently. Eighteen years after that encounter, parts of their story surfaced in her novel *Gigi*.[105] Later, crippled by arthritis, Colette spent each spring and summer from 1950 until her death in 1954 at the Hôtel de Paris in Monte Carlo. It was during the shooting at the hotel of a minor French film, *Monte Carlo Baby*, that Colette spotted a young actress called Audrey Hepburn and insisted she star in the Broadway adaptation of *Gigi*.

The spring in Saint-Tropez was, Colette wrote, 'tender and sweet-smelling', as lilac, iris and stocks bloomed. While the sea was still cold for bathing, the sand and sun were so warm 'that your skin tingles with excitement'. By the summer, the beach was too hot to cross, and Colette would retreat to the shade to write. Bel-Gazou, her daughter from her second marriage, was largely raised by an English nanny. She saw little of her mother. When she spent summers at La Treille Muscate, the girl was, Colette wrote, 'living like a little animal, bathing, sunshine, figs, honey, sleep and walks'.[106]

When he came to work on a portrait of Colette, André Dunoyer de Segonzac later recalled, lunch was 'laid on the terrace, in the shade of a trellis covered with wisteria and vine'. They enjoyed 'grilled rascasse, all crackly' and ravioli 'washed down by a fresh rosé from Saint-Tropez'. After that, they got down to work. Colette wrote of another occasion when the painter came to lunch, this time with several others to celebrate a local saint's day. Rascasse was on the menu once again – but stuffed and served with deep-fried aubergine, salad and several roast birds.[107] The meal was remembered in Colette's 1928 book *La Naissance du Jour* – that hymn to 'the indolent summer life' around Saint-Tropez. Its engagement with the untouched physical world enveloping the author is as vivid as the jottings of a botanist, and as intense as a Fauvist canvas. Nature reigns, while the scattered inhabitants enjoy a capricious and spontaneous life – shying away from the formal with impromptu gatherings that do not disturb their isolation and domestic peace.

⌖

As the summer season became established on the Riviera, new and delicate problems had to be redressed. Edna Murphey of Cincinnati had developed a solution for one of them in the early years of the century. Despite choosing a name that declared what it aimed to do, she invented a product that was difficult to market – as it tackled an almost unmentionable fact of life. At first, the *News* carried muted and reassuring advertisements for 'Odo-ro-no'. In 1924, it was 'an unfailing safeguard of personal daintiness' for 'the one spot which soap and water cannot keep immaculate'.[108] By 1926, the approach was more direct. Odo-ro-no was a 'liquid corrective for excessive perspiration'.[109]

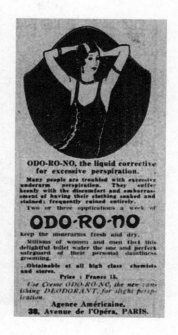

A 1926 advert for Odo-Ro-No.

In 1927, the new monthly, *Americans in France*, observed that the summer visitors were 'sunburned and athletic', and the *News* offered tips on 'How to Sun-Bathe'.[110] Walking on the beach at Juan-les-Pins, La Belle Otero was horrified by the sight of minimal bathing costumes, and wrote to the authorities.[111] The resort was very much in vogue – 'the Casino is crowded from morning until night and from night until morning. The beach is swarming with bathers.'[112] Juan-les-Pins became known as 'Pyjamaland', as it popularized a convenient, informal yet elegant way of dressing designed by Coco Chanel. 'Beach pyjamas' lent allure and freedom to the women who wore them, yet Chanel herself – the arbiter of fashion – was stopped from wearing them to establishments along the etiquette-conscious Riviera. In one story, she was to rendezvous with Bendor at Edouard Baudoin's casino in Juan-les-Pins. Always a fabulous model for her own creations, Chanel was wearing beach

Beach pyjamas.

pyjamas when she was halted by the doorman and upbraided – 'Mademoiselle Chanel, you are living proof that one must be not merely dressed but well-dressed.'[113] In another incident – perhaps in Monte Carlo – she was stopped for wearing a short evening coat. When Chanel pointed out that she had a full-length evening dress underneath and was admitted grudgingly, the doorman grumbled, 'All the same, I do not think you are dressed in the proper fashion.'[114] In Monte Carlo, beach pyjamas were illegal. A woman was arrested for wearing them, as an ancient Monégasque law forbade women to dress in male garments. The statute had never been repealed but, after the incident, the police were encouraged to turn a blind eye.[115]

After providing cannon fodder during the war, youth was increasingly treasured. In the *News*, the waspish Lady Lawford wrote that the Charleston is for the 'young and very young – I once saw a stout lady dance the Charleston: never in my life have I witnessed a more revolting sight... She grew purple in the face, the perspiration poured down, making rivers of what looked like custard pudding when mixed with face powder.' She added that 'a grey-haired man dancing the Charleston looks and must feel like a lunatic!'[116] The Riviera had become a world not for the aristocracy or rich septuagenarians, but for 'bright young things'. The tag was provided by the *Daily Mail*,[117] and the set was described by Cecil Beaton: Loelia Ponsonby, 'who is very amusing', and Zita Jungman, daughter of Beatrice Guinness, who 'would be so beautiful if her mother would allow her to make herself up'. There was also Zita's sister Theresa – always called 'Baby' – 'her cousin Elizabeth Sysonby and Lady Eleanor Smith, Lord Birkenhead's eldest daughter'.[118] They were playful, indulged, and forever seeking new outlets for their youthful energies. With consummate cynicism, Noël Coward wrote the song 'Poor Little Rich Girl', observing that leisure increased the wild search for pleasure. Parties and cocktails filled the days of the rich young things – but did they, he asked, have a future? One of France's biggest popular hits, 'J'ai Deux Amants', proposed that one lover was boring – having two was much more fun. The secret was to make either feel that the other was the serious romance. In *Les Girls*, an American revue that played Monte Carlo, the chorus sang that in their capacity as professional beauties they broke up homes – 'but what the hell'.[119] From the interconnecting compartments on the Blue Train, to the accessibility of the coast for a romantic fling, the Riviera was enjoying a new kind of sex appeal.

Despite the hypocrisy of pundits like Elsa Maxwell who – although a closeted lesbian herself – decried homosexuality, there was a strong and often openly homoerotic ambiance on the Côte d'Azur. It was partly the result of the number of sensitive and creative people who visited – as in Wilde's day – to escape from the barbaric laws that pertained in Britain. The pseudo-artistic colony at Cagnes was 'distinctly Hellenic', noted George Antheil,[120] the modernist composer who wrote the music for Man Ray and Fernand Léger's experimental film *Le Ballet Mécanique*. There were countless homosexual opportunities to be found in Villefranche when the fleet was in. Elsie de Wolfe, 'the Sapphic interior decorator',[121] made a lavender marriage with Sir Charles Mendl from the British embassy in Paris – she wanted a title and Mendl wealth. Wolfe, who lived on the Riviera, had been encouraged to become an interior designer by her friend and lover, the New York socialite and theatrical agent 'Bessie' Marbury.[122] American dancer Isadora Duncan, who had a long-term and fatal relationship with the Côte d'Azur, was involved with Mercedes de Acosta, the arch-lesbian lover of Marlene Dietrich and Greta Garbo.[123]

One of the most celebrated and long-term residents on the Riviera, W. Somerset Maugham, was a shy homosexual. His association with Cap Ferrat began in 1926 when he bought the Villa Mauresque, surrounded by nine acres. He employed a young gay American Art Deco architect, Barry Dierks, to strip off the faux-Moorish façade, remodel the interior and lay out a garden with a swimming pool. Maugham had made a mistaken marriage to Syrie, the daughter of the Victorian philanthropist Dr Bernardo. Syrie Maugham surrounded herself with frivolous homosexuals like Cecil Beaton, Rex Whistler and Oliver Messel, who were not to Maugham's taste.[124] He had fallen for a loud, rough American called Gerald Haxton, and there was great tension between Maugham's wife and his lover – who many consider responsible for the break-up of the marriage.[125] When drunk, Haxton was unpredictable and often violent. Maugham's nephew Robin was told that Gerald was 'always full of charm and full of liquor – in almost equal parts'. Once, at a party, Haxton – blind drunk – dived into an empty swimming pool and was hospitalized for months.[126]

Haxton was the perfect complement to the shy and quiet Maugham, whose stammer was always a problem, particularly when he had to call in bridge.[127] He was also a great travel companion. On one occasion, when a boat capsized in Borneo, Haxton saved Maugham's life and promptly suffered a non-fatal heart attack himself.[128] He was in Tahiti when Maugham secured Paul Gauguin's glass panel, painted as a thank you to the farmer who had looked after the artist when he had syphilis. The owner wanted to sell it in order to replace the door. He asked 100 francs, Maugham gave 200. It was shipped and installed in the square writing room at the top of the Villa Mauresque, to block out the beautiful and distracting view.[129]

Along with more and faster motor cars came rallies and new competitions. John o' Groats in the north of Scotland to Monte Carlo in seventy-three hours and fifty minutes created a record in 1926. Automobile manufacturers sent the latest models to competitions at Nice, Cannes and Monte Carlo, where 'beautifully gowned ladies or... impeccable chauffeurs' presented 'Hispanos, Voisins, Packards, Rolls-Royces, Talbots, Chryslers, Buicks and Farmans'. While sumptuous automobiles were still manufactured for the rich, by 1927 the increased number of cheaper cars led *The Times* to report that all driving on the Riviera was dangerous. That year saw a famous and fatal accident.[130]

After a jubilant and tempestuous career, the revolutionary dancer Isadora Duncan – who had mesmerized Diaghilev in St Petersburg in 1904 and thereby changed the course of dance in Russia[131] – was broke. Nonetheless, she rented a studio on the Promenade des Anglais. There was 'a sort of halo of joy about her', remembered Mary Desti, mother of the Hollywood film director Preston Sturges. They drove around Nice, singing 'Bye, Bye, Blackbird' at the top of their lungs and making plans for the future.[132] Brave or foolhardy in the face of adversity, Duncan needed to write her memoirs to make money. Staying at the Negresco, she was unable to check out because she could not pay her bill. Before shopping, she would go to Vogade in the Place Masséna for a crème de cacao laced with gin or vodka. She lingered in the sun. The shops shut for lunch, and – stranded – Duncan would order another aperitif.[133] Years of hard drinking had coarsened her looks. Her body was heavy, her hair hastily hennaed. From February until August, she worked on her memoirs – dictating them after she downed a few drinks. She went to Cap Ferrat to beseech her old flame Paris Singer to help her, but he had lost money speculating on the Florida land boom.[134] Although Duncan's debts were most probably being covered by Mercedes de Acosta, money worries gnawed at her dreams for the future.

One night, Duncan and Desti dined at Chez Tétou in Port-Juan, where she caught the eye of a handsome man twenty years her junior. As he drove off in a Bugatti, Isadora waved to him and, in return, he bowed. Isadora was thrilled. Turning to Mary Desti, she said desperately, 'You see, I'm still desirable.' The following night, they were invited to a party given to honour the French Dada artist Francis Picabia in the very same restaurant. Duncan asked Mme Tétou if she had the address of the young man with the Bugatti, as she wanted a car like that. Her head whirling, Isadora tracked him down. She went to the hairdresser and emerged radiant. She was going to see the 'Greek God' with the Bugatti.[135] When they met on 14 September, Duncan discovered he had been a flying ace, like Zelda's Jozan, but he was now a car salesman. She asked him to call for her at nine o'clock to take her for a spin. Before he arrived, Mary Desti was upset by a premonition and asked Isadora not to go – or, at least to wear a cape as the Bugatti was open-topped and the evening chilly.[136] Duncan preferred a pleated skirt and the long red Chinese shawl that Desti had painted for her. About to drive off with her 'god' in the car that would kill her minutes later, Duncan announced with assured amorous expectation, 'I am going to paradise.' *Americans in France* reported: 'The famous dancer came to an untimely end while trying out a new roadster. Her scarf caught in the rear wheel and strangled her.'[137]

That same year, the *News* started a series which ran over several seasons, 'Quaint Restaurants of the Riviera' – 'Places for Provençal Dishes'. Foreigners were at last developing a taste for the cooking at local inns. One such was an establishment that stood just outside the thick medieval gate of Saint-Paul-de-Vence. Opened in 1920 as the Café Robinson, with a terrace for dancing at the weekends, Paul Roux and his wife Baptistine made it into an attractive rendezvous for artists, writers and film personalities. Initially a rough-and-ready establishment, Roux's place, soon renamed La Colombe d'Or, was celebrated by Picasso as 'My kind of hotel; no name outside, no concierge, no reception, no room service and no bill.' Roux accepted pictures in lieu of payment, and the restaurant and hotel amassed a collection that included works by Léger, Rouault, Picasso, Braque, Dufy and Chagall. It hosted Edward, Prince of Wales, and later attracted regular guests such as the French actors Arletty, Simone Signoret and Yves Montand.[138] In the 1970s, it became a popular haunt for local resident and landmark American writer James Baldwin.

The monthly *Americans on the Côte d'Azur* was published in Cannes from 1927. It aimed to put people in touch with one another and provide legal contacts for the rising number of Americans wishing to buy property on the Riviera. The large American naval presence in the harbour of Villefranche, the paper suggested, gave visiting Americans 'a standing which they would not otherwise possess'.[139] Steamship companies reported that all their cabins from New York to Europe were booked months ahead, and many socialites and industrialists now arrived directly by ship in Monte Carlo. For those travelling via a northern port, the journey south could still be as eventful as those of the early travellers. Miss Frances McKee of Washington, DC was held up as masked bandits jumped her car and commandeered it for a robbery. Her handbag with her passport and letter of credit were gone. Still, she managed to get to Antwerp, where the consulate gave her substitute documents. She met up with her brother to motor to the Riviera 'in a roadster loaned by a friend'. After a head-on collision with an Italian automobile and a subsequent hospitalization, they proceeded on crutches by train to Cannes.[140]

In an interview in *Americans in France* of July 1927, the designer Charlotte Appert commented on current fashion habits. Ladies changed 'dresses several times in the course of the day. For morning and until tea-time, the sports costume is the preference, a very simple dress, often composed of a marinière, with long sleeves, a shirt and a little belt... But at five o'clock, our pretty chrysalid becomes a butterfly and dresses herself in light tissues, mousselines or lace.' Appert's avowed object was 'to dress a woman according to her style and beauty and to try to make her even more seductive'. Ironically, 'Virginal white' was all the rage, and the best evening wrap to suit – in Appert's opinion – was 'silver lamé bordered with ermine'.[141] In the *News* earlier that year, Lady Lawford had noted that as 'nearly all dresses... are on the short side... the clever woman... who studies her appearance, will adapt the mode to her requirements. This is where the fringed dresses are so useful, if one has not the ankles *sans reproche*.'[142] Betting on the fact that many French women did not have wonderful legs, Elsa Maxwell suggested lower hems to Jean Patou. Instead of following Chanel and her imitators, in 1924 Patou dropped hemlines by eight inches and his floor-length evening gowns 'formed the basis of a fortune even he could not dissipate'. Maxwell later recalled that Patou was 'the most flamboyant figure to invade the world of couture' with his 'animal magnetism and sex appeal for women'.[143] He had the fastest cars and boats, entertained lavishly, and gambled heavily at Monte Carlo.

Cannes had the largest number of fashion houses on the Riviera – Poiret, Patou, Lanvin, Molyneux, Worth, Doucet, Drecoll and Lucien Lelong.[144] Writing in *Vogue* in 1925, Colette lamented: 'Short, flat, geometrical and quadrangular. Feminine wear is fixed along the line of the parallelogram. And 1925 shall not see the comeback of soft curves, arrogant breasts and enticing hips.'[145] To complement the style, handbags to be carried under the arm were small and compact. Chanel, who had banished 'soft curves', opened a salon in Monte Carlo as she continued to dominate 1920s fashion.

During the summer, evening dress for men was stifling. What is more, the fashion for white 'Eton jackets' at Sporting Club galas often rendered clients indistinguishable from waiters.[146] Dress code was draconian. As with Lord Salisbury and his passport, Harpo Marx was refused entry to the Casino in Monte Carlo. He had no tie. In true Marx Brothers fashion, Harpo darted around the back, took off his sock, knotted it round his neck, and was admitted – only to lose a lot of money.[147] Ladies could still be barred for wearing cotton rather than silk stockings.[148] Dorothy Parker was refused entry for not even wearing them. With her celebrated wit she recalled, 'I went and found my stockings and then came back and lost my shirt.'

Harpo – who could talk off-screen – met George Bernard Shaw on Cap d'Antibes. The playwright had been invited to lunch with the formidable critic and wit Alexander Woollcott, but couldn't find him. Grabbing at Harpo's bathing towel to attract his attention, Shaw pulled too hard, and the scene played out between the writer and the naked comic. It was the luncheon host, Woollcott, who once remarked, 'Nothing risqué, nothing gained.' Marx and Shaw got on famously, and for the next few days Harpo drove the playwright all over the coast.[149] They visited Nice's Victorine film studios, where they became extras in a scene shot in a pool room that sadly ended up on the cutting-room floor.[150]

After the Great War, the Monte Carlo Casino had a new owner and a new kind of player who sought to control the game – both Greek. Sir Basil Zaharoff started life as a money-lender in a Greek market, then went to London – where he styled himself as 'Prince Gortzacoff' and married the daughter of a Bristol builder. One year and another name later, 'Z. Z. Williamson' was arms dealing in Cyprus. He sold munitions to the Balkan states and three submarines – one to Greece and two to their traditional enemy, Turkey. He bought shares in the Maxim, the first fully automatic machine gun, and throughout the First World War he made a fortune, salving his conscience by donating huge sums to Allied charities. Skilled at negotiating war loans, he was appointed director of various banks and became an advisor to Lloyd George. Having made his base in Monte Carlo, Zaharoff bought a controlling interest in the SBM, which ran the Casino, from the ailing Prince Albert. He doubled the minimum bet and watched profits rise. It was not his first commercial initiative on the Côte d'Azur. Zaharoff had set up brothels to entertain and compromise prominent figures. When a detective working for the French National Police was shot dead in his hotel room, it was rumoured he had been investigating the arms dealer. A verdict of suicide provoked by gambling debts was registered – even though the undercover agent left sound finances.[151]

In 1924, when the woman Zaharoff had loved for thirty-seven years was widowed, he married her. He sold his interest in the Casino to a consortium of French bankers, retaining ownership of the Hôtel de Paris, where he lived. Within a year, his wife became terminally ill and he devoted himself to her.[152]

Nicolas Zographos, the son of a Greek professor of political economy, was the leader of the 'Greek Syndicate' which shook up casino procedures. The syndicate – which first appeared at Deauville in 1922 – consisted of four men who took on high rollers. Their declaration, 'Tout va' – even if the stakes went sky-high – signalled they were prepared to cover any wager. This proved so attractive to so many top gamblers that the syndicate cut a deal with the SBM. They would enjoy tax exemption in return for the business they brought to the principality. Among their victims were André Citroën, the French car manufacturer, and the British band leader Ambrose, who started gambling in 1926 and lost £500,000 in the casinos of Deauville, Biarritz, Cannes and Monte Carlo.[153]

Although the Casino recovered from the war, its customers altered. There was a 'general lack of money among the aristocracy of Europe' – or what remained of it. Post-war restrictions on taking money out of certain countries constrained gamblers. The president of the International Sporting Club, General Polovtsov, ruefully observed that in 'Russia, of course, there is not any money to be taken out'.[154] To counter the dip in the Casino's revenue came the Americans, carried by a stock-market tsunami.

Betting in the Casino was keener in the winter than during the summer season.[155] Lartigue – who never liked Monte Carlo – remembered seeing the old Belle Époque courtesans still hanging around, eye make-up smudging across skin no longer taut. In 1986, he also told the journalist Mary Blume about the stench from a woman gambler who had placed a sponge between her thighs so that she would not have to leave the table to go to the toilet.[156] Monte Carlo itself, however, was still 'scrupulously clean'.[157] When Evelyn Waugh was in the principality during the cold winter of early 1929, it snowed every night, but teams in blue overalls cleared the streets, shook the snow from the branches of the trees, and pulled the protective coverings from flower beds each morning to reveal an instant spring.[158]

In 1927, Elsa Maxwell was hired by the principality to promote Monte Carlo as a summer resort. Already famous for creating scavenger hunts and holding murder and fancy-dress parties, Maxwell felt that the demise of the *demi-mondaine* had led to a decline in Monaco's popularity. Her ideas to recapture clientele included the creation of a new beach, a swimming pool and a summer casino.[159] Polovtsov was 'responsible for running the Beach', a role that could be 'extremely awkward'. It 'occasionally happens that negroes wish to bathe there'. He observed that in France there was no 'colour bar' and 'if the other bathers were all French, not the slightest objection would be made… English people and Americans, on the other hand, strongly object to mixing with negroes'.[160]

When the *News* welcomed the Ballets Russes back in April 1922, they wrote that 'it is many years now since Russian dancing first astonished the Western world and revolutionised the modern ballet, yet its attraction seems as powerful as ever'.[161] Nijinska was the season's star. The following spring, they returned with old favourites such as *L'Aprés-Midi d'un Faune*, *Petrushka*, *Schéhérazade* and *Dances from Prince Igor*.[162] From 1922 until Diaghilev's death in 1929, the troupe played Monte Carlo with increased frequency. During the opera season, the theatre was unavailable, yet the Ballets Russes was based in Monte Carlo rehearsing new material for their Paris and London seasons, in rooms beneath the Casino theatre. To take advantage of their presence, the authorities decided to let the troupe give a series of ballets in the music room of the Cercle Privé. This move was very 'much appreciated by that numerous public who love these Russian dancers and like a change from the interminable jazz dancing or the continual concerts'.[163] New ballets included *Chatte*, based on an Aesop fable and choreographed by the young George Balanchine. It featured Serge Lifar and 'the young dancer Alicia Markova'. Having started ballet in London's Finsbury Park to strengthen her limbs, she went on to become – along with Margot Fonteyn – one of the two British dancers accorded the title *prima ballerina assoluta*.

The opera continued to present exciting seasons under the skilled direction of Raoul Gunsbourg, who attracted many top singers to Monte Carlo. Caruso, Chaliapin, Ruffo, Schippa and Gigli were among those who performed in a wide range of operas. Wagner was given, along with familiar Italian, Russian and French works. *La Rondine*, revived in 1920 with Gilda dalla Rizza recreating her role as Magda, was presented in French. Contemporary works such as Honegger's *Judith* and Ravel's *L'Enfant et les Sortilèges* were seen and – with the music commissioned by Diaghilev for the Ballets Russes – the principality became an exciting centre for musical innovation.

In September 1924, after a spell in Biarritz amidst the sizeable Russian community, Igor Stravinsky settled in the Mont Boron quarter of Nice with his mistress, Vera – soon to become his second wife. During the second half of the 1920s, he worked on *Oedipus Rex* in collaboration with Jean Cocteau, and in 1930 on his *Symphony of Psalms*, taking inspiration – like Berlioz before him – from the seascape seen from the cliffs. Stravinsky's day would start with a swim in the sea. Then he would compose. In the afternoons, he would drive, write letters, and practise the piano.[164]

After the Revolution, most rich Russians had departed to uncertain fates. Many of those left on the coast were now in a sorry state, their community depleted. When the Carlton in Monte Carlo offered a Russian Christmas dinner on 7 January 1923, the *News* reported that all the 'old Russian aristocracy who can will be present'.[165] A decade earlier, Russian aristocrats would have filled establishments all along the coast on such a festive occasion. Now, once-wealthy Russians were forced to take work as doormen, taxi drivers, or extras at the Victorine Studios. A photograph appeared in the *News* of a Russian princess selling newspapers on the Promenade des Anglais.

The ballerina Mathilde Kschessinska – a former dancer in the Imperial Ballet and mistress of the tsarevich, the future Nicholas II – had settled on the Riviera with Grand Duke Andrei Vladimirovich on the eve of the Great War. They returned to Russia during the conflict only to flee again in 1920, arriving back in Cap d'Ail penniless. They had to mortgage their villa to pay the servants and the old gardener who had been looking after the estate during their six-year absence. Yet their prospects improved when Raoul Gunsbourg invited them to lunch with Diaghilev, who suggested Kschessinska star in his next Paris season. Although nearly fifty, she could have done it but declined – as she did an offer from the Paris Opéra. Eventually, tight finances necessitated a move to Paris in 1929, where Kschessinska opened a ballet school.[166]

For the most part, the Russians consisted of poor immigrant families. The novelist Romain Gary, who arrived in Nice aged thirteen, described his experiences as a poor Russian Jew in *La Promesse de l'Aube*. Gary was industrious and made his own way, after a childhood during which his adoring mother supported them by selling little Provençal dolls by day and reading palms in restaurants by night. Her scheme to sell her 'family jewels' to guests at the grander hotels involved an accomplice – 'a genuine Russian Grand Duke' whose connections to the late tsar and British royal family she exploited to the hilt. The ruined aristocrat accompanied her, silent and guilty, 'embarrassed' and 'unhappy'.[167] Many other Russians on the coast were living on charity. A lottery was organized on behalf of poor families in Cannes where the children's home took care of sixty Russian children. A grand gala ball was held 'in aid of the Russian Refugees along the Côte d'Azur',[168] and in 1925 the Ballets Russes – in their 'first and only appearance in Cannes'[169] – gave a gala in aid of the Franco-Russian Children's Home. From the cultural mix that was the Côte d'Azur, the Russians would effectively be absent for the following seventy-five years. In F. Scott Fitzgerald's *Tender Is the Night* – set in the late twenties – the narrator observes that 'there was the scent of the Russians along the coast – their closed book shops and grocery stores. Ten years ago, when the season ended in April, the doors of the Orthodox Church were locked, and the sweet champagnes they favoured were put away until their return. "We'll be back next season," they said, but this was premature, for they were never coming back anymore.'[170]

Remaining a favourite with royalty, in 1927 Cannes welcomed the King and Queen of Denmark and Manuel and Victoria, the former King and Queen of Portugal. Cannes also received King Gustav of Sweden, who was an enthusiastic embroiderer. Each year, as he left, he would present the mayor of Cannes with several cushions he had made. Erté claimed 'they were so ugly that the mayor hid them away until the King came back the following year'.[171] E. Phillips Oppenheim found King Gustav – who was also fond of tennis – a most cunning men's doubles player. His partner would be chosen for the length of his legs and youth, and the king would let him scurry all over the court, while he stayed put and returned the easy shots that came his way. When his athletic partner missed a ball, the king would loudly exclaim, 'Pity you didn't leave that one to me.'[172] As for mixed doubles, Oppenheim claimed the king would always choose a partner not solely for her skill but also for her appearance. Possible – though King Gustav had a penchant for his own sex.

Suzanne Lenglen, the tennis star, would swim out from La Garoupe to the small yacht – nicknamed 'the floating bed' – that Oppenheim kept for cocktails, gossip and the inexplicably long line of female admirers[173] who threw themselves at the bushy-eyebrowed,[174] dumpy little man. Oppenheim never saw Lenglen play, but 'in her delightfully modelled bathing-suit' he claimed she was 'the most beautiful figure of a woman I have ever seen in my life'.[175]

Lenglen's father was the secretary of the Nice Lawn Tennis Club, and from 'her earliest childhood' Suzanne 'was put through the most severe training in the game'. Her precise footwork resulted from being taught on a tennis court divided like a chessboard.[176] Winning her first championship in France when she was only fifteen, she also became ladies' champion of Wimbledon in 1919. She went on to win the championship five more times and Wimbledon's mixed doubles twice.[177] After a breakdown in 1921, Lenglen was back on form by the following spring.[178] She had no equal, and saw off challenges from the Californian Elizabeth Ryan and three leading British players – Mrs Chambers, Mrs Satterthwaite and Mrs Beamish.[179]

During the 1920s, the Riviera tennis tournaments were more important than any except Wimbledon, Forrest Hills and the French Championships. On 28 November 1925, the *News* observed that Lenglen was 'still keeping her regular form on the courts and though there are many who come each year and try and defeat her we look for nothing but triumphs for her again this year'.[180] Helen Wills, the American lady tennis champion, arrived by the Blue Train on 23 January 1926.[181] There was a flurry of expectation about a match that was inevitable – Lenglen, 'Champion of the World' vs Wills, 'Champion of the United States'. At Cannes, on 20 February 1926 – after 'three days' solid rain' – the contest took place. 'Miss Wills played splendidly' but 'Lenglen was... as usual utterly and completely mistress of the court', defeating Wills 6–3, 8–6 in the final of the ladies' singles championship.[182] After that, Wills played in many testing tournaments in the south, while Lenglen's doctor ordered her to rest.

On the eve of the First World War, young Alice Prin, later known as 'Kiki de Montparnasse', arrived in that quarter of Paris and started her working life as a salesgirl. Around the age of fourteen, she drifted into modelling for sculptors. She also claimed she could get two francs for showing her bosom to old men behind the Gare Montparnasse – 'Sometimes I got five francs. I have a terrific bosom.'[183] She later sang in nightclubs and became an exciting figure on the bohemian scene, posing for the more celebrated artists of the *École de Paris* – Moïse Kisling, Jules Pascin and Léonard Foujita. After the American photographer Man Ray arrived in Paris in the summer of 1921, he immortalized Kiki, often painting on her face or body before photographing her.[184]

In the early 1920s, Montparnasse was the avant-garde hub of Paris, attracting artists from all over the world. To complement its lively scene in winter, artists came south to the Côte d'Azur in summertime, where they relaxed, found new inspiration and changed the way in which the Riviera was seen. For Kiki, the bar of the Hôtel Welcome in Villefranche was a home away from home. It was there that she got into a fight with a local prostitute over access to American sailors, and hit a policeman who arrived to intervene. She was arrested and sentenced to six months in jail, until Man Ray came down from Paris to secure her release by paying a fine.[185]

The second floor of the hotel, which reeked of opium, was inhabited by a mix of homosexuals, prostitutes, artists, sailors and poets. Jean Cocteau – that artistic jack-of-all-trades, homosexual and occasional opium addict – spent a total of fifteen months living there on-and-off, between 1926 and 1929. Working in various media, Cocteau developed a talent for getting close to the centre of things. At the Murphys' barge party for *Les Noces*, desperate to be noticed, he dressed as a sea captain and moved around declaring, 'We're sinking! We're sinking!' In 1923, when his protegé – the young writer Raymond Radiguet – died, Cocteau turned to opium, which was neither expensive nor rare among artists and the upper classes at the time. Colette noted in *Ces Plaisirs* that the social choice at the time was 'a pipe of opium, a pinch of cocaine, or a cocktail'.[186] Just as Coco Chanel paid for Radiguet's funeral, so she paid for Cocteau to be treated for opium addiction at an exclusive clinic in Saint-Cloud from December 1928 to April 1929. It was, however, in the pale blue rooms of the Hôtel Welcome, with their views out over the gulf of Villefranche, that Cocteau's mood eased and he wrote his play *Orphée*.[187]

In contrast to the congested bars and nightspots of Montparnasse, a number of foreign artists found themselves drawn to the vistas and beaches of the Riviera. Apart from Murphy and Man Ray, the American painter Marsden Hartley came south in the mid-twenties and worked in Vence. Painters Vanessa Bell and Duncan Grant visited Cassis. For Bloomsbury, it had been the critic and painter Roger Fry who discovered the town in 1915, and he went back to paint there in the late twenties. The German George Grosz spent the spring and summer of 1927 on the coast at Marseille, but the landscape did not excite him as much as the wounded relics of war, prostitutes and sex-obsessed plutocrats of Weimar Berlin. The same year, Swiss artist Paul Klee spent time on the Île de Porquerolles off Hyères. The Dutch artist Kees van Dongen became a regular visitor to Cannes and Nice. As portraiture – especially of women – was an important part of his oeuvre, it is not surprising that he became popular with high society. Much later, he settled in Monte Carlo, where the Nouveau Musée National de Monaco now holds a large collection of his work.[188]

In February 1924, the *News* reviewed an exhibition of a 'business-like specimen of the modern artist' – Jean-Gabriel Domergue. The reviewer found 'some of his nude studies… frankly unpleasant'.[189] Inasmuch as they are brash pin-ups favouring peaky breasts and long-limbed women of Barbie-esque proportions, the reviewer was not wide of the mark. Domergue also arranged society events in Juan-les-Pins and decorated the Gondola Room at the new Sporting Club in Cannes, where tea could be taken to the sounds of jazz. He was very much part of the local scene, which – as it is described in the March 1928 issue of *Americans in Beautiful France* – appeared positively exhausting. From 9 to 12, golf at Mandelieu or tennis at the Carlton courts. From 12 to 1, a stroll along La Croisette. At 1, lunch at a good but unpretentious restaurant with an 'impressive wine list'. From 2 to 4, a motor drive. At 4, the Casanova for tea, with its band, and then upstairs to the gaming rooms to play baccarat. At 7, an aperitif and dance at the Provençal Bar of the Sporting Club or the Kit Kat. At 8.45, *Un Bon Garçon*, 'a gay musical comedy full of brains and pep' played in the Sporting Club theatre, which was 'a symphony of gold, grey and black'. At 11.45, another drink and 'a flutter'. At 1 a.m. back to the Kit Kat or the Casanova, which – from midnight onwards – 'ministers to the aristocracy and plutocracy at supper'.[190]

Domergue's paintings were a far cry from the best commercial art of the day. The pared-down design of the first decades of the century led to a dynamic period in poster art – clean, hard, uncluttered images engaging with the new sensation of speed and increased opportunities for travel. A good example was the work of the Ukrainian-born graphic designer Adolphe Jean-Marie Mouron, who called himself 'Cassandre'. He designed a sharp and energized range of posters for the Compagnie des Wagon-Lits. Likewise posters for the Blue Train dramatized its power and dynamism in a way that could never be matched by its speed.

As artists grew familiar with the south coast, some began to subvert its clichés. The Dadaist Francis Picabia deliberately undercut the luxurious, pleasurable idea of the south in a bleak image of the Promenade des Anglais – almost void of people, and devoid of beautiful Belle Époque villas and voluptuous foliage. Even his choice of materials for the painting was at odds with any comfortable notions about the scene it depicts – oil, feathers, macaroni, and leather stuck on canvas.[191] The idea of applying

Robert Mallet-Stevens, the Villa Noailles in Hyères.

found material to a picture was taken one stage further when the coast itself became part of the work. The Surrealist André Masson made disturbing sand paintings in Sanary between May 1926 and March 1927. Three years later, in Juan-les-Pins, Picasso covered objects found on the beach with sand, confounding a recognized shape with an unexpected texture, thus unsettling the spectator in a manner popular among the Surrealists.

In the most innovative architecture of the twenties, the clean lines of Modernism curtailed the excesses of Belle Époque affectation. White or light stone and reinforced concrete defined the desirable and luxurious house in the sun. The jagged landscape of the coast strikingly offset the purity of these Modernist homes. In towns and cities, the candour of the new architecture sat comfortably beside the mannerisms of previous ages. Like Chanel, Modernist architects renounced 'anything superfluous'. Simplicity, contoured to elegance – as seen in the Murphys' Villa America – was suited to the studied informality of life in the south.

An early commission for the young French architect Robert Mallet-Stevens was the Villa Noailles in Hyères, designed in such a way that wings could be added. The building, begun in the early twenties, evolved over a decade until it comprised 1,800 square metres with fifteen en-suite bedrooms, a swimming pool, a hairdressing salon and a squash court. The ensemble contained rather small rooms, some of which were furnished traditionally despite their angular Modernism. Yet its novelty and the fact that Charles and Marie-Laure de Noailles were great patrons of modern art meant that the villa acted as a magnet for modernity. Man Ray was invited there in 1929 to make his film *Les Mystères du Château de Dé*. With contemporary themes such as how speed changes the perception of landscape, and the new importance placed on fitness, the film is, above all, a celebration of the Mallet-Stevens structure, which appears deceptively spacious. The Vicomte de Noailles, fascinated by cinema, planned a birthday present for his wife with the young Spanish director Luis Buñuel. Conceived at the villa, filmed in Paris, the birthday present and surrealist masterpiece – *L'Age d'Or* – was immediately banned.

Across the gulf from Saint-Tropez, at Beauvallon, the lovers Natalie Barney and painter Romaine Brooks built the Villa Trait d'Union – the 'hyphenated villa'. There were two wings connected by a dining room – the common space and hyphen that joined close but separate existences. The austere wing, with its modern furnishings, was inhabited by the tidy portraitist Brooks, whose often-severe oeuvre was summarized by Truman Capote as 'all the famous dykes from 1880 to 1935'. The other wing, with its more cluttered interior, was occupied by the writer and influential salon hostess Natalie Barney. From when they met in 1915 until the death of Romaine Brooks in Nice in 1970, their relationship was open. Barney had many lovers.

After studying at the Slade in London and the Académie Julian in Paris, Eileen Gray became known for the 'modernity' of her designs. In 1923, Mallet-Stevens asked if she would like to work with him, 'because there is so little good modern stuff around'. She didn't feel ready to collaborate but, a year later, began dabbling in architecture with Jean Badovici, the editor of *L'Architecture Vivante*. Just over fifty in 1929, Gray, with the help of two assistants, built the most adventurous and striking modernist house on the

Looking out over the Mediterranean from the salon of E-1027. 'Bibendum' in the centre.

Riviera. Nestling on an inaccessible part of the rough coast near Roquebrune-Cap-Martin, it was constructed of material that starkly contrasted with the craggy rocks on which it was sited. As there was no road, materials were bought in by wheelbarrow. The ideas of Le Corbusier – horizontal windows and free-standing screens to create a malleable open plan – were added to those of Badovici. As Gray would not have persevered with the house without Badovici's encouragement, they called the result E-1027. This blunt, modernistic name derived from the place in the alphabet of their initials – E for Eileen, 10 for J, 2 for B, 7 for G. There was more wit inside. A chair constructed from tubes was named after the Michelin tire mascot, Bibendum. A one-armed chair was called the 'Non-Conformist'. Design ideas were innovative and ship-shape. Sailing thirty metres above the Mediterranean, the egregious house appears like a tiny ocean liner.[192]

That champion of modern economy, Coco Chanel, settled for a more traditional structure. Situated in five acres, 180 metres above E-1027, it afforded striking views over Menton and Monaco. Chanel had the house converted into a three-winged villa around a central courtyard – the ensemble modelled on the twelfth-century orphanage in Aubazine where she had been raised.

Consuelo Vanderbilt – who, as a young lady, had learned about the *demi-monde* in Monte Carlo – came back to the coast with her second husband and found 150 acres of land made accessible by the opening of the Moyenne Corniche. The negotiations to buy 'required diplomacy, patience and tact', as about fifty locals owned tiny parcels of the land. Jacques Balsan 'bantered and bartered' with the 'cunning and cautious' owners. The Balsans built their home, Lou Seuil, in a Provençal style, and gave cosmopolitan lunches on a terrace with a magnificent view overlooking Cap Ferrat. Once, out of twenty guests, there were seven nationalities present – English, American, French, Austrian, Polish, Belgian and Italian. The composer Lord Berners came to lunch and Consuelo spotted, on the front seat of his car, 'a small harmonium on which it was his habit to note motifs inspired by the countryside' as he drove about.[193] When Clementine Churchill was invited to lunch, she found that her hostess looked 'younger & more ethereal every year... her cheeks are pinker & her eyes brighter'.[194]

In Nice, a good deal of new architecture remained hybrid. Georges Dikansky was responsible for Art Deco buildings with exterior decoration employing mosaics, ceramics and powdered glass – all reminiscent of Art Nouveau. Yet Nice – by building the enormous and imposing Palais de la Méditerranée – revealed that it was keen to embrace a Modernism that reflected the indulgence of the 1920s. In the city, the four huge Art Deco cinemas built during the second half of the 1920s attested to the growing popularity of the 'Seventh Art'.[195] Its climate having something in common with California, the Côte d'Azur was beginning to attract Hollywood stars. Rudolph Valentino and his wife were regular visitors, and were seen 'frequently at the *thés dansants* at the Hôtel Negresco'.[196] Rex Ingram came from Hollywood to settle in Nice, where the Victorine Studios – rented out to different directors and productions – were gaining a reputation. Born in Dublin, Ingram studied art at

Yale and worked as an extra in the Vitagraph Studios in Brooklyn. His first full-length film was shot in 1916 and, in Hollywood five years later, he made his name by directing *The Four Horsemen of the Apocalypse*.

Having brought a number of his American crew with him, from 1925 to 1927 Ingram dominated production at the Victorine Studios, making four films. After his successful adaptation of the Vicente Blasco Ibáñez novel *Four Horsemen*, Ingram turned to the author's wartime espionage story, *Mare Nostrum*, which Ibáñez had written in neutral Monte Carlo. Production was lengthy – six months to shoot, another nine for post-production. Michael Powell, who went on to be a celebrated British director, was given his first job in film by Ingram – the opportunity arising as Powell's father owned the Voile d'Or hotel in Saint-Jean-Cap-Ferrat. As the shooting of *Mare Nostrum* dragged on, the producer, Metro Goldwyn Mayer, urged Ingram to abandon the project – the special effects were proving too costly and dangerous. In November 1925, the *News* reported that a crew member had been killed when a propeller he was operating to simulate a stormy sea came loose and struck him on the head.[197] Ingram kept filming and, a year later, *Mare Nostrum* became a hit in America.

As well as two other projects, Ingram directed the first film version of *The Garden of Allah*. Location took the unit to the oasis of Biskra – fourteen hours by train from Algiers. First, Ingram got lost in the desert, and then, in Tunis, in order to engage a dancer, he was forced to arrange for her divorce. Shortly afterwards Ingram gave up cinema, turned to Islam and sculpted until his death in 1950.[198] Matisse had been stimulated by Biskra in 1906, provoking his lifelong interest in Arab patterning and arabesque. Painting his odalisques in Nice during the 1920s, Matisse seemed caught up in the same passion for Arab design as Rex Ingram. When Diaghilev invited the painter to Monte Carlo to draw a portrait of the composer Sergei Prokofiev, for the programme of his ballet *The Love for Three Oranges*, the painter took the opportunity of borrowing one of Bakst's Middle Eastern costumes for *Schéhérezade*.[199]

Erich von Stroheim's 1921 extravaganza, *Foolish Wives*, was set in Monte Carlo – the ideal backdrop for an exploration of American gaucheness and European decadence in the years after the Great War. It was filmed in California using an impressive facsimile of the façade of the Casino complex, along with another and less convincing set constructed on the Monterey Peninsula to simulate views of the Mediterranean. Written, directed and starring the megalomaniacal von Stroheim, the filming of the first million-dollar movie made by Universal Pictures was fraught. Von Stroheim planned to present *Foolish Wives* in two long segments on successive evenings. The studio disagreed, and the film was cut to a mere three and a half hours, which was cut once again to please the censor.

Castlerosse eventually married Doris Delevingne at Hammersmith Register Office at 10.30 on 15 May 1928. His biographer suggested that 'she was probably on greater terms of intimacy with him than with anyone else in her lifetime… but they shocked each other. Each had weaknesses which they found hard to forgive – Castlerosse's dependence upon others for money, her dependence upon others for attention.' After the marriage, Beaverbrook refused to see his protégé and described the relationship between the Castlerosses as 'a cesspool'. Castlerosse was indebted. She was spending mightily. He was chasing other women and started circulating malicious gossip about his wife – 'older than she claimed', 'lurid past'. After a year of marriage, she was considering divorce. The relationship and the spectacle surrounding it became more violent. When Castlerosse tried to hit Randolph Churchill – one of Doris's lovers – he was stopped: 'Don't do that – I'm not your wife.'[200]

Highly successful after Delevingne provided inspiration for the heroine of his novel *The Green Hat*, Michael Arlen married Countess Atlanta Mercati in 1928 and bought a villa outside Cannes. Outselling Fitzgerald's *Gatsby*, *The Green Hat* – 'lushly written'[201] and at times contrived, is witty and pertinent about the society who read it. They were the 'bright young things' who, as Arlen noted in the novel, 'ignored everything but themselves, in whom they were not very interested'. The author explored the general loosening of what was openly permissible, observing that the purpose of a 'bestseller' – which is what *The Green Hat* proved to be – 'is to justify a reasonable amount of adultery in the eyes of suburban matrons'.[202] Syphilis is discussed openly. So is suicide. Sexual ambivalence is acceptable. One character doesn't mind boys being girls – 'as long as they were original'[203] – and, in a Parisian night-spot, we see elderly women 'dancing with young men of both sexes'.[204] Arlen captured the spirit of a spoilt age, a world that was out of reach for most. The *News* noted that the Bulgarian-born Armenian had 'a tendency to overdress and wear more jewellery than is customary with Englishmen'.[205] In Britain, he owned a yellow Rolls-Royce registered in Manchester so he could have 'MA' on the licence plates and take advantage of the new vogue for celebrity.[206] As Arlen's son claimed, 'the 1920s more or less invented it'.[207]

Just as *The Lancet* had talked up British resorts at the expense of the Riviera in the nineteenth century, so Beaverbrook's *Daily Express* conducted an 'odious campaign of calumny… against the Riviera'.[208] The *News* jibed that Beaverbrook himself was more than happy to relax in the hotels and villas of the coast.[209] The slanders of the *Express* included suggestions that clients of the American Bar at the Miramar hotel on La Croisette were being fleeced and pickpocketed. Petty crime, of course, existed. Yet, in Nice, most summonses were issued for misdemeanours – malfunctioning car lights, exceeding the speed limit, drunk driving, hanging laundry out 'to dry at a front window', 'using profane language, insulting a gendarme', watering the milk and leaving household rubbish in the street.[210]

The *News*, however, recorded an ominous shift away from the chic – 'Nice, which used to be a city of gardens is now becoming an immense block of re-inforced concrete'.[211] In Cannes, La Croisette was certainly losing a little of its graciousness, and becoming a paradise for hawkers selling 'artificial pearls and Oriental carpets, all "Very cheap, very good."'[212] There was also a local backlash against imported trends. An advert for an establishment near the aerodrome at the western end of the Promenade des Anglais appeared in *L'Éclaireur de Nice* – 'there is no good orchestra, no fairy like illuminations, no American Bar, the room is shabby, the gramophone is rusty, the discs are worn-out, the piano is out of tune, and the vocalist very husky. But one smiles all the same.' Cannes viewed such perverse 'competition... with supreme indifference'.[213]

The heavy rains of November 1926 created a crevasse above Roquebillière in the backcountry. It gave way in a landslide, carrying three million cubic metres of mud, rock and trees towards the village in the middle of the night on the 24th. Many inhabitants were able to flee but some were caught asleep, and nineteen were buried alive. Telephone lines were down. Nice had to be alerted by bicycle. As if the catastrophe were not enough, rebuilding became enmeshed in local political struggles indicative of the nascent squabbling in the region and in France as a whole. That year, the Parti Communiste was consolidating its presence in and around Nice. Labour unrest, as in Britain with its General Strike in May, was fermenting.

The American anarchist Emma Goldman, who had been deported from the United States, stayed at various places along the Côte d'Azur as she had the year before. A guest of Peggy Guggenheim and Laurence Vail at their villa on the Côte des Maures, she also worked on her hefty memoirs in Saint-Tropez in a house found by Frank Harris and partly paid for by Guggenheim. Harris introduced Goldman to George Bernard Shaw. Both ideologues 'talked so much and so fast that each forgot to listen to what the other was saying'.[214]

When, in 1927, the Italo-American anarchists Sacco and Vanzetti were sent to the chair after being unfairly tried and wrongly convicted, outrage ricocheted around the world. In Nice, a bomb was thrown at the American consulate, another was placed on a railway line outside the city, and one person was killed and six injured when a dance hall, popular with Americans, was bombed.[215] In one of the most luxurious resorts in the world, 1927 saw the workers' paper *Nice Ouvrier* launched. A fête was organized by the Parti Communiste in Menton,[216] while the *News* – the paper for wealthy visitors – took a swipe at champagne socialists. They reported a stay at the Grand Hôtel du Cap d'Antibes of 'Mr Oswald Mosley, the young Socialist MP and his equally Socialist wife, Lady Cynthia Mosley, a daughter of the late Marquis Curzon'. The visit by Mosley – not yet a fascist – might 'arouse the envy of some of their Socialist "comrades" who do not manage to enjoy such delightful holidays in ideal surroundings'.[217] Anomalies were becoming more apparent as the fizz of the 1920s was starting to go flat. Events in America – financial rather than political – would, in 1929, alter the short-term prospects of the Riviera.

London in the first weeks of 1929 was described by Evelyn Waugh as 'lifeless and numb'. Shrinking 'from the icy contact of a cocktail glass', people took the underground 'where they stood, pressed together for warmth, coughing and sneezing among the evening papers'. So cold was it that Waugh packed 'two or three solemn books'[218] – including Spengler's *Decline of the West*, recently translated into English – and headed to Monte Carlo to join a Mediterranean cruise. It was unusually cold when he arrived, and Waugh asked what 'made rich people so rigidly liturgical in their movements that they will come to Monte Carlo in the snow because that is the time ordained for their arrival in rubric and calendar'.[219] Boarding the ship, he wondered how his fellow passengers styled themselves – tourist or traveller. He was certain that the Englishmen on-board would like to flatter themselves that they were travellers, but Waugh decided that all on-board – himself included – were 'tourists'.[220]

As Waugh was sailing the Mediterranean, relaxing in a deckchair with *The Decline of the West* open on his lap, there was a tremor on the New York financial markets. Between 1923 and 1929, favoured stock such as the Radio Corporation of America – bucked by the growing popularity of the wireless – rose thirty-fold. Similarly, shares in AT&T, US Steel and Montgomery Ward were moving ever upward. Industrial activity was sluggish, unemployment high, yet investors wanting to surf the crest of the wave pushed stocks to new heights.

Waugh returned to Monte Carlo as the season was ending. The Ballets Russes had presented, among other things, *Le Chant du Rossignol* with music by Stravinsky, choreography by Balanchine, and curtain, set and costumes by Matisse. The company left at the end of April, never to return under the direction of Diaghilev – four months later, there would be a death in Venice.

Coco Chanel and Misia Sert were cruising along the Dalmatian Coast on Bendor's *Flying Cloud* when Misia received a telegram from Diaghilev – 'Am sick; come quickly. Serge.' Both women had given generous financial aid to the impresario. One crisis moment was at the Parisian dress rehearsal for *Petrushka*, which could not go ahead until the costume-maker was paid. Diaghilev found Misia sitting in the stalls and asked her if she had 4,000 francs. Not with her. Her chauffeur waiting by the car outside, Misia sped home and grabbed the money.[221] Shortly after, the curtain went up on one of Diaghilev's most popular ballets. On condition of anonymity, Chanel helped with the restaging of *Le Sacre du Printemps* – an offer which was perhaps prompted by the fact that in 1920 she had briefly given financial help to its composer Igor Stravinsky, who was, at the time, her lover.

Flying Cloud dropped anchor and the women visited Diaghilev at the Grand Hotel des Bains on the Lido. They spent an hour with the sick man and then put out to sea, where Chanel was rattled by a premonition. They returned to the Lido with the German doctor from their yacht.[222] Diaghilev was in a coma. During the early hours of 19 August, Father Irenaeus of the Greek Orthodox Church was summoned. Roused from his bed, then finding that the dying man was Russian and not Greek Orthodox, the priest became petulant. Misia started screaming until he capitulated and gave a brief absolution. Serge Lifar dressed the body and watched over it as a theatrical storm broke and lightning flashes streaked the dead man's face.[223] Diaghilev had always feared death by drowning, and he died in a city struggling to keep afloat. The coffin was embarked on a funerary gondola, which conveyed the dead impresario across the lagoon to the cemetery on the island of San Michele.

Diaghilev's tomb on San Michele, Venice – with pointe shoes and flowers in tribute.

During that summer of 1929, the Fitzgeralds were on the Riviera – where the ever-tolerant Murphys were the only people who had any time for them. Their hosts were, however, preoccupied by the health of their delicate eldest son, Patrick. Initially diagnosed by doctors in Antibes with bronchitis, Sara took Patrick to Villard-de-Lans in the hills near Grenoble. After three weeks there, the boy's health had not improved, so the Murphys took him to a specialist in Paris whose diagnosis proved more alarming. The nine-year-old Patrick was suffering from the disease that had haunted the Riviera throughout the nineteenth century – tuberculosis. The normally ebullient and witty Dorothy Parker wrote to columnist Robert Benchley from the Villa America on 7 November: 'I will draw that veil over the last few days of shutting up the place in Antibes. Because what is more horrible than a dismantled house where people have once been gay?'[224]

Patrick's illness changed the Murphys' lives – a change compounded by the stock market crash only weeks later. That would adversely affect Sara's annuity, and oblige Gerald to return to take control of Mark Cross through the stormy days ahead for a firm dealing in luxury goods. His career as a painter was over, as was their enchanted life on Cap d'Antibes.

The February tremors on the New York Stock Exchange had gone seismic. On 3 September, the market reached an all-time high. Just over a month later, the roller-coaster swooped. On Thursday 24 October, there was frenzied trading as prices dropped dramatically. The next day, sell orders carpeted the trading floor. By the close of the market, the overworked ticker-tape machines were hours behind with price quotations. Greed had ignored reality and, on 29 October, the stock market collapsed. As with the unlucky gamblers in Monte Carlo, there were suicides; F. Scott Fitzgerald wrote in the short 1931 essay 'Echoes of the Jazz Age': 'The ten-year period that, as if reluctant to die outmoded in its bed, leaped to a spectacular death in October, 1929'.

The impact on the Riviera was immediate. On 7 December, the *Cannes News* noted, 'there are far fewer visitors… than at this date last year, but in view of the serious and unsettled condition of the financial centres of the world we must not expect to see any very large influx of visitors before the end of this month at least. Americans in particular are naturally reluctant to come so far from home.'[225] The delicious cocktail mixed by the Americans, French and British on the Riviera seemed about to dry up. However, as the world stood on the brink of what has been called 'the devil's decade', there were degrees of optimism. A new aerodrome was under construction in Nice. The Blue Train – subject of a 1928 Agatha Christie novel – would, from 1929, circulate daily throughout the year. New carriages carrying only ten people were introduced.[226] A new Pullman Express left Paris at 8.15 in the morning and arrived at Cannes about 10.30 p.m.[227] – in time for a nightcap at the Kit Kat or Casanova. In mid-December, the hot topic was an all-talking programme of films at the Star Cinema. The Aga Khan took a new bride and bought the Villa Taormina on Cap d'Antibes – once home of the late Grand Duke Nicholas of Russia.

The invitation remained – come to the Riviera, where life would glitter and be gay.

9

Losing Paradise
1930–9

The first film to celebrate Nice in all its complexity premiered at the end of May 1930. Jean Vigo's short *À Propos de Nice* was made in 1929, the same year the brother of his cinematographer filmed the landmark documentary *Man with a Movie Camera* in Russia. Both films are silent evocations of cities – urban noise blaring from the power of the images.

Vigo declared that he wished to focus on 'the last gasps of a society so lost in its escapism that it sickens you'.[1] *À Propos* begins with fireworks, an aerial swoop over the city, the beach and the gaming table. Two tourist dolls arrive by toy train and are scooped up by a croupier – taken in like a gambling wager. The film proceeds to contrast wealthy tourists with local workers. Rich visitors are seen under palms, on pebble beaches, in cloche hats and silk stockings on hot café terraces along the Promenade des Anglais. Local washerwomen pound sheets. Socca-makers balance huge trays on their heads as they trot down the lanes of Old Nice from their ovens to their market stalls. Handicapped, a man in a self-propelled cart hawks the *Daily Telegraph*. The grotesque papier-mâché figures of carnival floats haunt the scene, and scream or chortle carnival's invitation to liberty and licence.

À Propos de Nice presents a city hanging in the balance. In the twenties, youth headed south to feel vital after the war. In wake of the Wall Street crash, the desperate headed to Monte Carlo to win back what they had lost. Yet for most, the effects of the crash were not immediate. It took a while for ruin to reach beyond Wall Street. By then, the fallout from irresponsible speculation became enmeshed in politics that grew uglier as the thirties progressed. In the meantime, the Riviera remained defiant, determined to absorb the hangover of the stock market catastrophe. During the winter season of 1929–30, casino takings in Cannes and Nice remained sound. There were elegant Art Deco pylons placed to light the Promenade des Anglais. An impressive 300,000-brick post office was built to serve a bustling city.[2] Cunard advertised weekly sailings from Monaco to North America, and frequent sailings to Southampton. *The Riviera Society Directory: Who's Who on the Riviera 1930–1* declared that 'to find details of yourself… is to have handed you the honour of social success'. It listed the addresses and phone numbers of prominent people such as Mr and Mrs Clews at the Château de la Napoule, and Frank Jay Gould and his wife – the kind of people who had staff to receive calls. Frank Harris withheld his number, and Nicolas Zographos of Greek Syndicate fame gave his address as the 'Yacht Vonna, Jetée Albert-Edouard'. The *Directory* listed six international regattas and advertised the Palais de la Méditerranée as the 'most sumptuous Casino in the World'.[3]

Art Deco pylons on the Promenade des Anglais, 1935. Photo by Jean Giletta.

In November 1930, the *News* reported that 'famous dress houses and other firms dealing with luxury trades have been open during the past summer and have had no reason to regret their experiment'. They praised the 'effective publicity campaign of Mr Frank Jay Gould's great organization', crediting Juan-les-Pins and Cap d'Antibes with sustaining the craze for summer.[4] The frivolity of the 1920s persisted as people took to racing against the Blue Train. Woolf 'Babe' Barnato was the son of an ex-circus performer who made a fortune diamond mining in South Africa. An accomplished sportsman who won the twenty-four-hour Le Mans race for three consecutive years from 1928, Barnato became one of the many drivers who raced the Blue Train to flaunt their audacity or promote their make of car. The first to beat the train in January 1930 was the Rover Light Six. In early March, an Alvis Silver Eagle arrived in Calais with a three-hour lead. Then, the owner of the Bentley Motor Company, Woolf Barnato, entered the fray and bet £100 that he could arrive at his club in London before the Blue Train reached Calais. On the afternoon of 13 March, minutes after the train pulled out of Cannes station, Barnato set off in his Bentley Speed Six. Torrential rain, fog, refuelling and a burst tire notwithstanding, he parked his car outside his club in St James's Street at 3.20 in the afternoon of the 14th – minutes before the Blue Train pulled into Calais.[5]

The *Menton and Monte Carlo News* sounded the alarm in November 1931 – 'to say that the financial difficulties in Europe and America will not affect us would be incorrect; it will make a difference. Many of our regular visitors and residents will not be able to spend the winter here owing to the depreciations in their investments.'[6] Britain was suffering from high unemployment, and when it came off the gold standard in September 1931, the exchange rate fell by over 20 per cent. Two months later, the *News* reported that hotels along the Riviera agreed to reduce charges so that British visitors could effectively pay the same price as the year before. Nonetheless, the paper claimed that, in Menton, the winter season of 1931–2 would 'be ranked as one of the most trying and most difficult that the town has ever experienced'.[7] The lists of arrivals published weekly in the paper were appreciably shorter, and advertising was down. In its first issue of 1932, amid the advertisements on the front page, the *News* advertised for advertisers.[8] That year, the Dow Jones Industrial Average was down 89 per cent from its 1929 peak. The 'Americans in Paris', kept solvent by money sent from the States, were forced to go home.

In communities along the coast, there was increasing anxiety that Europe was being promised economic security and order by two violently opposed political alternatives – fascism and communism. In the parliamentary elections for Cannes-d'Antibes of May 1932, the Communists won more votes than the Socialists. When Jean Médecin, mayor of Nice, organized an international tourist conference the following year, he was accused of focusing on tourism and ignoring the plight of locals.[9] The tourist slump had, of course, contributed to local misery. Frank Jay Gould's enterprises suffered as the Depression reduced the number of American visitors. The ill-fated Palais de la Méditerranée, which had lost a substantial amount of money during its first season, was damaged by fire in 1934. By the time it was repaired, there were so few visitors that it remained shut for the winter season. The Goulds themselves were rich enough to be insulated. Florence Gould – credited with introducing water-skiing to the Côte d'Azur – would drink and gamble the night away, yet be up by eight for sport. Their life together was free and easy. Florence later recalled that 'in the thirties everyone slept with everyone. It was amusing, it was practical.'[10]

Sexual freedom was a theme and a lifestyle for writers such as H. G. Wells and D. H. Lawrence, who spent time on the Riviera for different reasons. Spontaneity and the search for an ideal climate for tuberculosis had kept Lawrence and his wife, Frieda, on the move.[11] He had been suffering for years as the blood-spitting and haemorrhaging became more frequent. In 1928–9, the couple tried Bandol. At first, they stayed at the Hôtel Beau Rivage – where Katherine Mansfield had suffered her first haemorrhage – and then at the Villa Beau Soleil. Professionally, Lawrence was trying to negotiate the legal minefield surrounding his 'tender and phallic'

novel, *Lady Chatterley's Lover*. An unexpurgated edition had
been published in Florence, and he was preoccupied with finding
a Parisian bookseller or publisher. Of the 1,000 copies printed in
Italy, 500 were to be sent to America. The six sent to the London
literary agent Laurence Pollinger were confiscated, and the recipient
was visited by officers from Scotland Yard.[12]

Aldous Huxley observed that, by 1930, Lawrence no longer
wished to know how ill he was. He 'coughs more, breathes very
quickly and shallowly, has no energy'.[13] With his weight hovering
around forty-five kilos, Lawrence was not eating and wished to
flee 'moribund Europe'. However, on the advice of his London
doctor, he entered the Ad Astra sanatorium at Vence on 6 February.
Pain savaged his nights, yet the last week of Lawrence's life was
full. On 24 February, H. G. Wells visited. The Huxleys came to
help care for him on the 25th and 28th. The American sculptor
Jo Davidson arrived to do a clay bust. On the 27th, the Aga Khan
visited. He admired Lawrence's paintings.[14] Meanwhile, the dying
man was working on a review of Eric Gill's *Art Nonsense* in which
he described Gill's hectoring manner as sounding like 'a tiresome,
uneducated workman arguing in a pub'. On 1 March, Lawrence left
Ad Astra for the nearby Villa Robermond. He began to hallucinate
– 'I see my body over there on the table.' At the end, he implored
Frieda, 'Hold me, I don't know where my hands are. Where am I?'
Morphine was administered and, in the late evening of 2 March
1930, D. H. Lawrence died aged forty-four.[15]

The short and squeaky-voiced H. G. Wells had a formidable
intellect, energy and sexual drive. He wrote more than a hundred
books, hundreds of articles, and several film scripts. As a young
man, he had entertained a faith in the power of science to ameliorate
the human condition, but towards the end of his life he rather
thought that human barbarity would prevail. In between, he tried
'to save the world from itself' by predicting two devastating wars
in which tanks and rockets would be used as weapons.[16]

Sexually irrepressible, Wells had a long affair with, and a son by,
the novelist Rebecca West. Throughout the 1920s, West holidayed
at the Pension Josse in Antibes, and her observations about life on

the Côte d'Azur formed the world she created in her 1936 novel *The Thinking Reed*. Protagonists Isabelle and Marc are staying at a villa in Antibes. Their circle – apart from meeting, eating, lovemaking and sleeping – have little to do. When Isabelle's guests arrive – 'They had to be given cocktails, they often had to be asked to stay to lunch, and although they left in the afternoon about three, they were back in the early evening.' Such guests 'refused all succour offered to them by the mind, and there is simply not enough for the body to do unassisted during the whole twenty-four hours'. They are a rich set who have taken secular vows of 'wealth, unchastity, and disobedience to all standards' and any 'possibility of friendship was undermined by their promiscuous amities and sudden enmities'. They are afraid of communism, and worried that any radical shift in society will make them obsolete.[17]

Wells was a full-time philanderer. He married his second wife and ex-student Amy Robbins in 1895, and they remained married until her death from cancer in October 1927. Rebecca West was only one of Wells's lovers during that period. He met the colourful and elusive Moura Budberg during a visit to Russia in 1920. Disappointed by the obvious failure of the Revolution, Wells was much taken with Budberg but they would not meet again until the end of the decade.[18]

Russian by birth, Budberg had been the mistress of the celebrated English secret agent Robert Bruce Lockhart. She had also been Gorky's mistress, and perhaps even Stalin's. As a London socialite, she became close to many literary and political luminaries, and was a good friend of the Cambridge spy Guy Burgess, along with many figures in the British Communist Party. MI5 had her watched from the day she arrived in England in 1922, but despite the slurs of sexual rivals such as Rebecca West, extensive surveillance and her dubious connections, nobody could decide if Budberg was, indeed, an agent. To muddy the waters, after Burgess defected she denounced Anthony Blunt, but MI5 ignored the tip from a woman who was something of a fantasist and felt no compunction to tell the truth.[19] Budberg helped shape Wells's ideas about Russia, yet when the writer returned to the Soviet Union to meet Stalin and Gorky in

1934, Moura claimed she could not accompany him – she had not been there for ten years. In fact, she had travelled to Moscow three times during the previous twelve months.[20] The lie did nothing for a relationship during which Wells envisaged marriage.

Wells had been living with an emotionally overwrought former Jesuit nurse, the Dutch writer Odette Keun, in a house they had built in Grasse and over which there was a long and testy ownership dispute after they parted in 1933. At Christmas the following year, Wells stayed with Budberg at the Hermitage in Monte Carlo. When she returned to London in January, Wells was invited to dinner at the Negresco by Constance Coolidge, a forty-three-year-old American heiress and racehorse owner whom he had met at Somerset Maugham's. Constance had enjoyed almost forty lovers, and Wells – who fell for her – had been in love around fifty times. Before she returned to America, they shared a passionate week together.

Maugham found Wells 'fat and homely'.[21] In fact, he was volatile emotionally and needed physical love as one needs food and sleep. It was a craving he often resented. His sometime-neighbour Charlie Chaplin remarked that, after writing 1,000 words and answering correspondence, boredom set in. Wells claimed that was the moment for sex.[22] During the 1930s – in his seventies and early eighties – Wells integrated his compulsive sex drive with much hard work. In 1931, the year in which Aldous Huxley projected his bleak vision of the future in *Brave New World*, Wells was in Cannes working on *The Shape of Things to Come*, which dealt with the consequences of an economic slump and a world war.

A writer ignoring dystopian futures and wallowing in the luxury of the Riviera, with its allure for criminals, was the popular novelist E. Phillips Oppenheim. Interviewed by the *News*, Oppenheim humbly called himself 'a teller of tales rather than a novelist'. Asked if his stories were plotted, he replied, 'Oh dear no, I seldom know what's going to happen in the end.'[23] It shows. He wrote 150 books, and taking one at random – *Murder at Monte Carlo*, published in 1933 – we see his shortcomings. The dialogue is leaden and pedestrian. There is constant explaining, and Oppenheim repeatedly reminds the reader – and probably himself as he writes – what has happened so far.[24] His biographer Robert Standish claimed that there was 'in Phillips Oppenheim, as there has been in almost every man and woman who has found a place in tens of millions of human hearts, a wide streak of mediocrity'.[25] Oppenheim clearly wrote for money and enjoyed the fruits of his endeavours. The Oppenheims lived at the Villa Deveron in Cagnes-sur-Mer, with its tennis court and adjacent golf links. He wrote thirty novels at the villa, and the couple hosted cocktail parties at which Oppenheim mixed excellent White Ladys. When the pound tumbled in 1931, the Oppenheims went back to England – but soon returned to the Riviera, and settled in the Domaine de Notre Dame at Mougins.[26] Oppenheim resumed his Riviera lifestyle, with daily rounds of golf, cocktails and his admiring ladies, and – for a month each year – he took a suite with his wife at the Hôtel de Paris in Monte Carlo.

Another industrious writer was the Belgian Georges Simenon, whose crime novels were of an altogether higher calibre. In 1932, he published *Liberty Bar*, in which Commissaire Maigret comes south to solve a murder in Antibes. Simenon started visiting the coast in the mid-twenties, and continued to do so over several decades. He spent his mornings writing and his afternoons walking and watching the locals. Such research paid off. In contrast to Simenon's approach, F. Scott Fitzgerald described Oppenheim as 'a fat industrious man... who lived in a bathrobe'.[27]

In February 1934, Fitzgerald implored Maxwell Perkins, when advertising *Tender Is the Night*, 'Please do not use the phrase "Riviera" or "gay resorts". Not only does it sound like the triviality of which I am so often accused, but also the Riviera has been thoroughly exploited by E. Phillips Oppenheim and a whole generation of writers and its very mention invokes a feeling of unreality and unsubstantiality.'[28] Harvesting events that had played out in the mid-1920s, Fitzgerald was worried that the setting of the early part of the book might appear out of date.

The novel was begun in the wake of *Gatsby*'s 1925 success. But when it was finished eight years later, Fitzgerald was a changed man. During the intervening years, Zelda had suffered a breakdown and

American prosperity had evaporated. Writing the final draft back in the States, Fitzgerald found it necessary to fuel himself with gin. When the book was published, objections centred on his decision to write about a group of neurotic expatriates. Hadn't he heard of the Depression? As one reviewer put it, 'Dear Mr Fitzgerald, you can't hide from a hurricane under a beach umbrella.'[29]

It was the Murphys who had first brought Scott and Zelda Fitzgerald to the Riviera, and their dubious reward was to function as ill-managed models for Fitzgerald's uneasy protagonists, Dick and Nicole Diver. At the outset of the novel, Dick is based on Gerald Murphy, with his 'virtuosity with people'.[30] Inexplicably, he morphs into a far less attractive character based on Fitzgerald himself. Amanda Vaill has suggested, however, that Diver's hollowness in the second part may have more to do with Murphy's 'feelings of emptiness' than is generally supposed.[31] After all, Sara and Gerald's boys were ailing. Baoth would die of meningitis in 1935, and Patrick of tuberculosis in 1937.

Hemingway took Fitzgerald to task for his messy procedure. 'It started off with that marvellous description of Sara and Gerald... Then you started fooling with them, making them come from things they didn't come from, changing them into other people and you can't do that, Scott.' True to form, Hemingway put the boot in: 'Of all people on earth you needed discipline in your work and instead you marry someone who is jealous of your work, wants to compete with you and ruins you... I thought Zelda was crazy the first time I met her... and, of course, you're a rummy.'[32] The novel was a commercial failure, and its quality was debated by critics. The bulk of Fitzgerald's money came from his 160 magazine stories – the novels made comparatively little.[33] After years of riotous living, Scott died of a heart attack in 1940, and Zelda burned to death in an asylum fire in 1948. Calvin Tomkins, surveying the world the Murphys created in the south of France, observed that F. Scott Fitzgerald's 'life always attracted more attention than his work'.[34]

There was a freshness about a new literary generation enjoying its first contacts with the coast. For ten days in 1931, Jean-Paul Sartre was shown Marseille by Simone de Beauvoir, who was teaching there. When she was sent off to Nice to examine that year's *baccalauréat*, she found an enormous room with a balcony in the Place Masséna for ten francs a day. Her 'landlady was a heavily made-up woman in her fifties, all tricked out with satin dresses and jewelry, who spent every night at the Casino'. She would wake de Beauvoir at 6 a.m. before she went off to bed. Surprising someone who came from Paris, female candidates for the oral examinations would arrive in 'large straw hats, bare-armed, their naked feet thrust into sandals'. After a day examining, de Beauvoir 'would wander round the cafés or the little dance halls on the front. Nonchalant, she would "let strangers sit down" at her table and talk. "I was so enchanted by the mild night air, and the lights, and the soft lapping of the water, that nothing and no one could cause me annoyance."'

Interested in alternatives to the status quo, de Beauvoir became curious about the educational initiative of a teacher called Célestin Freinet, who lived in nearby Saint-Paul-de-Vence. Rather than demanding 'blind obedience' from his pupils, Freinet 'appealed to their friendship and initiative'. When priests incited the locals to throw stones at the schoolhouse windows in protest against such dangerous licence, the teacher held fast. De Beauvoir noted that his success 'bore out our most passionately held conviction: that freedom is an inexhaustible source of discovery, and every time we give it room to develop, mankind is enriched as a result'.[35]

Illustrious visitors enjoyed not only the restaurants, casinos and hotels, but also the hospitality of energetic hosts who built or owned outstanding villas along the coast. Winston Churchill was more than happy to accept invitations, and his hosts were thrilled. Consuelo Balsan recalled that he was one of their favourite guests at Lou Seuil. He spent 'his mornings dictating to his secretary'. In the afternoons, when he went off to paint along the coast, the cigar box was filled before he was driven to his chosen destination by the Balsans' chauffeur, 'accompanied by a detective the British government insisted upon providing'.[36] Churchill also enjoyed staying with an American actress who had scored a triumph in the late-Victorian London theatre – Maxine Elliott. Elliott had quit her native America, where her beauty made her 'just a chattel', and

Barry Dierks's Château de l'Horizon.

Barry Dierks's 1938 Villa Aujourd'hui.

had settled in England, where she found she could 'live like a lady' among people 'civilized enough' to appreciate her as a person. At the house of George Keppel, she was introduced to the cream of London society.

In November 1930, the *News* reported that Miss Maxine Elliott was 'building a large and particularly interesting villa on the edge of the sea a short distance to the west of Golfe-Juan'. The railway ran immediately behind, and 'to eliminate noise... some very massive stone walls have been erected', while the interior of the house was 'lined with a new sound-proof material' by the architect Barry Dierks.[37] After graduating from the Carnegie Institute of Technology in Pittsburgh in 1921, Dierks settled in Théoule-sur-Mer in 1925 with his partner, the British landscape gardener Eric Sawyer. Having declared his style with the white rooms of his own villa, Dierks made his reputation working on Somerset Maugham's Villa Mauresque and proceeded to design or remodel many Riviera homes. Maxine Elliott's Château de l'Horizon shared logistical problems with Dierks's later and most celebrated commission – the Villa Aujourd'hui of 1938, whose gentle curves were accommodated to the thin strip of land on which it was built.

Even before the Château de l'Horizon and its thirty-three-metre swimming pool were finished, Elliott started entertaining. As guests sat down to an informal outdoor lunch, the workmen on the scaffolding serenaded them with Provençal songs. When work was finished and Elliott shipped her Edwardian furniture from England and glutted his lucent, clean-lined interior, Barry Dierks burst into tears. Reporter and writer Vincent Sheean provided a peek at the rhythm of life at the chateau, which 'began late, seldom before eleven o'clock, often not till noon'. As the guests emerged, 'Lady C wore a patch or two of yellow; Lady P was older and less naked; Lord A wore practically nothing except a brilliant scarf around his neck'. Winston Churchill was expected. He became a frequent guest, and Maxine Elliott was careful to invite stimulating people whenever he visited. If some fool slipped through the net, they were met with gently barbed paternalism. Sheean recalled an occasion when a 'particularly vacuous guest' enquired in a piercing nasal voice: '"Winston, why is it they always seem to go to Geneva for their meetings? Seems to me they could pick out a nicer place." Mr Churchill paused in his mastication, looked at her benevolently from

Doris Delavigne and Winston Churchill on the rocks.

the shade of his big straw hat, and said as to a child: "Because, my dear, Geneva happens to be the seat of the League of Nations. You have heard of it, no doubt?"[38] Elliott's neighbour in Antibes, the Aga Khan, was invited as he had a deep appreciation of a politician whose strong personality combined the 'romantic, deeply emotional' with the 'common-sense... hard-headed and coolly calculating' – 'a majestic combination'.[39] Elsa Maxwell was invited because she shared Churchill's love of popular music. He also relished flightier moments with some of the notorious socialites of the day, such as Daisy Fellowes and Doris Castlerosse,[40] but – underlying all the fun – he was 'disgusted' by the *Daily Mail*'s 'boosting of Hitler',[41] and generally anxious about the deteriorating international situation.

When Churchill was staying at Max Beaverbrook's villa in 1929, Doris Castlerosse was there, and he painted her portrait. Four years later – both guests of Maxine Elliott – Churchill painted her again. According to Judith Mackrell – who became party to a well-kept family secret – Churchill briefly became her lover.[42] Doris Castlerosse was certainly active. She had recently been infatuated with the homosexual Cecil Beaton, whom she introduced to heterosexual lovemaking. Viscount Castlerosse was incensed yet unfailingly witty when he spotted them dining together – 'I never knew Doris was a lesbian!'[43] In October 1932, Castlerosse petitioned for divorce, 'a co-respondent being cited'. Beaton was subpoenaed but the petition was withdrawn, and the following March there was a deed of separation despite the fact that Castlerosse was still in love with his wife.[44]

The whole romantic rigmarole and the homosexual antics of the age were captured in Lord Berners's *roman-à-clef*, *The Girls of Radcliff Hall*, which he published privately under the name of 'Adela Quebec'. All the characters in the school where the book is set were based on real people. The headmistress, Miss Carfax, was Berners himself. His beloved Robert Heber-Percy was Millie. Cecily was Cecile Beaton, and Lizzie was the love of Beaton's life, Peter Watson, with whom Berners was also in love. Mr Dorrick, the dancing master, was Doris Castlerosse. When Miss Carfax/ Berners finds Lizzie/Watson in bed with another pupil, 'Her heart began to beat violently. The sight of the two girls clasped in each other's arms aroused a curious hitherto unknown emotion in her breast. She felt as if she was going to faint.' At Radcliff Hall, 'it was strictly forbidden for girls to sleep in one another's beds, presumably for hygienic reasons'. The pupil whose personality attracted Miss Carfax most of all was undoubtedly Cecily/Beaton. Meanwhile, Mr Dorrick/Doris Castlerosse – 'no novice in the art of love' – also had a 'decided penchant' for Cecily.

The short novel, with its schoolboy-ish jokes, captures the camp crushes and incessant jealousies of its world. It also functioned as a tribute to Berners's lover Robert Heber-Percy. 'The presence of Millie... brought a new interest into Miss Carfax's life. She had become convinced that there could be nothing more in life that could restore that wonderful sensation of ecstasy that she had so often experienced in her youth.' When it is discovered that 'Miss Carfax has a photograph of Millie in her drawers', another girl asks if 'the photograph is sewn in or just stuck in with a safety pin?' Miss Carfax finds Millie 'wild, unrestrained and a little crazy... Her movements were often violent but, although she was constantly breaking things, there was nothing clumsy about her movements... everything she did was redeemed by a peculiar gracefulness. She was like a young panther.' It is an accurate picture of Heber-Percy. Given the headmistress's pash for the pupil, Cecily/Beaton advises Millie/ Heber-Percy to take advantage of the 'very rich' Miss Carfax.[45]

Heber-Percy was not yet twenty-one when he met Lord Berners, who was then approaching fifty. From an upper-class Shropshire family, Heber-Percy was bisexual but preferred men. To Berners, the outstandingly beautiful young roustabout was 'a young panther' whom he cherished for hijinks rather than sex. Once, when Cecil Beaton was staying with them and wanted to know in which bedroom Percy slept, Berners swapped rooms and greeted Beaton in the middle of the night, 'Why Cecil, this is so sudden!' On one occasion, Doris Castlerosse asked Heber-Percy if they had slept together the previous evening – 'she simply couldn't remember'.[46] As for Berners, Heber-Percy only wanted to go to bed with him when drunk, although he lived with him for eighteen years – until the older man's death. When he brought a wife and child to Berners's country house, Faringdon, Heber-Percy pushed his host's patience to the limit.[47]

Lord Berners – who used Doris Castlerosse as the model for the improper wife in his play *The Furies*[48] – was one of the most colourful characters to spend time on the Riviera. His great passion was to turn the whole of life into an outrageous giggle. Not the most handsome creature – Cecil Beaton found him 'a ridiculous-looking man – like a particularly silly tailor's dummy'[49] – Berners was a composer, painter and a celebrated wit. On the subject of his own sexuality, and mocking the travel announcements of the rich, he wanted to place a notice in *The Times* – 'Lord Berners has left Lesbos for the Isle of Man'. Lady Colefax – who many people considered to be an indifferent hostess – had the irritating habit of sending invitations on postcards using initials to identify the other guests. Berners sought revenge by inviting her to luncheon 'to meet the P. of W.' When she arrived, Berners introduced her not to the Prince of Wales, but to the Provost of Worcester College, Oxford.[50]

Berners was staying with Emerald Cunard in the south of France in September 1927 when he discovered that the English artist Christopher Wood, whom he had met in Rome, was next door. Berners took Wood for jaunts to scenic spots along the Riviera, where they painted together. Berners had only just started painting and Wood found his approach pedantic but the result promising. For his musical compositions, Berners sought criticism from Stravinsky, who considered that the music he composed for Diaghilev's *The Triumph of Neptune* compared well with the French compositions commissioned by the impresario. Igor and Vera Stravinsky visited Berners at Faringdon, where meals were improvisations on a single colour and the pigeons circling above were tinted with harmless cosmetic dyes. When in 1930 George Balanchine devised a ballet called *Luna Park*, the music was by Berners and the decor by Christopher Wood, who that summer would throw himself under a train in Salisbury station.[51]

The formidable bundle of energy who helped Maxine Elliott decorate the Château de l'Horizon was the American interior designer Elsie de Wolfe. As she got older, Elsie became famous for her exercise regime, which was celebrated by Cole Porter in his 1934 song 'Anything Goes'. In the post-1929 world, the bite of Porter's lyrics was a tonic for a society cautioned. On the Riviera, where opium – 'a gentleman's drug' – was widely consumed and morphine was used by people like Coco Chanel, it hardly seemed that Porter was pushing the boundaries of what was acceptable with his cocaine lyric in the song 'I Get a Kick Out of You'. Frequently replaced with an array of anodyne lyrics on recordings, Porter's original was apt for the high living on the Riviera.[52]

Wealthy Cole Porter was blithe while satirizing the upper crust. Noël Coward, born into a modest family, was less comfortable. Nonetheless, he aspired to society, and four years after 'Anything Goes' he included Elsie de Wolfe in the array of guests in his song 'I Went to a Marvellous Party' – a celebration of the Riviera in-crowd to which Coward desperately wanted to belong. The song distilled incidents at several parties given by Elsa Maxwell, who claimed that 'any similarity between the names in the song and the names of my guests was purely intentional'.[53] Among those Coward evoked was an outrageously dressed Cecil Beaton. The photographer and designer never really took to Coward. A meeting between them in New York confirmed that the entertainer found it difficult to merge with the smart set. Beaton remembered that, although Coward 'talked hard… the entire time he didn't succeed in saying anything amusing or clever. He was extremely badly dressed in trousers too short and his face was sweating at every pore.'[54]

At the outset of the 1930s, the *Cannes News* reported that Coward was 'mixing work with pleasure by taking a holiday on the Riviera, where… Miss Gertrude Lawrence, who is to be the leading lady in his new play, is also staying. We understand that there are only four characters in his new comedy and throughout the whole of the second act Mr Coward and Miss Lawrence have the stage entirely to themselves.'[55] Coward and Lawrence were rehearsing *Private Lives* at La Capponcina on Cap d'Ail – the villa of the couturier Edward Molyneux, who was to design Gertrude Lawrence's gowns for the play.[56] Lawrence had shared an apartment in London with Doris Delevingne, and the violent quarrelling of Elyot and Amanda in *Private Lives* was inspired by the brawling in Doris's marriage. When her husband's mother, Lady Kenmare, was introduced to Coward at the first night and protested, 'No couple could possibly quarrel like that in real life,' Coward replied, 'You obviously don't know the Castlerosses.'[57]

Despite affairs and violent contretemps, the Castlerosse marriage raged on with the absurdity of those besotted but ill-suited. Castlerosse hired a detective to follow Doris to Paris. The resulting report was sufficiently incriminating to warrant divorce. Castlerosse could not proceed. The man whom the detective alleged spent eighteen hours in a room at the Ritz with Doris had been none other than the viscount himself. When in 1938 their divorce was, at last, made absolute, her life went to pieces. Early in the war – in debt and unhappy – Doris overdosed on sleeping tablets and never woke up. Three weeks after the inquest, and not long before he died in 1943, Castlerosse married the recently widowed Enid Furness.[58]

Although the Duke of Westminster had a bedroom at La Pausa, by the time the villa was finished, he was married to Loelia, daughter of Sir Frederick Ponsonby, Treasurer to the King and Keeper of the Privy Purse. Chanel, ever onward and upward, dismissed her time with Bendor – 'fishing for salmon is not life'. Over lunch one day, Sir Charles Mendl asked her why she had refused the duke's offer of marriage. With Gallic pride, she retorted, 'There have been many Duchesses of Westminster but only one Coco Chanel.'[59] By 1931, Chanel had taken up with a protégé of Paul Poiret – the illustrator and decorative artist Paul Iribe. Despite a furious sense of competition between them, people began to talk of the possibility of marriage. Those rumours were quashed when Iribe – aged fifty-two – died of a heart attack while playing tennis at La Pausa in 1935.[60]

In the autumn of that year, Chanel suffered the first great challenge to her supremacy in the fashion world. The curves that Colette had pined for in the mid-twenties returned in the flamboyant designs of the Italian Elsa Schiaparelli. As Erté remarked, Schiaparelli 'struck a blow against the dreary uniform created and maintained for years by Chanel. Chanel had created "Mrs Everybody", but Schiaparelli finally managed to resurrect individuality.'[61] With novelties like visible zippers, synthetic fabrics, wrap dresses, the use of 'shocking pink', and outrageous collaborations with the Surrealists, Schiaparelli became particularly popular with extrovert clients such as Hollywood stars and Daisy Fellowes. Nonetheless, Chanel the skilled businesswoman remained a vital force in design, and a generous person. Luchino Visconti bred racehorses but hankered for a more artistic milieu. Over lunch at La Pausa, Chanel introduced Visconti to Jean Renoir, and the following year the Italian joined his film crew – the first step in an important career as one of Italy's great directors.

As always, the pages of the *Menton and Monte Carlo News* revealed the tastes and preoccupations of the anglophone community. There was a new craze for miniature golf. The Palais de la Méditerranée had an indoor course, as did the Savoy Palace Hôtel – on its first floor, overlooking the sea.[62] Much of the *News* was devoted to tennis, golf, motor rallies, regattas, bridge tournaments, ping-pong games and crossword puzzles. 'Books to Read' and 'Travel Notes' occupied a good deal of space, and 'Winter Sports' began to be featured as skiing clubs opened in Menton. The paper noted that the children's 'physical culture lesson' on the beach was a highlight, and honoured the enthusiasm for sun-drenched exercise by advertising lecture topics such as 'How to Obtain Glorious Radiant Health'.[63] Amateur dramatics thrived. The Menton Players presented *The Naughty Wife* in which 'Miss Dorothy Crossthwaite made a charming Naughty Wife' and Darrell MacKnight's 'love making was well done, and his enunciation capital'.[64] There were *tableaux vivants* in aid of charity, but fewer reports of revelry, as if people were becoming jaded. The value of the pound was not the only thing that had devalued. On the Riviera, 'the term "old friend"' meant 'little more than "cocktail party acquaintance"'.[65]

There was, despite the slump, a determined effort to buoy things. In Monte Carlo, the new 'Open Sesame' nightclub was a cave accessed through pirate-guarded iron doors, which slid open as clients murmured the familiar formula that Ali Baba overheard. The dance floor had an illuminated border, and on the tables were 'bejewelled lamps and great champagne coolers which threw coloured lights on the golden beverage'. Music was provided by a gypsy orchestra and the Carolina Stomp Chasers. Every night, 'amusing gifts' were given 'to women guests'.[66] At the Knickerbocker – instead of familiar cocktails such as the dry martini – Russell, the Jamaican barman, mixed over twenty drinks including a Paradise, a Glad-Eye, a Monkey Gland, a Whip, a Grand Duke, a Depth Bomb, a Silver Streak and a Millionaire.[67]

British parlance – 'I say, topping band – what?' – was being replaced by transatlantic gab – 'She'll shoot the works, that bimbo.' The *1933 Supplement to the Oxford English Dictionary* added terms like 'gadget', 'anti-fat', 'vibro-massage', 'flapper', 'gangster', 'perm', 'talkies', 'yap' and 'lipstick'. As one commentator put it, 'when we Americans are through with the English language, it will look as if it had been run over by a musical comedy'.[68] Ominously, the *Supplement* also added the word 'fascism', which began to spread its ever-lengthening shadow towards paradise.

In purely romantic terms, the shadows seem to have lengthened for the 'perfect young ladies' of Sandy Wilson's *The Boy Friend* when they came back to Nice ten years later in Wilson's sequel, *Divorce Me, Darling*. Wondering how their marriages disintegrated, the characters from *The Boy Friend* find themselves – by a series of

Special 800th issue of *The Menton and Monte Carlo News.*

incredible coincidences – back where it all began. This 1960s show was nowhere near as successful as its refreshingly simple 1950s predecessor. Despite its gusto and its excellent pastiche of thirties popular music, *Divorce Me, Darling* ran for only three months in the West End.

Comparisons between then and now were also the subject of the 800th issue of the *Menton and Monte Carlo News*, published on 28 February 1931. The cover contrasted the fashions of 1897 and 1931, and people were asked for reminiscences. One long-term American resident remembered Monte Carlo's Café Riche in the Galerie Charles III. Upstairs there were private lodges and, one night, the rivals Otero and de Pougy had a large supply of champagne bottles sent up. Oscar Wilde was to arrive with Lord Alfred Douglas, and when they appeared the courtesans pelted them with the bottles. On another occasion, the eccentric owner of the *Herald*, James Gordon Bennett, drove a three-horse fiacre the length of the gallery, turned it round and charged for the entrance, where he was arrested. Such stories – doubtless apocryphal – were also far-fetched.[69]

In the early 1930s, only baccarat and *chemin de fer* were played at French casinos. For roulette, a player was obliged to go to Monte Carlo. Peter de Polnay, the Hungarian-born adventurer and novelist, wrote that 'few places were as dismal as the casino there filled with crippled old ladies, gouty dwarfs and such like creatures'.[70] In 1933, however, France voted to allow roulette, and Italy relaxed its attitude towards gambling. This, combined with the Depression, resulted in some rough years for the Casino. The financial crisis meant that in 1931–2 – for the first time – no shareholder's dividend had been paid. This happened again in 1935–6. The Casino was paying a hefty 73 per cent of its receipts to the principality. A new deal was signed in which the state covered the cost of Monaco's utilities and services, which, hitherto, had been paid by the Casino. There was also a shift in the relative presence of different nationalities. In the Sporting Club – ensuring exclusivity by limiting its membership to those who belonged to the principal clubs of the world – the 1935–6 season saw the English account for nearly 50 per cent of the admissions. By comparison, the American presence was slight, although they, along with the few remaining Russians, were generally the more adventurous gamblers.[71]

A novelty that attracted huge crowds to Monte Carlo was the Grand Prix Automobile de Monaco, which grew into one of the world's great contests. Known as the 'Race of a Thousand Corners',[72] with its challenging changes of elevation, the three-kilometre circuit

William Grover Williams in the lead during the first Monaco Grand Prix.

Poster for the second Monaco Grand
Prix

covered the streets of Monte Carlo and La Condamine. The first
race, in 1929, had been won by William Grover Williams, a British
driver who lived in the principality. Over the first decade, the average
top speed went from 86 to 107 kilometres per hour. In 1932,
tramway rails were removed and, in 1935, the road was resurfaced.
Italian drivers won three times and French and German twice. Five
of those winners drove Italian cars – Bugattis, Alfa Romeos and
Ferraris. Towards the end of the decade, Mussolini forbade Italian
drivers from competing in France and Monaco. Then, in 1939, the
international situation led to the cancelling of the Grand Prix.[73]

Under the joint direction of the mysterious and volatile Colonel
de Basil and René Blum, who had been producing plays in the
principality since the early 1920s, the Ballets Russes de Monte Carlo
rose from the ashes of Diaghilev's company with the handsome and
talented George Balanchine as principal choreographer. In 1932,
in their first season, they presented some old favourites such as
Les Sylphides and Petrushka, along with five new ballets including
Balanchine's Cotillon and Suite des Danses and Léonide Massine's
Jeux d'Enfants. Many of the dancers used the beach for practice,
and in 1933 Massine choreographed Beach. Like Le Train Bleu of

nearly a decade earlier, it was 'athletic, even acrobatic'. With sets by Raoul Dufy and evening gowns by Lanvin, it incorporated a tap dance and a foxtrot in what was really a tribute to the pursuits and style of the principality.[74]

Throughout the thirties, the company was plagued by strife.[75] Its name changed depending on the year and where it was playing. In London in 1934 it was billed as the 'Ballets Russes du Col. W. de Basil'. Claiming to be a Cossack colonel, de Basil had started a small dance troupe with his wife after the Great War. An accomplished publicist, he was also an autocrat who could not collaborate with René Blum. By 1936, they had fallen out and Blum created the short-lived Ballets de Monte Carlo with Fokine as choreographer and ballet master. After two seasons, this became the Ballet Russe de Monte-Carlo when Massine became artistic director and Serge Lifar its leading dancer.[76] The American choreographer Agnes de Mille later suggested that, during the nearly twenty-year existence of the Ballet Russe de Monte Carlo, Massine was overworked and 'a general air of preciosity, sterility and exhaustion pervaded the troupe'.[77]

Meanwhile, Colonel de Basil – with his enterprise and flair for publicity – guaranteed success for his company. He understood the impact that the so-called 'baby ballerinas' would make in both Europe and America. The collective name for the three dancers – discovered by Balanchine amongst the exiled Russian community in France – was not invented by de Basil but he knew how to exploit it. The dancers were remarkably young when Balanchine brought them to Monte Carlo in 1932. Irina Baranova and Tamara Toumanova were twelve and Tatiana Riabouchinska fourteen. Their considerable contribution to de Basil's highly publicized American tours in 1934–8 resulted in great success, and laid down important foundations for the development of ballet in America.[78]

The income of the Palais de la Méditerranée dropped 75 per cent between 1929 and 1933, the year that Hitler became chancellor of Germany and President Roosevelt launched the New Deal to combat the American Depression. In Nice, unemployment was spiralling.

On the streets of Paris, the bitter struggle between right and left played out in fatal clashes. On 6 February 1934, right-wing leagues converged on the Place de la Concorde to threaten the parliamentary government. When police fired on the armed crowd, sixteen people were killed and hundreds of demonstrators wounded. Two days later, the Nice branch of one of the protest groups, the Croix de Feu – a nationalist veterans' association – organized an 'impressive patriotic march' joined by royalists and fascists to honour those who fell in the Paris demonstration. The right-wing *L'Éclaireur de Nice* called it a good example of 'considered patriotism'.[79] In Paris, during the socialist and communist counter-demonstration on 9 February, a further nine people were killed. There were anti-fascist protests in Nice, Cannes, Grasse and Menton. In Nice, Virgile Barel – a shop owner and later a Communist member of the Assemblée Nationale – obtained 13.8 per cent of the vote in the municipal elections of 1935, the year that saw the creation of *Le Cri des Travailleurs des Alpes Maritimes*. Produced for the workers, the paper's circulation reached 17,000 the following year.

Unemployment hit two million in France as people considered extreme solutions offered by starkly opposed political systems. Yves Montand – who would emerge as a singer of considerable talent on the eve of the Second World War – grew up in a poor, communist Italian family in Marseille. His father was a member of an anti-fascist group, and Montand took part in the May Day march organized by the local communist paper, *Rouge Midi*, in 1935. He felt for the cause but didn't follow all his father's arguments. Already – aged fifteen or sixteen – he was obsessed by American cinema, especially Fred Astaire – whose tap-dancing he wished to emulate. The boy lived in the make-believe world of American films, thinking – at that time – that America was synonymous with justice.[80]

In May 1936, as Hitler reoccupied the Rhineland and there were stirrings of civil war in Spain, France elected its first Socialist prime minister – Léon Blum, brother of the man who administrated drama and ballet in Monte Carlo. Only the third time since the Revolution that the 'left' had come to power,[81] the workers reacted to victory with a general strike in May and June. That resulted in the socially significant Matignon Accords being voted swiftly and almost unanimously into law. They included a forty-hour working week, pay rises for the workers, the right to strike without retaliation, and two weeks' paid annual leave. The Under-Secretary of State for Sports and Leisure, Léo Lagrange, initiated cut-price rail tickets for people travelling over 200 kilometres and holidaying for at least five and no more than thirty-one days.[82] This made the Côte d'Azur accessible to people on paid holidays. The first such vacationers to arrive at Nice station to enjoy the *congés payés* were welcomed by a brass band and Virgile Barel – by then a Communist *député*. He believed that ordinary vacationers would play a role in the economic development of the region. But travelling to exotic places was not always a happy experience for poorer families, as they were not able to afford suitable clothing. If a modest family dared to visit the Riviera and attempted to kit themselves out in what they thought appropriate – 'white shorts, a *capeline* for the daughter, a very white shirt for papa and for mama a dress covered with flowers' – privileged visitors stared and sneered, 'What are they?' Many shops displayed signs refusing to admit and serve the new kind of visitors.[83] Meanwhile, the glorious countryside around Saint-Tropez was filled with *congés payés* campers. In August 1937, Colette 'saw thousands'.[84] La Treille Muscate became prey to the curious and the press. Then, as the international situation darkened, the south coast became vulnerable to an Italian invasion. Colette sold her house and headed north.

The limited budget of *congés payés* holidaymakers proved incapable of relieving the economic misery of the Riviera. In February 1936, *Le Cri des Travailleurs* published an article noting that Cimiez was dead – the Hôtel Regina was closed, while the Majestic, the Grand and other hotels had few guests even at the height of the season. Villas stood uninhabited or for sale – their owners living elsewhere.[85] Apart from unemployment, xenophobia and antisemitism were rife – Léon Blum was a high-profile target for abuse. In Antibes, there were signs nailed to trees vowing death to the Jews. In London, where many considered fascism a manner of containing communism, posters were seen proclaiming 'Better Hitler than Blum'.[86]

While people in Britain deliberated appeasement with Hitler, the country was distracted by a constitutional crisis that would play out, in part, on the Riviera – the singular romance between Edward, Prince of Wales and a divorced and remarried American, Mrs Wallis Simpson. The prince met her at a country house party in January 1931. At the time, he was the most eligible bachelor in the world – a man who enthusiastically embraced the fads and fancies of the rich in early thirties Britain. He was also in line to become emperor over a quarter of the world's population, and king of a depressed nation. The pressure of the pomp and circumstance and respect for the rules and traditions surrounding the crown fretted against the prince's sense of fun. As his interest and feeling for Wallis Simpson developed, he discarded mistresses and came to believe that she was the woman of his life. She was in no way outstanding, but she was loving and perhaps – with her head turned by the exceptional fate of 'Wallis in Wonderland' – not a little ambitious. But that ambition seemed to be focused on the man she loved, rather than on a personal desire to become queen. That option became clearly impossible, despite the couple's exploration of constitutional manoeuvres such as a morganatic marriage – whereby the king is crowned, but the woman he marries does not become queen. A procedure entertained in other European countries, it proved impossible under English law.

If Edward VII came to the Riviera for the winter season, the man born to be Edward VIII enjoyed summer in the south, where – as the thirties progressed – the romance developed between Wallis and her prince. It was in 1934, on holiday on Lord Moyne's yacht *Rosaura*, that Wallis claimed she fell in love with Edward. As their mutual dependence became manifest, the establishment were not unduly worried. Then, on 20 January 1936, George V died and Edward became king. Still married, Wallis Simpson remained Edward's habitual guest. Whether through sloppiness, self-indulgence or the distraction of the looming crisis, despatch boxes sent to the new king were left unlocked and Wallis came to be seen as a security risk.

The Foreign Office stopped sharing confidential reports. Intelligence had it that Wallis had been sharing low-level secrets – intentionally or unintentionally – with her friend Joachim von Ribbentrop at the German embassy in London. It was yet one more argument to rid the king of a woman who could never be a queen.[87]

An extended cruise in the eastern Mediterranean in August with Wallis and a handful of loyal friends was considered a mistake by the establishment, who rightly felt that, as the new king, Edward should be devoting more time to his job. Whenever Edward and his married lover went ashore, they were recognized and photos of them proved sensational in the American and continental press. When it became clear that Edward would not take the throne without the woman he loved at his side, and when in October 1936 that woman filed for divorce, the crisis came to a head. Lord Rothermere's *Daily Mail* and Lord Beaverbrook's *Daily Express* agreed to remain silent on the subject of Mrs Simpson's divorce and possible marriage to Edward. When the news broke, they positioned themselves – with the help of Winston Churchill – as a 'King's Party' to fight for Edward.

The lovers were separated during the proceedings, and it was agreed that they should not meet until the divorce became absolute in May 1937. For a man who could not bear to be parted from the woman he loved, this was – on top of the constitutional crisis – difficult to sustain. The king's friends and advisors thought it best for Mrs Simpson to leave the country. Sir Dudley Forwood, equerry to the Duke of Windsor from 1936 to 1939, felt that in England, she inspired 'intense loathing', adding that he feared 'she could have been murdered'.[88]

On 3 December, Wallis fled to France under the protection of Lord Perry Brownlow, Lord-in-Waiting to Edward VIII. She was to seek sanctuary at Lou Viei, the villa of her friends Herman and Kitty Rogers in Cannes. The journey was fraught, and when her car reached its destination – Wallis curled up on the floor, hiding under a rug – they found Lou Viei besieged by reporters. At the villa, Wallis had to stay indoors and keep away from the windows. Telephone operators – paid by the reporters – listened in on her

Wallis Simpson's statement from Cannes.

conversations. Lord Brownlow lodged a complaint, and the French Foreign Office sent two of its own operators down to Cannes to handle calls to and from the villa.[89]

Wallis begged the king not to abdicate. She prepared a short press statement declaring 'Mrs Simpson, throughout the last few weeks, has invariably wished to avoid any action or proposal which would hurt or damage His Majesty or the Throne. Today her attitude is unchanged, and she is willing, if such action would solve the problem, to withdraw from a situation that has been rendered both unhappy and untenable.'[90] When, at last, she ventured out in Cannes, the reaction of the English community resembled that of the erstwhile response to the arrival of the ex-convict and pederast Oscar Wilde. Edward's aunt, Queen Maud of Norway, heard that 'in Monte Carlo, all the English and French leave as soon as she walks in... I wish something bad would befall her!'[91] It was a sentiment expressed in the letters that arrived at Lou Viei each morning threatening physical violence and death.

Prime Minister Stanley Baldwin sent Mrs Simpson's lawyer by aeroplane to plead one last time for Wallis to withdraw. The abdication, however, was already underway. King Edward gave the government his irrevocable decision on 7 December. Under great strain, he telephoned Wallis to read a statement penned by his solicitor, Sir George Allen – 'The only conditions on which I can stay here are if I renounce you for all time. And this, of course, I will not do.'[92] On 10 December, Edward VIII signed the Instrument of Abdication, which became law the following day.

That night, Edward drove to Windsor to deliver the speech that Sir Walter Monckton and Winston Churchill had helped him to write. At Lou Viei, everyone – including the domestic staff – gathered round the wireless. Wallis was lying on the sofa with her hands shielding her tears.[93] Edward's message – loyal to both Crown and Wallis – was short and direct. 'You must believe me when I tell you that I have found it impossible to carry the heavy burden of responsibility and to discharge my duties as King as I would wish to do without the help and support of the woman I love.' Afterwards, Edward was driven to Portsmouth, from where the destroyer *Fury* took him to the continent. For the twenty weeks before her divorce from Ernest Simpson became absolute, Edward would remain at Schloss Enzesfeld in Austria while Mrs Simpson would stay on the Riviera until March 1937, when she moved to the Château de Candé in Touraine.

According to 'Fruity' Metcalfe, Edward was 'on the line for hours and hours every day to Cannes' – his phone bills for the period of separation were over £800. Metcalfe didn't think the talks went very well.[94] The Riviera telephone system was 'the worst in the world' – a claim, the *News* suggested, 'few would be inclined to dispute'.[95] Wallis certainly concurred – the 'circuit between Cannes and Austria was, in those days, hardly more than an acknowledgement of the possibilities of long-distance communication'.[96]

After the abdication, the reporters and photographers who had haunted Lou Viei became less present, and some measure of freedom was possible. Somerset Maugham invited Wallis for Christmas. She saw Sybil Colefax and visited Daisy Fellowes at her Cap Martin

villa, Les Zoraides. Wallis was becoming a member of Riviera society
– a role she would play, on and off, for years. The threatening letters
kept arriving. As she put it, 'there can be few expletives applicable to
my sex that were missing from my morning tray'. Her host, Herman
Rogers, kept a loaded pistol on his bedside table.[97]

Troubles for the couple were hardly over. There were tense
negotiations over finances and the question of what to call Edward,
let alone the woman he had chosen. He was pleased by the title
'Duke of Windsor', but burst out crying on Dudley Forwood's
shoulder when he found that Wallis was not to be accorded 'HRH'.[98]
There was also the matter of returning to England and finding a
suitable way for the duke to serve his country. These deliberations
dragged on until and beyond the couple's reunion and marriage at
the Château de Candé on 3 June 1937. It was a modest affair. Cecil
Beaton was the official photographer but not a single member of
the royal family attended the wedding. George VI wrote to inform
Edward that 'it would be harmful to the monarchy'. Thus began
an emotional, professional and physical exile. Edward, who came
from a cold home, became devoted to – if not obsessed by – the
woman with whom he found true love. The Aga Khan considered
the romance between the duke and Wallis to be 'one of the very
great love stories of all time'.[99] Elsa Maxwell put it 'way ahead of
Romeo and Juliet'.[100] While Edward was often deeply homesick
and bewildered by a life that had robbed him of the duties for
which he had been prepared, his need and love for Wallis never
diminished. The complexity and totality of the love was caught by
Wallis's hairdresser in Paris. He claimed that Edward remained 'an
adolescent' and found in her a 'mother, nurse and wife'.[101]

Certainly, Edward's judgement was not always sound. As a man
born to be king, he did not understand his suddenly diminished
importance. An ill-advised visit to Hitler's Germany took place
in October 1937. The duke, while showing a lively interest in the
Nazi experiment, made some critical remarks during his meeting
with Hitler which were deliberately mistranslated. Speaking good
German, the duke was aware of the chicanery. He advanced
arguments against war, which were dismissed, and the duke left in

distress. The papers – particularly the Nazi press – had a field day, and rumours started to circulate that there were political reasons for the British government's desire to rid the country of a dubious king. Yet the British political class of the day were hardly zealous in their opposition to Hitler. Churchill, one of the few alarmed by Nazi Germany, remained a steadfast friend to the duke.[102]

After months of financial wrangling, in the early weeks of 1938 the Windsors took out leases on two large properties – the Château de la Maye in Versailles, and the Château de la Croë in twelve acres of woodland fronting the sea on Cap d'Antibes. At first, they took a two-year lease, because they did not intend to stay away from England long. That summer was taken up with redecorating La Croë, and they stayed at the nearby Hôtel du Cap-Eden-Roc to escape the disorder when an 'avalanche' of furniture arrived from England.[103] Johnny Lucinge, the Riviera socialite and husband to 'bright young thing' Baba d'Erlanger, observed that Wallis 'was far from being beautiful'. She had particularly ugly hands – but she possessed 'true elegance' and had an eye for detail. He thought her more 'bourgeoise than royal', a 'wise-cracker' with 'a will of iron'. As for 'the Dook' – as Wallis called him – Lucinge suggested that he 'didn't particularly like France and never made any effort to understand it or to master the language'.[104] He enjoyed the fact that it was close to England, and that English friends frequently visited.

Although the Aga Khan found Edward serious 'even in the midst of flippant people',[105] the duke had a good sense of humour and a great deal of energy. The couple appeared happy on the Riviera, dining at the Hôtel de Paris in Monte Carlo and receiving and being received by many of the people they had enjoyed in London.[106] But Edward's diminished status brought unforeseen nuisances. He was jostled by eager diners and gamblers at the Palm Beach Casino in Cannes.[107] When the royal couple joined Winston Churchill for dinner at Maxine Elliott's, Churchill later observed, in a letter to his wife, that the duke was 'bright and charming' but now, no longer king, 'he had to fight for his place in the conversation like other people'.[108]

❖

While the Duke and Duchess of Windsor were invited to see Germany, much of its intelligentsia fled and settled in Sanary. The German colony had been developing since the late 1920s, when Bertolt Brecht and Kurt Weill spent time there, working on *The Threepenny Opera*. Thomas Mann's son, Klaus – a homosexual, drug-taking prodigy who, by the age of nineteen, had published a lesbian play, a homosexual novel and a book of poems – enjoyed Sanary when visiting Jean Cocteau at Toulon with his sister Erica. Klaus Mann detested the Nazis, and knew that if he remained in Germany, they would imprison or kill him. The brother of Thomas, Heinrich Mann, was also hounded by the Nazi press after the successful 1930 film adaptation of his novel *Professor Unrat: The Blue Angel* with Marlene Dietrich and Emil Jannings. Thomas Mann spent the summer of 1933 in Sanary, then visited several more times before moving to America. Optimistic after the execution of Ernst Röhm in July 1934, many Jewish intellectuals thought Nazism would implode and they would be able to return to Germany. In the event, as Hitler consolidated his position, over thirty German and Austrian writers and their families fled to Sanary.[109] As Sybille Bedford observed, the locals pocketed rents and tips and called them 'Boches, Jews, war-mongers and spies'.[110]

Aldous Huxley – another writer whose lungs consigned him to warm climates – bought a villa in Sanary in 1930, which a decorator mistakenly named 'Villa Huley' when he painted the address in bright green letters on the gate. The misnamed villa stood above the Plage de la Gorguette on the promontory between Bandol and Sanary. The sales of *Point Counter Point* were so good that Huxley and his wife not only bought the house in which they lived between 1930 and 1937, but also purchased a custom-built Bugatti which Maria Huxley drove like a maniac.[111] Speed was, Huxley observed, the only entirely novel sensation of his age.[112]

Huxley found the Germans 'rather a dismal crew'. When the American writer William Seabrook threw a drink-fuelled garden party, the Huxleys dressed informally and the host was stripped to the waist, while Heinrich Mann arrived in a starched collar and black coat. In fact, the Germans divided into two groups.

One formed round Thomas Mann, hallowing high culture with organized readings from *Joseph and His Brothers*, which Mann was writing at the time.[113] The other group formed around Lion Feuchtwanger, a lively raconteur who amused himself by totalling the syntactical errors in Hitler's *Mein Kampf*.[114] This group included communists such as Ernst Toller, journalists Egon Kisch and Arthur Koestler, and a high-level Communist International operative, Otto Katz.

Katz visited Feuchtwanger on holiday from running intrigues in the Spanish Civil War. The socialist struggle on behalf of the Republicans countered the pro-Franco fascist intervention which many saw as a dry run for the Second World War. Italian troops were in Spain. German Heinkels and Junker bombers – 150 aircraft and 5,600 men – formed the Condor Legion under Colonel Wolfram von Richthofen, cousin of the First World War flying ace. The struggle of the anti-fascists in the Spanish Civil War promised what George Orwell called in *Homage to Catalonia* the 'thrill of hope'. But by 1937, Otto Katz – with his slew of aliases – was playing a complicated game. In his propaganda work, he presented the Spanish conflict as the essential cause for concerned fellow travellers. Under the alias 'Rudolph Breda', he mesmerized the elite of Hollywood with his anti-Nazi escapades and laid the foundations for the Hollywood Anti-Nazi League. Wearing a trench coat, Katz/Breda moved around Tinseltown with a cigarette dangling from the corner of his mouth – Humphrey Bogart before the fact. He was the star attraction at a magnificent Hollywood dinner for the relief of the victims of Nazism, co-hosted by Dorothy Parker and Donald Ogden Stewart. Katz/Breda slowly stood up and surveyed the glittering diners, who were unusually quiet for actors. His performance – a mix of fact and fiction – was spellbinding, and it bequeathed a legend. Breda was not only a star turn in Hollywood, he also became a template – if not an archetype – for movie writers. He would figure as the central character, Muller, in Lillian Hellman's Oscar-winning *Watch on the Rhine*. He stood behind heroes such as Victor Laszlo in *Casablanca*. Like Katz, Laszlo was a Czech who took his struggle to Paris and his anti-fascist message to the world.

If Muller represented the quiet, patient, persistent Otto Katz, Victor Lazlo was Rudolph Breda superstar.

In Spain, overseeing propaganda, Katz brought those acrimonious friends from their Villa America days – Ernest Hemingway and John Dos Passos – to work with the communist filmmaker Joris Ivens. The resulting documentary, *The Spanish Earth*, was powerful and moving. Katz also lured volunteers to the International Brigades, which were a useful arena from which to recruit Soviet agents and a convenient context in which to eliminate Trotskyists and other undesirables. Some witnesses have claimed that Katz selected the victims of assassination; others, that he himself was the executioner. Hardly surprising that when he met Katz in Sanary, the philosopher Ludwig Marcuse called him a 'Prince of Darkness', a 'devilish string-puller' behind multiple intrigues.[115]

One of the most iconic films of the twentieth century came about after two Americans – Murray Burnett and his wife Joan Alison – came to the Riviera to relax. They visited a nightclub outside Nice, where a black pianist from Chicago called Rick was playing. The couple were resting after helping beleaguered Jews smuggle assets out of Nazi-occupied Austria. The nightclub and the frightening international outlook prompted a play called *Everybody Comes to Rick's*. That play was turned into a film called *Casablanca*, with its hero Victor Laszlo.

Sanary also played host to a German who was by no means a refugee from Hitler's Germany. Baron Hans Günther von Dincklage arrived there with his wife, the half-sister of Huxley's biographer Sybille Bedford. Dincklage was working in the German embassy in Paris and beginning to build intelligence networks supplying Berlin with information about German Jewish refugees in France. Sanary was obviously important. Posing as a tennis coach, Dincklage tried to get Lion Feuchtwanger's wife, Marta, to be a partner.[116] When Dincklage became involved with Coco Chanel, their association would later fuel questions about whether or not, and to what degree, the designer collaborated with the occupying Nazis during the Second World War.

The painter Moïse Kisling settled in Sanary in the 1920s. Today, much of his output appears derivative, but his contemporaries held him in high esteem. The Polish-born artist worked in Montparnasse before the First World War, in which he was badly wounded. From 1915, he convalesced in Saint-Tropez until the end of the war, when he returned to Paris. In Sanary, the Kislings enjoyed spending time with the Huxleys – who, when they left for America in 1937, gave Maria's red Bugatti to the painter.[117] Towns from Marseilles to Menton were popular with a widening range of artists. The German Max Beckman worked all along the coast in the 1930s. Wassily Kandinsky visited Les Sablettes, between Sanary and Toulon, in 1933. Throughout the remainder of the thirties, this great painter and pioneer of abstraction visited different places along the Riviera – La Napoule in 1935, Cap Ferrat in 1938, and La Croix-Valmer on the Côte des Maures near Saint-Tropez in 1939. During these years, Kandinsky sometimes added sand to texture the colours in his canvases.[118]

Less successful or lazy artists were targeted – along with a decidedly insalubrious Riviera – by Cyril Connolly in his 1936 novel *The Rock Pool*. The novel is set in the fictitious Trou-sur-Mer – 'Pits-on-Sea' – which before the plunge of the pound and the dollar was, the author tells us, an artists' colony worthy of the name 'Montparnasse by the Sea'. By the mid-thirties, however, it has been reduced to 'a lot of bums'. In the novel, Connolly, who lived at Six-Fours near Sanary, maps out the Riviera in terms of the successful writers who settled there: 'All along the coast from Huxley Point and Castle Wharton to Cape Maugham... anyone who could hold a pen in St. Tropez, Arlen in Cannes, and beyond Monte Carlo and the Oppenheim country.' But it is the tawdry contemporary scene and the rapacious history of the region that preoccupies the protagonist, Naylor. Visiting Juan-les-Pins, he remarks on 'the casino with its false smartness'. He sits in a café where 'tarts, gigolos and motor-car salesmen seemed the only public'. From Antibes, he contemplates the Mediterranean and its history – 'the dinginess, the corruption of that tainted inland sea... how many civilizations had staled on that bright promontory! Sterile Phoenicians, commercial-minded Greeks, destructive Arabs, Catalans, Genoese, hysterical Russians, decayed English, drunken Americans... everything that was vulgar, acquisitive, piratical and decadent in capitalism had united there, crooks, gigolos, gold-diggers and captains of industry through 25 centuries had sprayed their cupidity and bad taste over it... the tideless cloaca of the ancient world.' Naylor can see no evidence of human progress, and wonders if he is 'on the wrong side of Eden'. A glimpse of an over-exploited Juan-les-Pins, 'where the fetid waves of sunburn oil lapped tidelessly on the sand', is developed in a later book, *The Unquiet Grave*, in which Connolly gives a potent image of a pleasure ground when war is in the air.[119] Spotting an edition of a right-wing Nice newspaper, he writes, '*Éclaireur de Nice*: head-lines about the Spanish war soaked in sun-bathing oil' – paradise threatened by commercialism and conflict.[120]

France was surrounded by three right-wing states – Italy, Germany and Spain. Yet, in early 1938, the spirits of the tourist industry were buoyant. The *Riviera News* observed that 'Monte Carlo during the holiday season has been a veritable miniature *Debrett* and *Who's Who* as Britons have been so much in the majority'.[121] At the end of January, Raoul Gunsbourg presented Wagner's *Ring* and *Tristan und Isolde* at the Monte Carlo Opera, conducted by the orchestral leader from Bayreuth. The reviewer noticed a few empty seats, but thought that had more to do with operas which might 'not appeal to the light-hearted visitors' than any nascent anti-German sentiment.[122] A year later, as Nazism posed an increasing threat to peace, the *Riviera News* oddly ran a series from late January 1939 entitled 'News from Germany', with features on 'German Resorts' and German hospitality.

The Christmas season of 1937–8 saw famous people such as the actor Charles Laughton and the songwriter Irving Berlin staying at the Hôtel Bristol in Beaulieu. On New Year's Eve at the Sporting Club, the Duke and Duchess of Windsor – she 'in a black tulle dress with motifs in red sequins that toned with her ruby and diamond necklace and earrings' – were the guests of Reginald and Daisy Fellowes.[123] Fashion writers often called Daisy Fellowes 'the best-dressed woman in the world' – an accolade Elsa Maxwell attributed to flair rather than money.[124] Lady Diana Cooper – whose husband had a dalliance with Daisy – rather found her 'the very picture of fashionable depravity'.[125] Born Marguerite Séverine Philippine Decazes de Glücksberg, Daisy – after her mother's suicide – was raised by Winnaretta Singer, Princesse de Polignac. Cecil Beaton thought Daisy a bully – 'spoilt, capricious and even wicked'.[126] He also lauded her 'studied simplicity', a strange epithet for someone who wore extravagant hats – one shaped like a large high-heeled shoe – and who dressed in Schiaparelli pink, that designer's surrealist 'Lobster Dress', and a monkey fur coat embroidered with gold. Daisy furnished her villa, Les Zoraides, with the same outrageous taste with which she dressed – there were glitter-balls filling the stairwell and carpets of loud leopard print.[127]

In January 1938, Winston Churchill – first cousin of Daisy's second husband Reginald Fellowes – was staying at Maxine Elliott's. The Duke and Duchess of Windsor were dinner guests. Churchill wrote to Clemmie on 10 January, 'The Ws are very pathetic, but also very happy. She made an excellent impression on me, and it looks as if it would be a most happy marriage.'[128] A year later, Churchill was back at the Château de l'Horizon, where the Windsors were again invited for dinner and there was much discussion beforehand as to whether or not to curtsy to the duchess. A few days later, it was the Windsors turn to receive. Churchill wrote to his wife, 'Everything extremely well done and dignified. Red liveries, and the little man himself dressed up to the nines in the Balmoral tartan with dagger and jabot etc. When you think you could hardly get him to put on a black coat and short tie when he was Prince of Wales, one sees the change in the point of view.'[129] Adroitly, Churchill observed that the man who flouted royal protocol missed it bitterly. The duke's face appeared pinched. The worried frown revealed the anxiety of failing in his responsibility. In the mid-1950s, Edward R. Murrow – in a television series that must have been excruciating to that powerful journalist – would visit the Windsors' apartment in New York. As the duchess flounces and flutters, Edward appears strained – if not mortified.

The year between Churchill's January visits to the Château de l'Horizon was one of growing international peril. In March 1938, German troops crossed the Austrian border, and entered Vienna. Hitler incorporated Austria into Germany in the Anschluss. A month earlier, Foreign Secretary Anthony Eden had resigned over Prime Minister Chamberlain's friendliness towards a clearly belligerent Italy. At the end of September, Germany, Italy, France and Britain signed the Munich Agreement, which forced the Czechoslovak Republic to cede the strategically important Sudetenland to Germany. Attempting to appease and avoid a European war, Neville Chamberlain famously and naively claimed that he returned from Germany with 'peace for our time'. Six months later, Hitler violated the agreement and occupied Czechoslovakia.

The legendary Janet Flanner, Paris correspondent of the *New Yorker*, ominously reflected on the characteristics of the political dilemma facing the world: 'The functional speed of democracies is still that of the vehicles that bore the first argumentative democrats around liberty-loving lands. Fascism dates from the first third of the twentieth century. Like all startling political innovations, it reflects its period, and thus takes its tempo from the airplane.'[130] She was shrewd. In April 1939, Hermann Göring – supposedly holidaying in San Remo – was observed discreetly watching the traditional military parade in Nice. During the summer, there were rumours of spies being landed on Cap Ferrat and at Cap Martin. In early August, Simone de Beauvoir and Jean-Paul Sartre were holidaying along the coast. On the Île de Porquerolles they found no restaurant open, so they picnicked on grapes, wine and bread. By contrast, when Sartre was received by the writer and Popular Front activist André Malraux in a sumptuous villa at Saint-Jean-Cap-Ferrat, his host gave him a lunch of Chicken Maryland and confided that he 'was relying on Russian tanks and American planes to win the war'.[131] From the terrace of her house, Elsa Maxwell watched all the lights dim in Cannes, Nice and Juan-les-Pins – 'Hitler was massing panzer divisions and planes on the Polish border... the

Government ordered a black-out in anticipation of an air-raid'.[132] During that last month of peace, Picasso painted *Night Fishing at Antibes* – his largest canvas since his response to the fascist bombing of the Spanish town of Guernica. In the painting, the simple joys of Mediterranean life appeared ghosted and menaced, as if the painter anticipated the imminent collapse of what he called 'the world of yesterday'.

On 1 September 1939, Hitler invaded Poland. Two days later, France and Great Britain responded. Just before noon on 3 September, the telephone rang at La Croë. The Duke of Windsor was expecting to hear directly from his brother, King George VI, but it was the British ambassador in Paris. After the call, Edward walked to the edge of their swimming pool, and calmly told Wallis, 'Great Britain has just declared war on Germany, and I am afraid in the end this may open the way for world Communism.' He then dived into the water.[133]

Noël Coward's plays *Present Laughter* and *This Happy Breed* were due to open in Manchester on 11 September. During the last week of August, in the face of the appalling international situation, he went with his two leading ladies, Leonora Corbett and Joyce Carey, to Antibes to sunbathe and learn lines. Among the friends they visited were Somerset Maugham, Marlene Dietrich and Barry Dierks. There were, Coward remembered, 'picnics on the islands with *langoustes* cooked in garlic, and crisp French bread and vin rosé; motor trips to Nice and Monte Carlo and St. Tropez'. Before leaving for England, Coward went to visit Maxine Elliott, who was very ill. Coward knew he would not see her again. As his speedboat pulled away from the Château de l'Horizon, he caught a glimpse of Maxine leaning against one of the supports of her balcony, waving a white handkerchief.[134]

10

Refugees and Resistance
1939–45

The Riviera – where people go to relax and turn a blind eye – was chosen for an early demonstration of resistance to fascism. As Mussolini's Venice Film Festival had become a showcase for his political vision, the French wanted to counter-attack. Several locations were proposed for its first film festival in 1939, but Cannes was chosen – a jewel on a glittering coast which had much to offer illustrious visitors. Hotel owners – in a bid to extend their summer season – pressed for September as the ideal month. MGM chartered a 'steamship of stars' to carry its top names to Cannes – Gary Cooper, Douglas Fairbanks and Mae West among them.[1] Then France declared war. The festival was hastily rescheduled for Christmas. Then February 1940. Then Easter. But conditions only got worse.

In the summer months before the aborted festival, people returning in the dead of night from clubs and parties noticed troops on the move. In August, all available gas masks were distributed. The post functioned normally, but telephone lines were frequently blocked. Most visitors left before Britain declared war, yet nearly 2,000 British residents remained. Near the railway station in Monte Carlo, Baroness Orczy saw 'a crowd of close on a thousand men and women... pushing and jostling outside the door of the booking office'. Given her husband's age and ill-health, she hoped that they would be able to sit out the war at the Villa Bijou. Money should not have troubled the affluent author of the highly successful *Scarlet Pimpernel*, but Orczy's savings were blocked in English banks.[2] The baroness was relieved that British residents in the principality were placed under the protection of the neutral Monégasque government, which advanced them £10 a month to help meet the privations of war. This was a gesture – many were obliged to sell possessions in order to survive.[3]

British nurse Elsie Gladman had come to work at the Sunny Bank Hospital in Cannes in 1936. It was a small establishment operated by a matron and eight nurses. Their patients – residents and tourists – paid what they could. The visiting French physicians gave their services free when the need arose. Some patients were wealthy and would be sent home on the Blue Train, to which – at great cost – an 'invalid coach' could be hitched. But after the outbreak of war, that service ended.[4] The Blue Train was replaced by ordinary carriages – always packed, often full of soldiers, and travelling very slowly from lack of coal or in case of possible sabotage. Meanwhile, the Blue Train stood idle in a station in the Dordogne, except for one carriage that was taken to Limoges, where it was operated as a luxury brothel.[5]

Apart from her work at Sunny Bank, Gladman was active in the community. On one occasion, she was called to Elsa Maxwell's villa with a high colonic wash-out apparatus. Eight guests had spent their weekend chomping through hampers sent from Fortnum & Mason. Gladman later recalled that she was busy with her device for two days. When war broke out, the British consul advised her to leave. She complied, but returned in January 1940 to find the English community closing their villas and departing.[6]

The German exiles in Sanary were under threat. Lion Feuchtwanger was greatly attached to the 'warm intimacy' of the fishing village, but in a small town, two dozen aliens became the focus of rumour and gossip. When his secretary used her typewriter at night, she was suspected of sending messages to the Nazis. When his wife gave lifts to soldiers, she was held to be prising information from them. The German intellectuals were first forced to register as 'enemy aliens', then rounded up by the French authorities and incarcerated in a huge, abandoned brickworks near Aix-en-Provence. Feuchtwanger and his wife eventually escaped over the Pyrenees on foot to Spain, Portugal, and thence to the United States.[7]

Relief agencies in Marseille fought to secure passages for political refugees, artists and writers under threat of Nazi persecution. Varian Fry, head of the Emergency Rescue Committee, arrived in France with a priority list compiled by Albert H. Barr Jr, the first director of the Museum of Modern Art in New York. Moïse Kisling left Sanary for the US. Heinrich Mann, André Breton and Max Ernst were given passages to America. Marc Chagall and his wife were arrested in Marseille but were released under pressure.[8] Others, like the abstract artists Jean Arp, Sophie Taeuber and Sonia Delaunay, stayed, lying low in Grasse until the end of 1942, when they fled to Switzerland.[9] Charles Camoin narrowly avoided arrest by an Italian patrol while painting spring blossoms in Saint-Tropez – photographing or drawing the coast was prohibited.[10] Henri Matisse and Pierre Bonnard stayed on the Côte d'Azur and worked from home.

The legal separation from his wife, Amélie, caused Matisse great distress, and a hernia – problematic since childhood – flared up in May 1940. Remaining untreated for seven months, a complicating tumour necessitated a colostomy – performed in two stages and compounded by a near-fatal blood clot. Aged seventy-one, Matisse recovered slowly, and was obliged to find an alternative to painting. Working from bed or in a wheelchair, he began to play with colourful cut-outs and to draw with a paintbrush bound to the end of a long bamboo stick. In September 1941, Monique Bourgeois arrived to nurse him. She too had been through a series of crises. A refugee from Metz, her father dead and mother ill, she was recovering from tuberculosis when she came to care for the painter. Slowly, they both grew stronger. Matisse became well enough to cope with the constraints of wartime winter transport and visited Pierre Bonnard in Le Cannet, taking him paint and canvas. At length, Monique announced that she was taking the veil and – after her novitiate – would return to the Dominican nuns in Vence where she had convalesced. After Matisse settled in that town in 1943, she would re-enter the painter's life as Soeur Jacques-Marie, and become midwife to one of the greatest manifestations of religious art in the twentieth century.[11]

French writers such as André Gide settled in the south to avoid the restrictions and privations of life in the north. But it became increasingly clear that, in this war, the Côte d'Azur would be directly involved. Right-wing extremists prevented Gide from giving a lecture at a local university in May 1941. They also sought to destroy evidence of the English and American presence on the Riviera. Signs for streets such as George V, Quai des États-Unis and rue d'Angleterre were torn down. In March 1942, a statue of Queen Victoria was decapitated.[12] Baroness Orczy noted that the 'hatred of the British was fanned' by the local press – 'dirty rags all under German control'. In August 1940, *L'Éclaireur de Nice* declared that 'French instinct was never in favour of an alliance with England', following its claim with a litany of anti-British abuse.[13] There were right-wing conferences all along the Côte d'Azur, with titles such as 'England Will Pay' and 'Reconciliation between France and Germany'. As it had been in certain quarters in England in the 1930s, Nazism was perceived by many as a bastion against communism, and films such as *Against Bolshevism* drew huge crowds to the Majestic and Riviera cinemas in Cannes.[14]

Somerset Maugham watched as Cap Ferrat became deserted. Anti-aircraft guns and batteries were camouflaged among the trees. The peninsula was only a few miles from the Italian border, and British inhabitants realized that they were vulnerable in the event of an Italian invasion. From Maugham's staff of thirteen at the Villa Mauresque, only two remained – the French were conscripted and the Italians had gone home. English newspapers disappeared. There were blackouts. In order to move around, permits – which could take up to three days to obtain – were required.[15] Rapidly, luxury and ease became suffering and scarcity.

It was still possible to escape to England via Spain and Portugal, but the visa was expensive and the trip could take as long as ten weeks. For the remaining British residents, there was the promise of evacuation by sea. Converging on Cannes to await the British cruiser that was supposed to arrive, they found the *Ashcrest* and the *Saltersgate* – two coal boats – waiting in its place. One elderly gentleman from Sunny Bank got on and immediately got off. The nurses at the hospital were offered places but declined – colliers would offer impossible conditions for their patients.[16] Each boat – capable of transporting 400 people – had only one toilet. The Oppenheims decided against the voyage. The bad-tempered shipping magnate Lord Furness was gravely ill, and his third wife got him to the Carlton to await the cruiser. When he saw what the consul had managed to procure, he screamed, 'That's not a ship, that is a fucking cargo boat.'[17] Furness returned to Cap Ferrat, where his wife nursed him until his death four months later.

Maugham tried to persuade people to leave. Asked about the chances of reaching their destination, his reply was candid: '50/50'. Men were allocated the hold – where, on the *Ashcrest*, coal dust lay ankle-deep. Women and children packed together on deck. There was only coal-stained water with which to wash, and a luxury such as changing clothes was next to impossible. The butler of Maugham's neighbour was on-board. Such was the tenor of the age that he visited Maugham with a cup of tea at dawn, brushed down his grimy clothes, and brought a short-lived shine to his shoes.[18]

The colliers departed under French escort, which they lost when they put into port near the Spanish border with engine trouble. After that, their captains set a zigzag course to Gibraltar, where all passengers were vetted by the British authorities. With German submarines operating in the vicinity, the passage to England meandered. There were no lifejackets or rafts. A precautionary blackout against attack made the nights seem long.[19] The captain of the *Saltersgate* asked Maugham to divert the passengers by telling stories. The writer sat on the deck under the stars and imagined himself a storyteller out of the *One Thousand and One Nights*.[20] The voyage – which both colliers survived – took twenty days. As the *Ashcrest* chugged towards Liverpool docks, the Duke of Windsor's piper stood in the bow playing them into port.[21]

In late May 1940, the Duke and Duchess of Windsor returned to La Croë from Paris, where Edward had been attached to the British military mission. On 10 June – the day that Paris was abandoned to the Nazis – Italy declared war on England. The Windsors were entertaining the singer Maurice Chevalier when the declaration was broadcast, and their guest left in the middle of lunch to join his wife, the Jewish cabaret artist Nita Raya, at their home in La Bocca.[22] A few days later, the duke and duchess would be forced to leave. A convoy of four cars set off for Madrid. While not an ally of Hitler, Spain under General Franco was friendly towards the Axis powers, and Nazi agents could easily operate. After the couple arrived, a German spy was sent to the Ritz to warn the duke that the British secret service was out to assassinate him. Berlin was aware of Edward's sadness over the way he had been treated, and they were positioning to snatch him – the duke, Hitler had concluded, would prove a sympathetic puppet-king on England's throne after the war. The Windsors went on to Portugal where – to terrify Edward into asking for protection – Nazi thugs attacked their house. The new prime minister, Winston Churchill, was most anxious and drew up plans for the couple to sail from Lisbon on the American – and therefore neutral – SS *Excalibur* bound for the Bahamas. There, Edward would take up the safe and distant role of governor.[23]

In May 1940, the British consul in Menton moved into his office to sleep by his telephone and await the inevitable instruction to evacuate. It came a few weeks later, when Maréchal Pétain's French government signed an armistice with the Nazis. The consul burned archives and codes and fled to Nice.[24] On 21 June 1940, the Italians began their assault on Menton. This brief Battle of the Alps ended a few days later, when Italy also signed an armistice with France. The very English resort of Menton reverted to its Italian origins. Changes to names and fixtures were greater than anywhere else along the Italian-occupied Riviera. Road signs and shop names became Italian. The town hall – the Mairie – became the Palazzo del Comune. Italian letterboxes were installed throughout the town, as Menton became a showcase for fascist Italy. There was even an attempt to restart the tourist industry in early 1942, by refurbishing hotels in a manner that would attract holidaying Italians. At first, there was little sign of interest, but by the summer, visitors started

Menton: Fascist marches included the children of French residents and Italian occupiers.

to arrive. Cultural links were forged. A troupe from La Scala Milan was invited, and there were fascist marches that included the children of French residents and of Italian occupiers.[25]

With so many Italians or people of mixed descent living along the coast, the first occupation from June 1940 to September 1943 sometimes felt like having family to stay – not necessarily peaceful but with moments of warmth. Less than a hundred years earlier, the region had been part of the Kingdom of Sardinia, and Johnny Lucinge noted that the 'mixture of blood and cultural ties' made the Italian occupation 'seem quite gentle, almost invisible'.[26] Permitting sea-bathing between eight in the morning and nine at night during the summer of 1943, the Italians filled the Baie des Anges with grateful swimmers. Soldiers – young and far from home – mixed with the locals at dances, concerts and cinemas. Girls seemed more inclined to flirt with the Italians than with their Nazi successors. Elsie Gladman recalled that the Italians 'strutted about in their plumed headgear' but 'seemed more interested in contacting relatives, and showing off, than becoming a serious occupying force'.[27]

  Entering neutral Monte Carlo, troops were hailed by expatriate Italians lining the streets. Advised by his unpopular and pro-fascist Minister of State, Émile Roblôt, Prince Louis II calculated that – if the Axis powers prevailed – it would be prudent to ally himself with France's Vichy government. Despite the tolerant attitude taken by the Italians towards the Jews, the principality's long-serving opera director, Raoul Gunsbourg, was warned that he should go into hiding. With the help of the Résistance, he escaped into Switzerland.[28]

There were mass gatherings of French anti-Jewish groups in towns along the coast. Anyone with two Jewish grandparents was deemed Jewish, and barred from holding public office and from working in the cinema, theatre or the press. These professional constraints were extended, in June 1941, to a prohibition on work in trade, industry and the economy. A month later, further laws aimed to destroy all 'Jewish influence in the national economy'.[29] Yet, in the spring of 1941, Cannes was thriving as Jews from the north arrived.[30] Among the town's permanent or seasonal residents were many rich and notable Jews including the Rothschilds, the Lévitans, the German exile Baronne Friedländer-Fuld, and Reynaldo Hahn, the Belle Époque composer.[31] An oft-repeated joke was that there were sufficient Jewish residents in Cannes to justify renaming it 'Kahn'. The Casino in Monte Carlo – shut after French conscription reduced its staff – reopened for the wealthy refugees who fled south. In 1941–2, the SBM made great profits.[32] In Nice, the Palais de la Méditerranée had its best year.[33]

If collaborators had been swift to manifest their enthusiasm for Vichy, the Résistance was slow to organize. During 1940, there were calls for clandestine action, and the first groups were formed in the winter of 1941.[34] In the early days, their activity consisted of posting handbills denouncing Vichy, printing tracts and publishing underground newspapers throughout the region. In the southern, unoccupied zone, there were fewer wireless sets than in the north, but for those wedged between Mussolini and the pro-German Vichy government, gathering around the wireless to listen to the BBC was a way of finding out what was going on. The corporation's avowed aim was to 'break through the totalitarian darkness' with news bulletins and 'objective, analytical and informative talks'. Above all, from 1940, the BBC fostered the 'motivation' for resistance and created 'a fraternity among listeners'. Unlike the Nazi broadcasts, there was no sensational and shrill propaganda, no instructions or interdictions. The Vichy-imposed ban in October 1941 only testified to the efficacy of the BBC.[35] People continued to tune in illegally, and broadcasts became a useful way of sending information to those in occupied territory. The composer Elizabeth Poston even coded messages in her music which was broadcast from London.

As the resistance networks were consolidated in 1942, their tactics became more aggressive. They threatened and bombed the businesses of collaborators, sabotaged the infrastructure, and helped infiltrate British agents. Peter Churchill was landed on the south coast in January 1942. After three weeks of immersion in subversive activity – arms training, signalling, bridge demolition – the volunteers from the French Section of the War Office who appeared capable and courageous were selected for advanced training. Those not eliminated after that were given a parachute course, and told – time and time again – 'the less you know the better'.[36]

On his first mission to southern France, Churchill – code-named 'Michel' – arrived from neutral Spain via submarine. As it surfaced 800 metres from the shore, the headlights from isolated cars on the coastal road west of La Napoule dazzled the agent as he leapt into his kayak and attempted to negotiate the swell. Reaching shore east of his target, he slit the kayak and pushed it into the water. Fearing a curfew, Michel planned to stop and rest for the night just short of Théoule. It was too cold. Under the cover of a furious hailstorm, he walked through the town. Then, to avoid possible patrols around Cannes aerodrome, Michel chose a devious route. Guards at a bridge, swaddled and stamping to keep themselves warm, showed no interest. Passing through Cannes in the early morning, Michel noticed endless food queues forming. Snow had turned to sleet and – taking the coast road – he plodded on towards Antibes. He turned off to make for La Californie, where he found his first contact and rested until mid-afternoon. Returning to Antibes, Michel checked into a hotel, went for a drink, and devoured a local paper full of German propaganda. The next morning, his coffee was so vile 'he took his revenge by shaving in it'. He made contact

with Baron d'Astier de La Vigerie – code-named 'Bernard' – head
of the Lyon group Libération-Sud.[37] There were, by then, many
groups operating in the Alpes-Maritimes gathering information on
the occupying troops and the coastal defences, and infiltrating and
exfiltrating agents – twenty-six during 1942, fifteen of them British.
French networks like Ajax, Jove, Combat, Phalanx, Tartane and
Coty were complemented by British ones – Attorney, Donkeyman,
Jockey, Urchin; they smuggled messages to London and sprung
captured pilots from jail.[38]

The purpose of Michel's mission was to fund resistance groups.
He gave his contact 450,000 francs, and then proceeded to Marseille
where the port's cosmopolitan population meant the Gestapo was
everywhere. Nevertheless, Michel delivered the money to enable a
local network to prepare a jailbreak, and – before he returned to
England – learned that networks on the coast were in urgent need
of a trained radio operator with a set.

When Michel came back to France on three successive missions,
he was much concerned with obtaining accurate map markings
for parachute drops and rail sabotage, and with the problems
of keeping a sprawling and garrulous network tight. His second
mission delivered two radio operators. His third mission, in August
1942, involved meeting groups throughout the region. He was taken
to the chief of the south-eastern resistance movement, a painter he
found decorating sets in the theatre of the Cannes casino. 'Carte',
as he was called, complained that 'Julien' – one of the two radio
operators Michel had smuggled in – refused to send all his messages.
Michel insisted that contact must be kept to a minimum. Despite
urging precaution, Julien was later captured and executed.

Meeting so many people, Michel saw that the networks were too
sloppy. On a single day, he was introduced to two men whom – for
security reasons – he should never have met. Certainly, carelessness,
meetings in brasseries, loose talk and betrayal resulted in many
arrests.[39] After three successful missions, landing by parachute for
a fourth, Michel was betrayed and captured. He would survive the
war – freed from a German concentration camp by Allied troops
in 1945.[40]

A British resident who worked for the Résistance was Gerald Hakim, the English president of the Nice Ski Club and an alpinist of note. His group set up a network of agents who smuggled plans, photos and secret reports out of France. They also sent radio messages to London from the depths of the old marine biology laboratory founded by the Russians in Villefranche. Forced to leave Nice, Hakim settled in the Alps, where he was given a mission to find out what was going on in a chemical factory at La Roche-de-Rame, near Briançon.[41] Eventually arrested at his home, Hakim commented later that he was lucky to have been captured by the Italians and not the Germans – 'the Italians were human'.[42]

Yet, as resistance activity became more daring, the Italians hardened. In January 1943, the Italian secret police – the OVRA – installed itself in Cimiez, where it used the Villa Lynwood to detain and torture suspects. As the OVRA began a campaign of arrests – sometimes in cooperation with the Gestapo – the Résistance struck back. On 15 April, an OVRA agent was killed on the Boulevard Carnot. The officers' mess of the Genova Cavalleria regiment was bombed in early May. Three months later, an Italian soldier was killed and four were wounded by a bomb lobbed at a restaurant in the rue Paganini frequented by the military.[43] The OVRA intensified its activity. One victim later recalled his detention at the Villa Lynwood in May 1943. At first, he was handcuffed and left in a small cell. When asked what he had to confess, and having replied 'Nothing', he was taken to a rectangular room flooded with blinding light. Bound with chains that cut his hands and beaten with a club, he was ordered to walk round and round and round in a circle, frequently struck from behind to urge him to move faster. When he dropped, exhausted, his torturers doused him with cold water. 'Want to say something?' 'No.' He was kicked, beaten, and ordered to get up and stagger round for two days and nights without food. When he was brought before the director, he refused to cooperate and was returned to the rectangular room for seventy-two more hours of stumbling. By then, he was vomiting blood. His torturers kicked and beat him and left him for dead – yet he lived to describe the ordeal. Others did not.[44] In an OVRA villa at Antibes, a man died after being suspended by his testicles.[45] Twisting breasts and balls were effective techniques.

People who survived Italian interrogation or torture centres were imprisoned in Italy, deported to Nazi-occupied territory, or incarcerated in the concentration camp opened at Sospel in the backcountry. It held the first *résistants* to be arrested, along with non-French Jews and those Americans and English residents who had been forced to leave the coast.[46] Italian partisans operated in the mountain regions, and at Sospel, fifteen were tortured and shot. There were also increasing acts of violence outside the detention centres. Up in the hills, three young Frenchmen were lynched for showing disrespect to an Italian shopkeeper.[47]

The villas and hotels along the coast became casualties of the war. As hostilities commenced, Senegalese troops arrived to man anti-aircraft installations at La Croë on Cap d'Antibes. Maxine Elliott billeted eighteen *chasseurs alpins* at the Château de l'Horizon, and created a workshop to make clothing for families impoverished by conscription. After her death in 1940, Barry Dierks, who still possessed the keys to the property he had designed, used it as a safe house in which the Résistance could hold meetings. Under the successive occupations, it was inhabited by Italian and German officers as well as top Gestapo agents. Somewhat ironically, given her antisemitism, a secret cellar in Chanel's unoccupied villa, La Pausa, became a rest stop for the Résistance helping Jewish refugees to escape over the Alps.[48] The Villa Noailles, with its many small modern spaces, was commandeered by the Italians as a military hospital.[49] At the Château de la Napoule, where Henry Clews had died in 1937, his wife, Marie, stayed on throughout the war. During the Italian occupation, a tribunal indicted her for supporting the Allies, but her friendship with the daughter of the King of Italy, Princess Maria of Savoy, saved her. When, later in the war, the chateau housed a German artillery battery, the Louvre intervened to rescue Clews's sculptures from bombardment by storing them offsite.

Fashion was another predictable victim of war. Not only because of shortages but, on occasion, for ideological reasons. Vichy decreed that women were only allowed to wear trousers when cycling.[50] Where were they supposed to change? Longer bathing dresses were obligatory. Shorts were forbidden. Women would, once again, be forced to 'be women'.[51] Designers also fell on hard times. Cecil Beaton saw Paul Poiret on the Riviera wearing a suit made from a bathrobe.[52] Poiret's attempt at making a comeback had been unsuccessful. Poor and hungry, he waited patiently outside restaurants, hoping that the owners would give him food. When he died in Paris in 1944, Schiaparelli paid for his funeral.[53]

During the war, the Abwehr – perhaps through her lover Baron von Dincklage – learned of Chanel's desire to have her nephew André Palasse returned from a German POW camp. As an 'Aryan', Chanel also sought Nazi help to wrest control of Parfums Chanel from the Jewish Wertheimers. In exchange for their help, German military intelligence thought that – with her powerful connections – Chanel could prove useful. It has been suggested that, sometime in 1941, Chanel became Abwehr agent F-7124 – code name 'Westminster'.[54] Anne de Courcy suggested that it is 'difficult to believe that Chanel's pillow talk contained anything of real value to Germany'[55] – yet there would have been titbits of scandal about the rich and famous, not to mention her close knowledge of British society through her long association with Bendor. Evidence has also emerged that she undertook missions on behalf of those elements in the Nazi hierarchy who wished to sue for peace when the war began to turn against them. When in September 1944 she was interrogated by the Free French Purge Committee, she was hastily released – perhaps with the help of her friend Winston Churchill.[56]

In early November 1942, the armies of Great Britain and the United States landed on the shores of Morocco and Algiers, creating a base from which to attack Italy and Provence. That same month saw the entry of the German army into 'unoccupied' France. This meant that the remaining zone controlled by Italy – with its more sympathetic attitude – remained the only chance for Jews. Elsewhere, manhunts and deportations began as the Germans scoured the south. In December, as Vichy started to conscript Jews into labour battalions, it prohibited those who had entered France after 1 January 1938 from living within thirty kilometres of the coast. Later the same month, when the *préfet* of the Alpes-Maritimes, Marcel Ribière, decreed that Jews should prepare to leave for the 'interior territory' at short notice, the Italians objected and forced Vichy to back down. In the Italian zone, the largest concentration of Jews was in Nice and – from the beginning of 1943 – their situation was somewhat normalized when they were issued with temporary ID cards. Berlin was not happy. At the end of January, foreign minister Joachim von Ribbentrop insisted that 'it is important... that the Jews of foreign nationality residing in the Italian Occupied Zone of France, whether of Italian or of other citizenship, be eliminated'. The Nazis declared that 'by the end of 1943, not a single Jew should remain alive in Europe'. Impatient, Vichy intervened with a widespread manhunt. In the backcountry, the Italians reacted by freeing prisoners and preventing deportations to the death camps.[57]

By mid-July 1943, the Allies had landed in Sicily, and – on the 20th – their first air raids hit Rome. A month later, the Fascist Grand Council voted to oust Mussolini, and on 8 September 1943 Italy surrendered to the Allies. As Italian forces left France, Germany bargained with the release of a small number of Italian Jews under their control in return for the thousands of Austrian and German Jews in the Italian zone. Police Inspector-General Guido Lospinoso – a high-ranking officer responsible for 'race policy' – had been sent to Nice in March. Consistent with Italian resistance to the racial dictates of Berlin, Lospinoso started to move Jews from Nice to hill villages from which they could escape, over the Alps, to freedom. He was aided in this by an Italian-born Jewish banker, Angelo Donati, who – after the fall of Mussolini – made several trips to Rome to make arrangements to help Jews escape. By the time the Germans put a reward of one million marks on Donati's head, he himself had fled to Switzerland.[58]

The inhabitants of Nice were suffering from exhaustion and malnutrition. Trains full of fresh vegetables and fruit departed for Germany every day,[59] while most locals fed on salad and a few greens.[60] Staples such as milk, cheese and sugar were scarce. After the Allied occupation of North Africa, imports of olive oil, mutton, wine and eggs ceased.[61] In the spring of 1943, there were mass demonstrations against deprivation, while a black market – largely operated by foreigners and Jews – offered 'luxuries' such as potatoes, butter and flour. Karl Bitter – a German Jew pretending to be Hungarian – sold potatoes on the black market in Monte Carlo until he turned informer and made money blackmailing other Jews. Until his arrest after the war, Bitter was a leading racketeer, trading in gold, jewellery and foreign currency from a wicker chair beneath a parasol outside the Hôtel Métropole.[62]

On the black market, one tomato cost fifteen francs and a litre of oil over 2,000 francs. In restaurants in Nice, a menu would deliver a dish of hot water with a little beetroot, boiled lettuce as a main course, a salad without seasoning, and no dessert, for around fifty francs.[63] Simone Righetti was at teachers' training college in Nice from 1943 to 1945. Eating by the ration card which regulated the quantities of bread, oil, sugar and pasta to different age groups – more for the young, less for the aged – made for poor concentration. Righetti recalled endless tapioca, and mussels that were nothing but empty shells.[64] The big cities – Marseille, Toulon and Nice – were hit worst,[65] and when enterprising city-dwellers went on expeditions to the country to scavenge or buy from the peasants, they found the locals had nothing to sell.

A shortage of petrol meant that roads were deserted except for military or police vehicles. Bicycles became so important that theft incurred a jail sentence. A man found guilty of stealing seventeen of them was condemned to four years. Reacting against the deprivations of war and the fascist ideal of conformity, zazous – scruffy-haired boys, and girls cycling with their skirts unbuttoned – were seen on the streets of the larger cities. Concerts – both classical and popular – were given.[66] Charles Trenet – the optimistic voice of the Popular Front years who gave France his energizing song

'Boum!' and the world his perennial hit 'La Mer' – sang in Nice.
Mistinguett also performed, as she had done in the Great War.
Young Yves Montand – whose breakthrough moment had been
snatched by the commencement of hostilities – saw his first palm
trees when he went to sing in Nice. For a boy from an immigrant
family in Marseille, 'the Côte d'Azur was always "*là-bas*" – very
far away, a place where only foreigners went'. He never thought he
would ever see it. First there under the Italian occupation, he didn't
mind being shouted at – 'not like having a German yell at you'.[67]
Despite frequent electricity cuts, there were many functioning
cinemas along the coast. The American movies that Montand had
feasted on as an adolescent were, however, forbidden.

A ghostly presence from an earlier epoch, La Belle Otero – her
resources diminished by gambling losses – settled in a modest hotel
in Nice squeezed between a plumber's shop and a hairdressing
salon.[68] Her reduced circumstances added to her intolerance. Early
in the war, she attacked one of her neighbours in the street, with
cries of 'dirty Jew'. Later, she denounced a neighbour to the police
for selling chickens and eggs at excessive prices.[69] Raids began in
mid-August 1943, targeting airfields in the interior. During the
autumn, bombers hit the railway between Cannes and Fréjus,
the train depot at La Bocca, the bridges of the Var, and targets
around Marseilles and Toulon where many civilians were killed
or wounded.[70] La Belle Otero – incorrectly – was reported dead.

When the German occupation began on 9 September 1943 and
the Wehrmacht came marching into Nice, a curator at the Musée
Masséna described the troops as 'practically youngsters or very
old' – their 'uniforms and boots worn out'. Despite appearing 'low
spirited, sad and anxious', they possessed 'amazing discipline' in
carrying out their destructive tasks.[71] In Cannes, the English library
was ransacked – valuable books were sent to Germany, others
burned.[72] In Nice, that *fin-de-siècle* fantasy the Jetée-Promenade
was stripped of zinc, brass, bronze and electric cable by the
German Organisation Todt.[73] As the Nazis started to requisition
vehicles, at least one enterprising family buried their Citroën to

The German occupation of Nice.

await its resurrection after liberation.[74] Buildings close to the shore were evacuated – 192 in Cannes, 372 in Nice. As the defence of the coast began, blockhouses were built and concrete, wire and metal barricades were scattered along the beaches. Every night, the so-called Phantom Plane flew along the coast, monitoring the blackout.[75]

Intimidation began at once. From 11 September, anybody found in Nice in possession of a gun or ammunition would be executed immediately. In searching out Jews and miscreants, the Nazis were aided by the Milice, the unsavoury French paramilitary organization that assisted the Gestapo with their local knowledge. Torture centres were located at the Hôtel Hermitage and Villa Trianon in Cimiez, the Villa Montfleury in Cannes, the Villa Isnard in Grasse and the Villa Anaïs in Menton.[76] In Monte Carlo, the Gestapo settled in the Hôtel de Paris. The commanders of a Panzer regiment took over the Métropole.[77] Using Monaco as a rest area, Nazi officers complied with the Casino's request that they wear civilian clothes when gambling. The Third Reich also used the principality for financial dealings. Prince Louis created more than 300 holding companies to facilitate – and profit from – their operations.[78]

The Monégasques and certain enterprises were not so forthcoming. Rubble was scattered throughout the Hôtel Hermitage so it would be declared unfit for German troops. Its finest wines were hidden. Members of the Résistance helped captured pilots escape from the fortress on Mont Agel. Mrs Trenchard at the Scotch Tea House hid airmen on the run,[79] and a fortune teller called 'La Bohémienne' amused herself by gently mocking the invaders. She asked officers on leave from the Russian front if they would go back or prefer to kill themselves. If they went back, she predicted that while they were being trounced, the Allies would bomb their homes in Berlin. When wives came to join the officers, they would consult the clairvoyant about the fidelity of their husbands. La Bohémienne would reply, with a disconcerting shrug, 'All husbands are butterflies.'[80] While the officers on leave enjoyed the gaming tables and champagne's brief oblivion, the Monégasques were put to work fabricating defences.[81]

With the goal of total eradication, the Jewish question was a Nazi priority. On 10 September 1943, German security forces under SS-Hauptsturmführer Alois Brunner arrived in Nice to purge the region of Jews. They were aided in their work by right-wing collaborators who combed the town to scrutinize names on letterboxes and ferret out Jews. The fascist Parti Populaire Français began to raid homes. Police, Milice and French fascists would surround suspected addresses in the dead of night and pull terrified fugitives screaming from their beds. Sometimes, up to twelve people were found hiding in a small room – without food and with little hope. Black Citroëns circulated carrying 'physiognomists' supposedly able to determine a Jew by their facial features.[82] Meanwhile, an official at the Commissariat Général aux Questions Juives wrote, 'Since the entry of the German troops, the city of Nice has lost its ghetto-like appearance. Jews no longer walk in the streets; the synagogues are closed and the Promenade des Anglais offers the Aryan stroller many empty benches that until now had been occupied by Jews.'[83]

The first trainload was despatched from Nice on 11 September. Four days later, to improve efficiency, Brunner installed his force at the Hôtel Excelsior, which stood only 200 metres from the train station. When the prisoners arrived at the Excelsior, everything was taken from them. As they gathered in the lobby, names were called and the space slowly emptied. During the following three months, 1,820 victims left Nice station for Drancy,[84] the depot from which they were shipped to the German death camps. It is a testimony to the cunning of the local population that out of 30,000 Jews who had been in the Italian zone, Brunner deported fewer than 2,000.[85] Those taken by the Gestapo were tortured, to extract information about relatives and friends. One begged for a lethal injection. When it was refused, he threw himself out of a window.[86] Babies had their skulls broken. Pregnant mothers were killed. People who were circumcised and those with thick lips and big noses were taken north. No 'final solution' could afford to be less than thorough.

While collaborators were rewarded by the Nazis, the Résistance targeted the headquarters of collaborationist movements and the homes and businesses of their leaders. Saboteurs in Nice were active against the rail depot at Saint-Roch and the factory producing liquefied oxygen – important for Germany's developing missile technology. In the basements of Old Nice, teams were trained in radio operation and the use of explosives. Groups were busy gathering information about fortifications, observation posts and the mining of the coast in and around Nice. A doctor posed as pro-German to infiltrate Organisation Todt, which was building and maintaining coastal defences from Genoa to Marseille. This enabled him to gather details about the powerful Radio Monte Carlo transmitter that the Germans used to relay propaganda broadcasts. In February 1944, he and his wife, Sonya, were captured by the Gestapo. Under interrogation, her eye was gouged out while the doctor was strung up by his thumbs and beaten on his kidneys with a club. After the torture, Sonya was sent to Auschwitz and her husband to Mauthausen. They both survived.

Jean Moulin – who settled in Nice with forged documents and the cover of running an art gallery – had been asked by Charles de Gaulle to unify the fiercely independent resistance movements. As a result, Combat, Franc-Tireur and Libération joined forces in October 1942.[87] Marie-Madeleine Fourcade – who claimed the lifespan of a committed *résistant* was six months, yet who survived the war – divided the unoccupied zone into sectors. Her units used the new plastic explosives and time fuses in attacks, although most of their work consisted of observing troop movements.[88] The networks became larger, more organized, better financed and fitter, but there was no safety in numbers. Within a larger structure, a network such as the Groupes Francs in Nice used a six-man cell structure to limit damage, in case of arrest and torture.

Of those never known by name, so many were women. They committed to the fight in the knowledge that – if they were captured or killed – there would be hundreds more to take up the struggle for victory. Women became couriers, distributers of tracts and clandestine journals. They ascertained who was sympathetic to the Résistance in neighbourhoods close to the offices of the Milice or the Nazis. They photographed blockhouses and other shore defences with miniature cameras concealed in pendants. They hid airmen on the run. Josette Autrun, who worked at the telephone exchange in Grasse, disarmed a German soldier, took his gun, and captured five more soldiers before destroying the exchange.[89]

Matisse's daughter, Marguerite, joined the Francs-Tireurs et Partisans and worked as a courier until, in April 1944, she was arrested by the Gestapo in the north, taken to Paris and tortured so badly she tried to kill herself. Shortly afterwards, she was liberated.[90] Some were not so lucky. Hélène Vagliano worked in Cannes, helping refugees escape to Spain. As part of the Tartane network, Hélène lodged Allied agents and – as her friend Elsie Gladman noted – transmitted messages to various resistance groups from a radio she carried in a shopping bag on her bicycle. Just before the liberation, Vagliano was betrayed to the Gestapo, taken to their headquarters, tortured and mutilated. Her brother wrote to Elsie a few months later – Hélène's friends had asked her to hide but she had refused, not wanting her parents to be taken in her place. 'She was terribly tortured' but 'never betrayed a single person', he said. The day of the Allied landings at Fréjus, a woman who shared her prison cell remembered that 'Hélène danced with joy, kissed her and said, "Now I don't care what happens, my work is done."'[91] Hélène was one of the *résistants* shot in Cannes as the Nazis began their retreat.

Les Enfants du Paradis, a tender story of love frustrated and a poetic excursion into the worlds of early nineteenth-century Parisian crime and popular theatre, is often voted by cineastes as 'the best film ever made'. It is a miracle that it was made, yet the film's troubled production resulted in a masterpiece. Leaving aside the problems of materials and censorship, many of the cast and crew led dangerous double lives. The Victorine Studios in Nice, where Marcel Carné shot much of *Les Enfants*, was a hotbed of resistance. René Clément's 1942 documentary *Ceux du Rail* filmed the fortification work done by the occupation forces along the Paris–Lyon–Méditerranée track. From the production offices at the studio, useful sequences were smuggled through Spain into Gibraltar for the attention of the Allies.[92]

In making *Les Enfants du Paradis*, Carné relished working under the difficulties of the occupation, because he felt it showed that France's spirit remained undaunted. The problems were legion. Film and electricity were at a premium.[93] The production manager was a member of the Résistance, as were some actors, many extras and members of the crew. Others, however, collaborated with the Germans. When Carné was pressed to hire some German soldiers among his cast of many extras, he argued against this on aesthetic grounds and took on as few as possible. Alexandre Trauner, the set designer, and Joseph Kosma, who composed music for the film, were both Jewish. They worked while hiding in an old priory rented by the film's writer, Jacques Prévert, in the hills outside Tourrettes-sur-Loup.[94]

The film required a mock-up of the early nineteenth-century Parisian 'Boulevard du Crime' beneath the blue skies on the backlot of the Victorine Studios. Eighty metres long with twenty more in *trompe-l'œil*, the set comprised fifty façades between twelve and eighteen metres high. This required five tons of scaffolding, 350 tons of plaster and great quantities of wood – a tall order in wartime. Just as the carpenters, plasterers and painters completed their work and Carné started to shoot, the Allies landed in Sicily and the Axis powers became anxious about the threat to the southern French coast. As a result, the production was ordered up to Paris. Then, the armistice signed by Italy meant that finance from the Franco-Italian company Scalera had to be refused.[95] The film's producer André Paulvé, discovered to have Jewish origins, became a victim of Vichy's Comité d'Organisation de l'Industrie Cinématographique, which aimed to put film production 'on a rational and solid basis'– in other words, to eliminate the Jews who 'polluted' the movies. Paulvé survived and worked in cinema after the war, though his involvement with *Les Enfants* was over. Filming restarted in Paris at the Pathé studios in November 1943 until, two months later, the unit went south again to film the exterior sequences. Upon arrival, they discovered that violent winds had demolished some of their boulevard. Filming was delayed by weeks.[96]

Carné's cast presented problems. Marcel Herrand, who played the stylish criminal Lacenaire, was almost as unacceptable to the occupiers as the Jews because he was homosexual. The Vichy-controlled *préfet* of Nice had rounded up 2,000 prostitutes and homosexuals and incarcerated them at an internment camp near Sisteron in the Basse-Alpes. Robert Le Vigan, the actor cast to play the stoolpigeon Jéricho – turned out to be a collaborator, an antisemite who broadcast pro-fascist material on Radio Paris. Le Vigan shot only one scene before he fled to Austria. He was replaced by Pierre Renoir[97] – brother to one of France's greatest film directors and son of the Impressionist painter.

The popular star Arletty played the central character in *Les Enfants*, an enigmatic beauty with whom the four principal men fall in love. Privately, her life became entangled with the Nazi occupiers. Prévert would remember catching sight of her one day enjoying the company of two German officers. She had already had a passionate affair in 1941 with Hans-Jürgen Soehring, a German officer ten years her junior. It ended when he was sent to Monte Cassino and Arletty had an abortion. Arrested on 20 October 1944 for 'horizontal collaboration', Arletty was taken to the Conciergerie in Paris while a Free French Tribunal in Algeria condemned her – *absente reo* – to death. In response to her accusers, she declared, 'My heart belongs to France but my arse to the whole bloody world.' She missed the premiere of the film, which Carné controversially held up until after the liberation. By then – her death sentence commuted – Arletty was under house arrest at La Houssaye-en-Brie. She didn't work again until 1947, when her modest return to the stage was compromised by deteriorating eyesight.[98]

Many people who just got on with their careers were seen as playing into the hands of the Nazis – among them Serge Lifar and Jean Cocteau. The man who had been lunching with the Windsors the day Italy declared war on France, singer Maurice Chevalier, was brought before a Resistance tribunal for singing to the Nazis in occupied Paris and – a great propaganda coup – in Germany. Chevalier had hidden his Jewish wife, Nita Raya, and her parents in his house in La Bocca. The singer was acquitted by the tribunal, Chevalier maintaining that he performed for the Germans to protect his refugees.[99]

By the outset of 1944, the Nazis had eradicated the last semblance of normality in Nice. The Jardin Albert 1er and the hill of the fortress became camps with machine-gun nests and batteries ringed with barbed wire. The Kriegsmarine hollowed galleries beneath the fortress to site heavy guns. Circulation along the Promenade des Anglais and the Quai des États-Unis was forbidden, as the coast was mined against invasion. Tramway rails were ripped up and used to block the port and access to the main road east to Villefranche and Monte Carlo. The buildings of Les Ponchettes were camouflaged. Gaming rooms and theatres were shut. On 26 January, the Commissaire Général du Tourisme declared 'Tourism is dead.'[100]

In Saint-Raphaël, streets close to the seafront were cleared of inhabitants, and Cap Ferrat, the Îles d'Hyères and the Giens Peninsula were completely emptied. In Sanary, the Germans strengthened defences and destroyed hotels and houses – including the one where Thomas Mann had stayed. As the Allies started bombing, further damage was done to the small harbour.[101] In Monaco, Allied bombardment reduced the post office and the marble staircases of the *Établissement Thermal* to rubble.[102]

The winter of 1943–4 proved more difficult than the previous year, as air raids and resistance sabotage to railway lines further disrupted food supplies. To make matters worse, on 15 February 1944 regulations pertaining to the occupation in the north were applied in the south. For offences such as listening to enemy radio, communicating by wireless, spreading anti-German news or propaganda, taking photos or drawing outdoors, the offender would be condemned to forced labour. For violence or pillaging, the sentence was death. The administration of justice could be summary and brutal.[103] When two German officers and two soldiers were killed just outside Nice, Séraphin Tamia and Ange Grassi were taken at random, tortured, and hanged from lamp posts on the main approach to Nice station. Left dangling there for three days, traffic and pedestrians were routed past them to ensure that the maximum number of people would think twice.[104] In retaliation for other attacks against German soldiers, a curfew was imposed in early July. Cinemas, cafés and bars were closed. Nonetheless, the Résistance were going from strength to strength – in June, in the port of Nice, they sabotaged engineering work undertaken by Organisation Todt.[105]

As Allied bombing continued, a well-aimed torpedo from a British submarine hit a German minesweeper anchored in the bay of Monaco. The explosion sent debris hundreds of feet into the air, some raining down on the Baroness Orczy's garden at the Villa Bijou. On the morning after her roof was hit by Allied bombs, the German commanding officer rang the bell to ask whether 'the Baroness had not been too frightened by the bombardment and was well'.[106]

On 15 August, the Allies landed at Fréjus, Saint-Raphaël and Saint-Tropez. The 1st Airborne Task Force was dropped by parachute and glider under cover of darkness near the town of Le Muy, fifteen kilometres inland.[107] These were the flattest areas on a notoriously rocky coast. Given support from the sea by the

Séraphin Tamia hanged
by the Germans from a
lamppost on the approach to
Nice station.

British, the landing forces were largely American. So minimal was
the German resistance that 40 per cent of the losses suffered by
the 1st Airborne in Operation Dragoon occurred during the actual
droppings and landings.[108] The Germans concentrated their defences
in the strategic ports of Toulon and Marseille but – with help from
the local resistance groups – both were secured by the Allies within
two weeks of the American landings. In Cannes, there was shelling
of the German batteries near the summer and winter casinos on
17 August. By the 23rd, the Nazis started to retreat in scattered
groups – tired and dispirited. No longer would Jacques Lartigue
be disgusted by the sight of German officers dripping through the
lobby of the Carlton in bathing trunks.[109]

Prince Aly Khan found a German blockhouse obstructing the
main entrance to that hotel when he arrived with the Allies. Wishing
to stay the night, he went round to a side door and found his old
friend the manager. When he was offered the royal suite, Prince Aly
could see that the Riviera would soon return to normal. He went off
in a jeep to check on his father's villa on Cap d'Antibes and found

it in reasonable condition. He then reported to Lieutenant-Colonel Henry Cabot Lodge – commander of a special intelligence unit detailed to maintain contact with the Résistance and Free French troops – as the Americans advanced up the Rhône Valley.[110]

In Nice, from 20 August, resistance groups of all political colours called on the population to prepare for insurrection by paralysing the city with strikes – punishable, under German occupation, by forced labour. The printers who produced the right-wing *L'Éclaireur de Nice* were occupied. On 25 August, the Saint-Roch railway depot was shut down. Then, from 6 a.m. on the 28th – the day after American troops reached Saint-Laurent-du-Var – about 350 fighters in civilian clothing, armed with grenades, revolvers, machine guns, old rifles and knives, started to harass the Germans. They blocked the crossroads and main arteries out of the city. They struck against Radio Nice, the tram depot, and telephone exchanges in the centre and to the west of the city. The Germans threatened to burn Old Nice and bombard the centre of the city if the attacks continued. They intensified. The Résistance seized gendarmeries and turned captured enemy weapons against the occupiers. The leader of the group Loulou shot six Germans in the space of five minutes.

In the early afternoon, the Nazis kept their word and began to bombard Nice. The Allies continued their shelling from the sea. Just over twelve hours after the beginning of the insurrection, the Germans occupying the fort began to withdraw, as residents searched among the damaged buildings and broken trees for survivors. By 9 p.m., the Allied fleet had destroyed the blockhouses along the Promenade des Anglais.[111]

Two days later – as the Americans arrived in Nice and Beaulieu – the retreating Germans bombed railways and bridges, crippling a network already damaged by Resistance and Allied bombings. As the US Seventh Army moved up the Rhône, the Côte d'Azur slowly and painfully came back to life. Bomb disposal units began to disarm and remove mines. Six hundred were found along Monaco's tiny stretch of coast.

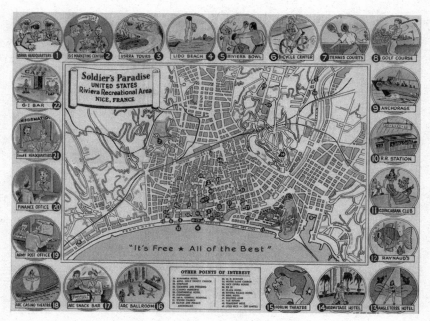

A map of Nice as a US soldier's 'paradise' after the liberation.

The Nazis may have been fanatical and vicious, but locals remembered them as sober. By contrast, the Americans were rowdy and often drunk. There was resentment as the liberators were well provisioned while the residents remained hungry. As the littoral became a recreational area, Cannes was kept for officers. Juan-les-Pins was designated for Red Cross women and nurses. Nice – where the Americans requisitioned twenty-eight hotels – was for the ordinary soldiers. Prostitutes arrived from across France. They were not allowed to accompany GIs into their hotels, so a trade in rooms rented by the hour became profitable. Complaints were made about the noise the Americans made at night, and military police were detailed to patrol the lively streets. There were arrests of pimps and prostitutes as the incidence of syphilis and gonorrhoea increased.[112]

To counter thoughtlessness and rowdiness, soldiers were given a booklet, *Don't Snafu Your Leave*. The pamphlet presented a series of cartoons and snatches of advice designed to keep GIs out of trouble: 'The Old Town is strictly off-limits'; 'You must wear dog tags when swimming' – most probably because of the mines. There were tips – 'Buggy rides cost beaucoup dough' – and calls for decent behaviour – 'Don't destroy hotel property'; 'Keep bottles out of sight', and avoid prostitutes. The word 'Snafu' – 'Situation normal: all fucked up' – satirizing the plethora of military acronyms, was a name attached to the none-too-bright Private Snafu. The character was created by Frank Capra and the author behind Dr Seuss for a series of fun, instructional cartoon shorts prepared for the army. Snafu was voiced by a vintage radio performer, Mel Blanc, who was the voice of cartoon characters such as Porky Pig, Bugs Bunny and, later, Barney Rubble in *The Flintstones*.

In Nice, cinemas were playing French and American films, and the opera restarted late in 1944. General Eisenhower came for a brief rest at Cap d'Antibes in August. Winston Churchill – who had watched the launching of Operation Dragoon from the deck of HMS *Kimberley* – returned to the coast to rest at Cap Martin in late September and early October. The Aga Khan reopened his villa, heralding the return of high life on the Riviera.

11

Glitz
1945–60

The film festival – postponed during the war – was optimistically scheduled for September 1945. Only three months after the signing of the armistice, there were still troops occupying the hotels where Cannes intended to welcome the film community. Defences and blown-out blockhouses littered hunks of concrete along the beaches. There were food queues. Estate agent John Taylor was working round the clock, visiting villas, assessing damage, making claims and supervising repairs.[1] The launch of what arguably would become the most important film festival in the world had to wait while grey, broken beaches once again became the Côte d'Azur.

By September 1946, the Blue Train was back in service, and brought the privileged to the first Cannes Film Festival.[2] Overall, there were too few trains coming south to carry the sudden swell of delegates and journalists. There were about a thousand of them, and the municipal casino – converted into a makeshift cinema – accommodated only 850. To complicate matters, the public was invited. Until they were banned for rowdiness, local citizens grabbed the best seats and refused to stop smoking during screenings. Many foreign films were delayed by a customs strike. Others never arrived. When they did, the screenings didn't make for easy viewing. Few had subtitles, and the reels of a Soviet film were shown in the wrong order. A projectionist offered to give it another chance and was awarded the Gold Medal for Services to Arts and Peace by the delegation from the USSR. When the reel order was fudged in a screening of Alfred Hitchcock's *Notorious*, the small American delegation threatened to go home. Hollywood was not in favour of international film festivals, and neither were the Americans altogether welcome at a time when – as part of their post-war cultural putsch – they were in bullying negotiations with the French to secure screenings of the backlog of American films banned during the occupation. The Russians understood what was happening – the festival was already a forum of international conflict. They won round one, presenting six feature films and four shorts – the only new American film was *Notorious*. At a reception hosted by the Soviets – in a scene worthy of the beginning of a Hitchcock movie – vodka flowed so freely that an American fell from the first-floor window.

Rather than 'a victory for France', Cannes was chaos. Critics complained they had been brought to a sunny place, only to be condemned to dark confines in which to watch fifty-two features and seventy-five shorts.[3] There were thefts of jewellery from hotel rooms, and thirty cars were stolen. All in all, it looked as if Cannes represented no threat whatsoever to the Venice Film Festival.

Among the films competing were David Lean's *Brief Encounter* and Charles Vidor's *Gilda*, starring Rita Hayworth and Glenn Ford. René Clément's *La Bataille du Rail* – thematically linked to his 1942 short *Ceux du Rail* – won the Prix International du Jury. The film was a dramatized account of how French railway workers in the Résistance had sabotaged Nazi trains. The Grand Prix went to Roberto Rossellini's *Roma Città Aperta*. Given the fact that, during the following decade, many items were pulled from the festival so as not to offend the sensibilities of competing nations,[4] those were brave and deserving choices for the top awards. Rossellini's unsensational yet shocking tribute to the determination of resistance networks and the courage of a Catholic priest in the face of the Nazi threat to vulnerable Roman citizens is a masterpiece. It set the competition's benchmark high.

Immediately after the war, Monte Carlo was drab and hotels scrambled to spend on grand refurbishments to lure back their clientele. When Churchill arrived in September 1945, he noted that the 'square in front of the hotel and the Casino is very empty and dead looking', although the welcome of the Monégasques was fervent. He ate on the terrace of the Hôtel de Paris facing the Casino. In a letter to his wife, Churchill reassured Clemmie that he 'did not transgress the 80 paces which separated me from that unsinkable institution'.[5] If the British population was grateful for his wartime leadership, many were enthusiastic for the social reforms proposed by the Labour Party. On 26 July, Churchill's government had been ousted by a majority of 146. Lord Beaverbrook, hosting Churchill's victory party at Claridge's, covered humiliation with a quip – the 'victory feast… now becomes a last supper'.[6]

Despite the entreaties of his grandson Rainier, Louis II of Monaco refused to rid himself of the pro-fascist Minister of State Émile Roblôt, and the prince's popularity remained low. German blockhouses in the gardens of the winter casino and along the shore added to the general air of melancholy. Charles Graves encountered a sad gigolo sitting by himself near the band in the Restaurant des Ambassadeurs. The man had been a dancer before the war, in which he had served as a Morse code operator. Refusing to become a black marketeer, he was now merely an unemployed gigolo in a place where visitors were no longer rich.[7]

To crown a career spanning nearly six decades, Raoul Gunsbourg came back as the director of the Opera. Monte Carlo's director of plays and operettas, René Blum, had been arrested in Paris in December 1941. After detention, he was shipped to Auschwitz concentration camp and murdered. The Ballets Russes de Monte Carlo under George Balanchine was in America. Although dancers dreamed of returning to Monaco, Balanchine was busy creating an 'American classicism' in a land of post-war opportunity.[8] Meanwhile, Massine's Ballet Russe de Monte Carlo remained in the principality and, in 1947, gave work to Serge Lifar, who had been disgraced and barred from the Paris Opéra in return for entertaining the Nazis.

The film director Michael Powell, who had first worked with Rex Ingram at the Victorine Studios, was back on the Côte d'Azur in 1947 to film ballet. *The Red Shoes* portrays the fatal love of a Svengali/Diaghilev impresario for his latest protégée. Adventurous in its effects, and boldly including an uninterrupted seventeen-minute ballet, the film nevertheless presents a rather arch take on the way in which ballet companies were run. Filmed at Pinewood Studios and on location, *The Red Shoes* affords glimpses of Monte Carlo in the late 1940s – grand, quaint, and remarkable for the lack of building on the backdrop of scrubby hills.

In the summer of 1946, the sixty-four-year-old Picasso and his twenty-four-year-old muse, Françoise Gilot, were living in a cramped house in Golfe-Juan. The couple enjoyed the deserted beach, spending time with the Polish photographer Michel Sima, who had returned from Auschwitz and Blechhammer to convalesce at the house of his friend Romuald Dor de la Souchère, curator of the all-but-empty museum at the Château Grimaldi in Antibes. As Picasso was looking for a place in which to work, Sima suggested that he might use the voluminous and empty rooms on the second floor of the chateau. When Picasso saw the space, he declared that he wouldn't just paint there, he would decorate the museum.

Picasso spent mornings on the beach and afternoons and evenings working in the chateau. He would lunch with Françoise at a small restaurant where the chubby owner walked back and forth carrying a basket containing a spiky species which was abundant on the submerged rocks and shelves around Antibes – the sea urchin. Picasso became obsessed by the delicacy, and the way in which the red-cheeked owner would stop, pull one from her basket, cut away the top and guzzle it.[9] *The Sea Urchin Eater* in the Château Grimaldi began as an almost realistic image, but Picasso gradually removed the descriptive details to reveal an absorbed, difficult posture which – in a kind of communion – focuses on the moment at which the flesh is consumed. Sea urchins – usually three – were included in many of the still lifes Picasso painted in Antibes.

He worked on plywood and fibro-cement with boat paint and the brushes used by decorators. Fine art materials were scarce and, apart from painting over some old canvases stored in the museum – as in the case of *The Sea Urchin Eater* – Picasso laid hard supports on the floor and worked with the fluid, drippy paint. Most of the images he produced at Antibes were made in a burst of activity during September and October 1946. In Paris, Picasso never drew fauns and mythical creatures, but he filled the works he painted in Antibes with images of Mediterranean antiquity. His large painting *Joie de Vivre* transformed a playful moment on the beach into an antique frolic. Françoise Gilot was the tambourine-playing nymph. Picasso became that wild and sexually charged half-man, half-beast – the centaur. Children were fauns playing. It is decorative, fun and life-affirming in face of a war-torn Europe, and nods at Matisse's 1905 *Bonheur de Vivre* which, four decades earlier, had celebrated the painter's opulent and warm-hearted encounter with the southern coast.

In nearby Vallauris, Picasso was drawn with childlike delight by the potter's 'blind palette'. Grey-black or red-brown colour applied after the biscuit firing is transformed – as if by magic – into a range of colours when a pot is baked in the kiln a second time. The Madoura pottery invited Picasso to make and decorate pots using the local red clay, which had been worked by craftsmen since Roman times. Picasso was taught and guided by the potters and, during the winter of 1947–8, produced about 2,000 pieces – the good, the bad and the ugly. His celebrity and phenomenal output helped revitalize the town's ceramic industry, which had been in decline since the First World War.

Picasso had not much liked Matisse in the early years of the century. Fauvist canvases with their expressionistic use of colour had secured Matisse's lead of the Parisian avant-garde. It was a role that the desperately ambitious Picasso coveted, and snatched when he developed Cubism. After the Second World War, both painters were living in the south – Picasso in his mid-sixties and Matisse in his seventies. As they began to see one another, Picasso grew to respect Matisse's enviable calm and balance. With Gilot, Picasso would visit his old rival, both in Nice and at Matisse's humble villa in Vence, opposite the convent where his old nurse and model was a novice.[10]

Soeur Jacques-Marie started to visit Matisse again. She spoke of a project for a chapel, and Matisse advised her to try her hand at designs for a stained-glass window. She produced a sweet, traditional image of the Virgin supported by little blond-haired angels. She also interested Matisse in the project, urging him to discuss it with a Dominican architect and with Père Couturier, who was – within the Church – a rare and vigorous champion of modern art. Matisse became fascinated by the problem of creating a feeling of spaciousness in a chapel only fifteen metres long, six metres wide and five metres high. He imagined that he could achieve 'a spiritual atmosphere in a reduced space' by banishing colour. White marble and tiles would, however, catch shifting projections of lemon yellow, green and ultramarine blue streaming through tall stained-glass windows. What Matisse did at Vence was to re-engage a site of Christian worship with nature and the elements – the yellow of the sun, the green of vegetation and the blue of sea and sky. The stone chosen for the altar was from Rogne near Aix, and its vesicular texture and warm colour against the white-marble chapel suggest bread – and hence the Eucharist.[11]

Picasso challenged Matisse about designing a chapel when he did not believe. It was, returned Matisse, 'a work of art... I put myself in the state of mind of what I'm working on. I don't know if I believe in God or not'. Françoise Gilot was, meanwhile, moved by the serenity radiating from the artist. Since his second operation, from which he had not expected to recover, Matisse had considered that he was living on borrowed time – 'Every day that dawns is a gift to me.'[12]

Matisse worked from the literal and descriptive towards a simplicity that hosts the ethereal. Cunningly, to the right of the altar, he used the support of white tiles to suggest the white Dominican habit in a large and simple brush drawing of St Dominic. In his search for serenity, however, Matisse did not shun drama. Disturbing the chapel's calm are the hectic, graffiti-like markings on the panel representing the Stations of the Cross. The fourteen images, traditionally disposed around a church, are here brought together on the back wall facing the altar in an affront – an urgent cacophony of Christ's agony. The lines are agitated – not graceful or peaceful, as elsewhere in the chapel. The spectator is drawn into the turbulence of the drama, and challenged to contemplate in order to make sense of the story. Towards the end of his work in February 1950, the artist wrote to Père Couturier that he feared his single panel for the Stations would be difficult for believers to accept. Nonetheless, Matisse was decided, claiming 'God held my hand.' The chapel was consecrated in 1951. Matisse commented, 'I want those entering... to feel themselves purified and lightened... This chapel is for me the conclusive achievement of a whole life of labour and the flowering of a huge sincere and difficult striving. It is not a labour I chose but rather one for which I was chosen... I regard it, despite all its imperfections... as my masterpiece.' He was using the term as late medieval apprentice craftsmen did – before achieving their mastership they had to produce a 'masterpiece'.

Three years later, Matisse died in his studio in Cimiez. He left the world with an affirmation of joy wrested from the need to see things anew. He revelled in the wonders of humanity – its music, its dance, its daily life, its exhilaration before nature – all re-baptized in colour and line. His artistic revolt and struggle declared a faith so fresh and refreshing it transcended with a simplicity that cost him – as he suggested in his comments on the chapel – an entire lifetime.

As Matisse had a chapel, Picasso had to have one too. In 1952 – outraged by the war in Korea – Picasso decided to decorate a tiny deconsecrated fourteenth-century chapel in Vallauris. He produced about 250 preliminary studies for the scenes, painted on plywood panels riveted to supports on the stone walls. Finished much earlier but opened in 1959, the chapel decoration is certainly not the Picasso of the powerful anti-war painting *Guernica*. If Matisse's chapel is airy, Picasso's is chthonic and claustrophobic, crowded with ciphers for war and peace. Picasso playing at being Picasso.

As Matisse and Picasso had a chapel, Cocteau also wanted one. In fact, he got two. During his longer and more regular winter sojourns on the Côte d'Azur between 1950 and his death in 1963, Cocteau embraced several decorative commissions. He was invited to brighten the wedding hall in the *mairie* of Menton. Peopling his spindly scenes with mythological figures such as Orpheus and Apollo, Cocteau 'tattooed' the white walls of his patron Francine Weisweiller's Villa Santo Sospir on Cap Ferrat. With typical exuberance, and using local motifs such as the capeline and the Phrygian sailor's cap, Cocteau painted the chapel of St Pierre in Villefranche, a stone's throw from the infamous Welcome Hôtel. Soon after the chapel opened, Noël Coward visited with Greta Garbo, remarking in his diary that he had not thought that all the Apostles resembled the actor Jean Marais – Cocteau's lover and muse. At the end of his life, Cocteau decorated another chapel – the overcharged Notre-Dame-de-Jérusalem in the hills above Fréjus. His flimsy version of the Last Supper includes a portrait of himself along with friends such as Coco Chanel and – once again – Jean Marais.[13]

The future Prince Rainier had taken an Easter break from his studies to return to Monaco in 1942. Despite the closure of many hotels and restaurants, Edith Piaf and Maurice Chevalier sang and Rainier – not yet nineteen – saw a young actress called Gisèle Pascal in the comedy *Vive le Théâtre*. He was smitten. When his studies took him to Paris, they began to see one another. After the war, the actress joined Rainier on the Côte d'Azur to share a villa on Cap Ferrat – Pascal accepting only films shot at the Victorine Studios in order to remain close to her lover. When the unpopular and ineffective Louis II died in 1949, his grandson became Rainier III. Despite Pascal's sacrifices, Rainier was uncomfortable with the morals and lifestyle of her theatrical friends, and asked her to give up work altogether. Such strains placed on the relationship were exacerbated by Rainier's power-hungry relatives, who disputed Louis II's will and spread stories about Pascal's inability to conceive. The romance disintegrated.[14]

If procedures at the Casino had been upset by the Greek Syndicate, it was a Greek shipping magnate who was going to shake up the principality itself. In 1950, Monte Carlo confronted one of its frequent crises, when the SBM suffered serious losses caused by a 75 per cent drop in visitors. The following spring, Aristotle Onassis and his wife leased the Château de la Croë and moored their yacht, *Olympic Winner*, in Monte Carlo harbour. Onassis was working clandestinely through a network of companies to secure a controlling interest in the SBM. He moved into the Hôtel de Paris and waited for his huge new yacht, *Christina O*, to be delivered. Gambling on the future of Monte Carlo, Onassis needed to give a new glitz to the principality, to secure a return on his immense investment. Meanwhile, Rainier – determined to assure Monaco's destiny – listened to the advice of his private chaplain, an American priest assigned by the Vatican. It was time for the prince to get married. A clever choice of bride would go a long way to solving Monaco's problems.[15]

London socialites, who marvelled at how quickly pre-war society reasserted itself, would – like those who had clung to Belle Époque manners on the Riviera – soon have their world disturbed. As in the aftermath of the First World War, youth clamoured to express itself. Noël Coward, now only moderately successful, sought to escape to what he remembered as the idyllic world of the Riviera, only to find a new caste of English visitor who seemed to him to be 'black-market profiteers'.[16] Many luminaries came back to a changed world. Somerset Maugham returned from America without Gerald Haxton, who had died in New York in 1944. The Villa Mauresque – occupied by Italian, German, British and American troops, and fired upon by the British fleet – was uninhabitable. The glass had gone, the roof was dodgy, the dogs had been eaten. The furniture removed from storage was in bad condition. Mercifully, the pictures survived.[17]

The Windsors came back to find a workforce of German POWs removing land mines from La Croë. Although the house had been used by both the Italians and the Germans, it had not suffered badly. Only the curtains, some oil paintings and a few items were missing.[18] However, the rhythms and the tone of life on the Côte d'Azur seemed to have changed. Gone were the days when Prince Jean-Louis de Faucigny-Lucinge – arriving early for lunch – caught sight of a timetable left in the hall – '12:30 Prince de Lucinge arrives, 12:35 we go down to bathe, a quarter to two lunch, 3 o'clock siesta, 4 o'clock so-and-so arrives' and so on.[19] When days were planned to be full and there were people on hand to fill them, life had been one long distraction. After the war – as the duchess recalled – 'the old familiar estates and villas seemed to be passing into unfamiliar hands; a new type of tourist was swarming in'.[20] The Windsors summered at La Croë until 1949, when they gave it up for good.

When Duff and Diana Cooper were staying aboard Daisy Fellowes's yacht in Monte Carlo, they parked their car on the quay. Woken the following morning by the news that their motor had plunged into the sea, Duff's somewhat strident reaction was that he 'strongly suspected sabotage, either by communists or drunken sailors'. The fact that his wife had left the handbrake off seemed neither here nor there.[21]

In the early fifties, the British community became marginalized or departed, and the ambiance of the coast was shaped not only by the French, but by American glitz and glamour. Playboys were a new breed, and their fast-moving lifestyle was rewriting the Riviera. They were young, good-looking and rich. If deficient in the first two categories, the third guaranteed their appeal. They liked sport and speed – anything that might give a frisson to their frivolous lives. They decorated themselves with diamond-draped women who showcased their generosity and wealth. Often, their women were rich or famous. Among the five wives of the Dominican playboy Porfirio Rubirosa were Doris Duke, the American tobacco billionaire, and Danielle Darieux, the French actress. Among his lovers, he counted Ava Gardner, Kim Novak and Rita Hayworth. Hungry for life, flirting with death, Rubirosa crashed his Ferrari 250 in the Bois de Boulogne in 1965, killing himself after an all-night bash at a Paris club.

Gianni Agnelli – heir to, then head of, the Fiat empire – was one of the richest men in Europe. He loved to jump from a helicopter into the waters off the Hôtel du Cap, then swim ashore to enjoy a cocktail with the women sunning themselves by the pool. Another speed-fiend, Agnelli was a daredevil driver who suffered a near-fatal accident between Èze and Beaulieu. He was linked romantically to Anita Ekberg, and to Jackie Kennedy in the summer before her husband was shot. If often fuelled by desperation, playboys exuded an aura of power and purpose. In 1953, their vices and desires led the originators of Hugh Hefner's new men's magazine – after rejecting *Top Hat, Sir* and *Satyr* – to settle on the title *Playboy*.

Prince Aly Khan was the son of Aga Khan III and Theresa Magliano, a dancer at the Opera Ballet in Monte Carlo whom the Aga Khan married in 1908. The prince's father was often absent and Aly spent much of his childhood in Turin with his mother's family, or in villas that his father had bought or rented for them along the Côte d'Azur. As a young adult, he had a playful, impetuous nature which – combined with his wealth and lifestyle – was attractive to women. The Aga Khan – married four times – did not always approve of his son's obsessive romantic adventures, but it was he who bequeathed to Aly a technique of lovemaking. A fascinated student of the erotic traditions of India, the Aga Khan believed that sexual relations improved the health and built up the stamina. He understood there could be only slight gratification for the man if the woman was not first satisfied. His son claimed that 'I think only of the woman's pleasure when I'm in love' – though, as Elsa Maxwell observed, love 'might only last one night'. Aly consumed women. The French singer Juliette Gréco went so far as to say, 'I don't know who didn't have an affair with Aly.' Another woman observed that 'you were really *déclassée, démodée*, nothing, you hardly counted, if you'd not been to bed with Aly'. He was exciting, caressing women tenderly while dancing, and whispering plans for wild, spontaneous excursions – flights on his twin-engine de Havilland, midnight speedboat rides, exotic destinations. Ultimately, it was the chase that thrilled him but – frequently faced with scant resistance – he employed the inherited wisdom of the ages to ensure the woman's satisfaction. He would make love for up to seven hours at a time, yet only allow himself to climax – at most – twice a week. That way, he sustained his stamina. In the rare moments when he was not pursuing women, Aly was a 'gentleman jockey' who loved horse racing as much as driving fast Lagondas – his playboy lifestyle a continual search for dangerous distraction.[22]

While the Riviera became the playground for playboys, Greek tycoons and jetsetters, the Cannes Film Festival was stumbling towards its glamorous and controversial future. Two years after its long-delayed opening in 1946, it was cancelled due to lack of funding – as it was again in 1950. The year in between saw the completion of the Palais – the festival's home until 1983. A popular, if imperfect, venue, on the final night of the 1949 festival its roof blew off in a freak storm. The 1,800 guests who had attempted to crowd into its 1,000-seat space returned to the Casino for the prize-giving – the Grand Prix going to Carol Reed's *The Third Man*.[23]

After 1950, a new train carried journalists and delegates south. The *Mistral* boasted four restaurant cars and a shop, as well as secretarial and hairdressing services. As it left Paris Gare de Lyon after lunch, it didn't arrive until after dark.[24] While efficient, it lacked the allure of the Blue Train, which gave passengers their first glimpse of the Mediterranean in the vibrant morning light. In 1951 – the first year that the Cannes Film Festival was held in the spring – the Blue Train made some changes. The restaurant was enlarged and a bar added. At 7.00 p.m., the passengers boarded the train in Paris. At 7.30, the bar opened as the train pulled out of the station – not to the sound of steam hissing, but to the sharp popping of champagne corks. There were two sittings for dinner at tables decorated with the flowers that would greet the travellers at their destination – orange blossom and mimosa.[25]

Cannes itself was trying to make a grand comeback after the war. What was left of the old British community – mainly former maids and butlers – was not wealthy. It was up to the tourist industry to attract new money. Lord Brougham's Villa Éleanore-Louise was converted into apartments. By 1950, there were 1,600 flats for rent, nearly 1,500 furnished rooms and 4,400 hotel rooms on offer. During the summer at the Carlton, there were more than sixty bartenders who served – between half-past six and 9 p.m. – over 4,000 drinks to the 2,000 clients in its several bars.[26] Nevertheless, between 1950 and 1960, visitors complained about the dirtiness of the streets, expensive beaches, and exorbitant bar prices.

As the Cannes Film Festival began to reorganize itself and Hollywood became less wary of international competitions,

American film producers and stars became a presence on the coast. In the hills above Cannes, Elsa Maxwell lived with her 'oldest friend', Dorothy 'Dickie' Fellowes-Gordon, in a farmhouse built in 1841. Their terrace afforded marvellous views, and they would invite people to dine around a large millstone converted into a low table. However uncomfortable it was, members of the 'celebrity circus' – the Windsors, Tyrone Power, Clark Gable, and film producers Darryl F. Zanuck and Jack Warner – were, over the years, happy to dine there.[27] At nearby Eden Roc, in one of the cabins attached to the hotel, Maxwell would drink champagne with Hollywood stars and play cards with the Aga Khan and Jack Warner.[28] When he lost in the casino, Warner would generously but ostentatiously buy champagne for everybody.

Warner bought the Villa d'Aujourd'hui on Cap d'Antibes. As it stood on a dangerous bend and close to the road, Maxwell maintained that he only purchased the property because the previous owner had put in a modern American kitchen. In Antibes alone, an incredible 400 villas were constructed between the liberation and 1950, the year in which the Murphys sold the Villa America to a Swiss electronics tycoon for $27,000.[29] Real estate prices dipped in the early fifties, then boomed again – but on a scale that would seem slight by the later standards of oligarchs, deposed dictators and arms dealers. Gregory Peck and David Niven bought villas on Cap Ferrat. Gary Cooper and his family were frequent guests at the Hôtel Cap d'Antibes, where they were much appreciated by the staff for their politeness and discretion. Producers and stars obviously needed periodic escapes from Hollywood to enjoy the diminishing aura of old-world charm.

Rita Hayworth was hoping for a reconciliation with her husband Orson Welles when she came to the Riviera in 1948.[30] Feeling gloomy about the likelihood of saving her marriage, when that great fixer Elsa Maxwell invited her to a party, she refused. Naturally shy, she had a history of chronic infatuation – Victor Mature, Glenn Ford, a first husband twice her age and then Orson Welles, who was too stimulated by his work to bother with making a home. Born to a Spanish dancer and a mother who had been a Follies girl, Hayworth

danced professionally as a child – appearing at New York's Winter
Garden Theatre before she was five. She deeply desired the chance
to settle down. Pressed, she again refused Maxwell's invitation to
a party at which the notorious playboy Prince Aly Khan would be
present. Maxwell persisted. Hayworth capitulated.

The star arrived late at the Cannes casino, inevitably turning
heads as she entered. Prince Aly asked Maxwell who she was. The
reply was that the apparition was to be seated next to him at dinner.
Aly knew the face. Indeed, he had seen her before. She had a string
of highly successful films behind her and, in Cairo during the war,
Aly had watched her play a temptress in *Blood and Sand* – three
times. The seating plan proved successful and, after Maxwell's party,
Prince Aly drove Rita Hayworth to the California nightclub above
Cannes, where they danced on the terrace. Hayworth had it in her
blood, but Aly – not a very good dancer – was thrown back on his
usual schemes for seduction. Someone wanting to make a home
should have been warned.

Having purchased the Château de l'Horizon from Maxine
Elliott's heirs for $29,000, Aly Khan invited Hayworth to visit.
With her divorce pending, she was much in demand. With fierce
competition from Hollywood and the Riviera fast set – the Shah
of Persia, Aristotle Onassis – Aly was thrilled by the chase. He
telephoned Hayworth at all hours, bombarded her with gifts and
flowers. He whisked her away on his private plane to Toledo, Lisbon
and Biarritz. They flew off to Hollywood and Mexico as Hayworth
waited for her divorce from Welles to come through.[31] When they
visited the Aga Khan, he asked if they had become devoted to one
another. When they replied in the affirmative, he advised them to
marry as soon as possible.[32]

It would be the fairy-tale romance of the late forties, and towns
along the Riviera began to compete to host the wedding. On
27 May 1949, the marriage was enacted in the *mairie* in the nearby
communist town of Vallauris, and the reception was held at the
Château de l'Horizon. Edith Piaf was to have sung but – indisposed
– her wartime lover and protégé Yves Montand performed in her
place. Gallons of Eau de Cologne were emptied into the swimming

pool. There were flowers, telegrams and – perhaps for Aly – a little sadness that his quest was over.[33]

Soon after their marriage – as Rita Hayworth settled down to what she hoped would be a life of domestic bliss – Aly was straining at the leash and out on the town. Hayworth locked herself in her room, put on Spanish music and danced. The Aga Khan now knew they were not a good match. His son loved to be surrounded by people, whereas Hayworth was seeking shelter from the stress of Hollywood. After she gave birth to their daughter, Yasmin, in December 1949, Aly's irrepressible lifestyle meant that the family spent time apart. He was as ill-suited to the responsibilities of fatherhood as he was to a monogamous marriage. Hayworth returned to Hollywood, and Aly jetted off on his latest romantic adventure.[34]

The actress Simone Signoret fell in love with Saint-Paul-de-Vence, and bought a small house in the village. She became a regular at the Colombe d'Or, where poet and screenwriter Jacques Prévert spent much time. In the summer of 1949, Yves Montand was playing Nice on 20 August and Cannes on the 21st. On his way south, he rested at the Colombe d'Or, where Prévert introduced him to the actress. Signoret was charmed when, in the informal atmosphere of Roux's establishment, Montand spontaneously started singing songs with words by Prévert – songs he would sing throughout his long career. The following morning, Montand drove off to rehearse in Nice and came back to the Colombe d'Or for lunch. Simone invited him to her little house in the village, where they took a siesta. After the concert, Montand returned for the night. The next day, Simone followed him to his concert in Cannes. It was the beginning of the end of her marriage to film director Yves Allégret. He had recently given her the leading role in a film scripted by Prévert that would – for the second time – not get made. Montand and Signoret began to spend a good deal of time in Saint-Paul-de-Vence, where, in December 1951, they married. Paul Roux was Montand's witness, and the marriage feast was held at his restaurant. Doves were released during the meal and one settled peacefully on Simone's head.[35] The marriage – not always untroubled – lasted until her death in 1985. When Montand died six years later, he was buried next to her in the Parisian cemetery of Père Lachaise.

The old, ad hoc Colombe d'Or was slowly refashioning itself into a celebrity haunt. In 1953, the owners bought the eighteenth-century house next door, creating bedrooms with Provençal furniture and outstanding paintings on the walls. The exquisite location and unique ambiance attracted writers and intellectuals such as Jean-Paul Sartre, Simone de Beauvoir and Raymond Queneau, who wrote sitting at a table once used by André Gide. It became a cherished destination for entertainers and actors coming down for the Cannes Film Festival – a journey that was becoming increasingly easy.[36]

By 1945, Nice had a one-runway airport that used a nearby villa as a terminal. The first commercial Paris–Nice flight that year took five hours and cost over 2,000 francs. With the train taking twenty-two hours and costing more than half as much, it was clear that flying to the Côte d'Azur would become popular. In June 1948, a British European Airways service flew London–Paris–Nice. Two years later, Nice airport would be processing a quarter of a million passengers a year.[37]

By 1953, the Cannes Film Festival had been glamorized by a publicity industry pushing sex, sex and more sex. The convenient beach provided an extendable space for photoshoots and a pretext to wear less. The festival made sensational use of its sunlit strip of nature fronted by hotels that were a byword in luxury. A very girlish eighteen-year-old Brigitte Bardot was photographed on the beach, in a bikini, having her hair plaited by that icon of American machismo, Kirk Douglas. The following year, this stunt was topped by the topless Simone Silva, B-movie actress and glamour model. Neither Silva nor her movies are remembered by anybody but film buffs. Her one claim to fame was snatched at Cannes in 1954. She had travelled to the festival with the express idea of giving her career a lift. She failed, but she did become the talk of the town when she posed with Robert Mitchum. Unexpectedly, she ripped off her top and cupped her bare breasts in her hands. Mitchum –

Simone Silva surprises Robert
Mitchum at Cannes.

unprepared for the stunt – looked on with horrified amusement.
Several photographers were injured in the scramble to get the hottest
shots, and festival authorities asked Silva to leave. The incident did
nothing for the growing American perception that Cannes was
somewhat lurid.[38]

There was a growing trend to associate the Riviera with sex. In
the 1950s, Simone de Beauvoir and Jean-Paul Sartre spent time in
Saint-Tropez. They had an open relationship and would tell one
another in minute detail what they got up to. In early 1953, Sartre's
lover was Michelle Vian, the translator and poet who collaborated
with her husband, Boris, on the writing of his novels. De Beauvoir's
lover was the writer and filmmaker Claude Lanzmann, seventeen
years her junior. That Easter, the two open restaurants on the
front stood next to one another. Lanzmann would sit in one and
eavesdrop, as de Beauvoir told Sartre everything that had happened
between them.[39]

Such freedoms were to help redefine Saint-Tropez. People came
down to holiday and dressed in the striped fishermen's tops and
espadrilles that had so delighted Gerald Murphy. In 1955, the

young novelist Françoise Sagan – flush from the success of *Bonjour Tristesse* – arrived in her Jaguar X440 convertible. Afraid of being alone, she embarked on a messy and self-indulgent summer – drinking enough to feel good without getting drunk, and attracting a crowd of hangers-on whose bills she paid and whose rowdy behaviour disturbed the village.[40] In her 1958 documentary *Du Côté de la Côte*, Agnès Varda – having noted that Saint-Tropez's population of 4,000 swelled to 50,000 in August – asks, 'What are they all looking for?'

It was a feature film that welded sex and Saint-Tropez in the public's imagination. Director Roger Vadim first saw Brigitte Bardot, aged fifteen, on the front cover of *Elle* magazine. By the time she came to star in *Et Dieu… Créa la Femme*, Bardot had made more than fifteen films, including the 1953 American *Act of Love* with Kirk Douglas and the 1955 British *Doctor at Sea* with Dirk Bogarde.[41] *Et Dieu… Créa la Femme* was filmed at the Victorine Studios and on location in the rather drab, dilapidated but working fishing village of Saint-Tropez in July 1956. The film trades on sexual stereotypes in its evocation of the fight between old and new attitudes, capturing the moment when French youth began to rebel against religious and social restraint. Bardot's spontaneous, unsophisticated sexuality particularly appealed to Americans – as Simone de Beauvoir noted, she became almost immediately 'an export product as important as Renault automobiles'.[42]

The orphan Juliette, played by Bardot, hates her work. She likes 'the sea, the sun, the hot sand'. She embodies the dissembling myth of the modern Côte d'Azur – a place for the young and free-spirited. Used to attracting attention, Juliette is casual and offhand in her attitude to men. She is tempted by an older, rich entrepreneur who – with a kind of playboy mentality – offers her 'the other side of the world'. His wish to build a casino in Saint-Tropez meets local resistance – a clash between local attitudes and entrepreneurs that would come to define the Côte d'Azur. Meanwhile, Juliette marries into a family of three brothers. After various trials, the film grudgingly upholds traditional values, as Juliette returns home with her husband in closing shots set against the untouched buildings

of old Saint-Tropez. In the preceding scene, Juliette lets her hair
down in a basement where she dances with abandon to the music
of a black band. It is a glimpse of the future Saint-Tropez, which
was – in part – triggered by a film made at a time when France was
moving towards a consumer culture. If Vadim's movie jump-started
the bikini industry, staid local authorities were flummoxed when
topless bathers put bottle tops over their nipples to avoid arrest.

By contrast, in 1954, Alfred Hitchcock was filming *To Catch
a Thief*, and Hollywood production codes allowed him no bikinis
on the beach. The film was based on a 1952 novel by David Dodge
that had been inspired by an authentic Riviera crime. In the villa
next door to the one Dodge had been renting – during a dinner
to which people like Schiaparelli, Elsa Maxwell, Lady Tavistock
and the Marquis de Ricci were invited – there was a massive jewel
robbery. The burglar Dario Sambucco, who was working under the
colourful alias of Dante Spada, was the thief. As Dodge disarmingly
commented, in Hitchcock's film all that remained of the original
novel was the title and the names of some of the characters. Happily,
he retained the copyright.

Filming took place at Paramount Studios in California and
along the Côte d'Azur, which – at times – was seen from the
air in Technicolor and in VistaVision, Paramount's answer to
Cinemascope. Technicolor had captured the Riviera before – both
in *The Red Shoes* in 1948 and in Walter Lang's 1951 film *On the
Riviera*, starring Danny Kaye and Gene Tierney. The latter was a
showcase for the considerable talents of Kaye, who played two
lead parts and who – in one song – did a very credible imitation
of Maurice Chevalier. Much of it was filmed in the studio, and
while it capitalizes on the flirtatious reputation of the Côte d'Azur,
it remains a minor Hollywood musical that could have been set
anywhere. By contrast, in *To Catch a Thief*, the location is integral
to the story.

Grace Kelly was Hitchcock's favourite star – 'Grace is,' he said,
'like a mountain covered with snow, and when the snow melts
you discover it to be a smouldering volcano.'[43] Co-star Cary Grant
was 'retired' – unable to find scripts with the wit of his earlier

comedies. Yet a new opportunity to film with Hitchcock was not to be missed. Grant described his working relationship with the meticulous perfectionist as almost telepathic. During the filming, Grace Kelly was in love with the designer Oleg Cassini, who had divorced the co-star of *On the Riviera*, Gene Tierney, leaving her free to become for Aly Khan what his father feared would be another Rita Hayworth. The fascination was – as so often for Aly Khan – brief. By 1954, they were no longer together.[44]

Many critics felt that *To Catch a Thief* was far from Hitchcock's best. Although slow to start, it was, as the *Washington Post* critic Richard L. Coe wrote, a picture 'in which everyone lives in glorious workless luxury on the French Riviera, looks wonderful, speaks amusingly and is unconcerned with transit strikes or hurricanes. I loved every minute of it.'[45] Hitchcock adored the south of France, and the film relies on a recipe of Riviera ingredients – a jagged and tormented coastline softened by pockets of affluence, where ostentatious wealth is a target for theft and where villas are often the reward for ill-gotten gains. It is a place where Englishmen behave with less restraint, and rich Americans search for even richer husbands. At the time in which the film was set – the late forties – the local population was still disturbed by the complications of the war. Many had scores to settle, and those tensions provoke the drama. The Corniche affords breath-taking views and reveals its dangers at speed. Unwittingly, the film foreshadowed Kelly's future. At one point, she parks her car in a lay-by overlooking Monte Carlo to picnic with Grant. She throws her arms in the air for joy and asks him if he has ever seen anywhere in the world that is quite so beautiful.

The coast – a God-given set – was used to such advantage that, in Paris two years later, the 'fine technicolor film' reminded the young poet Sylvia Plath of her brief trip to the Riviera a few months earlier. In her diary for 1 January 1956, Plath – who had spent a harrowing stint in 1953 as a guest editor of New York's fashion magazine, *Mademoiselle* – noted that, in Nice, 'painted bleached blondes pass by in high heels, black slacks, fur coats and sunglasses'.[46]

Hollywood had for years been the target of the anti-communist House Committee on Un-American Activities. In the early fifties,

Cannes became a refuge for the Hollywood victims of McCarthyism. In 1955, Betsy Blair – who had been blacklisted for a time – starred in Delbert Mann's *Marty*, which won that year's top prize. At the festival with her husband, Gene Kelly, she had a glorious moment: 'We, the winners, walked along the beach, barefoot in our evening clothes; a Soviet director, a communist or two, some fellow-travellers, a blacklisted director and his wife... Laughing, full of champagne and success, we felt the Left was invincible, that taking prizes at the festival in Cannes was only the beginning.' Despite the bimbo devouring paparazzi, Cannes was a serious international forum with a reputation for political argument and artistic disagreement. It was certainly not all about Diana Dors's mink bikini or French actress Françoise Deldick's topless promenade on a white charger in the lobby of the Carlton Hôtel. Yet, however much French critics like André Bazin found the 'worldly elegance' of Cannes 'puerile', part of the festival's *raison d'être* and hence its siting was intended to promote French chic.[47] The director François Truffaut – who later would take Cannes by storm – noted that the purpose of the festival was to fill hotels and casinos.

Having won the Best Actress Academy Award for *The Country Girl*, Grace Kelly was offered a part she refused and MGM suspended her. She also missed out on a couple of roles she coveted. Her nine films between 1951 and 1955 had made her a top Hollywood actress, but she was unsettled and uncomfortable about her numerous affairs. Her co-stars on *The Country Girl*, William Holden and the recently divorced Bing Crosby, had been her lovers – as had Gary Cooper and Clark Gable. Chance would have it that Cooper also had a brief affair with Gisèle Pascal before the actress broke with Rainier III. Kelly easily fell in and out of love, but she wanted marriage and children. To shake herself out of the doldrums, she accepted an invitation to Cannes in 1955. She travelled south with Pierre Galante, a writer working for *Paris Match* who asked Grace if she would agree to a photo shoot with Prince Rainier. She thought, why not? Rainier – wrestling with the financial problems of Monaco – felt there could be no harm in a little glamorous publicity.[48] After the shoot, Kelly remarked that she found the prince 'charming, quite charming – and shy'.[49]

Rainier – painstakingly reclaiming the respect of a population still smarting from the reign of Louis II – was struggling against the Onassis plan to remake Monte Carlo into a high-rolling, fast-living gambling resort. A fan of fast cars, Rainier had almost been killed in a serious accident in 1953. By the time of the photoshoot, he was in his early thirties – high time to get married. Tourism was on the increase, and a royal wedding might draw the curious to the principality. His chaplain, Father Tucker, drew up a list of possibilities which included Grace Kelly.

Grace Kelly and Rainier III began to correspond as various priests sounded out the likelihood of her accepting an offer of marriage. If Rainier proposed, he couldn't, as a prince, be seen to be refused. Prince and movie star met again on the set of *The Swan*, a remake of a 1925 silent film about the amorous court intrigues of a family wanting to reclaim their throne. Kelly had been vetted, approved and seemed willing to make the marriage. Still under contract to MGM, she reached the agreement that if she were to film *High Society* and the studio obtain exclusive rights to film the royal wedding, they would release her from all contractual obligations.[50]

Kelly's final film before marrying was about a girl who is destined to marry an overtly conventional and very boring wrong man, and who – at the eleventh hour – is rescued by her jazz-loving ex-husband. With a Cole Porter score including nine new songs, in a film uniting Louis Armstrong, 'crooner' Bing Crosby and new-generation singer Frank Sinatra, *High Society* is full of brio. While filming, Kelly wore her actual engagement ring from Rainier – 'a skating rink on her finger', quipped Celeste Holm, who played the photographer sent to cover the wedding. Towards the end of shooting, Holm was invited by Kelly to a lunch at which the prince was present. A guest asked, 'How big is Monaco?' Bad question, thought Holm. The prince replied, and the guest retorted, 'Gee, that's smaller than our back lot.'[51]

Meanwhile, there was much repairing, repainting and rejuvenating the Grimaldi palace in Monte Carlo for the wedding, which was set for 18–19 April 1956. Kelly arrived with members of her family and friends on the SS *Constitution*. From the moment she disembarked onto Rainier's yacht, which had sailed out to greet her, she played the part of the serene princess to perfection. In the MGM documentary covering the event, it is the prince who, at times, appears anxious. In newsreels, he appeared to fret – whereas, Celeste Holm noted, Kelly was 'a princess before she married that prince'. As the couple sped ashore amid a flotilla of small craft carrying reporters, Aristotle Onassis watched from his yacht while his plane showered the harbour with red and white carnations. He had high hopes of such a match changing the fortunes of the principality in which he had so heavily invested.

Although Rainier was disappointed by the poor return from the invitations he had sent out – Churchill, De Gaulle, Eisenhower and Buckingham Palace were among the refusals – those who accepted included the Aga Khan, Cary Grant, David Niven and the peevish publicity-seeker Norah, Lady Docker. The civil ceremony was at 11 a.m. on the 18th – the very day on which MGM chose to release *The Swan*. That evening, the opera gala – 'The Stars Dance for the Princess' – included Margot Fonteyn and Michael Soames, Serge Lifar and 'baby ballerina' Tamara Toumanova. At midnight, the lights in the principality were dimmed and Aristotle Onassis's hour-long firework display began – an extravagant spectacle that outdid the fabulous display Hitchcock had been obliged to use in *To Catch a Thief* as an explosive metaphor for lovemaking. On the 19th, the couple were married in the Cathedral of St Nicholas. Of the 1,500 journalists packing the principality, two unauthorized reporters disguised themselves as priests to gain entry. Climbing around behind the altar, one even used the transom of the cross to steady his camera.

By marrying, Princess Grace acquired a slew of titles – 142 in all. Even an actress used to learning lines could not possibly remember them all, but throughout the religious ceremony, the wedding lunch, the reception at the Hôtel de Paris and the newlyweds' departure on the prince's yacht for a six-week honeymoon cruise around Spain, Grace Kelly was a star. She had renounced the film industry, and her husband somewhat churlishly banned the projection of her films in

Monaco. Kelly successfully embarked on an unforeseen adventure, and the Principality of Monaco took on a new lease of life.[52]

Four days after the wedding, the Cannes Film Festival began. Prince Aly Khan met Kim Novak. One of the jury members was Arletty, who had come in from the cold. Despite the presence in the competition of masterpieces such as Satyajit Ray's *Pather Panchali* and Ingmar Bergman's *Smiles of a Summer's Night*, the top prize at Cannes – renamed the 'Palme d'Or' – went to Jacques-Yves Cousteau and Louis Malle for their documentary *The Silent World*. The film revealed the treasures and the horrors of an unexplored realm rendered accessible by Cousteau's refinements to the Aqua-Lung.

From his villa in Sanary, Cousteau had worked against the Italian occupation. After the war, he had set up the Underwater Research Group based in Toulon. He then leased the research ship *Calypso* from the British politician, businessman and philanthropist Thomas Loel Guinness for a token one franc a year. The film, made by a daring camera crew, was a celebration of the ship's many adventures – the observation of the exceptional bio-sonar faculties of the porpoise, the demonstration of the freedom afforded by a scuba device, a battle with frenzied sharks busy devouring a wounded baby whale, and the intrigue of exploring sunken ships. The Côte d'Azur would be able to open up in a new way, as Cousteau invited amateur divers into its translucent blue weightlessness. The choice of the flattest sections of the coast for the Allied landings in 1944 meant that there were a significant number of diveable wrecks from the war – PT boats, British and American minesweepers, landing craft, and the occasional aeroplane such as an American B-24 Liberator or German Heinkel He 111. While the film clearly promoted the new opportunities skin-diving offered on the Riviera, it remained an odd choice for the top prize.

Among Noël Coward's 'new caste of English visitor' was the brash Norah, Lady Docker. Born above a butcher's shop in Derby, the newspaper celebrity started out in life selling lampshades in a department store. Not wanting to stay in the shades, she then took work as a dance club hostess at London's Café de Paris. She married three millionaires – number two richer than number one. Number three – Sir Bernard Docker, managing director of the Birmingham Small Arms Company and chairman of Daimler cars – was even richer. With Norah's encouragement, Docker had Daimler produce a succession of increasingly showy cars – the Silver Flash, the Stardust and the Golden Zebra, with its zebra-skin upholstery. When asked about that, Norah replied that 'mink is too hot to sit on'. She owned six gold-plated Daimlers, whingeing that the gold was too thin.[53] Her tantrums and her craving for ostentation kept her newsworthy in austerity Britain.

A series of tiny crises in Lady Docker's relationship with Monaco began with her disappointment over a cabaret for a 1951 Red Cross gala. Telling Prince Jean-Louis de Faucigny-Lucinge – then president of the Sporting Club – that it was awful, led to an eventful evening during which she was snubbed by Lucinge. The Dockers were refused entry to the Casino. After they finally managed to slip in, they were not allowed to leave. In a hissy fit, Norah slapped a friendly casino official and then left.[54] The object of the snakes-and-ladders-like Monte Carlo Memorial Game – invented after the royal wedding – was to get from the Casino to the palace. Among the hazards along the way was 'Go to Lady Docker's yacht – drink champagne for three rounds'.[55]

Invited to the wedding of Rainier and Grace Kelly, the Dockers left for the cathedral in their Silver Stardust Daimler, but were instructed – as were all other drivers – to leave it in the car park and proceed by bus. Norah took umbrage. The night before, she had been outraged when forbidden to take a drink into the ballet gala.[56]

In her autobiography, Norah Docker manages to get the wrong year for the wedding.[57] Her chapter on Monte Carlo proceeds – sometimes inaccurately – through a series of inflated affronts and humiliations that should never have been visited on a couple of such consequence. Lunching at the Hôtel de Paris after an incident at the christening of Prince Albert, Norah tore up the little Monégasque-flag table decoration, snapping, 'To hell with the Monégasques.' This led to the couple being banned from Monaco and eventually

Winston Churchill painting on the Riviera.

the Alpes-Maritimes – or 'Alps de Maritime' as she calls it. The official reaction may have seemed petty, but perhaps the principality wanted rid of her.

Back home, Norah Docker's huffs and puffs of entitlement fuelled the anti-French carping of the popular English press, to whom she confided – a breathy little victim playing the room – 'I'm at war with Rainier.'[58] The *Daily Mirror* took her side, writing of 'the tetchiness of the bristling little Prince and his bride from Walt Disneyland'. Shameless, in her autobiography she admits that the Dockers left England and settled in Jersey 'to avoid tax and death duties'.[59] They should have played their cards right in Monte Carlo.

Clementine Churchill confided her dislike of the Riviera to her husband's private secretary, Anthony Montague Browne – adding that she felt Winston's enjoyment of it 'epitomised to me the shallowest side of his character'. After the war, Churchill had been thinking of buying a small villa on the Riviera, but when Lord Beaverbrook put La Capponcina at his disposal he gave up the idea. Beaverbrook had a Swiss chef and a good cellar, and Churchill could use the villa every winter – if he wanted – from 1 December through to the beginning of April. In 1955, when Churchill was staying with him, Beaverbrook noted that his guest stayed up late at night drinking brandy, was sluggish in the mornings and was speaking less distinctly than before. On one occasion, Churchill lunched in Saint-Paul-de-Vence and viewed the Matisse chapel afterwards. Churchill was finding it more difficult to paint, complaining that 'my arms won't let me'.[60]

Churchill's longstanding literary agent, Emery Reves, visited La Capponcina with his wife-to-be, the former top model Wendy Russell. They had bought La Pausa, and Churchill became their frequent guest until the end of the decade. He was working on the fourth volume of his *History of the English-Speaking Peoples*. Reves took exception to the 'schoolbookish' title and suggested *Great Moments in History*. The author would have none of it, and Reves said everybody would, of course, abide by Churchill's final decision, but showed him letters from foreign publishers revealing how badly the title translated – for instance *Histoire des Peuples de Langue Anglaise*, which, retranslated, becomes 'History of the Peoples of the English Language'. Churchill invoked Edward Gibbon in defence of his title. Reves pointed out that 'Decline and Fall' was more potent than 'History' and 'Roman Empire' more evocative than 'Latin-Speaking People'.[61]

During Churchill's spells at La Pausa, he enjoyed the serenity of a house filled with an impressive collection of French Impressionist and Post-Impressionist paintings. When there were no guests, Reves would play classical gramophone records after dinner in an attempt to refine Churchill's musical tastes.[62] When people were invited, the guests were – as they had been with Maxine Elliott – chosen to suit Churchill. Daisy Fellowes – 'wonderfully well maintained' – came to dinner with her young man and 'kept us all agog'. When that very 'able and masterful man' Aristotle Onassis dined, he surprised Churchill by kissing his hand.[63] Noël Coward came to lunch with Edward Molyneux, and noted in his diary that Churchill had wandering eyes and naughty thoughts about his glamorous hostess. Montague Browne felt that Coward's prurient remarks had something to do with Churchill's role in the entertainer's omission from the honours list.[64] Many people visited, from Konrad Adenauer, Chancellor of West Germany, to Greta Garbo and Somerset Maugham[65] – but, as Beaverbrook remarked, Churchill was at his best in a one-on-one conversation, 'otherwise he acted too much'.[66]

Churchill could spend up to a third of a year in the south – sometimes with his wife, often without. La Capponcina and La Pausa were havens, but he despaired of the creeping commercialism of the Côte d'Azur. Driving to Nice airport, he remarked on a large advert for sparkling Perrier water, captioned *L'eau qui fait Pschitt*, 'I've never spelled it that way.'[67]

The British painter Graham Sutherland spent time on the Riviera from after the war until the late sixties. In 1955, he purchased a villa designed by Eileen Grey at Menton. Strangely, his landscape painting was not stimulated so much by the south of France as it later would be by Pembrokeshire. Sutherland was, however, a controversial portrait painter, whose subjects included Riviera figures such as Somerset Maugham, Lord Beaverbrook and Winston Churchill. The 1949 portrait of Maugham conveys the intelligent discomfort of the author. Beaverbrook's portrait captures the powerful newspaperman used to influencing and persuading. It was – thought Beaverbrook – both an 'outrage' and a 'masterpiece'. Churchill detested his portrait commissioned by Parliament, to be presented to him on the occasion of his eightieth birthday in 1954. He had wished to be shown robed as a Knight of the Garter. Unfortunately, the commission stated otherwise and – by choosing Sutherland – the result was unlikely to be hagiographic. The painter revealed his sitters, warts and all. Lady Churchill found the depiction 'quite alarmingly like' her husband, but – knowing how much the image distressed him – controversially had it destroyed shortly after it was delivered.

Other foreign artists were working on the Riviera. The American colour-field painter Sam Francis found the radiance in his work not in his native California, but rather in Provence in the early 1950s. Marc Chagall returned to France after the war and settled first on Cap Ferrat and then in Vence. Perhaps inspired by the Matisse chapel, he began to contemplate a series of large Old Testament canvases. Nicolas de Staël was born in pre-Revolution St Petersburg, son of the governor of the Peter and Paul Fortress. Like so many Russians before him, de Staël was attracted by the warmth and light of the Mediterranean. Working furiously in what had been Picasso's post-war studio in Antibes, he produced 354 paintings during a six-month period in 1954–5. He spoke of 'flinging' himself into his work and of feeling 'dizzy'. After attending two Webern and Schöenberg concerts in Paris, he painted – between 12 March and the morning of the 14th – a huge 6-by-3.5-metre painting evoking the concert. Two days later he flung himself off the parapet of the Château Grimaldi.[68]

The Cannes Film Festival was under attack by the young journalist François Truffaut, who pilloried the selection of films and the motives for holding a festival which gave 'a very imprecise idea of what is most interesting in world cinema'. Truffaut's articles in the *Cahiers du Cinéma* and *Arts* were not only a catalogue of the festival's failings, but also suggestions for improvement. The festival was young, international and clearly had the potential to become a major player on the world stage – a worthy alternative to the Oscars, and an event that would sit comfortably alongside Venice and Berlin. On 4 May 1959, Truffaut's first film, *Les Quatre Cents Coups*, was screened. Its young star, Jean-Pierre Léaud, adopted – not for the last time – Truffaut's alter-ego, Antoine Doinel. The fourteen-year-old arrived at the festival on the overnight train from Paris. Carrying a battered suitcase in his hand and wearing a winning smile, he looked the lonely but eager outsider. The boy ended his appearance at the festival hoisted on the shoulders of a rapturous crowd. His director, Truffaut, had won the Best Director award, and opened the doors to the Nouvelle Vague which would influence the work of directors around the world. It would revivify French cinema and the Cannes Film Festival. Despite occasional accusations of diplomatic bias, Cannes was henceforth a byword for the best in cinema.[69]

The growing success of Cannes gave rise to the idea of jazz festivals. The first was held in Nice in June 1948, presenting –

among others – Louis Armstong and Mezz Mezzrow. A decade later, Cannes followed with a line-up that included Stan Getz, Ella Fitzgerald, Coleman Hawkins and Dizzy Gillespie. Soon afterwards, the festival that would become the most important on the Côte d'Azur was announced by the mayor of Antibes. Hosted in Juan-les-Pins from 1960, the festival was proceeded by a decade in which prominent musicians had played jazz in that resort. Just as the Riviera had become 'Montparnasse south' for the artists and writers of the 1920s, so Juan-les-Pins – with its Vieux-Colombier nightclub – became for musicians an extension of that exciting quarter of post-war Paris, Saint-Germain-des-Prés. At the Vieux-Colombier, Edith Piaf and Juliette Gréco sang, and the orchestra of Claude Luter and the band of Maxim Saury performed. Sidney Bechet appeared every year from 1950 until his death in 1959, and the venue was the site of the all-night wedding party of Bechet and Elizabeth Ziegler on 17 August 1951. Bechet had played the Riviera since 1927, when he was in the band at the Eldorado in Nice accompanying Josephine Baker and La Revue Nègre.[70]

In the palace at Monte Carlo, Princess Grace – sometimes feeling lonely – threw herself into her husband's initiatives for revitalizing the principality. Work was begun on a tunnel and underground train station, to create more space and cleanliness at street level. The princess persuaded Rainier to stop the cruel sport of pigeon shooting. The Grand Prix was thriving, and it was an arena in which the British presence on the Riviera remained imposing. In a career marked by sixteen wins in sixty-six Grand Prix races, Stirling Moss won the Monte Carlo race in 1956. Italian cars – Moss drove one that year – continued to dominate, but English models were gaining a reputation. In 1958, the French Maurice Trintignant – uncle of the film star Jean-Louis Trintignant – won the Grand Prix in a British Cooper T45, a car also driven by the Australian Jack Brabham, who came fourth. Brabham won in 1959, driving a Cooper T51. In 1960, Sterling Moss won again, driving a Lotus 18. Out of the nine cars classed, there were four British drivers.[71]

Rainier created the Monaco Development Council – emphasizing the tax-free status of the principality to lure foreign investors. President Charles de Gaulle took exception to a haven in which French people could take up residence and avoid paying French tax. In October 1959, de Gaulle gave Rainier an ultimatum – six months to rectify the situation, or lose the friendly status agreed between the two countries. France put up customs barriers, and the agreement reached – that French citizens living in Monaco could not escape French taxation – resulted in the removal of about 10 billion francs to Swiss banks.

To get away from the stress of ruling, Rainier bought an old farmhouse at Mont Agel, above the golf course. It had a swimming pool, horses, and a modern kitchen where Grace could cook when she used the property as a retreat. Missing the freedoms and challenges of her old life, she was tempted to work with Alfred Hitchcock and Cary Grant again – fascinated by the script for a psychological thriller to be called *Marnie*. When the Monégasques opposed the participation of their princess, she reluctantly gave up the idea.[72]

The prolonged impact of paid holidays was transforming the southern coast into a French destination. At Cavalaire, there were holiday camps that trade unions built for the benefit of their members in the industrial north. There were large campsites at Théoule, La Napoule, Juan-les-Pins, Cap Ferrat and Menton. There was even a small site with a restaurant in Cannes. In the late fifties, Sanary still thought of itself as a fishing village, whereas Le Lavandou had grown from Willa Cather's unmapped village of a hundred souls into a resort with forty hotels, service flats and a casino.[73] Its entertainments were brash, and calculated to draw an unsophisticated, even vulgar, clientele. There were competitions 'for the best bust, the most beautiful bottom, the plumpest thighs and the straightest knees'. Prizes included silk stockings and champagne. The resort also offered sports such as 'naked bathing by night, with searchlights playing on the sea'.[74]

As Nice prepared to celebrate the centenary of the annexation of the Comté de Nice by France, the curator of the Musée Masséna was appointed to research traditional costume for the dancing of the Provençal farandole in May and the parades of folk art in June. If Jean Vigo's *À Propos de Nice* had fanfared the 1930s, then Agnès Varda's *Du Côté de la Côte*, which was made in 1958 for the tourist industry, celebrated the democratized, technicolor coast of the 1950s. It also highlighted its cosmopolitanism – the Russian church at Nice, a Buddhist pagoda and Sudanese mosque at Fréjus, a Persian house at Monte Carlo, and an oriental palace at Menton. German and British holidaymakers were gently mocked for their frumpy beachwear. Sunburn on those scantily clad appeared raw. Nonetheless, the theme of paradise ran with determination through the film.

The Aga Khan – who, as a young man, had been perplexed by Queen Victoria's 'distinctly second-class servants' – died in 1957. In November of that year, his son Prince Aly was appointed Pakistani ambassador to the United Nations, but the impossibility of his making any noticeable impact frustrated him. He invited Senator John F. Kennedy and his wife, Jacqueline, to the Château de l'Horizon, giving them the 'Churchill' suite. The Kennedy marriage had been rocked by his frequent infidelities and her outrageous spending. During their stay, the couple resolved not to separate, in order to serve JFK's presidential ambition.[75]

Around this time, Aly Khan was losing his verve. Gianni Agnelli noticed the forty-seven-year-old trying to do things he had done at twenty-five. He considered Aly's publicity-seeking a surefire way of attracting lovers. But he also noticed that Aly's women were a little less glamorous and a little less eager. It all ended when Aly Khan killed himself in a car crash in the Bois de Boulogne in 1960, aged forty-eight.[76]

The verbal wit that had once embellished life on the Côte d'Azur had disappeared in the slipstream of the jet set's obsession with flaunting wealth. Noël Coward's 'poor little rich girls' had become Norah, Lady Docker. Gone were the sophisticated liaisons of yesteryear. In place of Viscount Castlerosse's waspish wit, there was gold-plated veneer for the tabloids. Coward had gone off to the Bahamas. He left behind a song – 'The Party's Over Now'.

12

Sunny But Shady
1960–90

The tourists visiting the Côte d'Azur were changing. In 1963, there were just over 64,000 British visitors, compared with 610,000 from France.[1] The *congés payés* had been extended to three weeks in 1956, and would be extended to four in 1969. Mass tourism took hold. With Nice airport handling a million passengers in 1964, 2.5 million a decade later, and 7.5 million in 1985, access was becoming easier. The SNCF's rapid *Mistral* train carried 450 passengers. Slowly, the Blue Train stuttered out of service. It had, over the years, attracted a growing body of crime fiction. Apart from Agatha Christie, who was drawn to murder in closed or confined circumstances, Georges Simenon's *Mon Ami Maigret* of 1949 saw the celebrated inspector reluctantly take the Blue Train with his Scotland Yard counterpart, Mr Pyke, as they travelled to solve a crime on the Île de Porquerolles, south of Hyères. In the 1960s, a thirteen-part television series based on the novel *Le Train Bleu s'Arrête Treize Fois* by Pierre Boileau and Thomas Narcejac offered a crime for each of the thirteen stations on the route.[2]

What is memorable about the last decades of the twentieth century is not so much who visited the Riviera, but the character of the coast to which they came. Local corruption and gangland wars made little overt impact on visitors, although tourists were unwittingly and passively implicated. The cronyism of local government and the tentacular mafia presence meant that facilities enjoyed by holidaymakers were sustained by the greed that nourishes crime. Paradise became a paradise for speculators. Rather than a new beginning, a familiar epithet for the 1960s, that decade on the Riviera could be seen as the beginning of the end.

The sixties started with a robbery from the Colombe d'Or in Saint-Paul-de-Vence. Paul Roux had died in 1955 and left his widow and their son, François, in charge. The restaurant continued to be a great favourite with artists, actors, writers and directors. It was still a casual, easy-come easy-go establishment – an attitude altered by the theft.

On the night of 31 March 1960, thieves watched as the Colombe d'Or went dark. They had cased the restaurant several days earlier, and loosened the screws on one of its shutters. Stealing twenty-one canvases – including a Braque, a Léger, a Miró and a Modigliani – they left a Picasso on the roadside as it didn't fit in their car. Only days earlier, the municipal museum in Menton had been targeted, and crooks got away with seven paintings.

Following leads from Corsican gangsters, the police were swiftly on the trail of the Colombe d'Or robbers. A talkative, unemployed baker boasted of his role in the heist, and the police hauled him in for questioning. He ratted on his accomplices who had planned the robbery – Lulu 'the Belgian', Denis 'the Corsican'. Altogether, there were six involved. Meanwhile, François Roux was summoned to a meeting in Cannes in the early hours of the morning, to identify the paintings. If he wanted to retrieve them, he should hide 10 million Mexican pesos near the Fontaine de Saint-Paul-de-Vence. Months passed. Rumours circulated that an Arab diplomat offered 15 million francs for the paintings, but the thieves – feeling the heat – offered to return the canvases in exchange for clemency. Following a tip-off, the twenty paintings were recovered from the left-luggage room in Marseille's Saint-Charles station.[3]

Just over a year later, thieves targeted the small, early-sixteenth-century Chapelle Notre-Dame de l'Annonciade in Saint-Tropez. It had been placed at the disposition of the rich industrialist and collector Georges Grammont to house his astonishing collection of largely local paintings. Transformed by the architect Louis Süe into a tiny museum, it opened in 1955 with nearly sixty works, including

The Musée de l'Annonciade,
Saint-Tropez.

sumptuously coloured views of Saint-Tropez by artists such as
Matisse, Signac and Bonnard. At 6 a.m. on 16 July 1961, the cleaning
lady arrived at the Musée de l'Annonciade and saw to her horror
that the impressive array of Fauvist paintings had disappeared. That
night, the guard watching over a museum that had never been fitted
with security alarms had gone to visit a sick relative.

A ransom was demanded – 500,000 francs. Each week, André
Dunoyer de Segonzac received a little cutting from a watercolour he
had made of Saint-Tropez, to show that the thieves meant business
when they said that without the ransom they would destroy
everything they had taken. Over agonizing months, as de Segonzac
jigsawed the tiny fragments of his painting, the police tried to trace
the canvases and catch the thieves. After a protracted war of nerves,
the robbers capitulated. On 16 November 1962, the Minister of
Culture, André Malraux, received a communication stating that the
robbers had left the fifty-six stolen works in a barn in a village near
Paris. A note was appended, begging that their generosity would be
recognized and earn them forgiveness.[4] The thefts in Menton, at the
Colombe d'Or and at the Musée de l'Annonciade, inspired gangs
who had lived off drug-dealing, prostitution, protection rackets
and gambling to consider art.

❖

On 11 April 1965, the press announced – correctly this time – the death of the courtesan La Belle Otero. A neighbour in the rue d'Angleterre, where she had lived in increasingly reduced circumstances, had smelled burning. Firemen and police had rushed to the scene and found an elderly woman, dressed, dead on her bidet. Fresh bread and two prepared dishes from a nearby *traiteur* sat on the table. The pan of water on the stove had boiled dry. Living on a municipal pension from Nice and two small pensions from the casinos of Monte Carlo and Cannes, Otero had told a journalist that no queen had ever lived like she did because she had 'been through so many kings'. Dying at ninety-six, Otero was buried in the Cimitière de l'Est. The mourners included her adopted son and the few locals who still cared for '*la belle des belles de la Belle Époque*'.[5]

Otero had been part of the world that Somerset Maugham evoked in his play *Lady Frederick* – Monte Carlo's rigid social divide, the class of *monde* and *demi-monde*. Despite living on Cap Ferrat for decades, Maugham wrote little about the Riviera. A notable exception was this play, set in a suite at the Hôtel Splendide in Monte Carlo in 1885 and first produced in London in 1907. The revival at the Savoy Theatre in November 1946 looked back from post-war austerity Britain on a lost world where the privileged rode every morning, drove in the afternoons and gambled half the night. When Charlie Mereston is asked what he is doing in Monte Carlo – hard-pressed to find any specific reason – he mentions the Casino. Charlie is preparing to take a seat in the House of Lords and desperately trying not to reveal any shred of talent. As the British like dull leaders, he observes that the nation's destiny could hardly be entrusted to a 'man whose speeches were pointed and sparkling' and whose mind was 'quick and agile'.[6] In the post-war production, such jibes gained in potency, as the electorate had ditched the eloquent Winston Churchill in the summer of 1945.

According to his nephew Robin, by the mid-1960s Maugham was a 'little frail old man, with a wizened, wrinkled face like a Chinese sage'. Although he hadn't written for a long time, Maugham was overwhelmed by fan letters and his royalties were undiminished.[7]

The bathmat designed for him by Matisse and the paintings were important,[8] but – tormented by a sense of failure – his wealth meant little. After the death of his lover Gerald Haxton, he had rarely given large parties, preferring dinners.[9] Over the years, he entertained an array of people – Arnold Bennett, Kenneth Clark, Ian and Ann Fleming, Churchill, Beaverbrook, the Windsors, Cecil Beaton, Evelyn Waugh, Marc Chagall, Rebecca West and Noël Coward, who, when he arrived, would greet his host as 'Cher maître'. Maxine Elliott – one of the inspirations for his story 'The Three Fat Women of Antibes' – was invited.[10] Maugham liked asking women to the Villa Mauresque because it helped conceal his homosexuality from the public.[11] In the winter of 1965, a bout of Asian flu leading to pulmonary complications took him to the Anglo-American Hospital on Mont Boron in Nice. He died there on 16 December in a room overlooking the bay of Villefranche, towards his home on Cap Ferrat. Matron Elsie Gladman noted that her patient could be 'stubborn'.[12]

Churchill also died in 1965. Nearly a decade earlier, while staying at La Pausa, he had blacked out, suffering a cerebral spasm. The attack was demoralizing and detrimental to his health. In the early sixties, the Churchills had opted for the ease of the Hôtel de Paris in Monte Carlo. He had lived long and effectively but, by the time of his death, many of his attitudes – belief in British colonial rule and 'Aryan stock' – were markedly out of date.[13]

At the end of the same year, Jean Médecin, the much-loved mayor of Nice, died. The Médecin dynasty had been in the area since the early sixteenth century and, before that, their lineage could be traced to a branch of the Florentine Medici family. Jean's father had been mayor of Villefranche and, in 1928, Jean had been elected mayor of Nice.[14] Over the decades, he wove a tight and tangled network of useful connections. Following his death, his son Jacques – elected mayor in 1966 – set the tenor of the region. A textbook case of the corruption that riddled France's Ve République – corruption which had seen two ex-presidents condemned to jail and one former prime minister incarcerated – Médecin would write a book in the early nineties, during his time imprisoned in Maldonado and Montevideo. After railing against the lefties and journalists who hounded him, Médecin listed everything that he had done for Nice – the urban autoroute, tunnels for heavy vehicles, the widening of the roads, pedestrian zones, and the construction of a university, twelve museums, the Palais des Congrés, theatres, stadiums, clubs, schools, social housing, elegant old folks' homes. There was also a Jewish centre and the enlargement of their cemetery. He mentioned those 'for the bastards who keep suspecting me of anti-Semitism'.[15]

Médecin coped with the large number of people arriving in the wake of what he called France's 'shameful withdrawal from Algeria'[16] – President de Gaulle's desire to give Algeria its independence from French colonial rule. The dissident paramilitary OAS – Organisation Armée Secrète – was formed to dissuade the French from ceding the colony. They launched attacks in Algeria and hit targets in France. General de Gaulle was in their sights. In the south, they struck in Nice, Cannes-la-Bocca and Vallauris at a time when a survey revealed that nearly 70 per cent of the region's population supported Algerian freedom.

Sympathetic to the extreme right, Jacques Médecin was popular locally but suspected and disliked elsewhere in France. He was always looking to improve his city, certain that everything he was destroying and building would make the Niçois richer. He was seen everywhere and had the gift of the gab – even enjoying short exchanges in Nissart.[17] His network of business relationships was based on mutual benefit and obligation.[18] His 'Latin' look – the moustache, thick eyebrows and yellow-tinted glasses – helped create the image of a man at home in the land of casinos, pimps and gangs.[19]

With its themes of 'spiritual aridity and moral decline' in upper-class Rome,[20] Federico Fellini's *La Dolce Vita* was awarded the Palme d'Or at the 1960 Cannes Film Festival. The following year, the top prize was shared between a French film and Buñuel's shocking *Viridiana*. A probe into the malaise of Roman society scandalized, but blasphemy impregnated with perverse eroticism was criminal. Buñuel's films were banned in Spain, and the Italian government –

acting upon Vatican outrage – condemned the director to a year's imprisonment should he ever set foot on Italian soil.[21] As the sixties progressed, Cannes consolidated its attack on old shibboleths – religious, aesthetic and political. Jacques Rivette's film based on Denis Diderot's novel *La Religieuse* was the scandal of 1966. Banned by the French state, when it was shown at Cannes it provoked a heated argument between the Gaullist government and the young French film directors of the Nouvelle Vague.[22] The term – first used by Françoise Giroud in the autumn of 1957 to describe the hopes and frustrations of French youth – was applied to radical filmmakers such as François Truffaut, Jean-Luc Godard and Claude Chabrol, who were changing the landscape of French films.

Two works were refused for the festival in 1968 – *Tell Me Lies*, Peter Brook's film of his Royal Shakespeare Company play/happening, *US*, and Eugene S. Jones's *A Face of War*. Both were deemed risky at a time when the Americans were negotiating with the North Vietnamese in Paris.[23] In the event, the festival – sympathetic to the student and worker revolt of May 1968 – was closed down on 19 May. Revolution, political struggle between liberal values and the extreme right, and the attempt to drop out of an unsympathetic society were themes explored at the festival in 1969. For the coveted Palme d'Or, jury president Luchino Visconti favoured *Z*, the Costa-Gavras film exploring the preconditions of the *coup-d'état* by the Greek colonels.[24] In the event, the film that won was Lindsay Anderson's *If...* It probes simmering revolution in the hothouse world of an English public school, until defiance fails as the empire strikes back.

Anderson was a guest at Le Nid du Duc, the hamlet owned by British New Wave film director Tony Richardson. Set amid the greenery of the Maures, Le Nid du Duc was a welcome escape from the hectic worlds of the Cannes Film Festival and the nearby resort of Saint-Tropez. In 1970, Anderson found the ambiance distinctly homosexual. Rudolf Nureyev – who had a villa at La Turbie above Monte Carlo – visited. David Hockney came with his then boyfriend, the American artist Peter Schlesinger. Among the canvases inspired by his stay was *Portrait of an Artist (Pool with two Figures)*, which sold at Christie's in New York in November 2018, fetching the highest price at that time for a work by a living artist – just over $90 million. When Lindsay Anderson went to shop in Saint-Tropez, he recoiled at the expense – 'but one has the impression that expense could never be a reason for *not buying* anything'. The following month, this man who had won the Palme d'Or at Cannes was back in Britain, casting a short commercial for Findus frozen foods.[25]

Confrontational in their approach, the local artists comprising the *École de Nice* worked in a variety of contemporary modes and supplanted the seventy-year-old tradition of visiting artists treating the coast. Their success resulted from the confluence of their talent, the Zeitgeist of modern art, and the fact they came from the Côte d'Azur. Yves Klein, Arman, Martial Raysse, and Ben Vautier called themselves 'Nouveaux Réalistes', echoed the Pop artists of the United States, and embraced and helped shape Conceptual and Performance Art. Above all, as they were Nice-based, they wanted their work to be the result of a 'permanent vacation'. Klein noted that 'gives us this spirit of nonsense'.[26] His development of a deep ultramarine blue which became his signature colour – International Klein Blue – was inspired by his life on the Mediterranean. The art of Martial Raysse, who echoed Klein's assertions about the endless vacation, presented the Riviera as playful, international, and susceptible to pop culture and kitsch consumerism.[27] His sculpture *Tree* in the Musée d'Art Moderne et d'Art Contemporain de Nice – its foliage created from plastic bottles found on the beach – has only gained in ecological significance in the sixty years since it was made.

One of the gambits used by the *École de Nice* to encourage people to see anew and question what constitutes a work of art, was simply to sign things. These 'appropriations', started by Yves Klein, were taken up by Arman, who signed the barrels of wine in the port of Nice, and Raysse, who signed the cosmetic shelves in a supermarket. Ben Vautier was photographed holding an empty frame through which Nice was visible. He wrote on the frame '*Ben signe Nice 1963*'.[28] Such 'appropriations' removed an object from one reality into another, underlining – as Marcel Duchamp had before them – the absurdity of defining and marketing art through the signature of the artist.

Much of the group's work can be directly related to the Côte d'Azur, yet its regard and appeal were international. The *École de Nice* became an impressive alternative to the Parisian avant-garde,[29] which by the early sixties had lost its dominant position as 'the capital of art' to New York. According to Klein, even New York was passé. He proposed a new axis: 'Nice–Los Angeles–Tokyo'.

Art as a tourist attraction was being developed along the Riviera. May 1960 saw the inauguration of the Musée National Fernand Léger at Biot. It was the region's first specifically constructed museum devoted to the work of a single artist. In 1964, the Minister of Culture, André Malraux, opened the Fondation Maeght just outside Saint-Paul-de-Vence. Marguerite and Aimé Maeght were art dealers, publishers and documentary makers, and their foundation was created to exhibit the work of twentieth-century artists who lived and worked in France. Designed by a Catalan architect, Josep Lluís Sert, the foundation consists of an asymmetrical cluster of buildings in local stone, rose brick and white concrete, which sit against the pine-covered hills. The Spanish artist Joan Miró made the ceramics, sculptures and fountains for the terraces, which also display works by other artists – an Alexander Calder stabile, the gaunt striding figures of Alberto Giacometti, and a fun if somewhat clunky kinetic work by Pol Bury.

Marc Chagall moved to Saint-Paul in 1966, one year before his eightieth birthday. Throughout the fifties and sixties, he worked on huge canvases illustrating major stories from the Old Testament. Absorbed by this theme for decades, Chagall was striving to compensate for the lack of a visual tradition in Judaism. He remarked, 'I have been fascinated by the Bible since my earliest childhood. I have always felt that it was the most fabulous source of poetic inspiration imaginable.' Influenced by the mystical strain in Hasidic Judaism, his interest resulted in seventeen large oils depicting scenes from Genesis, Exodus and the Song of Solomon, which Chagall and his wife gave to the French government. In

Jazz at Juan-les-Pins.

February 1969, the foundation stone was laid for the Musée Message Biblique in Nice. Opening in the summer of 1973, the canvases inspired by the first two books of the Pentateuch were not placed according to biblical chronology but in function of a colour logic. The abstract stained-glass windows treating the theme of creation, which Chagall made for the museum's lecture theatre, were placed so as to be read from right to left as in Hebrew writing.

Picasso moved into his last house, overlooking the bay of Cannes at Mougins, in 1962 – the year of the untimely death of the young Yves Klein. Picasso had become a visual magician, a celebrity. Until his death eleven years later, he continued to produce powerful works on themes that obsessed him – notably women. Among them were some fine works, but genius was somewhat eclipsed by showmanship.

The Murphys were remembered on the Jazz à Juan festival website as '*les Enfants du Jazz*' for their important role in bringing that music to the Riviera.[30] Held annually from 1960, the Antibes Juan-les-Pins Jazz Festival has thrived. Charlie Mingus, boycotting the

Newport Jazz Festival, appeared in its first season. Ray Charles established his reputation in Europe by performing at Antibes in 1961. Miles Davis recorded *Miles in Antibes* in 1963, with a young Herbie Hancock on the piano. In the mid-sixties, Duke Ellington, Ella Fitzgerald, Roy Eldridge and John Coltrane appeared as the venue became the Festival Européan de Jazz. Then, from 1975, it became the Festival International du Jazz Antibes-Juan-les-Pins, and in the 1990s, Jazz à Juan. The festival takes place over ten days in July, with most concerts held at La Pinède, an outdoor arena seating 4,000. Over the years, giants such as Erroll Garner, Stan Getz, Aretha Franklin, Chet Baker, Ahmad Jamal and Keith Jarrett have played, and the scope of the festival has steadily increased. In the 1960s, rock 'n' roll was invited, when Fats Domino, Chuck Berry and Little Richard performed.

On Wednesday, 30 June 1965, The Beatles played to 8,000 people at the Palais des Expositions in Nice with a programme that included 'Twist and Shout', 'A Hard Day's Night', 'I Feel Fine' and 'Ticket to Ride'. Just over two years later, Paul McCartney came back without his bandmates to film a sequence to accompany his song 'A Fool on the Hill' for the ill-fated Magical Mystery Tour. Shooting took place at dawn on the hills above Nice, but the images added little to the song.

At the beginning of the 1970s, UK supertax stood at 83 per cent with tax on unearned income at 98 per cent. On 5 April 1971 – the start of a new English tax year – the Rolling Stones fled to the south of France, where Keith Richards rented the Belle Époque Villa Nelcôte at the base of the Cap Ferrat peninsula. The rest of the group were spread about. Hating the Riviera in season, Charlie Watts rented in the Vaucluse.[31] Mick Jagger was in Saint-Tropez for his marriage in May.

During the sixties, rebellious and provocative Saint-Tropez had stiffened into a self-conscious resort where people went to be seen. Limited space and high prices initially secured an exclusivity that was soon destroyed by the sheer number of people wanting to be there. David Dodge noted that on Tahiti Beach 'the sheen of sun

The Villa Nellcôte.

oil… was blinding'. People slept during the day – on the sand under sunscreen, under trees in the shade. Nights were swilled with drink and danced away in cha-cha-chas and twists.[32] By May 1971, Saint-Tropez was still an 'in' resort – a place where you could make a glamorous splash for a big event, and where Mick Jagger married the Nicaraguan Bianca Pérez-Mora amid a media scrum. As Keith Richards wryly remarked, Jagger wanted a quiet wedding, so he chose Saint-Tropez in the middle of summer.[33] Although Bianca was four months pregnant, the couple had to fight through tight crowds to get to the civic ceremony. French marriage involves a declaration of ownership to be used in the case of divorce. Bianca nearly called the whole thing off when she found out how few assets were declared to be common. The couple were then mistakenly locked out of the religious ceremony – the fisherman's chapel of St Anne had been shut against the surge of photographers.

The reception was held at the Hôtel Byblos, built four years earlier on the highest hill of Saint-Tropez by a Lebanese businessman who had developed a crush on Brigitte Bardot.

Among the local guests were Bardot and Roger Vadim. Seventy-five others had been flown down from London in a plane chartered by Jagger. Paul McCartney and Ringo Starr – temporary enemies during a post-Beatles legal wrangle – kept away from each other. Keith Richards was out of his head and flat on his back. Bianca later declared that her marriage ended on her wedding day. Despite all the chaos, journalist David Hepworth claimed that the wedding marked 'the establishment of rock and roll as a viable branch of high society'.[34]

Meanwhile, Richards bought a speedboat – *Mandrax* – and the denizens of the Villa Nelcôte would speed along the coast for breakfast in Menton or over the border in Italy. The villa's cook, Fat Jacques, had connections with the Marseille underworld and soon became their drug dealer, bringing Richards huge sacks of lactose and small sacks of pure heroin. These had to be mixed to the gram – 97 per cent lactose to 3 per cent heroin. Get the proportion wrong – Richards warned – and you were in trouble.[35]

They were having a wild time. Richards and a couple of mates fought off some muggers in Villefranche. Go-karting in Cannes, Richards's kart flipped and he was dragged fifty metres down the tarmac, scraping all the skin from his back. Just off dope, he was given morphine. By July, however, Richards was getting itchy fingers. Deciding against studios in Nice or Cannes, the Stones recorded what many people consider their finest album, *Exile on Main St.*, in the damp, badly ventilated basement bunkers of the villa – hence the track 'Ventilator Blues'. They hooked up their eight-track mobile recording studio, started in the late afternoon and worked on through the night. The dampness affected the tuning of their instruments and their voices. Richards found the fumes of Jack Daniels beneficial.[36]

Recording was interrupted by the birth of Jade Jagger in Paris in October, and by the theft of Keith Richards's collection of vintage guitars from the villa later that month. When the recording was finished in December, the Stones were arrested on drugs charges. Only Richards and his partner, Anita Pallenberg, were convicted, but they escaped to the West Indies. It was rumoured that Jacques

Médecin – allegedly pal to some of the coast's big drug dealers – was behind the arrests.[37]

In the municipal elections of 1971, the slogan 'Nice-Médecin' – so simple, so repeatable – became a talismanic chant.[38] Médecin was consolidating power, and his tentacles were everywhere. Eager to make Nice modern and American, he targeted the impressive Art Deco Palais de la Méditerranée on the Promenade des Anglais. While international high rollers would go to Monte Carlo, Cannes, Beaulieu or to the nearby Ruhl, the casino in the Palais attracted retired people and local landlords. It was a sizeable company, with a staff of 350–400, yet Médecin informed the owner, Renée Le Roux, that it was too old-fashioned. It wasn't making enough money for the city. That needed to be changed.

After their encounter, things started to go awry. On 8 July 1975, the casino's bank lost nearly five million francs at Trente et Quarante. Most unusual. Driving home to Monte Carlo on 3 August, Le Roux stopped – as she often did – to post some letters. She was mugged from behind. Two days later, a fire broke out in the cloakroom of the cooking staff of the Palais. Ten days later, Le Roux surprised a colleague loading cartons of company records into his car. After he absconded with them, she was forced to obtain a court order to retrieve the documents. On 5 September, there was a fire in the Palais's nightclub Le Mécart, forcing it to close for repairs. A week later, several clients complained that the casino's roulette balls were loaded. When Le Mécart reopened, a gang of five, armed with bicycle chains and truncheons, started a fight. The damage forced the club to shut once more.[39]

When the Sun-Beach casino in Menton lost three million francs on 1 October 1975, the enquiry noted there were parallels with the five-million-franc loss at the Palais just three months earlier. Inculpated in the Menton incident was Daniel Guy – a real estate developer who had been convicted for theft and pimping in Switzerland. The others implicated were linked to Urbain Giaume, a drug-dealing Corsican mafioso.[40] Giaume – associated with Jacques Médecin through a building project for the Ruhl casino –

was friends with Jean-Dominique Fratoni, the man who ran that establishment. From 1964 to 1967, Fratoni had been in London, where his Victoria Sporting Club became one of the most successful gambling institutions in Europe. A childhood friend of Médecin, Fratoni returned to Nice with dreams of turning the city into a brash gambling resort.[41] When he secured the Ruhl concession, he gave it a Las Vegas makeover, with red carpets and the lavish use of gold and lacquer. A special gaming room, Le Louisiane, was kept for high rollers and offered – for the first time in France – chips of 500,000 francs. According to the Médecin-owned monthly *L'Action Nice-Côte-d'Azur*, the opening of the Ruhl casino transformed the city into the Mecca of gambling.[42]

Fratoni controlled casinos in Saint-Raphaël, Sainte-Maxime, the Sun-Beach in Menton as well as Le Casino Club and the Ruhl in Nice. Where did his money come from? Where did it go? Rich from drug trafficking and prostitution, the mafia needed somewhere to launder cash. Casinos are useful for that. Players who are complicit can 'lose' great sums of dirty money, collected for a laundering operation which channels illegal gains into respectable investments. The opposite can happen too. Players can 'win' large sums and leave with clean money. Close to the Italian border, the south of France was convenient turf for the mafia. With a man like Médecin in charge, organized crime could turn the coast into something resembling Chicago in the 1920s.

The only thing that stopped Fratoni from becoming the king frontman of casinos on the coast was the Palais. He visited Renée Le Roux and reiterated what Médecin had told her about the wasted opportunity. He wanted to buy the Palais; Le Roux did not want to sell. She found herself standing alone against the mafia-controlled casinos on the Côte d'Azur.

At the end of 1975, the equipment at the Palais was found wanting and Médecin instructed Le Roux to fix it.[43] His manner of favouring Fratoni was flagrant – 1–4 per cent municipal taxes for the Ruhl, 15 per cent for the Palais.[44] In mid-1976, when a low offer was made for the Palais, one of the partners in the bidding group was the ex-employee Le Roux had caught stealing archives.

Again, in March 1977, Médecin pestered Le Roux. Did the Palais respect the regulations for musical presentations? Three months later, *Nice-Matin* announced that the Fratoni group were 'taking over the Palais'. Le Roux had not sold. Fratoni had approached another major shareholder, Renée's daughter Agnès, who – unlike her siblings – agreed to part with her shares.[45]

Fratoni paid Agnès three million francs. Pressured by the family conflict and diagnosed with leukaemia, Agnès attempted to commit suicide twice. Then, in March 1978, a note was found in her apartment saying that her journey was finished: 'I stop there. All is fine.' She then disappeared. The note, coupled with the suicide attempts, persuaded police that she had killed herself. Her lover, Maurice Agnelet, had placed the money from the sale of the shares in a Swiss account. After fleeing to Canada, he was arrested upon his return to France in August 1983. On trial, he slipped up, claiming that he had not touched Agnès's money after her death. But death had never been established. Agnelet was sentenced to eighteen months in jail – but only for vote-buying and breach of trust.[46] On 12 June 1989, twelve years had elapsed since Agnès disappeared, and as her body had not been found, she was declared legally dead.[47] Through the persistence of Renée Le Roux, Agnelet was finally condemned for murder in 2007. In 2014, Agnelet's son confirmed that his father had indeed murdered Agnès Le Roux. Before she died in 2016, aged ninety-three, Renée Le Roux retrieved the three million francs Fratoni had paid her daughter.

Tax authorities investigating the Ruhl casino found that Fratoni had six million francs in his personal account that he was unable to explain. Between 1974 and 1979, 60 million francs passed through the account of the administrator of the Ruhl, Cesare Valsania. He was trafficking gold, money and drugs. Concluding that the Ruhl was the flagship of an organized crime operation wishing to invest in France through the intermediary of casinos, the Ministry of Finance filed a complaint for fraud to the tune of 210 million francs against Fratoni and his associates. Valsania fled and was arrested in Rome. Fratoni – sentenced for tax evasion and vote-buying – escaped to Paraguay, where he was given asylum by a friend of

Jacques Médecin. Facing thirteen years in prison and a huge fine in France, Fratoni broadcast from exile on Médecin's station, Radio Baie des Anges, claiming that he had been misjudged.[48]

The most spectacular crime on the coast in the mid-1970s was the work of a man with a military and criminal history and a Jean-Paul Belmondo charm. Albert Spaggiari had fought in Indochina, where he had been imprisoned for robbery. In Algeria, he had joined the right-wing OAS – the Organisation Armée Secrète – fighting against Algerian independence. That resulted in his being jailed for three and a half years for political terrorism. In 1962, Spaggiari was involved in an OAS plot that aimed to assassinate de Gaulle. The network was blown.[49] Taking life more easily, he settled outside Nice, raised chickens and became a photographer. In the summer of 1976, Spaggiari became a local hero when he broke into the Société Générale bank, stealing over 46 million francs from 337 strongboxes in what was called 'the robbery of the century'.

The idea was seeded by a drink in a bar with an ex-gendarme who was working as a teller at the bank in the Avenue Jean Médecin. He told Spaggiari about the astronomical sums deposited in their vaults. With his amiable manner, Spaggiari took to drinking in cafés around the Société Générale. He ingratiated himself with its employees and enquired – always smiling – about their work. He rented a strongbox and visited the bank regularly to make deposits. Alarm clocks set to go off at different hours were placed in his box to test the alarm system. The strongroom stood beneath an adjacent dress shop. Spaggiari's original idea was to work in the shop from Friday night to Monday morning, piercing a hole in the floor to gain access to the boxes. The Robin Hood motive for the robbery was to help some friends from the OAS and the extreme right who had fallen on hard times.

Casing the joint and trying to decide if he had chosen the best mode of access, Spaggiari was in the street that ran behind the bank when he spotted a technician descend through a manhole to the sewers. Nice's system was extensive and well-engineered – unlike the bank's strongroom, which Spaggiari knew from his clocks was not alarmed. From someone in city administration, he obtained sewer plans for the central sector of Nice and, one night, lifted the manhole cover and climbed down. The stench – unbearable to any ordinary mortal – was merely disturbing to a man who had hit upon the perfect plan.

Spaggiari needed a larger workforce than he could muster, so he enlisted the help of a gang from Marseille. By early April, they obtained an identical vehicle to those used by road maintenance teams. One evening, they parked at the corner of the rue de l'Hôtel des Postes and the rue Deloye, behind the bank. They were placing red cones and signs to signal roadworks when a police car drew up and asked about the job. Spaggiari and one of the gang had started playing the fool, to divert their questions, when a call came through for the officers to go and break up a fight. The robbers descended to explore the stinking underworld. Banging heads, shooing rats and – in places – crawling through excrement, they installed their heavy equipment at the point where they would start to drill.

The sewer sessions continued over several months, with Spaggiari calling their work environment 'the anus of the world'. By the early hours of Saturday 17 July, they broke through to the vault and started to solder the inside of the door through which the bank accessed their strongroom. The contents of the boxes were mixed – millions of francs, jewels, precious jade, an alarm clock, and a collection of pornographic photos of city notables. The Marseille gang wanted to pin the images to the wall for the police to see. Spaggiari told them to put the photos back. Though less nauseating than the sewers, the air was stifling and, by 2 a.m. on Monday morning, the robbers decided to stop. Rain had fallen, and the current in the sewers was strong. With water rising to chest level in places, escape was difficult for men carrying sacks of swag weighing up to sixty kilos.

Later that morning, when bank officials were unable to open the soldered door to the strongbox room, they decided to drill through the wall. After three hours, they got their first glimpse of the devastation. The following day, local headlines proclaimed the 'Break-in of the Century'.[50] Jacques Médecin's delighted reaction to such a spectacular heist was, 'Hats off!'[51] A reward of a million francs was posted for information leading to positive identification. Spaggiari packed his bags, went first to Spain and then to America. Later, as a photographer, he accompanied Médecin on one of his many trips to Japan. It was a large group, flying off to promote tourism on the Côte d'Azur, and Spaggiari's numerous suitcases passed customs unnoticed. He attempted to offload gold and objets d'arts to a fence in Kyoto and deposited sums in an Asian bank. A tip-off from an ex-girlfriend of one of the gang led the police to the thieves, and Spaggiari was arrested when he returned to Nice.

After four months in a cell, he was brought before Judge Richard Bouaziz. Over the course of several interviews, the rogue began to charm the judge. He did not reveal the name of any member of his gang, but told Bouazis about the compromising photos he had seen in the strongroom. At once, the judge asked the two police guards to leave the room, and Spaggiari seized his chance to escape, jumping through an open window that stood eight metres above the ground. He landed on a ledge below and then on the roof of a car. Miraculously, a motorcycle driven by the owner of a local nightclub popular with the right was waiting for him. Transferred to a Bentley in an underground car park, Spaggiari was driven to Paris by a smart lady who rode out fourteen police checkpoints.

Already popular for the sheer chutzpah of his theft, Spaggiari became a folk hero when he sent 5,000 francs to the owner of the car whose roof he'd dented when he jumped from the *préfecture*. While he was being sentenced *in absentia* to life imprisonment for theft, the mastermind – in a blond wig and dark glasses – was in Geneva giving interviews to *Paris Match*. He began to travel endlessly. In Rio, he had plastic surgery. He returned to France with a changed name and a script – Spaggiari adored cinema. By 1989, lung cancer was wasting him and he died in Italy in June. His wife illegally carried his body back into France, where he was buried.[52]

Questions remain about how Spaggiari obtained the plans to the sewer, where he got over twenty uniforms belonging to the municipal services, and how the escape motorcycle arrived below the judge's chambers with such meticulous timing. Spaggiari was called a Médecin 'hanger-on' and, in the press, the 'affair Spaggiari' became the 'affair Spaggiari-Médecin'.[53] After all, Médecin had deep sympathies with the OAS and the extreme right – the very people on whose behalf the robbery had been executed.

Always impressed by America and wanting to style the Côte d'Azur in its image, Jacques Médecin fell for Ilene, a blonde Californian, 'into nutrition, astrology and jewellery', at a Los Angeles house owned by his friend Max Factor.[54] It was summer 1977. Jacques and Ilene went shopping. They went to dinner. When he returned to France, Médecin couldn't stop thinking about the woman who claimed to be in line to inherit the Max Factor fortune. He was nearing fifty, and married with two daughters.

The mayor invited Ilene to Paris. Then, in the summer of 1978, without obtaining a French divorce, Médecin indulged in a quickie wedding in Las Vegas. The couple did business in LA and Médecin began placing money and buying houses. In Nice, rumours were rife, and after his divorce, Jacques and Ilene were properly married at the *mairie* of Nice in December 1979. Then things started to sour.[55] Ilene did not seem, after all, to be so close to the Max Factor fortune. She began to get bored with the poky little Riviera, where her command of French was colourful. Accustomed to the foul-mouthing of a husband famous for his 'verbal incontinence', at formal dinners Ilene would be thrown back on a limited vocabulary to pin an identity – 'Oh, you mean the asshole.'[56]

Like many crooked politicians, Médecin was a 'doer' – so long as a chunk of profit from what was done ended up in his pockets. While tourism was Nice's traditional source of income, Médecin – by 1973, not only mayor of Nice but president of the Conseil Général des Alpes-Maritimes – expanded the city's appeal as a business destination. He initiated plans for a huge conference hall – the Palais des Congrès Nice Acropolis – which opened in 1984 and went on to hold up to 300 events annually. Following the initiative of a group of prominent scientists, the city created a 6,000-acre science park – Sophia-Antipolis – to the north of the busy airport. At the same time, there was a decidedly unsavoury undercurrent

The Palais des Congrès Nice Acropolis with La Tête Carrée Library to the left.

to some legislation. Under Médecin, Nice had a law that allowed the city to pre-empt any purchase of property in the old town. This had nothing to do with the preservation of historic sites. The city earned a good profit from resale to their chosen purchaser, and the law kept out unwanted North African immigrants.

Criticism of Médecin came from an unexpected direction. It is rare for a foreigner to wade into the problems of a region, but the English novelist Graham Greene had been living seasonally at Antibes since 1966, when his doctors – familiar story – advised him against the cruddy winters of southern England.[57] No stranger to the world of organized crime in novels such as *The Third Man*, Greene reserved the Côte d'Azur – or 'Côte d'Ordure', as he called it – for lighter tragicomic tales set in off-season Antibes. His observations are always sharp – the English stay later in the season, shivering secretly; a lone Algerian staring out from the ramparts is 'looking for something, perhaps safety'.[58] In 1982, Greene published his pamphlet *J'Accuse: The Dark Side of Nice*, written in both English and French. Banned in France, it exposed police and judicial corruption in Nice – host to 'some of the most criminal organisations in the south of France'. Along with drug dealing and casino wars, gangs laundered money through the building industry and had links with the Italian mafia. Greene was outraged by the victimization of a friend, Martine, and as a novelist he worked from the observed and particular towards the larger picture.

The ex-husband of the friend in question was Daniel Guy, the crook incriminated in the 1975 Menton casino plot to aid Fratoni. Guy's associates – members of Urbain Giaume's gang – were serving time for trafficking forgeries. Poor while he was married to Martine, two years after the divorce Guy was driving a Rolls, a BMW and had built himself a villa on Mont Boron which he promptly put up for sale. The money for all this? His company had been chosen to market luxury flats. Martine's divorce had been particularly nasty. Guy lied, abducted their child and threatened her parents, knowing full well that, as a member of a powerful local gang, he would not be touched. When Guy smashed one of his lovers in the nose, she reported him to the police but was told that her complaint would just be stashed in a drawer like the rest of them. Punishment of a woman – wife or mistress – is one of the ways of the underworld, and Martine's difficulties continued. She wished to discuss some problems, so her lawyer invited her to the Ruhl nightclub. The following night, the lawyer asked Martine to the cinema then dinner, suggesting they go on to a well-known swinger's address in Cannes. The lawyer was, all this time, in contact with Guy, who was having Martine watched.

Greene started to receive suspicious phone calls, and his Antibes flat was broken into. He looked outside Nice for help, writing to the *grand chancelier* in order to return the insignia of his *Légion d'honneur*. When matters did not progress in the child custody battle, Martine and her parents went to the Cour de Cassation in Paris, which had difficulty obtaining files from Nice. Daniel Guy was simply being supported in his criminality by certain local police officers, magistrates, lawyers and officials of the city – 'the bureaucratic wall'.

Greene ends his tract by reminding the reader that its subtitle is 'The Dark Side of Nice'. With grand irony, he adds, 'For of course Nice had its sunny side also, but I can leave it to the Mayor of Nice, Monsieur Jacques Médecin, to talk about that side of the city.'[59]

The year that *J'Accuse* was published in England, Princess Grace of Monaco was killed. For a long time, she had been finding her role difficult. Cornered by her husband, who could be petulant and short-tempered, Grace largely suffered in silence. Occasionally, she snapped. When asked what she wanted as a tenth anniversary present, she replied, 'A year off.'[60] Missing her career, she kept in contact with Cary Grant and David Niven, who had a villa on Cap Ferrat overlooking Beaulieu. When the Nivens moved into La Fleur du Cap, the prince and princess came to celebrate the event and ended up sitting on packing cases eating sardine sandwiches.[61]

By 1982, Grace and Rainier's three children were grown-up. After their eldest, Caroline, made an unfortunate and short-lived marriage to the playboy Philippe Junot, Grace felt more protective towards her temperamental younger daughter, Stéphanie. In September 1982, the seventeen-year-old returned from Antigua with fifteen stitches in her head. She had been on holiday with the nineteen-year-old son of Jean-Paul Belmondo when she had a water-skiing accident. After a family weekend at their retreat at Roc Agel, Grace loaded a pile of clothes in the back of her green Rover. With Stéphanie, her mother and the dresses, there was no room for the chauffeur, and Grace, despite her deteriorating eyesight, said she would drive. The D37 running down to the Moyenne Corniche was steep and twisty, but the ride to the palace was short.[62]

On that dazzling morning of 13 September, as mother and daughter climbed into the front seats of the Rover, neither bothered to fasten their seat belts. Princess Grace was wearing glasses. Stéphanie later told doctors that after driving down the steep road for five minutes, Grace complained of a sudden pain in her head and slumped over the wheel of the car as it approached a sharp bend. A lorry following watched as the car started to veer and swerve across the road. Coming into the final hairpin bend before reaching Monte

Carlo, the brake lights failed to signal and the Rover appeared to accelerate until it smashed through the low barrier. The car plunged seventy metres over the side of the mountain and came to rest in the field of a farm. Stéphanie lay beneath the glove compartment, kicking at the door to get it open. Grace had been thrown into the back seat. Stéphanie, climbing from the car, yelled at a shocked farmworker to phone the palace. Her head wound had reopened. Then she collapsed, her spine injured. Her mother was taken to the Princess Grace Hospital, where there were no scanners to determine the gravity of the injuries to her head. In a matter of hours, her condition had stabilized sufficiently to move her to a clinic which had the appropriate equipment. However, her brain had been irreparably damaged in the accident, and the family decided that there was no reason to prolong her life artificially. At 10.10 p.m. on 14 September, Grace Kelly's life support system was switched off.

Despite the stand-offishness of some members of the Monte Carlo old guard, Princess Grace was much loved. When her death at the age of fifty-two was announced, Monégasques wept in the streets. The funeral was attended by representatives of many countries, including Mrs Nancy Reagan and Princess Diana, along with old friends from Grace Kelly's filmmaking days – Mr and Mrs Cary Grant and Frank Sinatra. Rainier was a ghost, and Stéphanie – shouldering the guilt of not having reacted quickly enough – faced accusations that she, in fact, had been driving the car.[63]

In 1982, a fifth week of *congés payés* was voted, and that put increased stress on the resources of a region desperately adapting to accommodate the staggering number of visitors. The year saw the opening of one of Médecin's pet projects – the large central shopping centre Nice Étoile, built on the site of the old Hospice de la Charité. West of Nice, in Villeneuve-Loubet, the enormous Marina Baie des Anges was under construction. The ensemble comprised four undulating blocks of residences on a forty-acre site. To many, it was a huge eyesore. Others joked that – like the Great Wall of China – the complex could be seen from the moon. For the developers, there was one tiny problem. An early-seventeenth-century munitions store stood in the middle of the site. Converted into a house, its owner refused to sell. Hanging on to his property, he even went on to profit from its location after the two construction companies became embroiled in a dispute when work started. The first refused access to the lorries of the second company, which was forced to negotiate a route through land attached to the house. The small property still stands – proving that even on the Côte d'Azur developers do not always get their way.[64]

The most eccentric private building was constructed above Théoule-sur-Mer between 1975 and 1989. The Palais Bulles was designed by the Hungarian Antti Lovag for an industrialist from Lyon. When he died, the couturier Pierre Cardin bought and enlarged it – adding a 500-seat outdoor theatre. The structure uses only curves and porthole windows, as Lovag considered the straight line an affront against nature. Cardin lived nearby and used the Palais Bulles solely for entertaining and fashion shows. After his death, there were hopes that the complex would be opened for public use but – listed in 2017 for $420 million – it is known by real estate agents as the property nobody will buy.[65]

The Château de l'Horizon was acquired in 1979 by the royal family of Saudi Arabia. They destroyed the chute from the pool to the sea, and gave the property a luxurious overhaul. They also purchased a large part of the adjacent wooded hill stretching down to the sea, and promptly built two new palaces in a green zone which prohibited construction. The Emir had offered the authorities whatever they wanted – a school, a retirement home – in return for permission to build. The bribes were never received.[66] All along the coast, developers and the rich of many nations were gobbling up protected green spaces.

Above all, it was the demand for smaller houses and villas that was stifling the Riviera. Dirk Bogarde – living in Grasse – watched a crazy situation develop as newcomers destroyed the very countryside they had come south to enjoy. New villas were crowding the land abandoned by peasants who moved to flats near the big towns, where they found work in supermarkets and on building sites. Cheap imported Turkish rose petals had deprived them of work in the Grasse perfume industry. Bogarde noted that birds also began to leave, as creeping construction left them with nowhere to nest. Birdsong gave way to grinding machinery. Meanwhile, the matinée-idol-turned-serious-actor who had worked with Luchino Visconti on *Death in Venice* and *The Damned* was threatened by another species: fantasizing women in transparent dresses revealing teasing black lingerie staggering towards his villa on high heels – women oblivious to the fact that Bogarde's partner was a man.[67]

In January 1984, Bogarde – summoned to a large suite in the Carlton hotel – was asked to become president of the next Cannes Film Festival. Over the decades, it had transformed from a bikini tease on the beach, through political and creative challenges, to become a serial shocker that raised the temperature of cinema. Bernardo Bertolucci's *Last Tango in Paris* was shown in 1971, and at the 1973 festival there were two films that outraged spectators. In Marco Ferreri's *La Grande Bouffe*, four well-known actors gather – using their own names – to eat and screw themselves to death in a Parisian house. The other film was Jean Eustache's *La Maman et la Putain* – a chatty and explicit discussion of sex, the word 'fuck' was iterated 128 times. Language aside, the film shocked in a devastatingly unexpected manner. The figure of the *maman* was based on Eustache's partner, Catherine Garnier, who did the costumes and make-up for the film, shot in the boutique where she worked. Garnier committed suicide after attending the first projection. The director never recovered and committed himself to a psychiatric hospital shortly afterwards, eventually shooting himself in 1981, aged forty-two.

Bogarde was charged with bringing back dignity to the festival by favouring more commercial, more 'American' films. His agent told him he must accept. Joseph Losey – who had directed Bogarde so expertly in *The Servant* and *Accident* – urged him to say no. He had been president in 1972 and knew it was a lousy job. Bogarde accepted. Heavily under guard, the jury discussed its prize options in a villa outside Cannes. When they announced their verdicts, there was horror that no American films had been chosen. *Paris, Texas*, directed by German wunderkind Wim Wenders won the Palme d'Or.[68]

At the Victorine Studios, the filming of the 1983 Bond film *Never Say Never Again* was hampered by the state of a dream factory that was in bad need of renovation. Even during the filming of Truffaut's *Nuit Américaine* a decade earlier, weeds had grown visibly across the back lot and the production had been troubled by the planes taking off from Nice airport. In what was one of the best comedies about the absurdities of filmmaking, the condition of the studios made a telling contribution. For the Bond production team, the difficulty of moving equipment through overgrown grass and the nicotine-stained screens in the projection room almost prompted the director to walk out. Médecin's friends were managing the studios and raking in the profits.[69]

James Baldwin had first lived in France between 1948 and 1957. With what LeRoi Jones described as his 'world-absorbing eyes', Baldwin was a powerful speaker and a piercing writer whose incensed humanity ably countered the aggression suffered by a homosexual black American. Desperation, racism and homophobia had driven him from a country where he was struck by 'an emotional poverty so bottomless, and a terror of human life, of human touch, so deep that virtually no American appears able to achieve any viable, organic connection between his public stance and his private life'.[70] His rhetoric was always sharp. Of the 'empty' and 'treacherous' film *Lady Sings the Blues*, Baldwin noted that it 'related to the black American experience in about the same way, and to the same extent that Princess Grace Kelly is related to the Irish potato famine'[71]. His darts hit bull's eyes. If his discourse was delivered live, he revealed the Shakespearean charisma of a mesmerizing preacher. When health took him south and he settled in Saint-Paul-de-Vence in 1971, it had been several decades since an important American writer had spent a good deal of time on the Riviera. In the twenties, they came south to enjoy the myth they helped create. In the case of James Baldwin, he adjusted to the rhythms that he found in Provence. Unique in staying sixteen years, he became part of the local community – which, in turn, became part of him.

It was after staying at the Colombe d'Or that the writer settled in the region. He became a close friend of the owners. Yvonne Roux spent hours talking with him, finding him 'the kindest man' she had ever met. Hoping to become an English teacher, Yvonne translated Baldwin's *Blues for Mister Charlie* into French, and a French piece that Baldwin wrote into English. They discussed women in fiction – a subject about which Baldwin's curiosity seemed boundless.[72] He became friends with Yves Montand and Simone Signoret, who helped Baldwin with the negotiations to rent some ground-floor rooms that had once been Georges Braque's studio.[73] The house was owned by Jeanne Faure, who lived upstairs with her brother. She hated anyone black. Eventually persuaded by the Roux family and by Signoret and Montand to accept Baldwin, Faure nonetheless barricaded the internal access from the rented part of the house. Baldwin's rooms gave onto a garden at the back. At the front, outside the kitchen, there was a place to eat beneath a straw canopy called 'the Welcome Table'. With his gentleness and charm, Baldwin won Faure over so convincingly that, when her brother died, she asked him to walk beside her in the funeral procession. Shocking, even in a village where Baldwin was roundly cherished, it was a sign of how Faure 'totally adored him'. When the writer was presented with the *Légion d'honneur* by President Mitterrand in June 1986, he invited his cook – who had never seen the capital – and his landlady, Jeanne Faure, to the ceremony.[74]

The Welcome Table was aptly named. Apart from several of Baldwin's lovers – the ashes of one who died of AIDS scattered in the garden – there were many visitors. Bobby Short, the gay cabaret singer and champion of African American composers who owned the lushly gardened Villa Manhattan in nearby Mougins, was a frequent visitor. Harry Belafonte came. Miles Davis visited, as did Toni Morrison, Maya Angelou and Nina Simone. Henry Louis Gates Jr – a young black Yale graduate – wanted to interview Josephine Baker, who was living in Monte Carlo. She agreed on condition that the young man brought Baldwin. Instead, Baldwin invited them to Saint-Paul for dinner. The evening became the basis for his last unfinished and unpublished play, *The Welcome*

Table – a tapestry of questions and discussions on the themes of race, gender, sexuality and nationality. Set at a celebration for Mlle Faure's ninetieth birthday, the central character is Edith, a Creole singer-dancer from New Orleans, based on Josephine Baker.[75]

Baldwin was accused by various black magazines of ignoring the plight of his people and living in paradise. The writer retorted, 'You don't ever leave home. You take your home with you. You better, otherwise you're homeless.' While writers enjoyed the Riviera, spending or bumming their way through it as visitors, Baldwin found a place in which to meditate on the 'home you take with you'. By living among the villagers, he reconnected with his southern American roots. He reflected on his historical situation through the acceptance he found in a Provençal village, among people enchanted by the warmth of his love. Even though he was homosexual. Even though he was black.

In June 1986, Baldwin's health started to deteriorate rapidly. Ten months later, his cancer of the oesophagus was diagnosed as terminal. Jeanne Faure had wanted Baldwin to have the house he loved when she died. Baldwin wanted it to become a haven for writers who would take their place at its Welcome Table. After his death on 1 December 1987, costs meant that by 2000 the house was lost. In 2017, hoardings advertising a projected luxury villa screened the site where the house had stood.[76]

It was his racist sympathies and poses that contributed to the fall of Jacques Médecin. One of his big projects for Nice was the Musée d'Art Moderne et d'Art Contemporain, which would feature the works of *École de Nice* artists. The mayor understood their importance – the 1978 inaugural exhibition of the landmark Centre Pompidou in Paris had been *À Propos de Nice*. In 1974, Ben Vautier had dismantled his shop, Laboratoire 32, which stood in the rue Tonduti de l'Escarène, and sold it to the Musée National d'Art Moderne. Over the years, Vautier had inevitably been drawn into the commercialism that absorbs attempts at anti-gallery strategies. His signing of his often simplistic, often flaccid maxims were reproduced on T-shirts and canvas bags sold in museums across the world. Médecin, while having no time for the anarchic aspect of the *École de Nice*, delighted in the commercial opportunities of the art world – particularly in the realm of cultural tourism.

The opening show at the Musée d'Art Moderne was to feature the local sculptor Arman, who withdrew at the last minute in reaction to the antisemitic sympathies of the mayor. The Minister of Culture refused to lend works, and French television and the Parisian press spurned the opening. Médecin's own monthly, *L'Action Nice-Côte d'Azur* – condemning this 'intellectual terrorism' – hailed the new museum as a brilliant cultural event. But one wonders where and how the city found its contractors. At the end of 1991, the museum had to close temporarily – its foundations cracking.[77]

Médecin presided over a culture of antisemitism. In 1984, the Jewish cemetery had been profaned. When Médecin made an antisemitic joke on national television, he added – in one of his bigmouth quips – that Jews represented only 4 per cent of his electorate, while the right-wing Front National represented 20 per cent. Three Jewish councillors resigned in the spring of 1990, when the mayor welcomed an FN rally to Nice at which the honoured guest was Franz Schönhuber, a former officer of the Waffen-SS and president of an extreme right-wing group in Germany.[78]

Nice, along with Toulon and Marseille, had become a hotbed of extreme-right sentiment occasioning inexplicable violence. On 13 June 1987, six young Niçois – not extremists and from all classes – lynched a Tunisian worker called Ammar Abidi. A police officer told *L'Événement du Jeudi* that they were representative of Nice. Extremism also resulted in carefully planned and cynical attacks. On the night of 8–9 May 1988, a gas-bottle bomb exploded in a lodging for immigrant workers in Cannes-la-Bocca, wounding and hurting fifty people. It was claimed to be the work of the 'groupe Massada' – a branch of the National Committee of Jews against the North African Invasion. Several other explosives targeted immigrant lodgings. They were, in fact, the work of a neo-Nazi party formed in 1987 by defectors from the Front National – their aim, to terrorize Arabs and praise/blame Jews for carrying out the attacks.[79]

Not everything had gone Médecin's way. His plans for the

destruction of the Palais de la Méditerranée and the building of a hotel and a twenty-five-metre-high parking lot had come to nothing. In June 1981, the Palais had been acquired by Kuwait Real Estate Investment, who wished to destroy the Art Deco edifice and construct offices, apartments and a shopping mall. The French Minister of Culture forestalled them by designating the façade a historical monument. The property would lie empty for years.[80]

In 1984, when Médecin was stopped at Los Angeles airport, his luggage was found to contain a number of undeclared jewels. An audit revealed 'inexplicable surpluses of bank credit' in his account. Meanwhile, the mayor was paying no tax and siphoning off sums from his city. Anomalies were noted in the accounting at the Nice Opéra. In 1990, Médecin – who had twice been found guilty of income tax evasion – was indicted for misuse of municipal funds. Charged with tax arrears of 20 million francs, the admiring Niçois observed, 'He'll get out of it, he has his ways.'[81] Still hugely popular in 1989, he stoked city pride by refusing to participate in the bicentenary celebrations for the French Revolution. Nice had not been a part of France at the time.

In the spring of 1990, police raided the Médecin house in Nice – 'like the Gestapo', observed his wife, Ilene. An unfortunate image, given her husband's political sympathies.[82] In September 1990, Médecin was in Japan for a ceremony twinning the pedestrian zones of Osaka and Nice. While he was there, the television station FR3 filmed an international removals van emptying the Médecin residence in Nice. Ilene left for the United States. Customs at Roissy airport in Paris found – in a case carried by a young Niçois bound for America but labelled for Médecin – 600,000 francs in notes. On 16 September, *Nice-Matin* published a letter the mayor had left with his lawyer. It announced his resignation.[83] At that very moment, he was on his way to Argentina, where he divorced Ilene and took up with a Uruguayan journalist. Then, after a spell in a French prison, he returned to South America and took up with another woman. By that time, pollution had settled over the Côte d'Azur.

13

White, Concrete Coast
1990–2023

Within a year of Princess Grace's death, Caroline married the son of a wealthy Italian industrialist, Stefano Casiraghi. When Casiraghi was killed in a powerboating accident, Caroline discovered that he had always had a mistress and was in debt.[1] The ever-restless Stéphanie pursued a suite of careers – model, pop singer and entrepreneur. Albert waited in the wings to become the ruler of the principality. Princess Grace had saved some of Monte Carlo's Belle Époque treasures but had not succeeded in stopping the developers. Towards the end of the twentieth century, the city appeared architecturally monotonous. There were auction houses but no interesting art galleries and no fine art museum. Video cameras monitored activity on the spotless streets, and the security system was so efficient that the border could be sealed within minutes. Mary Blume, the Paris correspondent of the *International Herald Tribune*, wrote that 'the only thing that made me laugh in Monte Carlo was when I called the palace and the music while I was put on hold was "Send in the Clowns"'.[2]

Today, the Grimaldi castle looks as brand-new as a child's cut-out model. Public toilets are of a cleanliness and quality that would not be out of place in the foyer of a smart hotel. The restaurants offer essays in precision dining. But while the old quarter of La Condamine has a certain charm and the Monégasques are friendly, the overall impression remains vapid. Attempts to improve the architectural allure of the principality result in buildings that pitch

Monte Carlo – architecturally monotonous.

The Grimaldi Castle – looks as brand new as a child's model.

Monte Carlo: The Café de Paris.

The Monaco Grand Prix circuit.

a more individual appeal, yet offer luxury apartments that, for the most part, assert wealth in a staid and characterless manner.

While visitors may marvel at the cleanliness and affluence, the major attractions remain the Musée Océanographique, founded by Albert I in 1910, the Grand Prix, and the ballet built on the ground-breaking work of Diaghilev. The Monaco Grand Prix has continued to thrill spectators. In one of the most testing circuits in Formula One, top speeds are not possible but those who master the circuit do well. England's Graham Hill and Germany's Michael Schumacher both won the race five times, and the Brazilian Ayrton Senna, six.

After Grace's death, Princess Caroline began to take over much of her mother's work. The Ballets de Monte-Carlo was created under her auspices. Pierre Lacotte and Ghislaine Thesmar put together a company of thirty-seven dancers, and focused on the creative collaboration between designer, composer and choreographer which had been the hallmark of the Diaghilev years. By 1990, the company was performing works by contemporary choreographers such as Maurice Béjart, Jiří Kylián, Jean-Christophe Maillot and William Forsythe. In 1997, Rainier

III and Caroline – Princess of Hanover after her marriage to Ernst August, Duke of Brunswick – opened the Atelier de Ballets de Monte-Carlo in Beausoleil. The three-floor, 4,000-square-metre space is used for classes, rehearsals and performances. During the 2009–10 centenary celebration of ballet in Monte Carlo, the company performed Nijinsky's *Le Sacre du Printemps* alongside a newer version by Maurice Béjart. The climax of the festivities was the visit by the Tanztheater Wuppertal in

Monte Carlo priorities.

December 2010. In memory of Diaghilev's impact on modern dance, and in homage to their artistic director Pina Bausch – who had died a year earlier – they presented her brilliant version of *Le Sacre*.[3]

Prince Rainier's aim was to keep the mafia out of the principality, but a tax-free haven could be nothing if not ideal for money laundering, and the legitimacy of certain companies registered in Monaco was questionable. In March 2000, a report by the Russian Foreign Intelligence Service concluded that the principality would become a key European centre for Russian money and finance. A haven was necessary for those who had snatched their wealth and could, in a trice, have it taken from them. In Russia, nothing changes except what changes overnight.

Rainier III died in 2005 and the new ruler, Albert II, began to enjoy 'good relations' with Vladimir Putin.[4] After Albert's 2006 participation in a Russian arctic expedition, Putin honoured him with a state dinner in Moscow. The following year, Putin offered the prince a three-bedroomed *dacha* constructed secretly by Russian builders at Roc-Agel. The gift – suggested Robert Eringer, founder of the short-lived Monaco Intelligence Service – was probably bugged to the rafters. In August 2007, Albert enjoyed a Siberian fishing trip with Putin – one of those recurring adventures at which the Russian president was photographed as a 'he-man of the wild'. Oligarchs were invited to prestigious charity galas in the principality.[5] Monaco presented a 2009 exhibition, 'Moscow: Splendours of the Romanovs'. Two years later, Dmitry Rybolovlev became president and major shareholder of the principality's football club, AS Monaco. To cap it all, 2015 was declared the 'Year of Russia' in Monaco. Prince Albert, all the while campaigning for financial transparency and a 'clean' Monte Carlo, allowed Putin's inner circle to use the principality as a 'hub for their financial affairs'[6] – a place where money could be laundered, and riches stashed safely.

When the Russians came to the Riviera during the nineteenth century, they were largely aristocrats who owed their wealth to the exploitation of the serfs who worked the agricultural land and extracted the mineral wealth of Russia. The oligarchs came, rich from the seizure of state assets that communism had appropriated on behalf of the people. Amassing sudden fortunes in gangsterish takeovers, oligarchs invested in Riviera gold – prestigious real estate – often choosing villas built in a style of architecture that the Revolution had suppressed. They started to arrive in the mid-1990s as Cyrillic was added to restaurant menus and estate agents began to employ Russian-speaking staff. Like their aristocratic forbears, they were lavish spenders. One of the earliest Russian buyers on Cap d'Antibes, banker Andrey Melnichenko, spent more than 10 million euros on his wedding celebration – flying in Christina Aguilera, Whitney Houston and Julio Iglesias to perform.[7] A Russian gas multimillionaire spent 90,000 euros on a dinner for ten, during an international real estate fair in Cannes. The coast was awash with such 'no questions asked' extravagance.

The 'Godfather of the Kremlin', Boris Berezovsky – once one of the most powerful men in Russia – bought the Château de la Garoupe in 1996. Close to Boris Yeltsin, whose electoral campaigns he funded, Berezovsky controlled automobile, petrol and television empires. The 1990s were rough in Russia. Gangs with persuasive firepower vied for control and blocked the evolution of a fair if bitterly competitive free market.[8] Berezovsky's chauffeur was decapitated while the 'Godfather' was saved by his Chechen bodyguards from several assassination attempts. By 2000, the French fiscal authorities had begun to take an interest in extravagant Russian acquisitions. The Château de la Garoupe was among those in which 'the origin of the money that financed the transactions was not clear'. Berezovsky owned a company in Beaulieu – Société d'Investissement France Immeubles – which screened his extravagant property deals. By 2005, when a Marseille judge seized the Château de la Garoupe,[9] Berezovsky had lost his clout in Russia after Vladimir Putin did a little house-cleaning and purged Moscow of those who opposed his reforms. The 'Godfather' took refuge in Britain, where he died in suspicious circumstances in 2013.

Putin's friend and Berezovsky's rival Roman Abramovich bought the Château de la Croë in 2001. Renovation – which involved over 180 companies and took four years – left only the original shell standing. Gone were the ghosts of the Windsors, Aristotle Onassis and his brother-in-law, the shipping magnate Stávros Niárchos. On Cap Ferrat, the most beautiful villas are in the hands of rich Russians, Chechens and Kazakhs. Such properties are under armed guard. Visitors come and go in bulletproof cars with darkened windows. A pro-Russian Ukrainian, Dmytro Firtash – linked to Semion Mogilevich, the 'boss of bosses' of Russian mafia networks – acquired Maugham's old Villa Mauresque in 2005 – 'a sunny place for shady people'.

During the Belle Époque, many hotels were built, owned or managed by foreigners – Swiss, German and English. The difference in the 2000s was that owners came from further afield and were developers rather than hoteliers. The Royal-Riviera at Saint-Jean-Cap-Ferrat was bought by an Indian group, the Fairmont in Monte Carlo was sold to a Saudi Arabian. The tired Hôtel Métropole in Beaulieu was acquired – through Metropole Holdings, based in the Bermudas – by rich Kazakhs, supposedly to renovate it. In fact, they wanted

Russian delicatessen in Beaulieu.

to demolish the structure and build a modern hotel. Despite local opposition and strict building and cultural laws, a study organized by the mayor of Nice, Christian Estrosi, and François Fillon – then Minister of Ecology and Sustainable Development under Nicolas Sarkozy – left the doors wide open. The mayor of Beaulieu denounced those who tried to obstruct an investment, which he considered essential to the well-being of his commune. In July 2011, the Kazakhs were given permission to demolish and construct a hotel two and a half times larger than the original. A protest blog led, in 2013–14, to the construction permit being annulled by the Tribunal Administratif de Nice.[10] The property remains unrestored and undeveloped.

While the Russians were living high on the hog, crime along the coast was thriving. Renée Le Roux listed activities that were clearly the harvest of the Médecin years. Police or customs officers were found guilty of association with criminals, theft, robbery and rape. At Menton, three customs officials were accused of accepting backhanders. Three CRS riot police were found guilty of arms dealing – from Kalashnikovs to small missiles. In 1990, twenty-five baggage handlers were arrested at Nice airport after years of complaints from passengers about theft.[11]

A mafia chief sought by a Calabrian judge was discovered working as a *pizzaiolo* on the Promenade des Anglais.[12] In the late 1990s, there were arrests for heroin dealing, money laundering and murder. While many gangs were involved – Serbo-Croat, Romanian,

Albanian, Armenian and Georgian mafias – the Italians were dominant.[13] In 1994, a member of the 'Ndrangheta, Giovanni Gullà, decided to cooperate in return for clemency. He told judges in Genoa about the Côte d'Azur, where there were seven mafia cells in towns along the coast including Antibes, Vallauris, Cannes and Grasse. Their control base was in Nice, and there was a transit room at Ventimiglia.

A panel for the unrestored Hôtel Metropole in Beaulieu.

Some mafiosi were merely hiding in France. At least seventy-five have been repatriated, including Walter d'Onofrio, a particularly dangerous member of the Neapolitan Camorra, who – when he was arrested in 2000 – was working as a cook in a school canteen in Cannes.[14] At Ventimiglia, the French handed over Antonio Lo Russo, who was arrested in Nice in April 2014. A member of the now-disbanded Lo Russo clan who ruled Scampia, a poor quarter of Naples, Antonio Lo Russo had been on the run for three years. His apprehension dealt a serious blow to organized crime in France, as did the arrest of Roberto Cima of the 'Ndrangheta in Vallauris in September 2010.[15]

Nice-Matin was full of robberies, knife fights at nightclubs, jewellery theft and petty crime. The 1990s saw a spate of bombings in Nice.[16] In 1995, a butcher's next to the *mairie* was blown up. The entry to a *discothèque* was hit by an explosion. The security-obsessed ageing population were more preoccupied by these items than by the financial scandals involving elected officials. Financial malpractice – unlike a shooting or a burglary – seems to carry no immediate threat, and comes cloaked in an aura of

Cranes stand tall along the Côte d'Azur.

luxury or privilege. Yet sometimes, fraud was so extensive that it hit the headlines. The mayor of Cannes from 1989 to 1997 is notable for being the most heavily sentenced elected official of the Ve République. Michel Mouillot was condemned for hiring ghost employees, forgery and use of forgery, the misuse of public funds, and for receiving bribes from the Cannes casinos. The three-million-franc 'gift' from the Carlton was designed to secure his permission for the installation of one-armed bandits.[17]

While the public turned a blind eye, civic buildings were badly maintained and there was much highly profitable speculation. Cranes stood tall along the Côte d'Azur. In 1990, *Le Nouvel Observateur* reported that one-quarter of the Alpes-Maritimes coastline was covered in concrete.[18] A glance at the aerial shots of *To Catch a Thief*, filmed in the mid-fifties, confirms how unspoilt the coast was only decades earlier. There was terraced arable land. Cap Ferrat appears almost uninhabited. Red-roofed Monte Carlo had no high-rise buildings. La Croisette in Cannes was manageable.

Moving into the twenty-first century, there were even more cars, more motorways, more fast-food chains and hypermarkets.

The coast became increasingly industrialized to cope with swelling numbers. There was fish farming in huge underwater tanks.[19] The Théâtre National de Nice, inaugurated in 1989 by Médecin, was slated for demolition in 2020 by Christian Estrosi, in order to extend the promenade of the Paillon. The building – like its neighbour, the Musée d'Art Moderne et d'Art Contemporain – had been badly built. A marble slab even tumbled from its façade. Tons of marble surfacing from the demolished theatre would be saved to restore parts of the adjacent art museum, or be stockpiled for future use. In any case, demolition and building remained big business. As Nice was chosen as one of the six French candidates for European Cultural Capital in 2028, Estrosi announced a 100-million-euro budget to renovate museums, relaunch the Victorine Studios and restore the Opéra. Meanwhile, the Riviera became an autoroute connecting access points to tiny, relatively unspoilt villages. Nice airport – the second busiest in France – handled over 13 million passengers in 2018. Carbon dioxide and nitrogen oxide are dumped across Nice's Baie des Anges as planes – often at 3–5-minute intervals – take off and land. The air is imperilled and the sea is hurt.

Around the millennium, when a phone was still a frequent way to book a hotel room, black visitors could be stonewalled. Such attitudes persist. In 2019, SOS Racisme found racial discrimination on the private beaches of the Côte d'Azur.[20] *Le Monde* noted it again in August 2022 at Juan-les-Pins.[21] In 2016, the *Guardian* reported that the model Naomi Campbell was refused access to an event to which she had been invited. As Campbell and her friend

Landing at Nice.

were being turned away, the doorman – who claimed the event was full – let white people pass.[22] Two years later, seventeen people were booked for a managerial dinner at a ritzy Cannes restaurant known for its love of big spenders. All business people and appropriately dressed, they arrived in two groups. The first was welcomed without fuss. The second group included people of mixed race and was not admitted.[23]

Reflecting the larger experience of the Riviera, the Cannes Film Festival has become a tightly organized question of 'hustling and waiting'. It has also become, over the years, a competition that brings to the attention of European cinemagoers many films from countries hitherto ignored. Truly international, the festival has pushed 'more "artistic films" towards mass awareness',[24] and offered a springboard for directors. Jazz à Juan thrives, and the constellation of museums – some great, some indifferent – is testimony to how many artists have lived and worked in this region and to how seductive art appears in the vivid Mediterranean light. The coast is increasingly congested but culture flourishes.

Music fortunes have accounted for some of the recent purchasers of magnificent villas – Tina Turner at Villefranche, Rod Stewart and ex-Rolling Stone Bill Wyman at Saint-Paul-de-Vence, where Wyman and his wife celebrated their twenty-fifth wedding anniversary at the Colombe d'Or. Sir Elton John chose a summer residence on Mont Boron in Nice. The villa – once a dark reddish-pink – was redone in pale yellow, giving it a welcoming lift. Bono bought his Villa Les Rose – squeezed between the railway line and the beach in Ezè-Bord-de-Mer – in 1993. In 2013, the singer's twenty-year association with the region allowed him to thank mayor Christian Estrosi for modernizing Nice while attempting to make it 'a green city under blue skies'.

The experience of being in the south gave U2's ex-manager Paul McGuinness the idea for the Sky television series *Riviera*. He is quoted as listing its ingredients – 'Rich people behaving badly in the sun, yachts, Maseratis, great clothes, beautiful women, art fraud, money laundering through auction houses, Russians, English people, American, French. Murder, adultery.' The first

Nice: The Negresco and the Promenade des Anglais at night.

series certainly pushed the right buttons, but it should have come with a health warning – the show's message is that being rich on the Riviera is a life-threatening experience. The matriarch of the central family makes Lady Macbeth look like a bridesmaid, and the final episodes of season one make the house of Atreus seem like a perfectly functioning family. The villain – Negrescu – is slanderously only one vowel away from sharing a name with Nice's most famous hotel. The critical response was muted. A *Times* reviewer described it as 'one of those shows about which one could almost write: "So bad it's good." But not quite because it's mostly just bad.'[25]

An image for the kind of frustration felt by many visitors to the Côte d'Azur in the twenty-first century is perhaps captured in the final scene of Prévert and Carné's *Les Enfants du Paradis*. We see Baptiste helplessly trapped in a carnival crowd that prevents him from catching up with Garance, the woman who promises him paradise on earth. In its flurry to accommodate millions of visitors on a tiny strip of coast, the Côte d'Azur remains a paradise only for a few. Bought by tech giants, advertising tycoons, soccer celebrities and designers, as well as pop stars and oligarchs, Belle Époque villas evoke the splendour of the Riviera's short, opulent past. All such people could – and some did – buy property in far-flung and less congested places, and yet they were still lured to the Riviera. For those blanching money, Monaco is certainly not the last resort. Tax havens exist where the sand is so white that even the beaches look laundered. Those purpose-built havens are at a far remove from the overcrowded Côte d'Azur, yet they lack the complex historical pull of the Riviera.

Today, many places along the coast are lost resorts. As the decades passed, Saint-Tropez boomed out its popularity, pulling the desperate into ever-more crowded streets, restaurants and clubs – the once-stylish resort living on cockeyed memories of the past. Yachts came and went. In August 1997, Princess Diana and Dodi Al Fayed were snapped by paparazzi enjoying themselves on his yacht moored off Pampelonne Beach. The photos created a front-page tabloid frenzy around the world. At the end of that month, they both died in a Parisian underpass. Today, a kind of hypnosis pervades the resort. Along the harbour front, visitors sip exorbitantly priced drinks and stare with envy at those lounging on the warm-toned wooden decks of yachts more often than not registered in tax-free havens.

Nice is too large and too complex to function solely for the amusement of those who EasyJet in for five days of fun. Its problems are those of urban France. As with Marseille, there is a large immigrant population negotiating a predominantly right-wing milieu. Smaller towns are bursting from the impossible summer numbers. Forest fires become ever more threatening. In 1990, one quarter of the forests on the Maures had gone up in flames.[26] Flashpoints will only get worse with global warming. August 2021 found 900 firefighters using helicopters and aircraft to contain a furious forest fire spreading with incredible speed in the direction of La Garde-Freinet.[27]

✧

Nice: Rubbish on the beach.

At the outset of the twenty-first century, terrorism struck paradise. Corsican separatists bombed the Nice tax and customs office in July 2003, injuring sixteen people. In February 2015, there was a non-lethal knife attack on soldiers guarding a Jewish community centre by a man vowing allegiance to Islamic State. Most devastating and cynical was the attack on the evening of Bastille Day – 14 July – in 2016. Islamic State claimed responsibility when Mohamed Lahouaiej-Bouhlel, a Tunisian resident of France with a history of psychiatric problems and domestic violence, ploughed his lorry through strollers enjoying the firework display along the Promenade des Anglais. Eighty-six people were killed and a further 458 were injured.

Veering on and off the pavement to avoid obstacles and inflict maximum damage, Lahouaiej-Bouhlel's killing machine hit ninety kilometres an hour. As it slowed near the Negresco, a cyclist attempted to clamber aboard the lorry only to be repelled by a threat from the terrorist's firearm. Seconds later, a motorcyclist threw his bike beneath the wheels of the truck before jumping onto the running board and beating the driver, who fought him off with the butt of his gun. At 10.35 p.m., as the lorry ground to a halt near the Palais de

Nice heatwave headlines in *Nice-Matin*.

la Méditerranée, two gendarmes shot and killed Lahouaiej-Bouhlel. Only seven months after the Paris bombings of November 2015, which included the massacre of 135 people at the Bataclan concert hall, it seemed as if France was under siege. Four years later, at nine o'clock in the morning on Thursday, 29 October 2020, a knife attack by Ibrahim Issaoui killed three people in the Notre-Dame Basilica on the Avenue Jean Médecin. All the while, the attacker – a twenty-one-year-old Tunisian national – was heard shouting 'Allahu akbar'.

The region opened up after Lord Brougham was stopped at the Sardinian frontier by a cholera outbreak. In 2020, the Riviera was shut down by Covid. Globally, during the pandemic, tourism was pushed back to levels unseen since 1990. For any region dependent on visitors, the virus was a disaster. During the first seven months of 2020, there was a 6.7-billion-euro drop in tourist revenue in Provence and the Côte d'Azur. Hotels – including the Negresco, the Carlton and the Majestic – were shut. The 2020 Cannes MIPIM – 'the world's leading property market' – was postponed. In Monte Carlo, there was no Grand Prix. Beaches were empty, cafés shut.

Nature sometimes has inconvenient, even painful ways to ask for something back. As life became more constrained, the air along the coast became purer, the light clearer. You could steal – from a rock overlooking the sea – a glimpse of a once upon a time world.

If its first foreigners were aged and ailing, the Riviera came to be a symbol of vitality. Later, as the region was hyped, a fantasy sprouted, seeded from its luxurious past. Money – big money, dirty money – was studded into every corner and aspect of the coast. Everybody had to be here, and there were too many everybodys building on land that should have been left alone. Today, tranquillity is best found in the discrete enclaves of untouched nature, or in modern villas with their cool white interiors from which wide windows offer that most precious vista in a crowded world – the infinity of sea and sky.

The marvel of the Riviera was constructed by the pleasures of its visitors and through the eyes of artists. After the fatal illnesses of two of their children forced Gerald and Sara Murphy to abandon Cap d'Antibes, Murphy wrote to F. Scott Fitzgerald, 'Only the invented part of our life – the unreal part – has had any scheme, any beauty.'[28] The Murphys created their world apart on a peninsula with an inescapable allure. All along this enchanted coast, writers and artists were changed by the cherished places they helped shape. As Colette wrote in the guestbook of the Colombe d'Or, 'Wait for me, dove, I'm coming back.'[29]

With fewer visitors in late spring, early autumn and during the mild winter, many coves and beaches offer hints of the inspirational appeal made by the Riviera. In the weeks just before the season begins or after it ends, the paths, pine woods and beaches skirting the Saint-Tropez peninsula are pristine and redolent of a less hectic time. Gentle breezes blow and light sparkles on the surface of translucent water that deepens into the 1,001 blues of a Côte d'Azur. Despite relentless building creeping up its slopes, the backdrop of steep, parched hills remains wild and exciting. In gardens and market squares, brash midday light is broken into the most fragile, soft and delicate warmth by the branches of plane trees and pines. At sunset along the coast, fire opal consumes the day. The sky becomes translucent then deepens into midnight blue. Sporadic stars appear and the sea's horizon merges with the night. The cool, quiet hours are punctuated by the distant laughter of late revellers, as blackness bleaches into dawn.

The Riviera has been a paradise for those who understood this azure coast as a gift of nature. Lord Brougham and his scientific experiments. Hector Berlioz and Friedrich Nietzsche on the hills above Nice. Katherine Mansfield at Bandol. The Impressionists, Fauves and their followers, whose eyes were opened by the Mediterranean light. Those who risked and gave their lives for the freedom to enjoy this enchanted place.

Under sentence of death, Katherine Mansfield wrote to her husband from Menton,[30] 'Wander with me ten years – will you, darling? Ten years in the sun. It's not long – only ten springs.'

Raoul Dufy, *La Jetée, promenade à Nice*, c. 1926.
Musée d'Art Moderne de la Ville de Paris.

French fashion magazine illustration of ladies at the bar
wearing evening gowns by Marcel Rochas, 1930.

Eileen Gray & Jean Baldovici – E-1027, Roquebrune, Cap St Martin.

'Côte-d'Azur All Year Round'.

'A New Blue Train'.

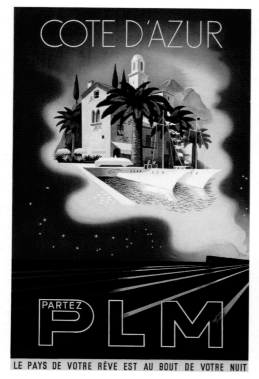

'Wake Up in Your Dreams'.

'Summer on the French Rivera'.

Grace Kelly and Cary Grant overlooking Monte Carlo in Alfred Hitchcock's *To Catch a Thief*.

Sunset over the Baie-des-Anges, Nice.

The beach at Cannes.

Saint-Tropez.

The Baie-des-Anges, Nice.

Monte Carlo views.

Juan-les-Pins.

The Riviera – trading off its past.

Casino Ruhl.

Notes

The Voices of Paradise

1 Léon Watripon, *Nice-guide: Nouveau Cicérone des Étrangers*, Nice, Imprimerie Administrative, Faraud et Congo, 1869, pp. 242–3.

2 Don Antonio de Beatis, *Voyage du cardinal d'Aragon en Allemagne, Hollande, Belgique, France et Italie (1517–18)*, Paris, Perrin, 1913, p. 245.

3 Charlotte Louise Hawkins Dempster, *The Maritime Alps and their Seaboard*, London, Longmans, Green and Co., 1885, pp. 35–6.

4 Tobias Smollett, *Travels through France and Italy*, London, 1776, Letter XXI, 10 November 1764.

5 John Ruskin, *Ruskin in Italy*, ed. Harold Shapiro, Oxford, Clarendon Press, 1972, p. 33.

6 Watripon, p. 32.

7 Laurent Germain, *Notes de voyage*, Toulon, 1878, p. 13.

8 Aga Khan, *The Memoirs of Aga Khan: World Enough and Time*, London, Cassell, 1954, pp. 13–14.

9 Allen Tate, 'The Mediterranean', in *New Verse*, vol. 1, no. 5, London, October 1933.

10 Ford Madox Ford, *Provence from Minstrels to the Machine*, London, Allen and Unwin, 1938, pp. 291–4.

11 Michael J. Arlen, *Exiles*, London, André Deutsch, 1971, p. 74.

12 Dodge, David, *The Rich Man's Guide to the Riviera*, London, Cassell, 1962, p. 5.

13 Dempster, p. 7.

14 Robert Louis Stevenson, *The Letters of Robert Louis Stevenson to His Family and Friends*, ed. Sidney Colvin, Vol. I, London, Methuen, 1901, Letter of 16 March 1884.

15 Mary Blume, *Côte d'Azur: Inventing the French Riviera*, London, Thames and Hudson, 1992, p. 33; Ford Madox Ford, p. 99.

16 Prosper Merimée, Letter of 11 December 1856, in Alexandre Hurel and Christelle Fucili (eds.), *Voyages sur la Côte d'Azur: Stendhal, Victor Hugo, Gustave Flaubert et al.*, Urrugne, Pimientos, 2004, p. 93.

17 General Petr Alexandrovich Polovtsov, *Monte Carlo Casino*, London, S. Paul., 1937, pp. 25–6.

18 Augustus J. C. Hare, *Winter at Mentone*, London, 1862, pp. 148–9.

1 Jagged, Tormented and Tiny

1 Jules Monod, *Nice, Monaco et Menton: Guide complet du touriste*, Nice, 1902, p. 81.
2 André Ripart, *Alpes Maritimes: Histoire géographie*, Nice, CRDP, 1991, pp. 17–19; Charles Lenthéric, *La Grèce & l'Orient en Provence: Arles, le bas Rhône, Marseille*, 5th ed., Paris, 1910, p. 360.
3 Adolphe Joanne, *Géographie du département des Alpes-Maritimes*, Paris, Hachette, 1900, p. 25.
4 Lenthéric, p. 381.
5 Joanne, pp. 25–6.
6 Lenthéric, pp. 371–2.
7 James Edward Smith, *A Sketch of a Tour on the Continent in the Years 1786 and 1787*, London, 1793, p. 179.
8 Sinclair Tousey, *Papers from over the Water: A Series of Letters from Europe*, New York, American News Company, 1869, p. 105.
9 Compagnie des Chemins de fer de Paris à Lyon et à la Méditerranée, *La Côte-d'Azur: de Marseille à Vintimille*, 1938, p. 3.
10 Aubin-Louis Millin, *Voyages dans les départemens (sic) du midi de la France*, Paris, 1807–11. Vol. II, pp. 476, 479; Edward Rigby, *Dr Rigby's Letters from France etc. in 1789*, ed. Lady Eastlake, London, Longmans, 1880, p. 142.
11 James Nash, *The Guide to Nice: Historical, Descriptive and Hygienic*, London, 1884, pp. 6–7.
12 John Richard Green, *Stray Studies from England and Italy*, London, Macmillan, 1876, pp. 36–7; Leslie Richardson, *Things Seen on the Riviera*, London, Seeley, Service & Co., 1924, p. 58.
13 Abbé Jean-Pierre Papon, *Voyage de Provence*, Paris, Moutard,

1787, p. 348; Françoise Cachin, *Saint-Tropez: Peninsula Maures Mountains*, Paris, Gründ, 1985, p. 4 (suggests the name may derive from *mauro*).
14 Joanne, pp. 30–34; Nash, pp. 55, 56.
15 Richardson, p. 76.
16 Jean-Baptiste Martel, *Catherine Ségurane: Véritable héroïne Niçoise*, Marseille, Editions Publiroc, 1933, p. 17; Nash, pp. 61–3.
17 Nash, p. 86.
18 Ibid., pp. 102, 109.
19 Dempster, pp. 101–2.
20 Joseph Addison, *Remarks on Several Parts of Italy, &c In the Years 1701, 1702, 1703*, London, Tonson, 1718, p. 13.
21 Didier Gayraud, *L'Age D'Or de Saint-Jean-Cap-Ferat*, Nice, Gayraud, 1983, p. 142.
22 Jean-Pierre Cassely, *Secret French Riviera*, Versailles, Jonglez Publishing, 2019, p. 79.
23 Smollett, *Travels*, Letter XVII, 2 July 1764.
24 Jean-François Albanis-Beaumont, *Travels through the Maritime Alps from Italy to Lyons*, London, T. Bensley, 1795, p. 102.
25 Adolphe Smith, *The Garden of Hyères: A Description of the Most Southern Point on the French Riviera*, London, 1880, pp. 88–9.
26 Monod, pp. 23–4.
27 Tristan Roux, *Promenade des Anglais: History and Reminiscences*, trans. Ungar, Éditions Gilletta, Nice Matin, 2006, pp. 6–7.
28 Dempster, pp. 124–31.

2 This 'Wild and Tremendous Region of the Globe'

1 Beatis, pp. 251–4.

2 John Evelyn, *The Diary of John Evelyn*, ed. Bray, London, Frederick Warne, 1879, p. 70.

3 Ibid., pp. 71–2.

4 Anon [Bromley, William], *Remarks in the Grand Tour of France and Italy Perform'd by a Person of Quality in the Year, 1691*, London, John Nutt, 1705, p. 19.

5 Joseph Addison, essay on the sea in *The Spectator* (1712), quoted in Lena Lenček and Gideon Bosker, *The Beach: The History of Paradise on Earth*, London, Pimlico, 1999, p. 55.

6 Jacques Casanova de Seingalt, *The Memoirs*, London, 1894, Episode 16, Chapters 3–5 of Volume IV, *In the South: 1725–98*.

7 L'Abbé Le Blanc, quoted by Ian Jack, 'Introduction' to Lawrence Sterne, *A Sentimental Journey*, Oxford, Oxford University Press, 1968, p. x.

8 Robert Kanigel, *High Season in Nice*, London, Abacus, 2003, p. 20.

9 Sterne, pp. 28–9.

10 Philip Thicknesse, *Useful Hints to Those Who Make the Tour of France in a Series of Letters*, London, 1768, p. 5.

11 Philip Thicknesse, *A Year's Journey Through France and Part of Spain*, Vol. 1, Dublin, 1777, p. 3.

12 Smollett, *Travels*, Letter I, 23 June 1763.

13 Ibid., Letters: II, 15 July; III, 15 August; IV, 1 September; VIII, 19 October; XII, 6 December 1763.

14 Thomas Nugent, *The Grand Tour*, Vol. IV, London, 1749, p. 174.

15 Smollett, *Travels*, Letter XII, 6 December 1763.

16 Ibid., Letter XIII, 5 January 1764; Letter XII, 6 December 1763.

17 Ibid., Letter XII.

18 Ibid., Letter XIII, 15 January 1764; Letter XXIV, 4 January 1765.

19 Ibid., Letter XVIII, 2 September 1764; Letter XIX, 10 October 1764.

20 Alain Corbin, *The Lure of the Sea: The Discovery of the Seaside in the Western World 1750–1840*, trans. Jocelyn Phelps, London, Penguin Books, 1995, p. 60.

21 Smollett. *Travels*, Letter XXIII, 19 December 1764.

22 Ibid., Letter XX, 22 October 1764.

23 Ibid., Letter XXI, 10 November 1764.

24 Johann Georg Sulzer, *Journal d'un voyage fait en 1775 & 1776 dans les pays méridionaux de l'Europe*, La Haye, 1781, p. 161.

25 Smollett, *Travels*, Letter XXIV, 4 January 1765.

26 Anne Edwards, *The Grimaldis of Monaco*, New York, William Morrow & Co., 1992, pp. 73–5.

27 Biddulph, Violet, *The Three Ladies Waldegrave*, London, Peter Davis, 1938, pp. 32 ff.; Nash, p. 111.

28 Jean-Pierre Bérenger, *Soirées Provencales*, 3 vols, Paris, Nyon, 1787, in *Voyages en France ornés de gravures avec des notes par La Mésangère*, Chapelle, 1626–86, Vol. 4, *Voyage en Provence*, Paris, 1798, pp. 8–9, 11.

29 Ibid., pp. 12–13.

30 Ibid., pp. 15–17.

31 Thomas Jefferson, letter to the Marquis de Lafayette of 11 April 1787, quoted in Roy and Alma Moore, *Thomas Jefferson's Journey to the South of France*,

New York, Stewart, Tabori & Chang, 1999, p. 99.

32 Jefferson, letter to William Short from Nice, 12 April 1787, in ibid., p. 100.

33 Arthur Young, *Travels During the Years 1787, 1788 and 1789*, Dublin, 1793, Vol. I, p. 379.

34 Ibid., p. 381.

35 Ibid., pp. 383, 387.

36 Rigby, pp. 135–8.

37 Millin, Vol. II, p. 449.

38 Hare, pp. 169–70.

39 Albanis-Beaumont, p. 1.

40 Ibid., p. 4.

41 Rigby, pp. 139, 144.

42 Smollett, *Travels*, Letter XVII, 2 July 1764.

43 Marie Ratazzi, *Nice La Belle: Monaco*, Paris, Degorce-Cadot, 1869, p. 51; Albanis-Beaumont, *Travels*, p. 103.

44 J. B. Davis, *The Ancient and Modern History of Nice*, London, Tipper & Richards, 1807, p. 14.

45 Ibid., p. 13.

46 Millin, p. 523; Davis, p. 7.

47 Albanis-Beaumont, pp. 117–18.

48 Millin, p. 562; Smollett, *Travels*, Letter XXII, 10 November 1764, p, 123.

49 Benjamin Silliman, *A Visit to Europe in 1851*, Vol. I, New York, G. P. Putnam, 1853, p. 233; *Sauvan, Honoré Maire de Nice*, Declaration of 24 September 1898 in the Musée Masséna, Nice.

50 Roux, *Promenades des Anglais*, p. 29.

51 Michael Dibdin, 'From Canova to Caro', in *Modern Painters, London*, 1992, pp. 42–5.

52 Watripon, pp. 96–7.

53 Ripart, pp. 66, 68.

54 Albanis-Beaumont, p. 105.

55 Young, *Travels*, p. 392.

56 Monod, p. 20; Michel de l'Hospital, quoted in André. Merquiol, *La Côte d'Azur dans la Littérature Française*, Nice, Dervyl, 1949, pp. 48–9.

57 Bérenger, p. 145.

58 Kanigel, p. 73.

59 Ripart, p. 69; Albanis-Beaumont, p. 103.

60 Watripon, p. 224.

61 Sulzer, p. 150.

62 Smollett, Letter XXXIX, 10 May 1765.

3 'Bathing in Sunshine', 1835–60

1 Victor Hugo, *Oeuvres complètes de Victor Hugo*, Vol II, Paris, P. Ollendorff, 1906–10, pp. 246–7.

2 Stendhal, excerpts from Stendhal, *Mémoires d'un Touriste*. Paris, Dupont, 1838, Vol. III, in Hurel and Fucili, pp. 243 ff.

3 George Sand, in Hurel and Fucili, p. 83.

4 John Murray (ed.), *A Handbook for Travellers in France: Part II*, London, John Murray, 1878, pp. 106–9; J. Henry Bennet, *Winter and Spring on the Shores of the Mediterranean*,

London, John Churchill, 1870, p. 21.

5 Hector Berlioz, *The Life of Hector Berlioz as Written by Himself in his Letters and Memoirs*, London, Dent, 1903, pp. 221–5.

6 Ibid., pp. 227–30.

7 Ibid., p. 225.

8 Brougham to Lord Wellesley, quoted in Patrick Howarth, *When the Riviera Was Ours*, London, Century Hutchinson, 1977, p. 17.

9 Ronald K. Huch, *Henry, Lord Brougham, The Later Years: The*

'Great Actor', Studies in British History 8, Lewiston NY, Edwin Mellen Press, 1993, pp. 24, 26–9.

10 Ibid., pp. 7–8, 20, 32.

11 Ibid., pp. 2–3; Charles Dickens to Marguerite Powers, 13 July 1847, in Storey and Fielding, *The Letters of Charles Dickens*, Vol. V, Oxford, Clarendon Press, 1981, p. 127.

12 Huch, p. 31.

13 Murray, *Handbook for Travellers*, 1878, p. 176.

14 Dempster, p. 39.

15 Rigby, p. 148.

16 Augustus Hare, *The Life and Letters of Frances, Baroness Bunsen*, Vol. II, London, 1882, p. 237.

17 Margaret Brewster, *Letters from Cannes and Nice*, Edinburgh, Thomas Constable, 1857, pp. 30–1.

18 Dempster, p. 58.

19 Stendhal, quoted in V. Del Litto, 'Stendhal, passant de la Côte d'Azur', in *Nice Historique*, no. 177, 1959, p. 124.

20 Huch, p. 174.

21 J. M., *Thomas Robinson Woolfield's Life at Cannes and Lord Brougham's First Arrival*, London, Kegan Paul, Trench, Trübner, 1890, pp. 54, 56.

22 Théodore de Banville, *La mer de Nice: Lettres à un ami*, Paris, 1861, letter of 15 May 1860, p. 149.

23 de Carli, *Conseiller du Touriste a Nice et dans ses environs*, Nice, Chez l'Auteur, 1864–5, p. 31.

24 Thicknesse, *Useful Hints*, p. 237.

25 Alan Sillitoe, *Leading the Blind: A Century of Guidebook Travel 1815–1914*, London, Macmillan, 1995, pp. 18–19.

26 Henry Morford, *Morford's Short-Trip Guide to Europe 1874*, New York, 1874, pp. 31–2.

27 John Murray (ed.), *The Handbook of Travel-Talk or Conversations in English,*

German, French and Italian, London, John Murray, 1844, p. 202.

28 Ibid., pp. 164, 188, 212, 258, 280.

29 William Miller, *Wintering in the Riviera with Notes of Travel in Italy and France*, London, Longman's, Green & Co., 1879, p. 157.

30 Murray, *Handbook for Travellers*, 1878, p. 108.

31 Brewster, *Letters*, pp. 32–3.

32 Kanigel, p. 82.

33 Antoine de Tourtoulon, *Lettres sur Nice et ses environs*, Montpellier, 1852, pp. 85–6.

34 Watripon, pp. 20, 30.

35 Albanis-Beaumont, pp. 89–90.

36 Rigby, p. 153.

37 Davis, p. 19.

38 William Farr, *A Medical Guide to Nice*, London, Ibotson and Palmer, 1841, p. 32; Léon Pilatte, *La Vie à Nice: Conseils et directions pour nos hôtes d'hiver*, Nice, Librarie Internationale, 1865, pp. 76ff., 87.

39 Watripon, pp. 78–9.

40 J. M., *Thomas Robinson Woolfield*, p. 12.

41 Jonathan Miles, *St Petersburg: Three Centuries of Murderous Desire*, Hutchinson, Penguin Random House, 2017, pp. 240, 249; David Magarshack, *Gogol: A Life*, London, Faber and Faber, 1957, pp. 76–7, 131.

42 Gogol, letter to the poet Vassily Zukovsky, quoted in Margarshack, *Gogol*, p. 225.

43 David Magarshack, *Turgenev: A Life*, London, Faber & Faber, 1954. pp. 103–6.

44 Ibid., p. 125; Donald McLeod, 'Composer of the Week – Pauline Viardot', BBC Radio 3, 14–18 June 2021.

45 Alexander Herzen, *Lettres de France et d'Italie (1847–1852)*, Geneva, Éditions des Enfants de l'Auteur, 1871, Letter of December 1847, pp. 92, 94.

46 Aileen Kelly, 'Introduction' to
Isaiah Berlin, *Russian Thinkers*,
1978; rev. ed. Penguin, London,
2013.

47 Herzen, *Lettres de France et
d'Italie*, Letter of 10 July 1850,
pp. 258, 270.

48 Herzen, quoted in Berlin, *Russian
Thinkers*, p. 100.

49 Herzen, *Lettres*, Letter of 10 July
1850, p. 268.

50 Herzen, quoted in Berlin, *Russian
Thinkers*, p. 243.

51 Alexander Herzen, *Childhood,
Youth and Exile*, Oxford, Oxford
University Press World Classics,
1980, p. 187; Aileen M. Kelly,
*The Discovery of Chance: The
Life and Thought of Alexander
Herzen*, Cambridge, MA and
London, Harvard University
Press, 2016, pp. 332–3.

52 Leo Tolstoy, Letter of 17 October
1860, quoted in Aylmer Maude,
*The Life of Tolstoy: The First
Fifty Years*, London, Archibald
Constable, 1908, pp. 200–1.

53 Leo Tolstoy, Diary for 13 October
1860, quoted in Maude, p. 200.

54 Maude, p. 207.

55 Ibid., pp. 191,193, 196, 200–9.

56 Michael Nelson, *Queen Victoria
and the Discovery of the Riviera*,
London & New York, I. B.
Tauris, 2001, p. 7.

57 Mérimée, Letter of 14 February
1859, in *Voyages sur la Côte
d'Azur*.

58 Roy Ellis, 'La Base Russe de
Villefranche', *Nice Historique*,
vol. 90, 1964, pp. 67–83; E.
Fricero, 'Les Russes au siècle
passé', *Nice Historique*, vol. 116,
1952, pp. 55–85.

59 Merimée, Letter of 11 December
1856, in *Voyages sur la Côte
d'Azur*, p. 93.

60 Perry, Captain John, *The State of
Russia Under the Present Czar*,
London, Benjamin Tooke, 1716,
pp. 72–3; Stevenson, *Letters*,
pp. 248, 266, 288.

61 Pilatte, p. 94.

62 Alexandre Dumas, *Une année à
Florence*, Arvensa ebook, 2015,
p. 81.

63 Clément Balme, *Mon voyage à
Nice*, Nice, 1863, pp. 55, 56.

64 Murray, *Hand-book for
Travellers in France*, 1848, quoted
in Sillitoe, pp. 4, 24.

65 Antoinette-Joséphine-Françoise-
Anne Drohojowska, *Une saison à
Nice, Chambéry et Savoie*, Paris,
Charles Douniol, 1860, p. 26.

66 Ralph Schor and Henri Courriére,
*Le Comté de Nice, la France
et l'Italie*, Actes du colloque
organisé à l'Université de Nice
Sophia-Antipolis, 23 April 2010,
Nice, Serre, pp. 157–8.

67 Ripart, p 73; Schor et Courriére,
pp. 24, 158; G. Boréa, 'Notes
d'un hivernant à Nice avant
l'annexion', *Nice Historique*, vol.
131, 1939, pp. 891.

68 Dempster, p. 59.

4 A Welcome to the World, 1860–90

1 Pilatte, pp. 97–8.

2 Polovtsov, p 76.

3 Davis, p. 146–7.

4 Smollett, *Travels*, Letter XIV,
20 January 1764; Albanis-
Beaumont, p. 106.

5 Hare, pp. 41–2.

6 Edwards, p. 107.

7 Tourtoulon, p. 67.

8 Polovtsov, p. 80.

9 Edwards, pp. 124–5.

10 Banville, p. 78.

11 Charles Graves, *The Big Gamble: The Story of Monte Carlo*, London, Hutchinson, 1951, p. 49.

12 Polovtsov, p. 85.

13 Edwards, pp. 126–9.

14 Polovtsov, p. 105.

15 J. M., *Thomas Robinson Woolfield*, pp. 16–17; Howarth, p. 32.

16 Mérimée, Letter of 17 December 1856, in *Voyages sur la Côte d'Azur*, p. 94; Archives communales de Cannes, *Chronique de l'Hôtellerie Cannoise*, Cannes, 2003, pp. 49–51.

17 Mérimée, in *Voyages sur la Côte d'Azur*, Letter of 18 February 1857, p. 95.

18 Brewster, p. 97.

19 Edward I. Sparks, *The Riviera: Sketches of the Health Resorts of the North Mediterranean Coast of France from Hyères to Spezia*, London, J. A. Churchill, 1879, pp. 75–6.

20 Nelson, *Queen Victoria*, pp. 42–3.

21 Howarth, pp. 21–2.

22 Angus Davidson, *Edward Lear: Landscape Painter and Nonsense Poet (1812–1888)*, London, John Murray, 1968, pp. 158, 170–2, 208; Mérimée, Letter of 27 February 1868, p. 147.

23 Mérimée, 13 January 1862, p. 120.

24 Lenček and Bosker, pp. 72–3, 93.

25 *Cook's Handbook to the Health Resorts of the South of France and the Riviera*, London, Thomas Cook & Son, 1878, p. 36.

26 Davis, p. 10.

27 Brewster, p. 111.

28 LeRoy Ellis, 'La Base Russe de Villefranche', *La Colonie russe dans les Alpes-Maritimes des origines à 1939*, Nice: Editions Serre, 1998, pp. 40–1.

29 Guy de Maupassant, *Sur l'Eau*, St. Remy-de-Provence, Equinoxe, 2005, pp. 35, 118.

30 Dempster, p. 355.

31 Thomas More Madden, *The Principal Health-Resorts of Europe and Africa for the Treatment of Chronic Diseases*, London, J. & A. Churchill, 1876, pp. ix–x.

32 Charles Dickens, *Bleak House*, London and New York, Penguin, 1996, p. 14.

33 Charles Dickens, *Pictures from Italy*, London and New York, OUP, c. 1905, pp. 31–2.

34 Sparks, p. 87.

35 Farr, p. 32.

36 Madden, p. vii.

37 Ibid., p. xiv.

38 *Cook's Handbook to the Health Resorts*, p. 43.

39 *Life on the Riviera: A Weekly Journal of Social and Political Life*, vol. 52, 24 November 1888, p. 942.

40 Davis, pp. xvii–xviii.

41 Miller, *Wintering in the Riviera*, p. 456.

42 Sparks, pp. 83, 125.

43 Monod, pp. 66–8.

44 Pilatte, p. 56.

45 Théophile de Valcourt, *Cannes et Son Climat*, Paris, Germer Baillière, 1866, p. 16.

46 Pilatte, pp. 67–8.

47 Reynolds Ball, *Mediterranean Winter Resorts*, quoted in Sillitoe, p. 133.

48 Dempster, p. 15.

49 Smith, *The Garden of Hyères*, pp. 24, 27–8.

50 Madden, pp. 40–1.

51 Murray, *Handbook*, 1878, p. 171.

52 Miller, *Wintering in the Riviera*, p. 455.

53 Fanny Stevenson, Letter to John Addington Symonds, January 1883, in *The Letters of Robert Louis Stevenson*, vol. II, London, Methuen, 1911, p. 95.

54 Stevenson, *Letters*, p 248.

55 Ibid., p. 266.

56 Ibid., pp. 264, 288.

57 Ibid., p. 306.

58 Bernard C. Meyer, *Joseph Conrad: A Psychoanalytic Biography*, Princeton, NJ, Princeton University Press, 1967, pp. 35–7.

59 Joanne, pp. 20–22.

60 Sparks, p. 262.

61 William Cope Devereux, *Fair Italy, the Riviera and Monte Carlo*, London, Kegan Paul Trench & Co., 1884, p. 52.

62 Sparks, pp. 289–90.

63 Miller, *Wintering in the Riviera*, pp. 222–3.

64 Bennet, *Winter and Spring*, pp. vii–viii.

65 Ibid., pp. 4, 68.

66 Ibid., pp. 165–6.

67 Hare, *Winter at Mentone*, pp. xvii, 145.

68 Ibid., p. 144.

69 Ibid., p. 147.

70 Ibid., pp. 172–3, 203.

71 Madden, p. 96.

72 Journal of Queen Victoria, RA/ QV, Windsor Castle, 16 March 1882, quoted by Nelson, *Queen Victoria*, p. 23.

73 Xavier Paoli, *My Royal Clients*, London, Hodder and Stoughton, 1911, p. 331.

74 Ibid., p. 333.

75 Michaela Reid, *Ask Sir James: The Life of Sir James Reid, Personal Physician to Queen Victoria*, London, Hodder and Stoughton, 1987, p. 48; Victor Mallet (ed.), *Life with Queen Victoria: Marie Mallet's letters from Court 1887–1901*, London, John Murray, 1968, p. 152.

76 Frank Harris, *My Life and Loves (1922–7)*, London, W. H. Allen, 1964, p. 658.

77 Nelson, *Queen Victoria*, p. 35.

78 Journal of Queen Victoria, RA/ QV, Windsor Castle, 12 April 1882, quoted by Nelson, *Queen Victoria*, p. 36.

79 Charles Yriate, quoted in Charles Martini de Chateauneuf, *M'en Aviso: Menton a la Belle époque*, Breil-sur-Roya, Les Éditions du Cabri, 1990, p. 116.

80 Devereux, pp. 39, 46.

81 *Guide-Bleu: Nice pratique et pittoresque*, Nice, Gauthier and Co., 1893–4, p. 11.

82 Ibid., pp. 132–3.

83 Watripon, p. 73.

84 *Cook's Handbook*, 1878, pp. 27.

85 *Guide-Bleu*, p. 151.

86 Ibid., pp. 134–5.

87 *Guide-Bleu*, p. 144; Wartripon, p. 80; Élisée Reclus, *Les villes d'hiver de la Méditerranée et les Alpes maritimes: Intinéraire discriptif et historique*, Paris, Hachette, 1864, p. 193.

88 Murray, *Guidebook*, 1878, p. 182.

89 Jean-Paul Potron, 'La Librairie Visconti', in *Nice Historique*, vol. 247, 1997, pp. 122–34.

90 Watripon, pp. 77–8.

91 Ibid., p. 54.

92 Monod, p. 21; Watripon, p. 53.

93 Roux, p. 19.

94 Watripon, non-paginated adverts.

95 de Carli, p. 75.

96 Watripon, non-paginated adverts.

97 Miller, *Wintering in the Riviera*, p. 5.

98 Smith, *The Garden of Hyères*, p. 131, and unpaginated adverts.

99 Ibid., p. 134.

100 Madden, p xvii.

101 Watripon, non-paginated adverts.

102 Watripon, pp. 78–9.

103 Dempster, pp. 3, 6.

104 Morford, p. 32.

105 Andrea Mrena, *Histoire de la colonie russe sur la Côte-d'Azur*, Agth eBooks, 2017, n.p.

106 Charles Graves, *Royal Riviera*, London, William Heinemann, 1957, p. 56.

107 Fricero, *Nice Historique*, vol. 116, 1952, p. 67.

108 Dempster, p. 25.

109 Germain, p. 8.

110 Jean-Rémi Bézias, 'Frédéric Stackelberg (1852–1934) ou la

révolution importée', in *Destins niçois: Actes du colloque de Nice*, Cahiers de la Méditerranée, 1997/55, pp. 31–41; Ellis, pp. 124–5.

111 Ellis p. 126; Mrena, n.p.

112 Bashkirtseff, Marie, ed. Pierre Borel, *Cahiers intimes – inédits*, Tome I Paris: Les Éditions du Monde Moderne, 1925. Entries for March and May, 1877, pp. 298, 303–4.

113 Marie Bashkirtseff, *Journal de Marie Bashkirtseff*, Vol. I, Paris, Charpentier, 1890, p. 34.

114 Marie Bashkirtseff, *Lettres*, Paris, Charpentier, 1891 p. 26.

115 Bashkirtseff, *Journal*, 4 May 1877.

116 Ibid., 1 January 1876.

117 Graves, *Royal Riviera*, pp. 52–3.

118 'Preface' by François Coppée, in Bashkirtseff, *Lettres*, p. vi.

119 Julian Young, *Friedrich Nietzsche: A Philosophical Biography*, Cambridge, CUP, 2010, p. 387.

120 Friedrich Nietzsche, *Unpublished Letters*, New York, Philosophical Library, 1959, Letter of February 22nd, 1884.

121 Young, *Friedrich Nietzsche*, p. 336.

122 Curtis Cate, *Friedrich Nietzsche*, London, Hutchinson, 2002, p. 437.

123 Young, *Friedrich Nietzsche*, p. 388.

124 Ibid., p. 389.

125 Ibid., p. 395.

126 Cate, pp. 446, 457, 467; Nietzsche, Letter to his sister February 1886, in Nietzsche, Friedrich, ed. Levy and Ludovici, *Selected Letters of Friedrich Nietzsche*, London, Heinemann, 1921, pp. 177–8.

127 Cate, pp. 491–2.

128 Ibid., pp. 487, 490.

129 Ibid., p. 491.

130 Young. *Friedrich Nietzsche*, p. 359.

131 *Le Tremblement de terre de la Riviéra, 23 février 1887*, Paris, F. Baranger, 1887.

132 Graves, *Royal Riviera*, p. 116.

133 Polovtsov, p. 45.

134 William. F. Goldberg and George Piesse, *Monte Carlo and How To Do It*, London, 1891, p. 108.

135 Cate, p. 493.

136 Nietzsche, *Selected Letters*, p. 189.

137 Cate, p. 493.

138 Jean-Louis Caserio and Charles Martini de Châteauneuf, *Le Tremblement de terre de 1887 à Menton*, Menton, Société d'art et d'histoire du Mentonnais, 1987, p. 6.

139 Cate, p. 512.

140 Young, *Friedrich Nietzsche*, pp. 387, 404.

141 Morford, pp. 243–44.

142 Ibid., pp. 30, 32, 44.

143 *Cook's Handbook*, 1881–2, advertisements and p. 53; Nash, advertisements, n.p.

144 Reclus, pp. 362–3.

145 Tousey, pp. 106, 108.

146 Stéphanie-Félicité de Genlis, *Adèle et Théodore ou Lettres sur l'Education*, Paris, Lambert et Baudoin, 1782, Vol. 2, pp. 242–3; Merquiol, pp. 39–40.

147 Tousey, p. 106.

148 Dempster, pp. 20–22.

149 Sparks, p. 144.

150 Graves, *Royal Riviera*, p. 55.

151 Nelson, *Queen Victoria*, p. 79.

152 Maupassant, *Sur l'eau*, p. 161.

153 Mikhail Evgrafovich Saltykov, *A Family of Noblemen: The Gentlemen Golovliov*, Project Gutenberg ebook, 2013, p. 250.

154 André Compan, *Histoire de Nice et son Compté*, Nice, Éditions Serre, 1982, p. 398.

155 *Life on the Riviera*, 24 November 1888.

156 Edwards, p. 131.

157 Tousey, p. 110.

158 Jean-Lucien Bonillo et. al., *Charles Garnier and Gustave Eiffel on the French and Italian Rivieras: The Dream of Reason*, Marseille, Éditions Imbernon, 2004, pp. 90, 116.

159 Bonillo, p. 130; Edwards p. 156.
160 Bonillo, p. 132.
161 Karl Marx, *Lettres d'Alger et de la Côte-d'Azur*, trans. Gilbert Badia, Pantin, Le Temps des Cerises, 1997, pp. 93–4, 98, 104.
162 Dempster, pp. 289–90.

163 Germain, p. 65.
164 *Cook's Handbook*, 1879, p. 58.
165 Symonds, quoted in Nelson, *Queen Victoria*, p. 32.
166 Devereux, pp. viii–ix, 49, 341.
167 Green, pp. 64–5, 66, 70.

5 The Belle Époque, 1890–1914

1 Dumanoir and Barrière, *Les toilettes tapageuses*, Paris, 1856.
2 Robin W. Doughty, 'Concern for Fashionable Feathers', *Forest History Newsletter*, vol. 16, no. 2, July 1972, pp. 4–11.
3 Sara Bowman, *A Fashion for Extravagance*, London, Bell and Hyman, 1985, p. 105.
4 Hebe Dorsey, *The Belle Epoque in The Paris Herald*, London, Thames and Hudson, 1986, p. 124.
5 Paoli, p, 207.
6 Anny Latour, *Kings of Fashion*, trans. Mervyn Savill Latour, London, Weidenfeld and Nicolson, 1958, pp. 78, 80, 124–5.
7 Consuelo Vanderbilt Balsan, *The Glitter and the Gold*, New York, Harper and Brothers, 1952, p. 66.
8 Dorsey, pp. 124, 126; Bowman, p. 56.
9 Bowman, p. 12.
10 Latour, pp. 164–5.
11 Dorsey, pp. 124.
12 Ibid, p. 137.
13 Ibid, p. 155.
14 Ibid, pp. 25–6.
15 *Paris Herald*, Sunday Supplement for 7 July 1901, in Dorsey, p. 150.
16 Erté, *Things I Remember: An Autobiography*, London, Peter Owen, 1975, p. 22.
17 Bowman, p. 18.
18 Joanne, p. 43.
19 Aga Khan, pp. xi–xii, 41, 42.
20 Mallet, p. 47.

21 Nelson, *Queen Victoria*, p. 58.
22 Éliane Perrin, *L'Age d'or de la parfumerie à Grasse: D'après les archives Chiris (1768–1967)*, Aix-en-Provence, Édisud, 1996; Reclus, p. 154.
23 Nelson, *Queen Victoria*, p. 58.
24 Constance Flower Battersea, Baroness, *Reminiscences*, London, Macmillan, 1922, p. 116.
25 Mallet, pp. 24, 42.
26 Battersea, p. 114.
27 Nelson, *Queen Victoria*, pp. 59, 66.
28 Mallet, p. 44.
29 Ibid., p. 50.
30 Nelson, *Queen Victoria*, p. 145.
31 Ibid., pp. 87, 106.
32 Jean Cocteau, *Souvenir Portraits: Paris in the Belle Époque*, trans. Jean Browner, London, Robson Books, 1991, p. 136.
33 Paoli, p. 20.
34 Mallet, p. 154; Nelson, *Queen Victoria*, p. 90.
35 Victor Bethell, *Ten Days at Monte Carlo at the Bank's Expense*, London, Heinemann, 1898, p. 72.
36 Paoli, pp. 334, 350.
37 Emmuska Orczy, Baroness, *Links in the Chain of Life*, London, Hutchinson, 1947, p. 87.
38 *Anglo-American Gazette* (aka *Anglo-American News List and Fashionable Visitors List*), 23 December 1899 and 20 January 1900.
39 Queen Victoria, quoted in Nelson, *Queen Victoria*, p. 106.

40 *Menton and Monte Carlo News*, Menton, 1897–33, 26 January 1901.

41 *Anglo-American Gazette*, 4 November 1899, 11 November 1899, 23 December 1899.

42 Paoli, pp. 201–2, 208.

43 Harris, pp. 658, 660, 666, 668.

44 Charles Castle, *La Belle Otero: The Last Great Courtesan*, London, Michael Joseph, 1981, p. 139.

45 Ibid., pp. 116–17.

46 Marie-Hélène Carbonel and Javier Figuero, *La véritable biographie de La Belle Otero et de la Belle Époque: 'Ruine-moi mais ne me quite pas'*, Paris, Fayard, 2003, p. 388.

47 Denis Judd, *Edward VII: A Pictorial Biography*, London, Macdonald and Jane's, 1975, pp. 29–30.

48 Balsan, p. 95.

49 Harris, p. 622.

50 Mallet, p. 153.

51 Eustace Reynolds-Ball and C.A. Payton (eds.), *Sport on the Riviera*, London, 1911, p. 16.

52 Paoli, p. 208.

53 Graves, *Royal Riviera*, pp. 81–2.

54 Nelson, *Queen Victoria*, p. 46.

55 Dorsey, pp. 55–6.

56 Paoli, p. 207.

57 Harris, p. 367.

58 Ibid., p. 466.

59 Oscar Wilde, *The Picture of Dorian Gray*, Chapter 2.

60 Théophile Gautier, *Lettre à la présidente: Voyage en italie, 1850*, Au Château de la misère, 1890.

61 Blume, *Côte-d'Azur*, p. 62.

62 Harris, pp. 643–4.

63 Anton Chekhov, *Letters of Anton Chekhov*, ed. Avrahm Yarmolinsky, London, Jonathan Cape, 1974, Letter of 1 November 1897.

64 Ibid., Letter of 14 December 1897.

65 Ibid., Letter of 28 February 1898.

66 Ibid., Letter of 13 March 1898.

67 Ibid., Letter of 10 November 1897.

68 Ibid., Letter of 4 January 1898.

69 Emile Zola, in *Le Figaro*, 5 December 1897.

70 Chekhov, *Letters,* two letters of 4 January 1898: one to F. D. Batyushkov, the other to A. S. Suvorin.

71 William Fortescue, *The Third Republic in France 1870–1940: Conflicts and Continuities*, London, Routledge, 2000, pp. 50–73.

72 Chekhov, *Letters,* Letter of 15 April 1891.

73 Bethel, p. 32.

74 Arnold Bennett, *Paris Nights and Other Impressions of Places and People*, New York, George H. Doran, 1913, pp. 178–9.

75 Bethell, pp. vii–viii, 14, 16, 23.

76 Polovtsov, p. 8.

77 Balsan, p. 64.

78 Polovtsov, pp. 8–11.

79 Bethell, pp. 33–5.

80 Fred Gilbert, 'The Man Who Broke the Bank at Monte Carlo', 1891.

81 Polovtsov, pp. 159, 162–4.

82 *Menton and Monte Carlo News*, 25 March 1899.

83 Kenneth Clark, *Another Part of the Wood: A Self Portrait*, London, John Murray, 1974, pp. 23–4.

84 Goldberg and Piesse, pp. 71, 97.

85 Bethell, p. 165.

86 *Anglo-American Gazette*, 4 November 1899.

87 Queen Victoria, quoted in Nelson, *Queen Victoria*, p. 30.

88 Willa Cather, *Willa Cather in Europe: Her Own Story of the First Journey*, New York, Alfred A. Knopf, 1956, pp. 154–5, 157, 169.

89 Chekhov, *Letters*, Letter of 15 April 1891.

90 Dorsey, pp. 87–8.

91 Bethell, p. 132.

92 Ibid., pp. 129–30.

93 *Paris Herald*, 26 September 1896, in Dorsey, pp. 40–1.
94 Bethell, p. 131.
95 Aga Khan, p. 107.
96 Virginia Rounding, *Grandes Horizontales*, London, Bloomsbury, 2004, p. 236.
97 Balsan, pp. 61–2.
98 Ibid.
99 Rounding, p. 2.
100 Claude Conyers, 'Courtesans in Dance History: *Les Belles de la Belle Époque*', in *Dance Chronicle*, vol. 26, no. 2, 2003, pp. 219–243.
101 Balsan, p. 61.
102 Rounding, p. 225.
103 Daisy Fürstin von Pless, *From My Private Diary*, London, John Murray, 1931, pp. 205–6.
104 Carbonel and Figuero, pp. 28, 41, 44, 96, 224.
105 Conyers, p. 221.
106 Castle, p. 87.
107 Ibid., pp. 117–18.
108 Ibid., pp. 73, 147.
109 Carbonel, p. 224.
110 Ibid., p. 244.
111 Ibid., p. 225.
112 Ibid., p. 388.
113 Colette, quoted in Castle, pp. 121, 124–5.
114 Jean Chalon, *Liane de Pougy: Courtisane, princesse et sainte*, Partis, Flammarion, 1994, p. 73.
115 Balsan, p. 61.
116 Graves, *Royal Riviera*, p. 132.
117 Howarth, p. 117.
118 Dorsey, pp. 128–9.
119 Benstock, Shari, *Women of the Left Bank: Paris 1900–1940*, Austin, University of Texas Press, 1986, pp. 47, 269, 273.
120 Tilburg, Patricia A., *Colette's Republic: Work, Gender and Popular Culture in France, 1870–1914*, New York, Berghahn Books, 2009, p. 5.
121 Liane de Pougy, *Idylle Saphique*, Chatenay-Malabry, Alteredit, 2006.
122 Pougy, quoted in Carbonel, p. 105.
123 Conyers, p. 227.
124 *Menton and Monte Carlo News*, 1 November 1897.
125 Ibid., 13 November 1897.
126 Ibid., 11 December 1897.
127 Ibid., 19 February 1898.
128 Ibid., 24 December 1898.
129 Ibid., 26 February 1898.
130 Ibid., 2 April 1898.
131 James Abbott McNeill Whistler, 'Ten O'Clock Lecture', 1885.
132 John Ruskin, *Fors Clavigera* 1871–4, Letter 79, 18 June 1877.
133 Harris, p. 607.
134 Aubrey Beardsley, *Last Letters of Aubrey Beardsley*, London, Longmans, Green and Co., 1904, pp. 67, 69, 72.
135 Aubrey Beardsley, *The Letters of Aubrey Beardsley*, ed. Duncan Maas, London, Cassell, 1971, pp. 393, 395, 402, 407, 412, 423, 436, 439; Alan Hollinghurst, 'Quite Mad and a Little Indecent', in *Apollo*, July/August 2016.
136 Conrad, quoted in Martin Ewans, *European Atrocity, African Catastrophe: Leopold II, the Congo Free State and its Aftermath*, London, Routledge Curzon, 2002, p. 2.
137 Barbara Emerson, *Leopold II of the Belgians: King of Colonialism*, London, Weidenfeld and Nicolson, 1979, p. 270.
138 Paoli, p. 274.
139 Ewans, p. 157.
140 Ibid., p. 3.
141 Ibid., pp. 177–8.
142 Ibid., p. 193.
143 Paoli, p. 259.
144 Pless, *What I Left Unsaid*, London, Cassell and Co., 1936, p. 110.
145 Mallet, p. 106.
146 Nelson, *Queen Victoria*, p. 100.
147 Emerson, p. 269.
148 Gayraud, pp. 83–90.
149 Ewans, p. 235.
150 Gayraud, p. 106.
151 Erté, p. 49.

152 Georges Fontaines, *La Côte d'Azure en l'an 1897*, Lyon, 1897, p. 55.
153 Sillitoe, p. 132.
154 Dorsey, pp. 7, 8, 13, 15.
155 Graves, *Royal Riviera*, pp. 105–6.
156 Dorsey, pp. 8, 13.
157 Howarth, p. 162.
158 Graves, *Royal Riviera*, pp. 106–7; Bethel, pp. 42–3.
159 Polovtsov, pp. 37–8.
160 Dorsey, p 8.
161 Balsan, p. 64.
162 Dorsey, p. 18.
163 Ibid., p. 22.
164 Ibid., p. 34.
165 Ibid., p. 23.
166 *Anglo-American Gazette*, 13 January 1900.
167 Fontaines, pp. 33, 35.
168 Roux, p. 44.
169 Cocteau, *Souvenir Portraits*, p. 92.
170 Paoli, p. 351.
171 Graves, *Royal Riviera*, pp. 86, 89.
172 Balsan, p. 153.
173 Judd, p. 9.
174 Polovtsov, p. 46.
175 Évelyne Maushart, *1891–93, L'alliance Franco-Russe: L'escadre russe à Toulon, Bandol, Ollioules, Hyères, St Tropez*, Toulon, Éditions Mnemosis, 2016.
176 Harris, p. 802; Polovtsov, p. 51.
177 Carbonel, p. 283.
178 Bonillo et. al., p. 136.
179 Pless, *From My Private Diary*, p. 272.
180 Edwards, pp. 163, 166–8, 170, 175.
181 Bronislava Nijinska, *Bronislava Nijinska: Early Memories*, trans. Irina Nijinska and Jean Rawlinson, New York, Holt, Rinehart and Winston, 1981, pp. 332–33, 335.
182 *Menton and Monte Carlo News*, 15 April 1911.
183 Misia Sert, *Two or Three Muses*, London, Museum Press, 1953, p. 113.
184 Aga Khan, p. 109.
185 Nijinska, pp. 339–56.
186 Ibid., pp. 416, 422, 427, 430–1.
187 *Le Figaro*, 30 May 1912, p. 1.
188 Bowman, p. 14; Latour, p. 169; Dorsey, p. 126.
189 Latour, p. 181; Erté, pp. 25–6, 29; Bowman, pp. 15, 19–20.
190 Latour, p. 174.
191 Catherine Parpoil and Grégory Couderc, *Paul Poiret, Couturier-Perfumer*, Paris, Somogy, 2013, pp. 11–12, 15.
192 Latour, p. 174.
193 Erté, pp. 24, 26.
194 Pless, Private Diary, pp. 204–6.
195 Polovtsov, p. 35.
196 *Guide-Bleu: Nice Pratique et Pittoresque*, p. 163.
197 Reynolds-Ball, p. 2.
198 Tilburg, p.15; Fortescue, p. 107.
199 Dorsey, p. 133.
200 *Anglo-American Gazette*, 4 November 1899.
201 Mallet, p. 161.
202 Pless, p. 137.
203 *Menton and Monte Carlo News*, 20 April 1912.
204 Aga Khan, pp. 41–2.
205 Patrick Verlinden, *Sporatlas Monaco: Toutes les coudses, les dates, les champions – le Grand Prix de Monaco, Le Rallye Monte-Carlo*, Éditions les 7 Collines, 1999, p. 279.
206 Roux, p. 36.
207 Miles, *St Petersburg*, pp. 311–22, 326.
208 Polovtsov, pp. 24–5.
209 Nijinska, p. 338.
210 Henri Clouzot, *Henri Clouzot à la Côte-d'Azur*, Saint-Benôit-du-Sault; Éditions Tarabuste, 2005, p. 33.
211 Edwards, pp. 180–1.
212 Howarth, p. 186.

6 Painting the Warmth of the Sun

1 *Menton and Monte Carlo News*, 21 January 1899.
2 Bethell, pp. 106–7.
3 Mallet, p. 51.
4 *Menton and Monte Carlo News*, 28 January 1899.
5 John House, *Monet: Nature into Art*, London and New Haven, Yale University Press, 1986, p. 23.
6 Monet, Letter to his companion Alice Hoschedé, quoted in House, p. 23.
7 Murray, *Guidebook*, 1848, quoted in Sillitoe, p. 118.
8 Vincent van Gogh, Letter to Emile Bernard of March 1888, in Van Gogh, *Letters to Emile Bernard*, London, Cresset Press, 1938.
9 Monet, quoted in House, p. 25.
10 House, pp. 150, 211.
11 Van Gogh, *Letters to Emile Bernard*, Letter of c. 20 June 1888.
12 Kenneth E. Silver, *Making Paradise: Art, Modernity and the Myth of the French Riviera*, Cambridge, MA, MIT Press, 2001, p. 34.
13 Paul Cézanne, Letters to Joachim Gasquet, in *Joachim Gasquet's Cézanne: A Memoir with Conversations*, London, Thames and Hudson, 1991, pp. 158, 163, 166, 168; Cézanne's letters to his son in Gerstle Mack, *Paul Cézanne*, London, Jonathan Cape, 1935.
14 Silver, p. 26.
15 Judi Freeman et. al., *The Fauve Landscape*, New York, Abbeville Press, 1990, p. 246.
16 Reclus, pp. 93, 94, 96.
17 Cachin, p. 26; Jim Ring, *Riviera: The Rise and Rise of the Riviera*, London, Faber and Faber, 2011.
18 Guy de Maupassant, 'Rencontre', *Le Gaulois*, 26 May 1882.
19 Colette, *La Naisance du jour*, Paris, Flammarion, 1984, p. 68.
20 Louis Vauxcelles, quoted in Roger Benjamin, 'Metaphor and Scandal at the Salon', in *The Fauve Landscape*, p. 243.
21 Ibid.
22 Hilary Spurling, *The Unknown Matisse: Man of the North 1869 – 1908*, London, Penguin, 2000, p. 337.
23 Ibid., p. 294.
24 Roger Cardinal, *Expressionism*, London, Paladin, 1984.

7 The First World War, 1914–18

1 Erté, pp. 34–6.
2 Edwards, p. 187.
3 *Menton and Monte Carlo News*, 22 January 1916.
4 Ibid., 26 February 1916.
5 Ibid., 22 January 1916.
6 Olivier Vernier, 'Espionnage et péril Germanique à Nice pendant la guerre de 1914', *Nice Historique*, vol. 230, 1990, p. 67.
7 Ralph Schor (ed.), *Nice pendant la Guerre de 1914–1918*, Aix-en-Provence, Le Pensée Universitaire, Publications des Annales de la Faculté des Lettres, 1964, pp. 28–31, quoting the *Journal de Nice* of 14 August 1914, pp. 46–7.
8 Ibid., pp, 35–8.
9 Ibid., p. 81.
10 Ibid., p. 80.
11 Christiane de Livry and Simon François, *Hotel du Cap-Eden-Roc, Cap d'Antibes*, New York, Assouline, 2007, p. 27.

12 Archives communales de Cannes, *Chronique de l'Hôtellerie Cannoise.*

13 Gayraud, pp. 21, 23, 25, 77.

14 Silver, *Making Paradise*, p. 42. *Bather* is in the Philadelphia Museum of Art.

15 Schor, pp. 96–8.

16 Renée d'Ulmès, *Auprès des blessés*, Paris, A. Lemerre, 1916, pp. 7, 16.

17 Ford Madox Ford, pp. 272–3.

18 Ulmès, pp. 7, 19, 26, 29–30.

19 Schor, p. 84.

20 Ulmès, pp. 35–6.

21 Schor, pp. 41, 47, 100.

22 *Menton and Monte Carlo News*, 29 January 1916.

23 Carbonel and Figuero, p. 276; Erté, p. 49; Castle, p. 169.

24 Schor, pp. 143–4, 159.

25 Marie-Paule Renaud, *Katherine Mansfield en France*, Fontainebleau, Impression Hassler, 2004, pp. 52–3; Katherine Mansfield, *Passionate Pilgrimage: A Love Affair in Letters,* London, Michael Joseph, 1976, pp. 7, 10, 30.

26 Mansfield, p. 57.

27 *Menton and Monte Carlo News*, 29 January 1916.

28 Ulmès, p. 6.

29 Ibid., p. 62.

30 Schor, p 136; Ulmès, p. 8.

31 Ulmès, pp. 14, 65.

32 *Menton and Monte Carlo News*, 19 February 1916.

33 Ibid., 4 March 1916.

34 Ibid., 25 March 1916.

35 Ibid., 16 March 1918.

36 Ibid., 12 January 1918.

37 Ibid., 25 March 1916.

38 Orczy, pp. 140–1.

39 *Menton and Monte Carlo News*, 29 January 1916.

40 Ibid., 25 March 1916.

41 Schor, pp. 161–3.

42 *Menton and Monte Carlo News*, 19 February 1916.

43 Schor, pp. 72–3, 76, 187, 189, 191–2.

44 *Menton and Monte Carlo Gazette*, 13 January and 5 May 1917; Schor, pp. 222, 225. 293.

45 *Menton and Monte Carlo News*, 12 February 1916.

46 Ibid., 24 and 31 March 1917.

47 Schor, pp. 207, 288–90.

48 Miles, *St Petersburg*, pp. 354–62; Stackelberg, quoted in Schor, p. 298.

49 LeRoy Ellis, *La Colonie Russe dans les Alpes-Maritimes*, pp. 169–70.

50 *Menton and Monte Carlo Gazette*, 29 December 1917; Schor, pp. 274–5.

51 Hilary Spurling, *Matisse, The Master: A Life of Henri Matisse*, Vol. II, London, Penguin, 2006, p. 205; Silver, p. 44.

52 Françoise Gilot and Carlton Lake, *Life with Picasso*, Harmondsworth, Penguin, 1966, p. 260.

53 Mansfield, pp. 61, 71.

54 *The Times*, London, 30 May 1917.

55 *Menton and Monte Carlo News*, 16 March 1918.

56 Ibid., 23 March 1918.

57 Schor, pp. 292, 363.

58 *Menton and Monte Carlo News*, 27 April 1918.

59 Schor, pp. 278–282; *Menton and Monte Carlo News*, 28 December 1918 and 4 January 1919.

60 Erté, pp. 37–9, 43–44, 50.

61 Katherine Mansfield, Letters to Murry of 21 January 1920 & February 23rd 1921 in *Passionate Pilgrimage*.

62 Spurling, *The Master*, p. 223.

63 *Menton and Monte Carlo News*, 9 March 1918.

8 'The British-American Riviera Colony', 1922–9

1 Linda Wagner-Martin, *Zelda Sayre Fitzgerald: An American Woman's Life*, Basingstoke: Palgrave Macmillan, 2004, p. 71.

2 Elsa Maxwell, *I Married the World*, London, William Heinemann, 1955, pp. 159–60.

3 Wilson to Arthur Mizener, 4 April 1950, in *Edmund Wilson: Letters on Literature and Politics 1912–72*, quoted in Linda Patterson Miller (ed.), *Letters from the Lost Generation: Gerald and Sara Murphy and Friends*, New Brunswick, NJ, Rutgers University Press, 1991; Malcolm Cowley, *Exile's Return: A Narrative of Ideas*, New York, W. W. Norton & Co., 1934, p. 7.

4 Duff Cooper, *The Duff Cooper Diaries 1915–1951*, ed. John Julius Norwich, London, Weidenfeld and Nicolson, 2005, p. 139.

5 *Menton and Monte Carlo News*, 4 and 11 February, 15 April 1922.

6 Ibid., 27 January 1923.

7 Mary Soames (ed.), *Speaking for Themselves: The Personal Letters of Winston and Clementine Churchill*, New York and London, Doubleday/Transworld, 1998, Letter of 7 February 1921, p. 231.

8 Ibid., Letter of 18 February 1921, p. 226.

9 *Menton and Monte Carlo News*, 7 January 1922.

10 Ibid.

11 Ibid., 29 March 1924.

12 Archives communales de Cannes, *Chronique de l'Hôtellerie Cannoise*, Cannes, 2003; Graves, *Royal Riviera*, p. 89; British Pathé, 'The Cannes Peace Conference 1922', YouTube.

13 *Menton and Monte Carlo News*, 10 March and 10 April 1923.

14 Ibid., 23 February 1924.

15 Ibid., 17 November 1923.

16 Ibid., 7 November 1925 and 6 November 1926.

17 Ibid., 21 April 1928.

18 Howarth, p. 151.

19 *Menton and Monte Carlo News*, 8 November 1924.

20 Sir Frederick Treves, *The Riviera of the Corniche Road*, London, Cassell, 1921, p. 110.

21 Erté, p. 50.

22 *Menton and Monte Carlo News*, 15 December 1923.

23 Michael Nelson, *Americans and the Making of the Riviera*, Jefferson, NC, McFarland, 2008, pp. 25, 54–8, 65.

24 Clark, p. 203.

25 Grace Kellogg, *The Two Lives of Edith Wharton: The Woman and her Work*, New York, 1965, p. 258.

26 Balsan, pp. 272–3.

27 Clark, pp. 203–5.

28 Edith Wharton, *The House of Mirth*, New York, Charles Scribner's Sons, 1905, pp. 293, 326, 347.

29 Edwards, pp. 168–9.

30 Marie Clews, *Once Upon a Time at La Mancha*, Beverly, MA, Memoirs Unlimited, 1998, pp. 1, 4–5, 7, 16, 66–7.

31 Henry Clews, *Mumbo Jumbo*, London, Grant Richards Ltd., 1923, pp. 10, 13, 15, 16, 64.

32 Marie Clews, pp. 49, 75, 80.

33 Julian Hale, *The French Riviera: A Cultural History*, New York, OUP, 2009.

34 Roberte Dallo, *Art Déco: Une Méditerranée Heureuse*, Nice, Éditions Gilletta, 2015, p. 64.

35 *Cannes News*, 16 November 1929.

36 *Menton and Monte Carlo News*, 19 November 1927 and 10 December 1927.

37 Maxwell, *I Married the World*, p. 153; Nelson, *Americans*, p. 69.

38 Amanda Vaill, *Everybody Was So Young: Sara and Gerald Murphy, A Lost Generation Love Story*, New York, Broadway Books, 1999, pp. 17, 28, 36, 44, 50–1, 62, 73, 87.

39 Calvin Tomkins, *Living Well is the Best Revenge: Two Americans in Paris 1921–1933*, London, André Deutsch, 1972, p. 25.

40 Vaill, p. 109.

41 De Livry, p. 16.

42 Lartigue, Diary May 1920, quoted in Raphaël Dupouy and Dany Lartigue, *La Riviera de Jacques Henri Lartigue*, Le Lavandou, 2007.

43 Vaill, p. 121.

44 Tomkins, p. 31.

45 Deborah Rothschild (ed.), *Making it New: The Art of Gerald and Sara Murphy*, Exhibition Catalogue, Berkeley and Los Angeles, University of California Press, 2007, pp. 42–5.

46 Jean Des Cars and Jean-Paul Caracalla, *Le Train Bleu et les Grands Express de la Riviera*, Paris: Denoël, 1988, pp. 57, 60.

47 Colette, *The Pure and Impure* (*Ces Plaisirs*, 1932), trans. Briffault, Harmondsworth, Penguin, 1971, p. 93.

48 Des Cars and Caracalla, pp. 60, 67, 70.

49 Blume, *Lartigue's Riviera*, p. 28.

50 *Menton and Monte Carlo News*, 8 November 1924.

51 Ibid., 17 January 1925.

52 Murphy to Calvin Tomkins, 31 January 1964, quoted in Miller, *Letters from the Lost Generation*.

53 Elsa Maxwell, *R.S.V.P.: Elsa Maxwell's Own Story*, Boston and Toronto, Little, Brown and Co., 1954, p. 91.

54 Ronald Berman, *Fitzgerald's Mentors: Edmund Wilson, H. L. Mencken and Gerald Murphy*, Tuscaloosa, University of Alabama Press, 2012, pp. 72–3.

55 Rothschild, p. 49.

56 Ibid., pp. 49, 50–1, 55, 58.

57 Leslie Field, *Bendor: The Golden Duke of Westminster*, London, Weidenfeld and Nicolson, 1983, pp. 177–8, 185.

58 Anne de Courcy, *Chanel's Riviera*, London, Weidenfeld and Nicolson, 2020, p. 34.

59 Michael Segalov, 'The Smell of Success: How Chanel No 5 Gained a Sprinkling of Stardust', *Observer*, 20 November 2021.

60 Courcy, pp. 31–2, 37.

61 Field, pp. 181, 185, 186, 199.

62 Archibald MacLeish, 'The Art of Poetry', interview in *The Paris Review*, vol. 14, no 58, p. 70, quoted in Vaill, p. 6.

63 Donald Ogden Stewart, *By A Stroke of Luck!: An Autobiography by Donald Ogden Stewart*, New York, Paddington Press Ltd., 1975, pp. 117, 133.

64 Wagner-Martin, p. 16.

65 Andrew Turnbull, *Scott Fitzgerald*, London, The Bodley Head, 1962, pp. 84–5.

66 Ibid., pp. 100–1, 118.

67 Sally Cline, *Zelda Fitzgerald: Her Voice in Paradise*, New York, Arcade, 2003, p. 146.

68 John Dos Passos, *The Best Times: An Informal Memoir*, New York, Open Road Distribution, 2015, p. 149.

69 Cline, p. 150.

70 F. Scott. Fitzgerald, *F. Scott Fitzgerald: A Life in Letters*, ed. Bruccoli, New York, Simon and Schuster, 1995, pp. xxi, 79–80.

71 Turnbull, p. 137.

72 Vaill, p 146; Cline, p. 148.

73 Leonard Mosley, *Castlerosse*, London, Arthur Barker, 1956, pp. 50–1, 58–60, 128.

74 Quoted in Courcy, p. 22.

75 Judith Mackrell, *The Unfinished Palazzo*, London, Thames and Hudson, 2018, p. 169.

76 Leonard Mosley, p. 78.
77 Michael Arlen, *The Green Hat*, London, Capuchin Classics, 2008, p. 24.
78 Leonard Mosley, pp. 78, 81, 82–4.
79 Richardson, *Things Seen on the Riviera*, p. 14.
80 *Menton and Monte Carlo News*, 29 March 1924.
81 Ibid., 22 March 1924.
82 Ibid., 18 April 1925.
83 Treves, pp. 10–11.
84 *Menton and Monte Carlo News*, 20 February 1926.
85 Ibid., 3 March 1923.
86 Fernand Léger, 'Contemporary Achievements in Painting', 1914, extracted in Charles Harrison and Paul Wood, *Art in Theory 1900–90: An Anthology of Changing Ideas*, Oxford, Blackwells, 1992, p. 157.
87 Woolf, Virginia, *The Waves*, ed. Herbert, Sellers and Blyth, Cambridge: CUP, 2011, p. 128.
88 Léger, 'Contemporary Achievements in Painting', 1914.
89 'American's Eighteen-Foot Picture Nearly Splits Independent Artists', *New York Herald Tribune* (Paris), 8 February 1924.
90 Rothschild, pp. 56–8.
91 Cline, p. 145.
92 Fitzgerald, Letter to Maxwell Perkins Salies-de-Béarn, 20 February 1926, in Fitzgerald, *A Life in Letters*, p. 137.
93 Kellogg, pp. 252–3.
94 Dos Passos, p. 149.
95 Cline, pp. 183–4; Ean Wood, *Headlong Through Life: The Story of Isadora Duncan*, Lewes, The Book Guild Ltd., 2006, p. 370.
96 Linda Miller, *Letters from the Lost Generation*, p. 13.
97 Fitzgerald, *A Life in Letters*, p. 82.
98 Dos Passos, p. 155.
99 Cline, pp. 172–3.
100 Dos Passos, pp. 141, 206.
101 Balsan, p. 274.
102 Gertrude Stein, in a questionnaire for *transition* magazine, quoted in Benstock, p. 12.
103 Fitzgerald, *A Life in Letters*, letters to Maxwell Perkins of 20 February and 15 March 1926, p. 139.
104 Joanna Richardson, *Colette*, London, Methuen, 1983, pp. 103–4, 118.
105 Ibid., p. 121.
106 Ibid. pp. 124–5, 127.
107 Colette, *La Naisance du jour*, p. 55; Richardson, pp. 125, 129.
108 *Menton and Monte Carlo News*, 5 January 1924.
109 Ibid., 2 January 1926.
110 Ibid., 19 November 1927.
111 Carbonel and Figuero, p. 365.
112 *Americans on the Côte-d'Azur aka Americans in Beautiful France*, Cannes, 1927–8, June and July 1927.
113 Blume, *Côte-d'Azur*, p. 90.
114 Polovtsov, pp. 27–8.
115 Ibid., p. 18.
116 *Menton and Monte Carlo News*, 19 March 1927.
117 Field, p. 213.
118 Hugo Vickers, *Cecil Beaton: The Authorized Biography*, London, Weidenfeld and Nicolson, 1985, pp. 74, 82.
119 Graves, *Royal Riviera*, p. 164.
120 Hugh Ford, *Four Lives in Paris*, San Francisco, North Point Press, 1987, p. 76, quoted in Blume, *Côte-d'Azur*.
121 Vickers, p. 110.
122 Mary S. Lovell, *The Riviera Set*, London, Little, Brown, 2017, pp. 75, 131.
123 Joan Acocella, 'Introduction' to Isadora Duncan, *My Life*, New York, Boni and Liveright, 1927, and also p. 376.
124 Selena Hastings, *The Secret Lives of Somerset Maugham*, London, John Murray, 2009, pp. 314–5.
125 Alec Waugh, *My Brother Evelyn and other Profiles*, London, Cassell, 1967, p. 279.

126 Robin Maugham, *Conversations with Willie: Recollections of W. Somerset Maugham*, London, W. H. Allen, 1978, pp. 28–9, 43, 50.
127 Alec Waugh, pp. 283–4.
128 Ibid., p. 51.
129 Hastings, p. 218.
130 *Americans on the Côte-d'Azur aka Americans in Beautiful France*, June 1927; *Menton and Monte Carlo News*, 6 February 1926.
131 Miles, *St Petersburg*, p. 299.
132 Mary Desti, *The Untold Story: The Life of Isadora Duncan 1921–1927*, New York, H. Liveright, 1929, pp. 244–5.
133 Blume, *Côte-d'Azur*, p. 83.
134 Wood, pp. 379, 386.
135 Desti, pp. 246–7, 266.
136 Ibid., p. 270.
137 *Americans on the Côte-d'Azur*, September 1927.
138 Martine Buchet, *La Colombe d'or: Saint-Paul-de-Vence*, Paris, Assouline, 1993, pp. 9, 14, 28.
139 *Americans on the Côte d'Azur*, 4 April 1927.
140 Ibid.
141 Ibid., July 1927.
142 *Menton and Monte Carlo News*, 15 January 1927.
143 Maxwell, *I Married the World*, pp. 146–8.
144 *Menton and Monte Carlo News*, 6 November 1926.
145 Colette, quoted in Bowman, p. 114.
146 Polovtsov, p. 28.
147 Nelson, *Americans*, p. 111.
148 Polovtsov, p. 26.
149 Nelson, *Americans*, p. 111.
150 Blume, *Côte d'Azur*, p. 83.
151 Howarth, pp. 111–12.
152 Edwards, pp. 63–5, 197–8.
153 Charles Graves, *None but the Rich: Life and Times of the Greek Syndicate*, London, Cassell, 1963, pp. 11–12, 98–100.
154 Polovtsov, p. 14.
155 Graves, *Royal Riviera*, p. 180.
156 Blume, *Lartigue's Riviera*, pp. 18–20.
157 *Americans on the Côte-d'Azur*, July 1927.
158 Evelyn Waugh, *When the Going Was Good*, Harmondsworth, Penguin, 1951, p. 16.
159 Maxwell, *I Married the World*, pp. 11, 154–55.
160 Polovtsov, p 17.
161 *Menton and Monte Carlo News*, 22 April 1922.
162 Ibid., 7 April 1923.
163 Ibid., 7 February 1925.
164 Hale, p. 158; *Menton and Monte Carlo News*, 13 February 1926 and January 1928.
165 *Menton and Monte Carlo News*, 6 January 1923.
166 Mathilde Kschessinska, *Dancing in Petersburg*, trans. Haskell, Alton, Dance Books Ltd., 2005, pp. 203, 205, 211.
167 Romain Gary, *La Promesse de l'Aube*.
168 *Menton and Monte Carlo News*, 24 February 1923.
169 Ibid., 4 April 1925.
170 F. Scott Fitzgerald, *Tender in the Night*, London, Collins, 2011, pp. 22–3.
171 Erté, p. 51.
172 E. Phillips Oppenheim, *The Pool of Memory*, London, Hodder and Stoughton, 1941, p. 89.
173 Robert Standish, *The Prince of Storytellers: The Life of E. Phillips Oppenheim*, London, Peter Davies, 1957, p. 9.
174 Graves, *Royal Riviera*, p. 200.
175 Ibid., p. 106.
176 Balsan, p. 281.
177 Ysabel De Witte, *Riviera Celebrities*, Menton: Menton and Monte Carlo News, n.d., p. 25.
178 *Menton and Monte Carlo News*, 1 April 1922.
179 Howarth, p. 146.
180 *Menton and Monte Carlo News*, 28 November 1925.
181 Ibid., 23 January 1926.
182 Ibid., 20 February 1926.

183 Kiki de Montparnasse, *Souvenirs Retrouvés*, Paris, José Corti, 2005, p. 101.
184 Simonetta Fraquelli, 'Montparnasse and the Right Bank: Myth and Reality', in Wilson et. al., *Paris: Capital of the Arts 1900–1968*, London, Royal Academy of the Arts, 2002, p. 112.
185 Blume, *Côte d'Azur*, p. 101.
186 Colette, *Pure and Impure*, p. 15.
187 Cocteau, *Souvenir Portraits*, pp. 92–3.
188 Silver, pp. 50, 79, 85, 101.
189 *Menton and Monte Carlo News*, 9 February 1924.
190 *Americans on the Côte-d'Azur*, March 1928.
191 Silver, pp. 63–4.
192 Peter Adam, *Eileen Gray: Architect / Designer*, London, Thames and Hudson, 1987, pp. 21, 26, 133, 174, 191–2, 200.
193 Balsan, pp. 256, 261, 277.
194 CSC to Churchill, 8 March 1925, in Soames, *Speaking for Themselves*.
195 Dallo, pp. 54, 66.
196 *Menton and Monte Carlo News*, 29 December 1923.
197 Ibid., 28 November 1925.
198 Anne-Elisabeth Buxtorf, *Les studios de la Victorine 1919–29*, Nice, Cinémathèque, 1998, pp. 191–4, 230.
199 Spurling, *The Master*, p. 244.
200 Mackrell, pp. 178–81.
201 Arlen, *Exiles*, p. 70.
202 Arlen, *The Green Hat*, pp. 99–100.
203 Ibid., p. 103.
204 Ibid., p. 148.
205 *Menton and Monte Carlo News*, 21 April 1928.
206 Alec Waugh, p. 262.
207 Arlen, *Exiles*, p. 72.
208 *Menton and Monte Carlo News*, 1 February 1930.
209 Ibid., 27 February 1926.
210 *Cannes News*, 7 and 14 December 1929.
211 *Menton and Monte Carlo News*, 4 December 1926.
212 Ibid., 21 January 1928.
213 *Cannes News*, 23 November 1929.
214 Robert McAlmon, *Being Geniuses Together: An Autobiography*, London, Secker and Warburg, 1938, p 262; Blume, *Côte-d'Azur*, p. 105.
215 Nelson, *Americans*, p. 109.
216 Les amis de la liberté, *Dictionnaire historique et biographique du communisme dans Les Alpes-Maritime, xxe siècle*, Sophie-Antipolis, 2011.
217 *Menton and Monte Carlo News*, 14 April 1928.
218 Waugh, *When the Going Was Good*, p. 11.
219 Ibid., pp. 64–5.
220 Ibid., pp. 16–17.
221 Misia Sert, *Two or Three Muses*, trans. Budberg, London, Museum Press, 1953, pp. 128–9.
222 Field, p. 206.
223 Serge Lifar, *Ma Vie: From Kiev to Kiev*, London, Hutchinson, 1970, pp. 74–5.
224 Vaill, pp. 210–14; Rothschild, p. 68, quoting Dorothy Parker to Robert Benchley, 7 November 1929.
225 *Cannes News*, 7 December 1929.
226 *Menton and Monte Carlo News*, 19 January 1929.
227 *Cannes News*, 14 December 1929.

9 Losing Paradise, 1930–9

1 Jean Vigo, address to the Groupement des Spectateurs d'Avant-Garde quoted by Maximilien le Cain, 'Jean Vigo' in *Senses of Cinema.Com*, July 2002.

2 Dallo, pp. 59, 137.

3 *The 'Riviera Society Directory': List of Notable Residents and Visitors – Who's Who on the Riviera 1930–1*, Nice, 1931, pp. 49, 173, and adverts.

4 *Menton and Monte Carlo News*, 15 November 1930.

5 Wikipedia, 'Blue Train Races'; 'Woolf Barnato'; 'Bentley'.

6 *Menton and Monte Carlo News*, 14 November 1931.

7 Ibid., 23 April 1932.

8 Ibid., 2 January 1932.

9 Kanigel, p. 183.

10 Nelson, *Americans*, pp. 150–1.

11 D. H. Lawrence, *The Letters of D. H. Lawrence*, London, Heinemann, 1932, p. xx.

12 Lawrence, *Letters*, Harmondsworth, Penguin, 1950, p. 93.

13 Huxley, Letter of 13 July 1928, quoted in Meyers, Jeffrey, *D. H. Lawrence: A Biography*, New York, Alfred A. Knopf, 1990, p. 376.

14 Meyers, pp. 378–9.

15 Lawrence, *Letters*, p. 852.

16 Andrea Lynn, *Shadow Lovers: The Last Affairs of H. G. Wells*, Cambridge, MA, Westview Press, 2001, pp. xvi, xviii.

17 Rebecca West, *The Thinking Reed*, London, Virago Modern Classics, 1984, pp. v, 6, 10, 56, 87, 147.

18 Lynn, pp. 106–7.

19 Miles, *St Petersburg*, pp. 378–9.

20 Lynn, pp. 26–28.

21 W. Somerset Maugham, *The Vagrant Mood: Six Essays*, London, Heinemann, 1952, pp. 210–11.

22 Lynn, pp. 11–12.

23 *Menton and Monte Carlo News*, 14 November 1925.

24 E. Phillips, Oppenheim, *Murder at Monte Carlo*, Milton Keynes: Lightning Source, n.d.

25 Standish, p. 57.

26 Ibid., pp. 78, 100, 132; Oppenheim, *The Pool of Memory*, p. 95.

27 Fitzgerald, *A Life in Letters*, quoted from Fitzgerald's 'Early Success', 1937.

28 Fitzgerald to Maxwell Perkins, 3 February 1934 in Fitzgerald, *A Life in Letters*, p. 246.

29 Philip Rahv, 'You Can't Duck a Hurricane Under a Beach Umbrella', *Daily Worker*, 5 May 1934.

30 Tomkins, p. 12.

31 Vaill, p. 229.

32 Ernest Hemingway, Letter to Scott Fitzgerald of 28 May 1934, quoted in Hemingway, *Selected Letters*, ed. Carlos Baker, New York, Charles Scribner's Sons, 1981.

33 Bruccoli, Introduction to Fitzgerald, *A Life in Letters*, pp. xxi–xxii.

34 Tomkins, *Living Well*, p. 11.

35 Simone de Beauvoir, *The Prime of Life*, trans. Green, Cleveland and New York, The World Publishing Company, 1962, pp. 93–4, 111.

36 Balsan, pp. 274–5.

37 *Cannes News*, 15 September 1930; *Menton and Monte Carlo News*, 15 November 1930.

38 Vincent Sheean, *Between the Thunder and the Sun*, London, Macmillan, 1943, pp. 22, 37.

39 Aga Khan, p. 89.

40 Lovell, pp. 103–4.

41 Churchill writing from the Château de l'Horizon, 22 August 1934, quoted in Soames, p. 359.

42 Mackrell, p. 204, n. 28.

43 Vickers, p. 162.

44 Leonard Mosley, pp. 113, 115.

45 Adela Quebec (Gerald Hugh Tyrwhitt-Wilson, Lord Berners), *The Girls of Radcliff Hall*, printed for the author for private circulation only, n.d., pp. 18–20, 27, 47–8, 51; Vickers, p.171.

46 Mark Amory, *Lord Berners: The Last Eccentric*, London, Chatto and Windus, 1998, pp. 124, 126.

47 Ibid., p. 130.

48 Mackrell, p. 197.

49 Vickers, p. 74.

50 Diana Mosley, *A Life of Contrasts: The Autobiography of Diana Mosley*, London, Gibson Square Books, 2009, pp. 98–9, 106.

51 Amory, pp. 108, 115; Igor Stravinsky and Robert Craft, *Memories and Commentaries*, London, Faber, 1960, pp. 83–4.

52 Robert Kimball (ed.), *The Complete Lyrics of Cole Porter*, New York, Da Capo, 1992, pp. xxi-xxi.

53 Elsa Maxwell, *The Celebrity Circus*, London, W. H. Allen, 1964, p. 105.

54 Cecil Beaton, quoted in Vickers, p. 114.

55 *Cannes News*, 31 July 1930.

56 Noël Coward, *The Letters of Noël Coward*, ed. Barry Day, New York, Alfred A. Knopf, 2007, p. 140.

57 Leonard Mosley, pp. 95–6.

58 Ibid., pp. 142, 144, 160; Mackrell, p. 223.

59 Field, p. 198.

60 Courcy, p. 72.

61 Erté, p. 103.

62 *Menton and Monte Carlo News*, 14 March 1931.

63 Ibid., 23 April 1932.

64 Ibid., 22 March 1930.

65 Standish, pp. 7–8.

66 *Menton and Monte Carlo News*, 16 January 1931.

67 Ibid., 31 January 1931.

68 Finley Peter Dunne aka Mr. Dooley, American humourist.

69 *Menton and Monte Carlo News*, 28 February 1931.

70 Peter de Polnay, *A Door Ajar*, London, Robert Hale, 1959, p. 58.

71 Polovtsov, pp. 40–1, 125–6.

72 Graves, *Royal Riviera*, p. 170.

73 Verlinden, pp. 17, 22–3.

74 Victoria Tennant, *Irina Baranova and the Ballets Russes de Monte Carlo*, Chicago, University of Chicago Press, 2014, pp. 24, 26, 34.

75 Jack Anderson, *The One and Only: The Ballet Russe de Monte Carlo*, London, Dance Books Ltd., 1981, p. 4.

76 Lifar, p. 144.

77 Agnes de Mille, *Dance to the Piper: Memoirs of the Ballet*, London, Columbus Books, 1987, p. 269.

78 Kathrine Sorley Walker, *De Basil's Ballets Russes*, Alton, Dance Books Ltd., 2010, pp. 4, 16, 50, 60.

79 *L'Eclaireur de Nice*, 9 February 1934 in Ralph Schor (ed.), *Nice et les Alpes-Maritimes de 1914–1945: document d'histoire*, Nice, Centre Regional de Documentation Pedagogique de Nice, 1974.

80 Yves Montand, *Montand raconte Montand*, Paris, Éditions du Seuil, 2001, pp. 36–8, 41.

81 Julian Jackson, *The Popular Front in France: Defending Democracy 1934–8*, Cambridge, Cambridge University Press, 1988, p. ix.

82 Kanigel, pp. 184–6.

83 Roger Bordier, *J'étais enfant en 1936*, Paris, Éditions de Sorbier, 1986, p. 33.

84 Blume, *Côte-d'Azur*, p. 120.

85 *La Cri des Travailleurs des Alpes-Maritimes*, 15–16 February 1936, in Schor, *Nice et les Alpes-Maritime de 1914–1945*.

86 Benstock, p. 405.

87 *Whatever Happened to the Windsors?*

88 Sir Dudley Forwood, interviewed in ibid.

89 Wallis Windsor, pp. 270–1.

90 Ibid., p. 274.

91 Courcy, p. 87.

92 Wallis Windsor, p. 279.

93 Ibid.

94 Howarth, p. 83.

95 *Menton and Monte Carlo News*, 16 February 1929.

96 Wallis Windsor, p. 289.

97 Ibid., pp. 281, 282, 287.

98 Sir Dudley Forwood, interviewed in *Whatever Happened to the Windsors?*

99 Aga Khan, p. 249.

100 Maxwell, *The Celebrity Circus*, p. 173.

101 Interviewed in *Whatever Happened to the Windsors?*

102 Michael Bloch, *The Secret File of the Duke of Windsor*, Bath, Chivers Press, 1989, p. 163; *Whatever Happened to the Windsors?*

103 Wallis Windsor, pp. 312–3; Bloch, pp. 95, 185, 188.

104 Jean Louis Faucigny-Lucinge, *Un gentilhomme cosmopolite*, Paris, Perrin, 1990, p. 157.

105 Aga Khan, p. 247.

106 *Riviera News*, 1 January 1938.

107 Graves, *Royal Riviera*, p. 179.

108 Churchill, quoted in Lovell, p. 160.

109 Martin Mauthner, *German Writers in Exile 1933–40*, London, Valentine Mitchell and the European Jewish Publication Society, 2007, pp. 1– 2, 10, 37, 55.

110 Sybille Bedford, *Aldous Huxley: A Biography*, London, Chatto amd Windus, 1973, p. 276.

111 Ibid., pp. 224, 230.

112 Blume, *Côte-d'Azur*, p. 88.

113 Bedford, pp. 276–77.

114 Jonathan Miles, *The Nine Lives of Otto Katz*, Bantam Press, 2010, p. 299.

115 Ibid., pp. 240, 245, 253–4, 262–7, 299–300.

116 Courcy, pp. 98–9.

117 Bedford, pp. 327, 335.

118 Silver, pp. 61, 68.

119 Cyril Connolly, *The Rock Pool*, Paris, Obelisk Press, 1936, pp. 13–5, 20, 31, 32, 36, 65, 117–18.

120 Cyril Connolly, *The Unquiet Grave: A Word Cycle*, London, Hamish Hamilton, 1951, p. 84.

121 *Riviera News*, 1 January 1938.

122 Ibid., 29 January 1938.

123 Ibid., 8 January 1938.

124 Maxwell, *I Married the World*, p. 134.

125 Quoted in Courcy, p. 101; Cooper, *Diaries*, p. 150.

126 Vickers, p. 216.

127 Courcy, p. 101.

128 Churchill, Letter of 10 January 1938, in Soames, pp. 431–2.

129 Churchill, Letter of 18 January 1939, in ibid., p. 448.

130 Janet Flanner, 22 October 1938.

131 Beauvoir, pp. 391–3.

132 Maxwell, *I Married the World*, p. 211.

133 Wallis Windsor, p. 321.

134 Noël Coward, *Autobiography*, London, Methuen, 1986, p. 321.

10 Refugees and Resistance, 1939–45

1 Kieron Corless and Chris Darke, *Cannes: Inside the World's Premier Film Festival*, London, Faber, 2007, pp. 12–15.
2 Orczy, pp. 202–3, 208.
3 Charles Graves, *Riviera Revisited*, London, Evans Bros, 1948, p. 15.
4 Elsie Gladman, *Uncertain Tomorrows*, London, Excalibur Press, 1993, pp. 17–18, 21.
5 Des Cars and Caracalla, pp. 97–8.
6 Gladman, pp. 20, 22.
7 Lion Feuchtwanger, *The Devil in France: My Encounter with Him in the Summer of 1940*, London and New York, Hutchinson, pp. 5, 13–14; Mauthner, p. 14.
8 Hanna Diamond, *Fleeing Hitler: France 1940*, Oxford and New York, OUP, 2007, p 196; Spurling, *The Master*, p. 396.
9 Silver, p. 147.
10 Spurling, *The Master* p. 413.
11 Ibid., pp. 390, 398, 402, 411.
12 Jean-Louis Panicacci, *En territoire occupé: Italiens et Allemands à Nice, 1942–44*, Paris, Vendémaire Éditions, 2012, p. 12.
13 Orczy, p. 208.
14 Panicacci, *Les Alpes-Maritime dans la guerre*, p. 113.
15 W. Somerset Maugham, *Strictly Personal*, London, Heinemann, 1942, pp. 49, 64; Lovell, p. 202.
16 Gladman, pp. 26–8.
17 Courcy, pp. 145–6.
18 Maugham, *Strictly Personal*, pp. 144, 159–60, 181.
19 Courcy, pp. 147–149.
20 Robin Maugham, pp. 65–7.
21 Courcy, p. 150.
22 Lovell, p. 214.
23 *Whatever Happened to the Windsors?*
24 Courcy, pp. 142–3.
25 Panicacci, *L'occupation italienne: Sud-Est de la France, juin 1940–septembre 1943*, Rennes, Collection Histoire Presses Universitaire de Rennes, 2010, p. 54.
26 Faucigny-Lucinge, p. 175.
27 Gladman, p. 24.
28 Edwards, pp. 207–8.
29 Daniel Carpi, *Between Mussolini and Hitler: The Jews and the Italian Authorities in France and Tunisia*, London, Brandeis University Press, 1994, pp. 69–70.
30 Panicacci, *Les Alpes-Maritime dans la guerre*, p. 111.
31 Ibid., p 157.
32 Graves, *Riviera Revisited*, p. 7.
33 Panicacci, *En territoire occupé*, p. 82.
34 Panicacci, *Les Alpes-Maritime dans la guerre*, pp. 124, 126.
35 Martyn Cornick, '"Fraternity Among Listeners"', the BBC and the French Resistance: Evidence from Refugees' in Diamond, Hanna and Kitson (eds.), *Vichy, Resistance, Liberation*, Oxford: Berg, 2005, pp. 101–3, 105.
36 Peter Churchill, *Of Their Own Choice*, London, Hodder and Stoughton, 1952, pp. 9, 14.
37 Ibid., pp. 55, 70–88, 90–6, 132.
38 Panicacci, *Les Alpes-Maritime dans la guerre*, p. 129.
39 Panicacci, *En territoire occupé*, p. 66.
40 Peter Churchill, *Duel of Wits*, London, Hodder and Stoughton, 1953, pp. 12, 97–8, 107, 109, 318.
41 Gerald Hakim, *Un Anglais dans la Résistance*, Paris, Presses de la Cité, 1998, pp. 62, 69.
42 Panicacci, *L'Occupation italienne*, p. 309.
43 Panicacci, *En territoire occupé*, pp. 62, 67.
44 Ibid., p. 242.

45 Panicacci, *Les Alpes-Maritime dans la guerre*, p. 227.
46 Ibid., p. 225.
47 Panicacci, *L'Occupation italienne*, p. 184.
48 Lovell, pp. 218, 224, 327.
49 Silver, p. 151.
50 Panicacci, *En territoire occupé*, p. 176.
51 Courcy, p. 161.
52 Cecil Beaton, *The Glass of Fashion*, 1954, quoted in Latour, p. 184.
53 Bowman, p. 25.
54 Hal Vaughan, *Sleeping with the Enemy: Coco Chanel, Nazi Agent*, London, Vintage Digital, 2011.
55 Courcy, p. 235.
56 Ibid., p. 266.
57 Carpi, pp. 72, 79–80, 87–8, 93, 95, 104, 106–7, 139.
58 Schor, *Nice et les Alpes-Maritimes*; Carpi, pp. 136, 138, 149, 171.
59 Gladman, p. 34.
60 *L'Eclaireur de Nice*, 9 April 1943, in Schor, *Nice et les Alpes-Maritimes*.
61 Panicacci, *En territoire occupé*, pp. 81, 87.
62 Graves, *Riviera Revisited*, p. 16.
63 Panicacci, *En territoire occupé*, pp. 16, 93.
64 Simone Righetti, *La guerre au quotidien*, Nice, Éditions du Losange, 2006, pp. 39, 43–44.
65 Paul Gaujac, *La Guerre en Provence*, Lyon: Presse univeritaire de Lyon, 1998, p. 33.
66 Panicacci, *En territoire occupé*, pp. 96–98.
67 Montand quoted in Blume, *Côte-d'Azur*, p. 135.
68 Castle, p. 176.
69 Carbonel and Figuero, p. 377.
70 Gaujac, pp. 37–8.
71 Quoted in Panicacci, *En territoire occupé*, p. 107.
72 Gladman, p. 36.
73 Panicacci, *En territoire occupé*, p. 113.
74 Gladman, p. 30.
75 Graves, *Riviera Revisited* p. 10.
76 Panicacci, Jean-Louis, *La Résistance azuréenne*, Nice: Éditions Serre, 1994, p. 89.
77 Ibid., p. 8.
78 Edwards, p. 210.
79 Graves, *None but the Rich*, pp. 138–9.
80 Graves, *Riviera Revisited*, pp. 72–5.
81 Orzcy, p. 217.
82 Panicacci, *En territoire occupé*, p. 118.
83 Quoted in Carpi, p. 189.
84 Panicacci, *En territoire occupé*, pp. 118, 122.
85 Carpi, p. 188.
86 Courcy, p. 226.
87 Panicacci, *La Résistance Azuréenne*, pp. 11, 26.
88 Fourcade, Marie-Madeleine, *L'Arche de Noé: Réseau Alliance 1940–45*, 1968; Paris, Plon, 1989, p. 438.
89 Panicacci, *La Résistance Azuréenne*, pp. 69, 73.
90 Spurling, *The Master*, pp. 420, 422.
91 Gladman, pp. 39–40.
92 Panicacci, *En territoire occupé*, p. 61.
93 Laurent Mannoni and Stéphanie Salmon, 'Les Enfants du Paradis' – Marcel Carné – Jacques Prévert, Paris, la Cinémathèque française, Éditions Xavier Barral, 2012, p. 23.
94 Ibid., p. 41.
95 Geneviève Sellier, *Les Enfants du Paradis*, Paris, Nathan, 1996, p. 13.
96 Ibid.
97 Mannoni and Salmon, pp. 167, 169.
98 Ibid., pp. 146–8.
99 Berruer, Pierre. *Maurice Chevalier – raconté par François Vals*. Paris: Plon, 1988, p. 45.
100 Panicacci, *En territoire occupé*, pp. 111–14, 167.
101 Gaujac, p 35; Mauthner, p. 15.

102 Graves, *Riviera Revisited*, p. 12.
103 Panicacci, *En territoire occupé*, p. 108.
104 Gladman, p. 38.
105 Panicacci, *La Résistance Azuréenne*, p. 98.
106 Orzcy, p. 218.
107 Hale, p. 29.
108 Howarth, pp. 207–8.
109 Blume, *Lartigue's Riviera*, p. 28.
110 Leonard Slater, *Aly: A Biography*, London, W. H. Allen, 1966, pp. 20, 107–8.
111 Panicacci, *En territoire occupé*, pp. 183, 188, 195–7; *La Résistance Azuréenne*, pp. 130–1, 133, 136.
112 Kanigel, pp. 215–16; Panicacci, *Les Alpes-Maritime dans la guerre*, p. 374.

11 Glitz, 1945–60

1 Graves, *Royal Riviera*, p. 208.
2 Des Cars and Caracalla, p. 105.
3 Corless and Darke, pp. 11–12, 16–21.
4 Ibid., pp. 22–3.
5 Churchill, Letter of 24 September 1945, in Soames.
6 Beaverbrook, quoted in David Kynaston, *Austerity Britain 1945–51*, London, Bloomsbury, 2007, p. 76.
7 Graves, *Riviera Revisited*, pp. 41, 117.
8 Anderson, pp. 95, 105, 120, 127.
9 Gilot and Lake, pp. 130–3.
10 Ibid., p. 255.
11 Henri Matisse, M.-A. Couturier and L.-B. Rayssiguier, *La chapelle de Vence: Journal d'une création*, Geneva, Editions d'Art Albert Skira, 1993, pp. 9, 12, 15.
12 Gilot and Lake, pp. 252–4.
13 David Gullentops (ed.), *Jean Cocteau et la Côte-d'Azur*, Paris, Non Lieu, 2011, pp. 5, 31.
14 Edwards, pp. 215–16.
15 Maxwell, *The Celebrity Circus*, pp. 24, 25.
16 Coward's Diary, August 1946, quoted in Kynaston, p. 78.
17 Robin Maugham, pp. 80–1.
18 Wallis Windsor, p. 363.
19 Faucigny-Lucinge, quoted in Blume, *Côte-d'Azur*, p. 123.
20 Wallis Windsor, p. 364.
21 Cooper, *Diaries*, February 1951.
22 Slater, pp. 6, 11, 26, 127–9.
23 Corless and Darke, pp. 23–4.
24 Howarth, p. 47.
25 Des Cars and Caracalla, p. 110.
26 Graves, *Riviera Revisited*, p. 121.
27 Maxwell, *I Married the World*, p. 10.
28 Graves, *Royal Riviera*, p. 225.
29 Blume, *Côte-d'Azur*, pp. 143, 145.
30 Lovell, p. 263.
31 Slater, pp. 6, 117, 136, 138, 141–2.
32 Aga Khan, p. 313.
33 Slater, pp. 153, 159.
34 Aga Khan, p. 313; Slater, pp. 162–4.
35 Nathalie Grzesiak, *Yves Montand-Simone Signoret: Une passion engagée*, Paris: Acropole, 2001, pp. 74–5, 91.
36 Buchet, p. 80.
37 Kanigel, pp. 210–11; Howarth, pp. 46–7.
38 Corless and Darke, pp. 54–7.
39 Hale, p. 127.
40 Bertrand Meyer-Stabley, *Françoise Sagan: Le tourbillon d'une vie*, Pygmalion ebook, 2014.
41 Ring, pp. 177–8.
42 Quoted in O'Neill, Rosemary, *Art and Visual Culture on the French Riviera 1956–1971: Ecole de Nice*, Farnham, Ashgate Publishing, 2012, p. 27.
43 Hitchcock, quoted in Edwards, pp. 235–6.

44 Slater, p. 187.
45 Richard L. Coe, 'Catch a Smile and a Thief', *Washington Post*, 1955, p. 30.
46 Sylvia Plath, *The Journals of Sylvia Plath, 1950–1962*, ed. Kukil, London, Faber and Faber, 2000, pp. 550, 563.
47 Corless and Darke, pp. 38, 42–3.
48 Edwards, p. 221.
49 Ibid., p. 244.
50 Edwards, pp. 240–1, 247–9.
51 Celeste Holm presenting *High Society* DVD featurette, 'Cole Porter in Hollywood: True Love'.
52 Edwards, pp. 253–4, 257–60.
53 Graves, *Royal Riviera*, pp. 242–4.
54 Norah Docker, *Norah: The Autobiography of Lady Docker*, London, W. H. Allen, 1969, pp. 164–6.
55 Graves, *Royal Riviera*, p. 264.
56 Docker, p. 171.
57 Ibid., p. 168.
58 British Movietone News, 'Sir Bernard and Lady Docker Arrive Home', 26 April 1958, YouTube.
59 Docker, pp. 172–6, 179, 181.
60 Kenneth Young, *Churchill and Beaverbrook: A Study in Friendship and Politics*, London, Eyre and Spottiswoode, 1966, pp. 301, 305–6.

61 Gilbert, Martin. *Winston Churchill and Emery Reves: Correspondence 1937–1964*, Austin, University of Texas Press, 1997, pp. 18, 347–9, 352–3.
62 Anthony Montague-Browne, *Long Sunset: Memoirs of Winston Churchill's Last Private Secretary*, London, Indigo, 1996, pp. 216–17.
63 Churchill, Letter of 17 January 1956 from La Pausa, in Soames.
64 Montague Browne, p. 218.
65 Ibid., pp. 227–9.
66 Young, p. 315.
67 Montague Browne, p. 229.
68 Danièle Giraudy, *Guide du Musée Picasso Antibes*, Antibes, Hazan, 1987, pp. 68–70.
69 Corless and Darke, pp. 99, 101; Emmanuel Laurent (dir.), *Deux de la vague*, Films à trois, 2009.
70 Nelson, *Americans*, pp. 171, 173.
71 Verlinden, *Sporatlas Monaco*.
72 Edwards, pp. 268–9, 274–6.
73 Churchill, *All About the French Riviera*, London, Vista Books, 1970, pp. 47, 68, 76, 81.
74 Graves, *Royal Riviera*, p. 17.
75 Slater, pp. 274–5; Lovell, p. 366.
76 Slater, pp. 224, 276.

12 Sunny But Shady, 1960–90

1 Howarth, p. 212.
2 Des Cars and Caracalla, pp. 128, 136.
3 Roger-Louis Bianchini, *Crimes and arnaques sur la Côte-d'Azur*, Nice, Éditions Giletta, Nice-Matin, 2003, pp. 15–17; Hugh McLeave, *Rogues in the Gallery: The Modern Plague of Art Thefts*, pp. 34–8.
4 McLeave, pp. 38–9, 44.

5 Castle, *La Belle Otero*, pp. 176, 185; Carbonel and Figuero, pp. 392, 396–7.
6 W. Somerset Maugham, *Lady Frederick: A Comedy in Three Acts*, London, Samuel French, 1947.
7 Robin Maugham, p. 3.
8 Hale, p. 80.
9 Robin Maugham, pp. 3, 18.
10 Robert Calder, *Willie: A Life of W. Somerset Maugham*, London, Heinemann, 1990, pp. 206–7.

11 Robin Maugham, p. 26.

12 Gladman, appendices.

13 Priyamvada Gopal, 'Why can't Britain handle the truth about Winston Churchill?', *Guardian*, 17 March 2021.

14 Jacques Derogy and Jean-Marie Pontaut, *Enquête sur les ripoux de la Côte*, Paris, Fayard, 1994, p. 410.

15 Jacques Médecin, *Un lynchage exemplaire: Mitterand m'a tuer*, Paris, Première Ligne, 1994, pp. 28–9.

16 Ibid.

17 Raoul Mille, *Un dynastie foudroyée*, Paris, Albin Michel, pp. 156, 192.

18 Derogy and Pontaut, pp. 409, 411.

19 Mille, p. 156.

20 Corless and Darke, p. 72.

21 Ibid., p. 83–5.

22 Ibid., pp. 88–90.

23 Ibid., p. 127.

24 Ibid., pp. 138, 141.

25 Lindsay Anderson, *The Diaries*, ed. Paul Sutton, London, Methuen, 2004, pp. 239, 240, 244.

26 Rosemary O'Neill, *Art and Visual Culture on the French Riviera 1956–1971: The École de Nice*, Farnham, Ashgate Publishing, 2012, pp. 3, 19.

27 Ibid., p. 119.

28 Laurent Jeanpierre and Christophe Kihm, 'La recherche de l'azur', in *L'Art contemporain et la Côte-d'Azur: un territoire pour l'expérimentation 1951–2011*, Dijon, les Presses du réel, 2011, p. 55.

29 O'Neill, pp. 2, 218.

30 Rothschild, p. 166.

31 Keith Richards, with James Fox, *Life*, London, Weidenfeld and Nicolson, 2010, pp. 289, 291, 307.

32 Dodge, pp. 35, 183.

33 Richards and Fox, p. 292.

34 Various web sources – search Mick and Bianca Wedding.

35 Richards and Fox, pp. 297, 300.

36 Ibid., pp. 296, 298–99.

37 Ring, pp. 210–12.

38 Mille, p. 168.

39 Renée Le Roux, *Révélations: Entretiens avec Mme. Renée Le Roux réalisés à Paris, Nice et Monte-Carlo en 1997, 1998 et 1990 recueillis par Alain Roullier*, Nice, France Europe Éditions Livres, 1999, pp. 13, 17, 67, 74–7.

40 Ibid., p. 78.

41 Mille, p. 199.

42 Le Roux, pp. 58, 66.

43 Ibid., p. 81.

44 Derogy and Pontaut, p. 376.

45 Le Roux, pp. 91, 111, 115, 125, 137.

46 Ibid., pp. 135, 161–2, 280–3.

47 Blume, *Côte-d'Azur*, p. 150.

48 Le Roux, pp. 183, 277, 280–3, 291, 299; Blume, *Côte-d'Azur*, p. 150.

49 Gilbert Picard, *Spaggiari or Le casse du siècle*, Paris, FleuveNoir, 1992, p. 213.

50 Ibid., pp. 58–62, 64–6, 81–8, 106, 115–16, 120, 122.

51 Derogy and Pontaut, p. 408.

52 Picard, pp. 128, 139–43, 150–1, 158, 164–8, 166.

53 Mille, p. 197.

54 Blume, *Côte-d'Azur*, pp. 15–16.

55 Mille, p. 186.

56 Ibid., pp. 204–5.

57 Ring, p. 200.

58 Graham Greene, 'May We Borrow Your Husband?' and 'Beauty' in *May We Borrow Your Husband? And Other Comedies of the Sexual Life*, 1967, London, Vintage, 2000, p. 8.

59 Graham Greene, *J'Accuse: The Dark Side of Nice*, London, The Bodley Head, 1982, pp. 7 & 1–29.

60 Ring, pp. 204–5.

61 David Niven, *The Moon's a Balloon*, New York, Putnam & Sons, 1972, p. 356.
62 Edwards, pp. 283, 296–8.
63 Ibid., pp. 298, 302–3.
64 Cassely, pp. 173–4.
65 Nadja Sayej, 'What Will Happen to Pierre Cardin's Iconic Palais Bulles', *Architectural Digest*, 12 February 2021.
66 Hélène Constanty, *Razzia sur La Riviera: Enquête sur les requins de la Côte-d'Azur*, Paris: Fayard, 2015, pp. 73–77.
67 Dirk Bogarde, *Backcloth*, London, Viking, 1986, pp. 248–50.
68 Ibid., pp. 291–294; Corless and Darke, pp. 181–2.
69 Hale, p, 159.
70 James Baldwin, notes for a projected book, 'Remember this House', from Raoul Peck (ed.), *I Am Not Your Negro*, London, Penguin Classics, 2017, p. 71.

71 James Baldwin, *The Devil Find's Work*, quoted in David Leeming, *James Baldwin: A Biography*, New York, Henry Holt, 1994, p. 333.
72 Magdalena J. Zaborowska, *Me and My House: James Baldwin's Last Decade in France*, Durham, Duke University Press, 2018, p. 129.
73 Buchet, p. 132; Leeming p. 313.
74 Leeming, p. 312; Zaborowska pp. 130, 132, 313.
75 Leeming, pp. 320, 334, 367, 372–3.
76 Ibid., p. 368; Zaborowska, pp. 131, 140.
77 Blume, *Côte-d'Azur*, p. 154.
78 Mille, p. 215.
79 Derogy and Pontaut, pp. 516–17.
80 Le Roux, pp. 272, 298–9.
81 Blume, *Côte-d'Azur*, p. 153.
82 Médecin, p. 206.
83 Mille, pp. 225, 226, 232.

13 White, Concrete Coast, 1990–2023

1 Edwards, pp. 305, 309.
2 Blume, *Côte-d'Azur*, p 175.
3 Jean-Christophe Maillot, *Les ballets de la compagnie de Monte-Carlo: 30 saisons chorégraphiques des ballets de Monte-Carlo 1985–2015*, Paris, Somogy, 2015.
4 Luke Harding, 'Pandora Papers Reveal Hidden Riches of Putin's Inner Circle', *Observer*, 3 October 2021.
5 Robert Eringer, 'Prince Albert Lets Putin turn Monaco into his pet Principality', Santa Barbara News Press, 10 April 2022; 'Vladimir Putin goes Fishing', *Guardian*, 14 August 2007.
6 Harding, 3 October 2021.
7 Constanty, p. 148.
8 Miles, *St Petersburg*, pp. 463–4.
9 Constanty, pp. 135–42.

10 Ibid., pp. 173–88.
11 Le Roux, pp. 104–5.
12 Constanty, p. 221.
13 Jean-Michel Verne, *Riviera Nostra: L'emprise des mafias italienne sur la Côte-d'Azur*, Paris, Nouveau Monde éditions, 2017, p. 18.
14 Ibid., p. 227.
15 Constanty, pp. 217–20.
16 Le Roux, p. 292.
17 Ibid., pp. 34–7.
18 Blume, *Côte-d'Azur*, p. 194.
19 Ibid., pp. 166–7.
20 June Raclet, SOS Racisme, 30 July 2019 and 11 June 2020.
21 Carla Monaco, 'Sur la Côte-d'Azur, les plages privées à l'épreuve des tests de discrimination raciale', *Le Monde*, 1 August 2022.

22 Kevin Rawlinson, 'Naomi Campbell says hotel turned her away because she is black', *Guardian*, 30 July 2019.

23 Social media site.

24 Corless and Darke, p. 228.

25 Carol Midgley, 'Riviera Review – if only they had all been blown up on that yacht', *The Times* 24 May 2019.

26 Blume, *Côte-d'Azur*, p. 164.

27 *Guardian* and *AFP*, 17 August 2021.

28 Murphy to F. Scott Fitzgerald in August 1935, quoted in Tomkins, pp. 124–5.

29 Buchet, p. 127.

30 Mansfield, Letter of 28 November 1920.

Bibliography

Adam, Peter, *Eileen Gray: Architect / Designer*, London, Thames and Hudson, 1987.

Addison, Joseph, *Remarks on Several Parts of Italy, &c, in the Years 1701, 1702, 1703*, London, J. Tonson, 1718.

Albanis-Beaumont, Jean-François, *Travels through the Maritime Alps from Italy to Lyons*, London, T. Bensley, 1795.

Amory, Mark, *Lord Berners: The Last Eccentric*, London, Chatto and Windus, 1998.

Anderson, Jack, *The One and Only: The Ballet Russe de Monte Carlo*, London, Dance Books Ltd., 1981.

Anderson, Lindsay, *The Diaries*, ed. Paul Sutton, London, Methuen, 2004.

Anon, *Cook's Handbook to the Health Resorts of the South of France and the Riviera*, London, Thomas Cook and Son, 1878.

Anon, *Guide-Bleu: Nice pratique et pittoresque*, Nice, Gauthier and Co., 1893–4.

Anon, *Le Tremblement de terre de la Riviéra, 23 février 1887*, Paris, F. Baranger, 1887.

Anon, *The Diaghilev-Lifar Library: Catalogue of Sale Nov 28–Dec 1 1975*, Monte Carlo, Sotheby, Parke, Bernet, 1975.

Anon [Bromley, William], *Remarks in the Grand Tour of France and Italy: Perform'd by a Person of Quality in the Year, 1691*, London, John Nutt, 1705.

Anon, *The 'Riviera Society' Directory: List of Notable Residents and Visitors – Who's Who on the Riviera 1930–1*, Nice, 1931.

Archives communales de Cannes, *Chronique de l'hôtellerie cannoise*, Cannes, 2003.

Arlen, Michael J., *Exiles*, London, André Deutsch, 1971.

Arlen, Michael, *The Green Hat*, 1924; London, Capuchin Classics, 2008.

Balme, Clément, *Mon voyage à Nice*, Nice, 1863.

Balsan, Consuelo Vanderbilt, *The Glitter and the Gold*, New York, Harper and Brothers, 1952.

Banville, Thédore de, *La mer de Nice, lettres à un ami*, Paris, 1861.

Bashkirtseff, Marie, *Journal de Marie Bashkirtseff*, Paris, Charpentier, 1890.

——, *Lettres*, Préface par François Coppée, Paris, Charpentier, 1891.

Battersea, Constance Flower, Baroness, *Reminiscences*, London, Macmillan, 1922.

Beardsley, Aubrey, *The Letters of Aubrey Beardsley*, ed. Maas, Duncan and Good, London, Cassell, 1971.

——, *Last Letters of Aubrey Beardsley*, London, Longmans, Green and Co., 1904.

Beatis, Don Antonio de, *Voyage du cardinal d'Aragon en Allemange, Hollande, Belgique, France et Italie (1517–18)*, Paris, Perrin, 1913.

Beauvoir, Simone de, *The Prime of Life*, trans. Peter Green, Cleveland and New York: The World Publishing Company, 1962.

Bedford, Sybille, *Aldous Huxley: A Biography*, London, Chatto and Windus, 1973.

Bennet, J, Henry, *Winter and Spring on the Shores of the Mediterranean*, 1861; London, John Churchill, 1870.

Bennett, Arnold, *Paris Nights and Other Impressions of Places and People*, New York, George H, Doran, 1913.

Benstock, Shari, *Women of the Left Bank: Paris 1900–1940*, Austin, University of Texas Press, 1986.

Bérenger, Jean-Pierre, *Soirées Provencales*, 3 vols, Paris, Nyon, 1787, in *Voyages en France ornés de gravures, avec des notes par La Mésangère*, Chapelle 1626–86, Vol. 4, *Voyage en Provence*, Paris, 1798.

Berlin, Isaiah, *Russian Thinkers*, 1978; London, Penguin, 2013.

Berlioz, Hector, *The Life of Hector Berlioz as Written by Himself in his Letters and Memoirs*, London, Dent, 1903.

Berman, Ronald, *Fitzgerald's Mentors: Edmund Wilson, H. L. Mencken and Gerald Murphy*, Tuscaloosa, University of Alabama Press, 2012.

Berruer, Pierre, *Maurice Chevalier: Raconté par François Vals*, Paris, Plon, 1988.

Bethell, Victor, *Ten Days at Monte Carlo at the Bank's Expense*, London, Heinemann, 1898.

Bézias, Jean-Rémi, 'Frédéric Stackelberg (1852–1934) ou la révolution importée', in *Destins niçois: Actes du colloque de Nice*, Cahiers de la Méditerranée, 1997/ 55.

Bianchini, Roger-Louis, *Crimes and arnaques sur la Côte-d'Azur*, Nice, Éditions Giletta Nice-Matin, 2003.

Biddulph, Violet, *The Three Ladies Waldegrave*, London, Peter Davis, 1938.

Bloch, Michael, *The Secret File of the Duke of Windsor*, Bath, Chivers Press, 1989.

Blume, Mary, *Côte-d'Azur: Inventing the French Riviera*, London, Thames and Hudson, 1992.

——, *Lartigue's Riviera*, Paris and New York, Flammarion, 2002.

Bogarde, Dirk, *Backcloth*, London, Viking, 1986; Penguin, 1987.

Bonillo, Jean-Lucien, et al., *Charles Garnier and Gustave Eiffel on the French and Italian Rivieras: The Dream of Reason*, Marseille: Éditions Imbernon, 2004.

Bordier, Roger, *J'étais enfant en 1936*, Paris, Éditions de Sorbier, 1986.

Borel, Pierre *Cahiers intimes: Inédits*, ed. Marie Bashkirtseff, Paris, Les Éditions du Monde Moderne, 1925.

Bowman, Sara, *A Fashion for Extravagance*, London, Bell and Hyman, 1985.

Brewster, Margaret, *Letters from Cannes and Nice*, Edinburgh, Thomas Constable, 1857.

Buchet, Martine, *La Colombe d'or: Saint-Paul-de-Vence*, Paris, Assouline, 1993.

Buxtorf, Anne-Elisabeth, *Les studios de la Victorine 1919–29*, Paris, Association française de recherche sur l'histoire du cinéma, Nice, Cinémathèque, 1998.

Cachin, Françoise, *Saint-Tropez: Peninsula Maures Mountains*, Paris, Gründ, 1985.

Calder, Robert, *Willie: A Life of W. Somerset Maugham*, London, Heinemann, 1990.

Carbonel, Marie-Hélène, and Javier Figuero, *La véritable biographie de La Belle Otero et de la Belle Époque: 'Ruine-moi mais ne me quite pas'*, Paris, Fayard, 2003.

Carpi, Daniel, *Between Mussolini and Hitler: The Jews and the Italian Authorities in France and Tunisia*, Waltham and London, Brandeis University Press, 1994.

Casanova de Seingalt, Jacques, *The Memoirs*, London, 1894, Episode 16, Chapters 3–5 of Vol. IV, *In the South, 1725–98*.

Caserio, Jean-Louis, and Charles Martini de Châteauneuf, *Le Tremblement de terre de 1887 à Menton*, Menton, Société d'art et d'histoire du Mentonnais, 1987.

Cassely, Jean-Pierre, *Secret French Riviera*, Versailles, Jonglez Publishing, 2019.

Castle, Charles, *La Belle Otero: The Last Great Courtesan*, London, Michael Joseph, 1981.

Cate, Curtis, *Friedrich Nietzsche*, London, Hutchinson, 2002.

Cather, Willa, *Willa Cather in Europe: Her Own Story of the First Journey*, New York, Alfred A, Knopf, 1956.

Chalon, Jean, *Liane de Pougy: Courtisane, princesse et sainte*, Paris, Flammarion, 1994.

Chekhov, Anton, *Letters of Anton Chekhov*, ed. Avrahm Yarmolinsky, London, Jonathan Cape, 1974.

Churchill, Peter, *Duel of Wits*, London, Hodder and Stoughton, 1953.

——, *All About the French Riviera*, London, Vista Books, 1960.

——, *Of Their Own Choice*, London, Hodder and Stoughton, 1952.

Clark, Kenneth, *Another Part of the Wood: A Self Portrait*, London, John Murray, 1974.

Clews, Henry, *Mumbo Jumbo*, London, Grant Richards Ltd., 1923.

Clews, Marie, *Once Upon a Time at La Mancha*, Beverly, MA: Memoirs Unlimited Inc., 1998.

Cline, Sally, *Zelda Fitzgerald: Her Voice in Paradise*, New York, Arcade, 2003.

Clouzot, Henri, *Henri Clouzot à la Côte-d'Azur*, Saint-Benôit-du-Sault, Éditions Tarabuste, 2005.

Cocteau, Jean, *Opium: The Diary of His Cure*, trans. Margaret Crosland, 1930; London and Chicago, Peter Owen, 1957.

Cocteau, Jean, *Souvenir Portraits: Paris in the Belle Époque*, trans. Browner, 1935; London, Robson Books, 1991.

Colette, *La Naisance du jour*, Paris, Flammarion, 1928; paperback, 1984.

Colette, *Ces Plaisirs*, 1932; *The Pure and the Impure*, trans. Herma Briffault, Harmondsworth, Penguin, 1971.

Colvin, Sidney, *The Letters of Robert Louis Stevenson*, vol, II, London, Methuen, 1911.

Compagnie des chemins de fer de Paris à Lyon et à la Méditerranée, *La Côte-d'Azur: de Marseille à Vintimille*, 1938.

Compan, André, *Histoire de Nice et son Compté*, Nice, Éditions Serre, 1982.

Connolly, Cyril, *The Rock Pool*, Paris, Obelisk Press, 1936.

——, *The Unquiet Grave: A Word Cycle*, London, Hamish Hamilton, 1945; rev. ed., June 1951.

Constanty, Hélène, *Razzia sur la Riviera: Enquête sur les requins de la Côte-d'Azur*, Paris, Fayard, 2015.

Cooper, Duff, *The Duff Cooper Diaries 1915–1951*, ed. John Julius Norwich, London, Weidenfeld and Nicolson, 2005.

Corbin, Alain, *The Lure of the Sea: The Discovery of the Seaside in the Western World 1750–1840*, trans. Jocelyn Phelps, London, Penguin Books, 1995.

Corless, Kieron, and Chris Darke, *Cannes: Inside the World's Premier Film Festival*, London, Faber and Faber, 2007.

Courcy, Anne de, *Chanel's Riviera*, London, Weidenfeld and Nicolson, 2019; paperback, 2020.

Coward, Noël, *Autobiography*, London, Methuen, 1986.

——, *The Letters of Noël Coward*, ed. Barry Day, New York, Alfred A. Knopf, 2007.

Cowley, Malcolm, *Exile's Return: A Narrative of Ideas*, New York: W. W. Norton and Co., 1934.

Dallo, Roberte, *Art Déco: Une Méditerranée heureuse*, Nice: Éditions Gilletta, 2015.

Davidson, Angus, *Edward Lear: Landscape Painter and Nonsense*

Poet (1812–1888), 1938; London, John Murray, 1968,

Davis, I. B. *The Ancient and Modern History of Nice*, London, Tipper and Richards, 1807.

de Carli, *Conseiller du touriste à Nice et dans ses environs*, Nice, Chez l'Auteur, 1864–5.

De Livry, Christiane, and François Simon, *Hotel du Cap-Eden-Roc, Cap d'Antibes*, New York, Assouline, 2007.

De Polnay, Peter, *A Door Ajar*, London, Robert Hale, 1959.

Dempster, Charlotte Louisa Hawkins, *The Maritime Alps and their Seaboard*, London, Longmans, Green and Co., 1885.

Derogy, Jacques, and Jean-Marie Pontaut, *Enquête sur les ripoux de la Côte*, Paris, Fayard, 1991; paperback, 1994.

Des Cars, Jean, and Jean-Paul Caracalla, *Le Train Bleu et les grands express de la Riviera*, Paris, Denoël, 1988.

Desti, Mary, *The Untold Story: The Life of Isadora Duncan 1921–1927*, New York: H. Liveright, 1929.

Devereux, William Cope, *Fair Italy, the Riviera and Monte Carlo*, London, Kegan Paul, Trench and Co., 1884.

Diamond, Hanna, *Fleeing Hitler: France 1940*, Oxford and New York, OUP, 2007.

Dickens, Charles, *Bleak House*, 1852–3; London and New York, Penguin, 1996.

——, *Pictures from Italy*, 1846; London and New York, OUP, c. 1905.

Docker, Norah, *Norah: The Autobiography of Lady Docker*, London, W. H. Allen, 1969.

Dodge, David, *The Rich Man's Guide to the Riviera*, London, Cassell, 1963.

Dorsey, Hebe, *The Belle Epoque in the Paris Herald*, London, Thames and Hudson, 1986.

Dos Passos, John, *The Best Times: An Informal Memoir*, 1966; New York, Open Road Distribution, 2015.

Drohojowska, Antoinette-Joséphine-Françoise-Anne, *Une saison à Nice, Chambéry et Savoie*, Paris, Charles Douniol, 1860.

Dumanoir et Barrière, *Les toilettes tapageuses*, Paris, 1856.

Duncan, Isadora, *My Life*, New York, Boni and Liveright, 1927.

Dupouy, Raphaël, and Dany Lartigue, *La Riviera de Jacques Henri Lartigue*, Le Lavandou, 2007.

Edwards, Anne, *The Grimaldis of Monaco*, New York, William Morrow and Co., 1992.

Ellis, LeRoy, *La Colonie russe dans les Alpes-Maritimes des origines à 1939*, Nice, Éditions Serre, 1998.

Emerson, Barbara, *Leopold II of the Belgians: King of Colonialism*, London, Weidenfeld and Nicolson, 1979.

Erté, *Things I Remember: An Autobiography*, London, Peter Owen, 1975.

Evelyn, John, *The Diary of John Evelyn*, ed. William Bray, London, Frederick Warne, 1879.

Ewans, Martin, *European Atrocity, African Catastrophe: Leopold II, the Congo Free State and its Aftermath*, London, Routledge Curzon, 2002.

Farr, William, *A Medical Guide to Nice*, London, Ibotson and Palmer, 1841.

Faucigny-Lucinge, Jean Louis, prince de, *Un gentilhomme cosmopolite*, Paris, Perrin, 1990.

Feuchtwanger, Lion, *The Devil in France: My Encounter with Him in the Summer of 1940*, London and New York, Hutchinson, 1942.

Field, Leslie, *Bendor: The Golden Duke of Westminster*, London, Weidenfeld and Nicolson, 1983.

Fitzgerald, F. Scott, *F. Scott Fitzgerald: A Life in Letters*, ed. Matthew J.

Bruccoli, New York, Simon and Schuster, 1995.

——, *Tender in the Night*, 1934; London, Collins Paperback, 2011.

Fontaines, Georges, *La Côte d'Azur en l'an 1897*, Lyon, 1897.

Ford Madox Ford, *Provence from Minstrels to Machine*, London, Allen and Unwin, 1938.

Fortescue, William, *The Third Republic in France 1870–1940: Conflicts and Continuities*, London, Routledge, 2000.

Fourcade, Marie-Madeleine, *L'Arche de Noé: réseau Alliance 1940–45*, 1968; Paris, Plon, 1989.

Freeman, Judi, et al., *The Fauve Landscape*, New York, Abbeville Press, 1990.

Gary, Romain, *La promesse de l'aube*, 1961; *Promise at Dawn*, trans. John Markham Beach, London, Penguin Classics, 2018.

Gasquet, Joachim, *Joachim Gasquet's Cézanne: A Memoir with Conversations*, London, Thames and Hudson, 1991.

Gaujac, Paul, *La guerre en Provence*, Lyon, Presses univeritaires de Lyon, 1998.

Gautier, Théophile, *Lettre à la présidente: Voyage en italie, 1850*, Au Château de la misère, 1890.

Gayraud, Didier, *L'Age D'or de Saint-Jean-Cap-Ferrat*, Nice, Gayraud, 1983.

Genlis, Stéphanie-Félicité de, *Adèle et Théodore ou Lettres sur l'Education*, 3 vols, Paris, Lambert et Baudoin, 1782.

Germain, Laurent, *Notes de voyage*, Toulon, 1878.

Gilbert, Martin, *Winston Churchill and Emery Reves: Correspondence 1937–1964*, Austin, University of Texas Press, 1997.

Gilot, Françoise, and Carlton Lake, *Life with Picasso*, 1964; Harmondsworth, Penguin Books, 1966.

Giraudy, Danièle, *Guide du Musée Picasso Antibes*, Paris, Hazan, 1987.

Gladman, Elsie, *Uncertain Tomorrows*, London, Excalibur Press, 1993.

Goldberg, William, F, and George Piesse, *Monte Carlo and How to Do It*, London, 1891.

Graves, Charles, *None but the Rich; Life and Times of the Greek Syndicate*, London, Cassell, 1963.

——, *Riviera Revisited*, London, Evans Bros, 1948.

——, *Royal Riviera*, London, William Heinemann, 1957.

——, *The Big Gamble: The Story of Monte Carlo*, London, Hutchinson, 1951.

Green, John Richard, *Stray Studies from England and Italy*, London, Macmillan, 1876.

Greene, Graham, 'May We Borrow Your Husband?' and 'Beauty', in *May We Borrow Your Husband? And Other Comedies of the Sexual Life*, 1967; London, Vintage, 2000.

——, *J'Accuse: The Dark Side of Nice*, London, The Bodley Head, 1982.

Grzesiak, Nathalie, *Yves Montand-Simone Signoret: Une passion engagée*, Paris, Acropole, 2001.

Gullentops, David (ed.), *Jean Cocteau et la Côte-d'Azur*, Paris, Non Lieu, 2011.

Hakim, Gerald, *Un Anglais dans la Résistance*, Paris, Presses de la Cité, 1968.

Hale, Julian, *The French Riviera: A Cultural History*, New York: OUP, 2009.

Hare, Augustus, *Winter at Mentone*, London, 1862.

——, *The Life and Letters of Frances, Baroness Bunsen*, Vol. II, London, 1882.

Harris, Frank, *My Life and Loves*, 1922–7; London, W. H. Allen, 1964.

Hastings, Selena, *The Secret Lives of Somerset Maugham*, London, John Murray, 2009.

Hemingway, Ernest, *Selected Letters,* ed. Carlos Baker, New York, Charles Scribner's Sons, 1981.

Herzen, Alexander, *Childhood, Youth and Exile,* Oxford, Oxford University Press World Classics, 1980.

Herzen, Alexandre, *Lettres de France et d'Italie (1847–1852),* Geneva, Éditions des Enfants de l'Auteur, 1871.

House, John, *Monet: Nature into Art,* London and New Haven, Yale University Press, 1986.

Howarth, Patrick, *When the Riviera Was Ours,* London, Century Hutchinson, 1977.

Huch, Ronald K., *Henry, Lord Brougham: The Later Years,* Lewiston, NY, The Edwin Mellen Press, 1993.

Hurel, Alexandre, and Christelle Fucili (eds.), *Voyages sur la Côte d'Azur: Stendhal, Victor Hugo, Gustave Flaubert et al.,* Urrugne, Pimientos, 2004.

Jackson, Julian, *The Popular Front in France: Defending Democracy 1934–8,* Cambridge, Cambridge University Press, 1988.

Jeanpierre, Laurent, and Christophe Kihm, 'La recherche de l'azur' in *L'Art contemporain et la Côte-d'Azur: un territoire pour l'expérimentation 1951–2011,* Dijon, les Presses du réel, 2011.

Joanne, Adolphe, *Géographie du département des Alpes-Maritimes,* Paris, Hachette, 1900.

Judd, Denis, *Edward VII: A Pictorial Biography,* London, Macdonald and Jane's, 1975.

Kanigel, Robert, *High Season in Nice,* London, Abacus, 2003.

Kellogg, Grace, *The Two Lives of Edith Wharton: The Woman and her Work,* New York, 1965.

Kelly, Aileen M., *The Discovery of Chance: The Life and Thought of Alexander Herzen,* Cambridge, MA, Harvard University Press, 2016.

Khan, Aga, *The Memoirs of Aga Khan: World Enough and Time,* London, Cassell, 1954.

Kiki de Montparnasse, *Souvenirs Retrouvés,* Paris, José Corti, 2005.

Kimball, Robert (ed.), *The Complete Lyrics of Cole Porter,* New York, Da Capo, 1992.

Kschessinska, Mathilde, *Dancing in Petersburg,* trans. Arnold Haskell, 1960; Alton, Hants., Dance Books Ltd, 2005.

Kynaston, David, *Austerity Britain 1945–51,* London, Bloomsbury, 2007.

Lartigue, Jacques-Henri, and Mary Blume, *Lartigue's Riviera,* Paris, Flammarion, 1997.

Latour, Anny, *Kings of Fashion,* trans. Mervyn Savill, London, Weidenfeld and Nicolson, 1958.

Lawrence, D. H., *Letters,* Harmondsworth, Penguin, 1950.

——, *The Letters of D. H. Lawrence,* London, Heinemann, 1932.

Le Roux, Renée, *Révélations: Entretiens avec Mme, Renée Le Roux réalisés à Paris, Nice et Monte-Carlo en 1997, 1998 et 1990 recueillis par Alain Roullier,* Nice, France Europe Éditions Livres, 1999.

Leeming, David, *James Baldwin: A Biography,* New York, Henry Holt, 1995.

Lenček, Lena, and Gideon Bosker, *The Beach: The History of Paradise on Earth,* London, Pimlico, 1999.

Lenthéric, Charles, *La Grèce and l'Orient en Provence: Arles, le bas Rhône, Marseille,* 5th edn., Paris, 1910.

Les amis de la liberté, *Dictionnaire historique et biographique du communisme dans Les Alpes-Maritime, XXe siècle,* Sophie-Antipolis, 2011.

Lifar, Serge, *Ma Vie: From Kiev to Kiev,* London, Hutchinson, 1970.

Lovell, Mary S., *The Riviera Set,* London, Little, Brown, 2016; paperback, Abacus, 2017.

Lynn, Andrea, *Shadow Lovers: The Last Affairs of H. G. Wells*, Cambridge, MA, Westview Press, 2001.

M., J., *Thomas Robinson Woolfield's Life at Cannes and Lord Brougham's First Arrival*, London, Kegan Paul, Trench, Trübner, 1890.

Mack, Gerstle, *Paul Cézanne*, London, Jonathan Cape, 1935.

Mackrell, Judith, *The Unfinished Palazzo*, London, Thames and Hudson, 2017; paperback, 2018.

Madden, Thomas More, *The Principal Health-Resorts of Europe and Africa for the Treatment of Chronic Diseases*, London, J. and A. Churchill, 1876.

Magarshack, David, *Gogol: A Life*, London, Faber and Faber, 1957.

——, *Turgenev: A Life*, London, Faber and Faber, 1954.

Maillot, Jean-Christophe, *Les ballets de la compagnie de Monte-Carlo: 30 saisons chorégraphiques des ballets de Monte-Carlo 1985–2015*, Paris, Somogy, 2015.

Mallet, Victor (ed.), *Life With Queen Victoria: Marie Mallet's letters from Court 1887–1901*, London, John Murray, 1968.

Mannoni, Laurent, and Stéphanie Salmon, '*Les Enfants du Paradis*' – Marcel Carné – Jacques Prévert, Paris, la Cinémathèque française, Éditions Xavier Barral, 2012.

Mansfield, Katherine, *Passionate Pilgrimage: A Love Affair in Letters*, ed. Helen McNeish, London, Michael Joseph, 1976.

Martel, Jean-Baptiste, *Catherine Ségurane, véritable héroïne niçoise*, Marseille, Editions Publiroc, 1933.

Martini de Châteauneuf, Charles, *M'en avisou: Menton à la Belle époque*, Breil-sur-Roya, Les Éditions du Cabri, 1990.

Marx, Karl, *Lettres d'Alger et de la Côte-d'Azur*, trans. Gilbert Badia, Pantin, Le Temps des Cerises, 1997.

Matisse, Henri, M.-A. Couturier and L.-B. Rayssiguier, *La chapelle de Vence: Journal d'une création*, Geneva, Editions d'Art Albert Skira, 1993,

Maude, Aylmer, *The Life of Tolstoy: The First Fifty Years*, London, Archibald Constable, 1908.

Maugham, Robin, *Conversations with Willie: Recollections of W. Somerset Maugham*, London, W. H. Allen, 1978.

Maugham, W. Somerset, *Lady Frederick: A Comedy in Three Acts*, London, Samuel French, 1947.

——, *Strictly Personal*, London, Heinemann, 1942.

——, *The Vagrant Mood: Six Essays*, London, Heinemann, 1952.

Maupassant, Guy de, *Sur l'Eau*, St Remy-de-Provence, Equinoxe, 2005.

Maushart, Évelyne, *1891–93, l'Alliance Franco-Russe: L'escadre russe à Toulon, Bandol, Ollioules, Hyères, St Tropez*, Toulon: Éditions Mnemosis, 2016.

Mauthner, Martin, *German Writers in Exile, 1933–40*, London, Valentine Mitchell and the European Jewish Publication Society, 2007.

Maxwell, Elsa, *I Married the World*, London, William Heinemann, 1955.

——, *R.S.V.P.: Elsa Maxwell's Own Story*, Boston and Toronto, Little, Brown and Co., 1954.

——, *The Celebrity Circus*, London, W. H. Allen, 1964.

McAlmon, Robert, *Being Geniuses Together; An Autobiography*, London, Secker and Warburg, 1938.

McLeave, Hugh, *Rogues in the Gallery: The Modern Plague of Art Thefts*, Boston, 1981.

Médecin, Jacques, *Un lynchage exemplaire: Mitterand m'a tuer*, Paris, Première Ligne, 1994.

Merquiol, André, *La Côte d'Azur dans la littérature française*, Nice, Dervyl, 1949.

Meyer-Stabley, Bertrand, *Françoise Sagan: Le tourbillon d'une vie*, Pygmalion ebook, 2014.

Meyer, Bernard C., *Joseph Conrad: A Psychoanalytic Biography*, Princeton, NJ: Princeton University Press, 1967.

Meyers, Jeffrey, *D. H. Lawrence: A Biography*, New York, Alfred A. Knopf, 1990.

Miles, Jonathan, *St Petersburg: Three Centuries of Murderous Desire*, Hutchinson, Penguin Random House, 2017.

——, *The Nine Lives of Otto Katz*, Bantam Press, 2010.

Mille, Agnes de, *Dance to the Piper: Memoirs of the Ballet*, 1951; London, Columbus Books, 1987.

Mille, Raoul, *Un dynastie foudroyée*, Paris, Albin Michel, 1991.

Miller, Linda Patterson, *Letters from the Lost Generation: Gerald and Sara Murphy and Friends*, New Brunswick, NJ, Rutgers University Press, 1991.

Miller, William, *Wintering in the Riviera with Notes of Travel in Italy and France*, London, Longman's, Green and Co., 1879.

Millin, Aubin-Louis, *Voyages dans les départemens (sic) du midi de la France*, Vol. II, Paris, 1807–11.

Monod, Jules, *Nice, Monaco et Menton: Guide complet du touriste*, Nice, 1902.

Montague-Browne, Anthony, *Long Sunset: Memoirs of Winston Churchill's Last Private Secretary*, London, Indigo, 1996.

Montand, Yves, *Montand raconte Montand*, Paris, Éditions du Seuil, October 2001.

Moore, Roy and Alma, *Thomas Jefferson's Journey to the South of France*, New York, Stewart, Tabori and Chang, 1999.

Morford, Henry, *Morford's Short-Trip Guide to Europe 1874*, New York, 1874.

Mosley, Diana, *A Life of Contrasts: The Autobiography of Diana Mosley,* (1977) London, Gibson Square Books, 2009.

Mosley, Leonard, *Castlerosse*, London, Arthur Barker, 1956.

Mrena, Andrea, *Histoire de la colonie russe sur la Côte-d'Azur*, Agth eBooks, 2017.

Murray, John (ed.), *The Handbook of Travel-Talk: or Conversations in English, German, French and Italian,* London, John Murray, 1844.

Murray, John (ed.), *A Handbook for Travellers in France: Part II,* London, John Murray, 1878.

Nash, James, *The Guide to Nice: Historical, Descriptive and Hygienic,* London, 1884.

Nelson, Michael, *Queen Victoria and the Discovery of the Riviera,* London and New York, I. B. Tauris, 2001.

Nelson, Michael, *Americans and the Making of the Riviera,* Jefferson N.C., McFarland, 2008.

Nietzsche, Friedrich, (eds, Levy and Ludovici), *Selected Letters of Friedrich Nietzsche,* London, Heinemann, 1921.

Nietzsche, Friedrich, *Unpublished Letters,* New York, Philosophical Library, 1959.

Nijinska, Bronislava, *Bronislava Nijinska: Early Memories,* trans. Irina Nijinska and Jean Rawlinson, New York, Holt, Rinehart and Winston, 1981.

Niven, David, *The Moon's a Balloon,* New York, Putnam and Sons, 1972.

Nugent, Thomas, *The Grand Tour,* Vol. IV, London, 1749.

O'Neill, Rosemary, *Art and Visual Culture on the French Riviera, 1956–1971: The École de Nice,* Farnham, Ashgate Publishing, 2012.

Oppenheim, E, Phillips, *Murder at Monte Carlo*, 1933; Milton Keynes, Lightning Source, n.d.

——, *The Pool of Memory*, London, Hodder and Stoughton, 1941.

Orczy, Emmuska, Baroness, *Links in the Chain of Life*, London, Hutchinson, 1947.

Panicacci, Jean-Louis (ed.), *La Résistance azuréenne*, Nice, Éditions Serre, 1994.

——, *En territoire occupé: Italiens et Allemands à Nice, 1942–44*, Paris, Vendémaire Éditions, 2012.

——, *L'Occupation italienne: Sud-Est de la France, juin 1940–septembre 1943*, Rennes, Collection Histoire Presses Universitaire de Rennes, 2010.

——, *Les Alpes-Maritime dans la guerre: 1939–1945*, Sayat, de Borée, 2013.

Paoli, Xavier, *My Royal Clients*, trans. Teixeira de Mattos, London, Hodder and Stoughton, 1911.

Papon, Abbé Jean-Pierre, *Voyage de Provence*, Paris, Moutard, 1787.

Parpoil, Catherine, Grégory Couderc and Musée International de la Parfumerie, *Paul Poiret, Couturier-Perfumer*, Paris, Somogy, 2013.

Peck, Raoul, from texts by James Baldwin, *I Am Not Your Negro*, London, Penguin Classics, 2017.

Perrin, Éliane, *L'Age d'or de la parfumerie à Grasse: D'après les archives Chiris (1768–1967)*, Aix-en-Provence, Édisud, 1996.

Perry, Captain John, *The State of Russia Under the Present Czar*, London, Benjamin Tooke, 1716.

Picard, Gilbert, *Spaggiari or Le casse du siècle,* Paris, FleuveNoir, 1992.

Pilatte, Léon, *La vie à Nice: Conseils et directions pour nos hôtes d'hiver*, Nice, Librarie Internationale, 1865.

Plath, Sylvia, *The Journals of Sylvia Plath, 1950–1962*, ed. Karen V. Kukil, London, Faber and Faber, 2000.

Pless, Daisy Fürstin von, *From My Private Diary*, London, John Murray 1931.

——, *What I Left Unsaid*, London, Cassell and Co., 1936.

Polovtsov, General Petr Alexandrovitch, *Monte Carlo Casino*, London, S. Paul, 1937.

Potron, Jean-Paul, *Les 30 Glorieuses: Nice 1945–1975*, Nice, Éditions Gilletta, 2016.

Pougy, Liane de, *Idylle Saphique*, 1901; Chatenay-Malabry, Alteredit, 2006.

Quebec, Adela [Gerald Hugh Tyrwhitt-Wilson, Lord Berners], *The Girls of Radcliff Hall*, printed for the author for private circulation only, n.d. (1937?).

Rafferty, Paul, *Churchill peint la Côte-d'Azur*, Paris, Albin Michel, 2021.

Ratazzi, Marie, *Nice La Belle, Monaco*, Paris, Degorce-Cadot, 1869.

Reclus, Élisée, *Les villes d'hiver de la Méditerranée et les Alpes maritimes: Intinéraire discriptif et historique*, Paris, Hachette, 1864.

Reid, Michaela, *Ask Sir James: The Life of Sir James Reid, Personal Physician to Queen Victoria*, London, Hodder and Stoughton, 1987.

Renaud, Marie-Paule, *Katherine Mansfield en France*, Fontaine-bleau: Impression Hassler, 2004.

Reynolds-Ball, Eustace and C. A. Payton (eds.), *Sport on the Riviera*, London, 1911.

Richards, Keith, with James Fox, *Life*, London, Weidenfeld and Nicolson, 2010.

Richardson, Joanna, *Colette*, London, Methuen, 1983.

Richardson, Leslie, *Things Seen on the Riviera*, London, Seeley, Service and Co., 1924.

Rigby, Edward, *Dr. Rigby's Letters from France etc, in 1789*, ed. Lady Eastlake, London, Longmans, 1880.

Righetti, Simone, *La guerre au quotidien*, Nice, Éditions du Losange, 2006.

Ring, Jim, *Riviera: The Rise and Rise of the Riviera*, London, Faber and Faber, 2011.

Ripart, André, *Alpes Maritimes: Histoire géographie*, Nice, CRDP, 1991.

Rothschild, Deborah (ed.), *Making it New: The Art and Style of Gerald and Sara Murphy*, Exhibition Catalogue, Berkeley and Los Angeles, University of California Press, 2007.

Rounding, Virginia, *Grandes Horizontales*, London, Bloomsbury, 2003; paperback, 2004.

Roux, Tristan, *Promenade des Anglais: History and Reminiscences*, trans. Catherine Ungar, Éditions Gilletta, Nice Matin, 2006.

Ruskin, John, and Harold Shapiro, *Ruskin in Italy: Letters to his Parents, 1845*, Oxford, Clarendon Press, 1972.

Schor, Ralph, *Nice pendant la guerre de 1914–1918*, Aix-en-Provence, Le Pensée Universitaire, Publications des Annales de la Faculté des Lettres, 1964.

—— (ed.), *Nice et les Alpes-Maritimes de 1914–1945: Document d'histoire*, Nice, Centre Regional de Documentation Pedagogique de Nice, 1974.

——, and Henri Courriére, *Le Comté de Nice, la France et l'Italie*, Actes du colloque organisé à l'Université de Nice Sophia-Antipolis, 2010.

Sellier, Geneviève, *Les Enfants du Paradis*, Paris, Nathan, 1996.

Sert, Misia, *Two or Three Muses*, trans. Moura Budberg, London, Museum Press, 1953.

Shackleford, George Green, *Thomas Jefferson's Travels in Europe 1784–9*, Baltimore and London, Johns Hopkins University Press, 1995.

Sheean, Vincent, *Between the Thunder and the Sun*, London, Macmillan, 1943.

Silliman, Benjamin, *A Visit to Europe in 1851*, Vol. I, New York, G. P. Putnam, 1853.

Sillitoe, Alan, *Leading the Blind: A Century of Guidebook Travel 1815–1914*, London, Macmillan, 1995.

Silver, Kenneth E. *Making Paradise: Art, Modernity and the Myth of the French Riviera*, Cambridge MA: The MIT Press, 2001.

Slater, Leonard, *Aly: A Biography*, London, W. H. Allen, 1966.

Smith, Adolphe, *The Garden of Hyères: A Description of the Most Southern Point on the French Riviera*, London, 1880.

Smith, James Edward, *A Sketch of a Tour on the Continent, in the Years 1786 and 1787*, London, 1793.

Smollett, Tobias, *Travels Through France and Italy*, London, 1766.

Soames, Mary (ed.), *Speaking for Themselves: The Personal Letters of Winston and Clementine Churchill*, New York and London, Doubleday/ Transworld, 1998.

Sparks, Edward I., *The Riviera: Sketches of the Health Resorts of the North Mediterranean Coast of France from Hyères to Spezia*, London, J. A. Churchill, 1879.

Spurling, Hilary, *Matisse the Master: A Life of Henri Matisse*, Vol. II, London, Penguin, 2006.

——, *The Unknown Matisse: Man of the North 1869–1908*, London, Penguin, 2000.

Standish, Robert, *The Prince of Storytellers: The Life of E. Phillips Oppenheim*, London, Peter Davies, 1957.

Starke, Mariana, *Travels in the Europe*, 8th edn, London, John Murray, 1833.

Stendhal, *Mémoires d'un touriste*, Vol. III, Paris, Dupont, 1838.

Stengers, Jean, *Le Congo: Mythes et réalités*, Bruxelles, Éditions Racine, 2008.

Sterne, Lawrence, *A Sentimental Journey*, 1768; Oxford, Oxford University Press, 1968.

Stevenson, Robert Louis, *The Letters of Robert Louis Stevenson to his Family and Friends*, Vol. I, ed. Sidney Colvin, London, Methuen, 1901 and 1911.

Stewart, Donald Ogden, *By A Stroke of Luck!: An Auto-biography*, New York, Paddington Press Ltd., 1975.

Stravinsky, Igor, and Robert Craft, *Memories and Commentaries*, London, Faber and Faber, 1960.

Sulzer, Jehan Georg, *Journal d'un voyage fait en 1775 and 1776 dans les pays méridionaux de l'Europe*, La Haye, Plaat, 1781.

Tennant, Victoria, *Irina Baranova and the Ballets Russes de Monte Carlo*, Chicago, University of Chicago Press, 2014.

Thicknesse, Philip, *A Year's Journey Through France and part of Spain*, Vol. 1, Dublin, 1777.

——, *Useful Hints to Those Who Make the Tour of France in a Series of Letters*, London, 1768.

Tilburg, Patricia A., *Colette's Republic: Work, Gender and Popular Culture in France, 1870–1914*, New York, Berghahn Books, 2009.

Tomkins, Calvin, *Living Well is the Best Revenge: Two Americans in Paris 1921–1933*, London, André Deutsch, 1972.

Tourtoulon, Antoine de, *Lettres sur Nice et ses environs*, Montpellier, 1852.

Tousey, Sinclair, *Papers from over the Water: A Series of Letters from Europe*, New York, American News Company, 1869.

Treves, Sir Frederick, *The Riviera of the Corniche Road*, London, Cassell, 1921.

Turnbull, Andrew, *Scott Fitzgerald*, London, The Bodley Head, 1962.

Ulmès, Renée d', *Auprès des blessés*, Paris, A. Lemerre, 1916.

Vaill, Amanda, *Everybody Was So Young: Gerald and Sara Murphy – A Lost Generation Love Story*, New York, Broadway Books, 1999.

Valcourt, Théophile de, *Cannes et Son Climat*, Paris, Germer Baillière, 1866.

Van Gogh, Vincent, *Letters to Emile Bernard*, London, Cresset Press, 1938.

Vaughan, Hal, *Sleeping with the Enemy: Coco Chanel, Nazi Agent*, London, Vintage Digital, 2011.

Verlinden, Patrick, *Sporatlas Monaco: Toutes les coudses, les dates, les champions – le Grand Prix de Monaco, Le Rallye Monte-Carlo*, Éditions les 7 Collines, 1999.

Verne, Jean-Michel, *Riviera Nostra: L'emprise des mafias italienne sur la Côte-d'Azur*, Paris, Nouveau Monde Éditions, 2017.

Vickers, Hugo, *Cecil Beaton: The Authorized Biography*, London, Weidenfeld and Nicolson, 1985.

Wagner-Martin, Linda, *Zelda Sayre Fitzgerald: An American Woman's Life*, Basingstoke, Palgrave Macmillan, 2004.

Walker, Kathrine Sorley, *De Basil's Ballets Russes*, 1982; Alton, Dance Books Ltd., 2010.

Watripon, Léon, *Nice-Guide: Nouveau cicérone des étrangers*, Nice, Imprimerie Administrative, Faraud et Conso, 1869.

Waugh, Alec, *My Brother Evelyn and other Profiles*, London, Cassell, 1967.

Waugh, Evelyn, *When the Going Was Good*, 1946; Harmondsworth, Penguin, 1951.

West, Rebecca, *The Thinking Reed*, 1936; London, Virago Modern Classics, 1984.

Wharton, Edith, *The House of Mirth*, New York, Charles Scribner's Sons, 1905.

Windsor, Wallis, *The Heart Has Its Reasons: The Memoirs of the Duchess of Windsor*, London, The Companion Book Club, 1958.

Withey, Lynne, *Grand Tours and Cook's Tours: A History of Leisure Travel 1750–1915*, London, Aurum Press, 1998.

Witte, Ysabel de, *Riviera Celebrities*, Menton and Monte Carol News, n.d.

Wood, Ean, *Headlong Through Life: The Story of Isadora Duncan*, Lewes: The Book Guild Ltd., 2006.

Woolf, Virginia, *The Waves*, ed. Herbert, Sellers and Blyth, 1931; Cambridge, CUP, 2011.

Young, Arthur, *Travels During the Years 1787, 1788 and 1789*, Dublin, 1793, Vol. I.

Young, Julian, *Friedrich Nietzsche: A Philosophical Biography*, Cambridge, CUP, 2010.

Young, Kenneth, *Churchill and Beaverbrook: A Study in Friendship and Politics*, London, Eyre and Spottiswoode, 1966.

Zaborowska, Magdalena J., *Me and My House: James Baldwin's Last Decade in France*, Durham, Duke University Press, 2018.

Articles and Essays

Boréa, G., 'Notes d'un hivernant à Nice avant l'annexion', *Nice Historique*, vol. 131, 1939, pp. 81–91.

Conyers, Claude, 'Courtesans in Dance History: *Les Belles de la Belle Epoque*', *Dance Chronicle*, vol. 26, no. 2, pp. 219–243, 2003.

Cornick, Martyn, '"Fraternity Among Listeners", The BBC and the French Resistance: Evidence from Refugees', in Diamond and Kitson (eds.), *Vichy, Resistance, Liberation: New Perspectives on Wartime France*, Oxford, Berg, 2005.

Del Litto, V., 'Stendhal, passant de la Côte d'Azur', *Nice Historique*, vol. 177, 1959.

Dibdin, Michael, 'From Canova to Caro', in *Modern Painters*, London, 1992, pp 42–5.

Doughty, Robin W. 'Concern for Fashionable Feathers', *Forest History Newsletter*, vol. 16, no. 2, July 1972, pp. 4–11.

Ellis, Roy 'La Base Russe de Villefranche', *Nice Historique*, vol. 90, 1964.

Eringer, Robert, 'Prince Albert Lets Putin turn Monaco into his Pet Principality', Santa Barbara News Press, 10 April 2022.

Fraquelli, Simonetta, 'Montparnasse and the Right Bank: Myth and Reality', in Wilson et al., *Paris: Capital of the Arts 1900–1968*, London, Royal Academy of the Arts, 2002.

Fricero, E. 'Les Russes au siècle passé', *Nice Historique*, vol. 116, 1952.

Gopal, Priyamvada, 'Why can't Britain handle the truth about Winston Churchill?' *Guardian*, 17 March 2021.

Harding, Luke, 'Pandora Papers Reveal Hidden Riches of Putin's Inner Circle', *Observer*, 3 October 2021.

Hollinghurst, Alan, 'Quite Mad and a Little Indecent', *Apollo*, July/August 2016.

Léger, Fernand, 'Contemporary Achievements in Painting', 1914, extracted in Charles Harrison and Paul Wood, *Art in Theory 1900–90: An Anthology of Changing Ideas*, Oxford, Blackwells, 1992.

Matisse, Henri, *Chapelle du Rosaire of the Dominican Nuns of Vence*, Vence, 1996, Offprint from the 1951 Christmas issue of *France Illustration*, n.p.

Monaco, Carla, 'Sur la Côte-d'Azur, les plages privées à l'épreuve des tests de discrimination raciale', *Le Monde*, 1 August 2022.

Potron, Jean-Paul, 'La Librairie Visconti', *Nice Historique*, vol. 247, 1997.

Rahv, Philip, 'You Can't Duck a Hurricane Under a Beach Umbrella', *Daily Worker*, 5 May 1934.

Rawlinson, Kevin, 'Naomi Campbell says hotel turned her away because she is black', *Guardian* 30 July 2019.

Sayej, Nadja, 'What Will Happen to Pierre Cardin's Iconic Palais Bulles', *Architectural Digest*, 12 February 2021.

Segalov, Michael, 'The Smell of Success: How Chanel No 5 Gained a Sprinkling of Stardust', *Guardian*, 20 November 2021.

Tate, Allen, 'The Mediterranean', *New Verse*, vol. 1, no. 5, October 1933.

Vernier, Olivier, 'Espionnage et péril Germanique à Nice pendant la guerre de 1914', *Nice Historique*, vol. 230, 1990.

Vigo, Jean, address to the Groupement des spectateurs d'Avant-Garde, quoted by Maximilien le Cain, 'Jean Vigo', SensesOfCinema.com, July 2002.

Wikipedia has been useful on many occasions.

Newspapers and Periodicals

Americans on the Côte-d'Azur aka Americans in Beautiful France, Cannes, 1927–8.

Anglo-American Gazette, aka *Anglo-American News List and Fashionable Visitors List*, Nice, 1874–1910.

Cannes News (issued in connection with the *Menton and Monte Carlo News*), Menton, 1929–33.

Life on the Riviera, A Weekly Journal of Social and Political Life, London and Nice, 1888 (+).

Menton and Monte Carlo News, Menton, 1897–33.

Paris Herald, Paris, 1887–1924.

Riviera News (a fusion of *Menton and Monte Carlo News* and *Riviera Review and Cannes News*), Menton 1933–49.

Documentary and News

Bextor, Robin (dir.), *Whatever Happened to the Windsors?* Duke / New Wave Pictures, 2006.

British Movietone News, 'Sir Bernard and Lady Docker Arrive Home', 26 April 1958, YouTube.

British Pathé, 'The Cannes Peace Conference 1922', YouTube.

Celeste Holm presenting *High Society* DVD featurette, 'Cole Porter in Hollywood: True Love'.

Geller, Daniel, and Dayna Goldfine (dirs.), *Ballets Russes*, New York, 2005.

Gerault, Yvonne and Didier, Baussy-Oulianoff (dirs.), *Le Train Bleu*, choreography by Bronislava Nijinska, restaged for the Paris Opera Ballet Company in 1993 by Irina Nijinsdka and Frank D. Ries in *Picasso and Dance: The Story of a Marriage*, Arte / La Sept / NCC, 1993.

Laurent, Emmanuel (dir.), *Deux de la vague*, Films à trois, 2009.

Nears, Colin (dir.), *Paris Dances Diaghilev*, NVC Arts / la Sept, 1990.

Varda, Agnès (dir.), *Du côté de la côte*, 24 mins, commissioned by the l'Office National du Tourisme, Argos Films (then Ciné Tamaris), 1958.

Vigo, Jean (dir.), *À propos de Nice*, silent short film, 1929.

Music and Radio

Daniderff, Léo, Marcel Bertal and Emile Ronn, 'Sur les bords de la Riviera', popular song, 1913.

Gilbert, Fred, 'The Man Who Broke the Bank at Monte Carlo', popular song, 1891.

McLeod, Donald, 'Composer of the Week – Pauline Viardot', BBC Radio 3, 14–18 June 2021.

Porter, Cole, 'Within the Quota', on *Overtures, Ballet: Within the Quota*, John McGlinn, London Sinfonietta, EMI Classics, 1991.

Messager, André, and Sacha Guitry, 'J'ai deux amants', from the operette *L'amour masqué*, 1923.

The Rolling Stones, *Exile on Main St.*, studio album, May 1972.

Films

Demy, Jacques, *La Baie des Anges*, Sud-Pacifique Films, 1963.

Frankenheimer, John, *Ronin*, United Artists, 1988.

Hitchcock, Alfred, *To Catch a Thief*, Paramount Pictures, 1955.

Lang, Water, *On the Riviera*, Twentieth Century Fox, 1951.

Powell, Michael, and Emeric Pressburger, *The Red Shoes*, The Archers, 1948.

Truffaut, François, *La nuit américaine*, Films du carrosse, 1973.

Vadim, Roger, *Et Dieu … créa la femme*, 1956.

Acknowledgements

A gigantic thank you to Catherine for her sharp eye, kind heart and wisdom. Being French, she has an impeccable knowledge of English grammar. A real collaborator – without Catherine, I could not have written the book. A big thank you to Marjotte for her expertise.

Many thanks to Thorsten Orr for his tennis knowledge and general kindness, and to Alain Keit for chats about French song. Also a big thank you to Amélie Louveau, Pascale Krémer, Cécile and Stéphane, Dom Soltysik, Julia Hamer-Hunt, Karen Hewitt and Claire Rickard as well as to all the people along the Riviera with whom I've chatted over the years and all the writers who have left vivid impressions of that paradise. A special thank you to the consultants, doctors, nurses and staff at the Churchill Hospital in Oxford and the Royal United Hospital in Bath. To Dr Jim Murray in particular.

Also, gratitude to Virginie Aubry at the Centre National de la Danse in Paris. As ever, I thank the more than helpful staff at the Bodleian Library in Oxford who were especially resourceful during the Covid lockdown, and to the fabulous staff of the Bibliothèque Nationale in Paris who make that stunning library such a special place to work.

A very big thank you to my agent, Julian Alexander – for his belief in the project and for placing it at the wonderful Atlantic Books. To my editor there, James Nightingale, enormous thanks for his zeal, intelligence and efficacy – a joy to work with. Also, much gratitude to Gemma Wain for her excellent, inspired and caring copy-editing.

And once more, to Catherine.

Illustrations

Black-and-white images

First colour section

1. The azure coast – a gift of nature. (*Jonathan Miles*)
2. Hercule Trachel, *The Bay of Villefranche*. (*Musée Masséna, Nice*)
3. The Russian Fleet in the Bay of Villefranche. (*Source unknown*)
4. The Les Ponchettes walkway above the *Cours* in central Nice. Henri Harpignies, 1887. Musée des Beaux-Arts de la Ville de Paris, Petit Palais. (*PWB Images/Alamy Stock Photo*)
5. The St Nicholas Orthodox church, Nice, 1912. (*Jonathan Miles*)
6. The conservatory, Palais de Masséna, Nice, 1898–1901. (*Catherine Louveau*)
7. Claude Monet, *Corniche near Monaco*, 1884. (*Rijksmuseum, Amsterdam*)
8. Claude Monet, *Old Fort at Antibes*, 1888. Barberini Museum, Potsdam. (*Vicimages/Alamy Stock Photo*)
9. Paul Signac, *Saint-Tropez in a Storm*, 1895. Musée de l'Anonciade, Saint-Tropez. (*Peter Horree/Alamy Stock Photo*)
10. Pierre Bonnard, *With Signac & Friends*, 1924. (*Kunsthaus, Zurich*)
11. Henri Manguin, *The Siesta*, 1905. Villa Flora, Winterthur. (*Wikimedia*)
12. Edvard Munch, *At the Roulette Table in Monte Carlo*, 1892. Munch Museet, Oslo. (*Google Art Project*)
13. Léon Bakst, set design for Diaghilev's *Schéhérazade*, 1910. (*Photo by Universal History Archive/UIG/Getty Images*)
14. Georges Barbier, Paul Poiret dresses, 1912. (*Photo Researchers/Alamy Stock Photo*)
15. French Art Deco book plate, 1920s. (*Retro AdArchives/Alamy Stock Photo*)
16. *Le Train Bleu* choreographed by Nijinska for Diaghilev. Costumes by Coco Chanel. Paris Opera Production, 1992. (*Pierre Verdy/AFP via Getty Images*)

Second colour section

1. Raoul Dufy, *La Jetée, promenade à Nice*, c. 1926. Musée d'Art Moderne de la Ville de Paris. (*Album/Alamy Stock Photo*)
2. French fashion magazine illustration of ladies at the bar wearing evening gowns by Marcel Rochas, 1930. (*Lordprice Collection/Alamy Stock Photo*)
3. Eileen Gray & Jean Baldovici – E-1027, Roquebrune, Cap St Martin. (*Jonathan Miles*)
4. 'Côte-d'Azur All Year Round'. (*Source unknown*)
5. 'A New Blue Train'. (*Archivart/Alamy Stock Photo*)
6. 'Wake Up in Your dreams'. (*JJs/Alamy Stock Photo*)
7. 'Summer on the French Rivera'. (*Archivart/Alamy Stock Photo*)
8. Grace Kelly and Cary Grant overlooking Monte Carlo in Alfred Hitchcock's *To Catch a Thief*. (*Collection Christophel/Alamy Stock Photo*)
9. Sunset over the Baie-des-Anges, Nice. (*Catherine Louveau*)
10. The beach at Cannes. (*Jonathan Miles*)
11. Saint-Tropez. (*Jonathan Miles*)
12. The Baie-des-Anges, Nice. (*Jonathan Miles*)
13. Monte Carlo views. (*Jonathan Miles*)
14. Juan-les-Pins. (*Catherine Louveau*)
15. The Riviera – trading off its past. (*Jonathan Miles*)
16. Casino Ruhl. (*Art Kowalsky/Alamy Stock Photo*)
17. Glimpses of paradise. (*Jonathan Miles*)

Index

A Note About the Author

Jonathan Miles enjoyed a nomadic childhood in England, America and Canada. Having taken a first from University College, London, he received his doctorate from Jesus College, Oxford. Among his books are *The Medusa, The Shipwreck, the Scandal and the Masterpiece*, which was published to international acclaim and is now in development as a full-length film. More recently, *St Petersburg: Three Centuries of Murderous Desire* – a History Book of the Year in *The Times* – was the first volume in an informal trilogy about iconic places created by strangers. *Once Upon A Time World* – the second in that series – is born of Jonathan's engagement with the French Riviera stretching back over three decades. He and his wife divide their time between France and Italy.

www.jonathanmiles.net